Brigham Young's Homes

Brigham Young's principal residences, the Lion House and Beehive House, in the early 1860s. Photo by Savage and Ottinger.

Brigham Young's Homes

Edited by

Colleen Whitley

with contributions from

Sandra Dawn Brimhall, Marianne Harding Burgoyne, Mark D. Curtis,
Randall Dixon, Judy Dykman, Elinor Hyde, Jeffery Ogden Johnson,
and Kari K. Robinson

UTAH STATE UNIVERSITY PRESS
Logan, Utah

Utah State University Press
Logan, Utah

Manufactured in the United States of America
Printed on acid-free paper

08 07 06 05 04 03 02   1 2 3 4 5 6 7 8

Library of Congress Catloging-in-Publication Data
Brigham Young's Homes / edited by Colleen Whitley ; with contributions from Sandra
    Dawn Brimhall . . . [et al.].
    p. cm.
Includes bibliographical references.
    ISBN 0-87421-441-6 (pbk. : alk. paper)—ISBN 0-87421-442-4 (cloth : alk. paper)
    1. Young, Brigham, 1801–1877—Homes and haunts I Whitley, Colleen, 1940– II
    Brimhall, Sandra Dawn, 1953–
    BX8695.Y7 .B56 2002
    289.3'092—dc21

Contents

Preface   VII

1   Determining and Defining "Wife": The Brigham Young Households   1
JEFFERY OGDEN JOHNSON

2   Brigham Young's Birthplace and New York Residences   13
MARIANNE HARDING BURGOYNE

3   A Missionary's Life: Ohio, Missouri, England, and Illinois   39
MARIANNE HARDING BURGOYNE

4   Wives in Wagons: Winter Quarters and the Trek West   69
JUDY DYKMAN AND COLLEEN WHITLEY

5   Settling in Salt Lake City   82
JUDY DYKMAN AND COLLEEN WHITLEY

6   The Beehive and Lion Houses   124
W. RANDALL DIXON

7   The Brigham Young Farm House   147
ELINOR G. HYDE

8   The Gardo House   173
SANDRA DAWN BRIMHALL AND MARK D. CURTIS

9   Beyond Salt Lake City   202
JUDY DYKMAN, COLLEEN WHITLEY, AND KARI K. ROBINSON

Epilogue *Preserving the Past*   212

Appendix A *Brigham Young's Houses*   215

Appendix B *Wives of Brigham Young*   219

Appendix C *Women Sometimes Named as Young's Wives*   228

Notes   231

Bibliography   249

About the Authors   255

Index   257

Once when Brigham Young was simultaneously president of the Church of Jesus Christ of Latter-day Saints, governor of Utah Territory, and head of the territorial militia, a visitor methodically addressed him by all of his assorted ecclesiastical, governmental, and military titles. Young replied, "Sir, you have omitted my most cherished titles—carpenter, painter, and glazier."[1] Brigham Young is most frequently remembered as a colonizer and builder on a massive scale. He led the dispossessed Latter-day Saints across hundreds of miles of plains and mountains, then directed their settlement in the Great Basin. He supervised the building of religious structures, organized the distribution of land in newly founded cities, and dispatched pioneer companies to build permanent settlements from San Bernardino, California, to Fort Bridger, Wyoming. He instigated and directed public works, including the Salt Lake Theater, the Council Hall, the public baths at the warm springs,[2] the territorial prison, and various roads, bridges, and railroads. Yet Brigham Young was also a builder on a very personal level, and for him some of the most important projects he ever made or directed to be made were his own homes.

Whether his projects were large-scale or small, whether he built them with his own hands or directed the labors of others, Brigham Young recognized the value of both public and private buildings and demonstrated ingenuity and skill in making them functional, beautiful, and sturdy. "For Brigham, every activity of man's daily life was a part of religion."[3] Houses were places for the necessary functions of life—eating, sleeping, working—but they were also places to pray, to study scriptures, and to promote the growth of the souls who lived in them.

In this book dedicated researchers have identified, described, and explained the uses of each of the many homes Brigham Young established for his wives and families. Such a study allows us a better perspective on this remarkable man and his equally remarkable family. We can also see into the times in which they lived, recognize the values on which they operated, and understand a little better how they managed to build a thriving civilization, time and again, in the face of opposition most of us will never have to know.

One of the greatest difficulties in listing Brigham's houses, however, is determining which of the various claimants to his former ownership are accurate. Several places are reputed to be Brigham's homes, but fail to meet some fairly rudimentary criteria. For example, someone reported the building that formerly housed the Waking Owl Bookstore near the University of Utah was one of Brigham's homes. However, when the owner established that the original house was built twenty-one years after Brigham's death, we eliminated that one from our list. Other homes owned by family members, especially by his son, Brigham Jr., are sometimes assumed to have been Brigham Sr.'s. In addition, Brigham Young owned a great deal of property on which no home was ever built during his lifetime, but homes there now are sometimes assumed to be his.

Identification of some locations is, of necessity, inexact. Many early cabins and temporary houses had no addresses in the sense we use them now. Other locations were stated imprecisely, probably because they were intended only as temporary expediencies to be torn down within a few years. Other problems stem from the loss of Brigham Young's original will. Only copies remain, some of which have obvious errors.[4]

Despite any confusion in sources, we have been able to assemble a great deal of information about the homes in which Brigham housed himself and his families during his lifetime: architectural designs, exact or approximate addresses, maps, floor plans, details of life in the homes, names of subsequent owners, and current use of the building or the property. Few of Brigham Young's homes remain standing today, and none are used for their original purposes. Preserved as museums, reception centers, or otherwise open to visitors, the few that are available provide examples of the architecture and lifestyle of the period. They do not simply stand as monuments to Brigham Young or to early Mormon pioneers, but give all of us a chance to connect ourselves with our communal past, a connection essential as our own society evolves and changes.

In addition to the main text, photos and three appendices augment the essential information on Brigham Young's homes and families. Appendix A summarizes the information available for each of Brigham Young's known homes. He needed so many homes simply because he had such a large family. He is probably the best-known practitioner of Mormon plural marriage, commonly called polygamy. Although popular culture tends to lump all of Brigham's wives into an amorphous group, they were actually women of vastly different temperaments and tastes with assorted talents and abilities. While a few are discussed briefly in the text, appendix B lists all fifty-six of the women married or sealed to Brigham during his lifetime.[5] That appendix also contains information on each woman's known marriages to other men and her children by each husband. Additionally, the note for each wife contains sources for information about her that extend far beyond the necessarily limited items included in the appendix itself.

Several other women have been included in various lists of Brigham's wives, although no hard evidence of such marriages exists. Appendix C lists what is known about some of these women, again with a note on each woman containing extensive sources of information.

This task has been, understandably, enormous. A book like this is possible only because several people and organizations have provided the necessary information and expertise. The entire project stems from the fertile brain and thoughtful contacts of Judy Dykman, who also helped author several chapters. The authors, of course, each wrote their own chapters; in addition they read, corrected, and suggested improvements in other chapters. Randall Dixon and Jeffery Johnson have been especially gracious in sharing their seemingly unlimited knowledge of Brigham Young and early Utah history. Kari Robinson has offered the histories and genealogies of the Brigham Young Family Organization. Marianne Burgoyne has traveled thousands of miles researching, examining, and photographing Brigham's early homes. Artists and photographers have shared their talents and their products. The archives and personnel of several repositories have also been extremely helpful: the Utah State Archives, the LDS Church Archives, the LDS Church Museum of Art and History, and especially the Utah State Historical Society. John Alley of Utah State University Press has given his usual excellent advice and encouragement, and my husband, Tom, has been infinitely patient with the chaos resulting from piles of research. I am deeply grateful to all of them.

I have built a great many houses, both for myself and for others. I have never built two houses alike, and I do not expect to in time or eternity, but I mean to improve every time I begin.

Brigham Young

Chapter 1

Determining and Defining "Wife"
The Brigham Young Households
Jeffery Ogden Johnson

Utah satirist Al Church, among other suggestions on how to survive as a gentile in Utah, offered this tip: "Ask guides at the Beehive House how many wives Brigham Young had. (Of my last four tours, the answer has averaged 21.)"[1]

The volunteer guides at the Beehive House have no corner on the confusion market. Ann Eliza Webb, a disgruntled wife suing Brigham Young for divorce and hefty alimony, defrayed her expenses by writing a mildly scandalous potboiler called *Wife Number Nineteen* in which she claimed (incorrectly) to be the last and (also incorrectly) the nineteenth.[2] She was actually number fifty-three. Stanley Hirshson's major biography of Brigham Young, *The Lion of the Lord*, gives the number of wives as seventy.[3] The research that produced this number is unfortunately no more accurate than that in the rest of the book. In 1940, the Young family produced a widely used pamphlet, "Brigham Young's Wives, Children and Grandchildren,"[4] that gives the number as twenty-seven, a number popularized by Irving Wallace in his *The Twenty-seventh Wife*,[5] a fictionalized biography of Ann Eliza Webb Young. Finally, Leonard J. Arrington's award-winning biography *Brigham Young: American Moses* divides the wives into three groups: (1) the sixteen wives who had children by Brigham Young, (2) nine others whom "Brigham Young held out to be wives" but who had no children by him, and (3) "some thirty women" who were sealed to him for eternity only, but whom he does not name.[6]

From all this confusion, this chapter attempts to identify the number of wives, to suggest some reasons for the ambiguities of the term "wife," and to document the wives Brigham Young married over the course of his life. (Also see appendix B at the end of this book.)

An earlier version of "Determining and Defining 'Wife'" originally appeared in *Dialogue: A Journal of Mormon Thought* 20 (fall 1987), used here by permission.

When Joseph Smith announced that Latter-day Saints would follow the principle of plural marriage, Brigham Young observed, "I was not desirous of shrinking from any duty, nor of failing in the least to do as I was commanded, but it was the first time in my life that I had desired the grave." Nonetheless, he went on to marry or be sealed to fifty-six women. Used by permission, Utah State Historical Society, all rights reserved.

The first purpose is the easiest: fifty-six women were sealed to Brigham Young. Then why did it take 109 years after Brigham's death and a great deal of scholarly research to derive a clear number? One reason is Brigham Young's own reluctance. His Victorian sensibilities apparently made it hard for him to talk about so sexual a subject, and his Yankee independence bristled at the invasion of his privacy. He himself, on one of the few public occasions when he discussed the topic, reported in 1870 that he had sixteen wives.[7] But usually he tried to avoid the question. He gave instructions to the Historian's Office that "he did not wish but little history of his family given."[8]

On another occasion, he complained mildly: "Ladies who come into my office very frequently say, 'I wonder if it would hurt his feelings if I were to ask him how many wives he has?' . . . I would as lief they should ask me that question as any other; but I would rather see them anxious to learn about the Gospel."[9]

A second reason for the confusion is the remarkable number of variations in the types of ecclesiastically recognized liaisons that occurred. Brigham Young's fifty-six sealings—meaning a ceremony performed by priesthood authority that linked a man and a woman—could be of two types. The most common—and the only one currently practiced—is a ceremony that seals a man and a woman for time (mortal life) and eternity. A second form could seal a woman to one man for time and another for eternity. Such ceremonies usually occurred when a widow was sealed to her dead husband for eternity and to a living husband for time in the same ceremony. It was understood that any children by the second husband would be considered the progeny of the first husband. In the early days of the church, these relationships were commonly called proxy marriages.

However, the two forms of sealing did not exhaust the possible relationships. In both forms of sealing, the husband and wife could either establish a conjugal relationship or the ceremony could remain unconsummated. In Brigham Young's case, a significant number of sealings may have been nonconjugal, since the only incontrovertible proof of cohabitation after this lapse of years is either personal documentation (none exists) or the birth of a child, and Brigham Young fathered children by only sixteen of his wives. This does not necessarily mean he did not have conjugal relationships with some of the other forty wives, but the topic of where he spent his nights was apparently not a matter of household discussion. His daughter, Susa Young Gates, in her recollections observes, "[Even] if I would, I could tell nothing of my father's marital relations, for they were regarded in the family as most sacred. And no one ever knew aught about these matters, which should be preserved in the holiest silence of the human heart."[10]

Corroborative evidence of nonconjugal status is that Brigham Young, in an 1859 interview with Horace Greely, states: "I have some aged women sealed to me upon the principle of sealing which I no more think of making a wife of than I would my Grand Mother."[11] Twelve of the forty were over forty-five when they married him, and six were more than ten years older than Brigham.

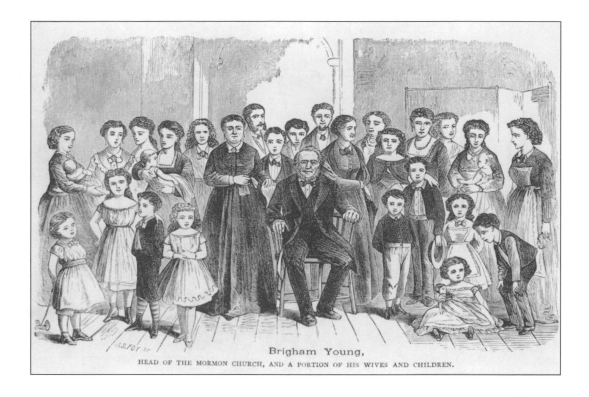

Brigham Young,

HEAD OF THE MORMON CHURCH, AND A PORTION OF HIS WIVES AND CHILDREN.

A third complication was whether a sealed wife became part of Brigham Young's households. I have considered that women members of Brigham Young's households, if they resided with other wives, received financial support from Brigham Young and/or were publically recognized as a wife. Twenty-three of his wives, by my count, belonged to his households. Of course, a woman sealed to Brigham Young and living in his household would not necessarily be a conjugal wife.

One might well ask why a woman would seek or accept sealing to a man under some of the more unconventional circumstances I have explained. Much of the motive lies in an understanding of the doctrines of plural marriage, a theological discussion which has been amplified elsewhere. Latter-day Saints (LDS) introduced to the doctrine of plural marriage in Nauvoo understood that it was part of the promised "restoration of all things" that included a reestablishment of the family structure of such ancient prophets as Abraham, Isaac, and Jacob; that it was the "higher law" of the afterlife which they were being called by God and his prophet to live in this life; and that it was an ordinance necessary to salvation. Not only would it determine relationships with beloved kinfolk in the next life, but Latter-day Saints believed a priesthood sealing between worthy partners was also essential for both men and women before they could be saved. In an 1845 sermon, Brigham Young alluded to this doctrine in those terms when he assured his listeners that "no woman can be perfect without a man to lead her . . . and I say to every man upon the face of the earth: if he wishes to be saved he cannot be saved without a woman by his side." He identified this doctrine as "Joseph Smith's spiritual wife system."[12]

In addition to these persuasive doctrines, the economic realities of the American frontier made it virtually obligatory for a woman to be married; and

MORMONDOM—A FRESH SUPPLY OF WIVES—GOING OUT TO THE SETTLEMENTS.

SCENES IN AN AMERICAN HAREM.

BRIGHAM YOUNG AND HIS FAMILY ON THEIR WAY TO CHURCH.

the cultural norms of the society also reinforced the view that the institution of marriage inevitably accompanied adulthood.

Brigham Young was a married man when he encountered Mormonism, and he would, as it turned out, have two wives before he ever had a plural one. He married his first wife, Miriam Works, on 8 October 1824 when he was twenty-three years old and she was eighteen. They had two daughters, then joined the LDS Church in April 1832. A few months later Miriam died of consumption at the age of twenty-seven. In Kirtland, Brigham met Mary Ann Angell. They were married on 10 February 1834, four months before her thirty-first birthday. She mothered Brigham's young daughters and, over the next seven years, gave birth to six additional children, including a set of twins.

Brigham Young learned about plural marriage in Nauvoo from Joseph Smith, and there is no reason to question his own report that he reacted negatively. Greeley asked him, "Is the system of your Church [plurality of wives] acceptable to the majority of its women?" and Brigham Young answered, "They could not be more averse to it than I was when it was first revealed to us as the Divine will. I think they generally accept it, as I do, as the will of God."[13] He made similar statements on other occasions.

MARTHA BOWKER.

Wives Sealed to Brigham Young during Joseph Smith's Lifetime:
June 1842–May 1844

Between the time that Brigham Young first learned of the doctrine of plural marriage and the time Joseph Smith died—just under two years—he was sealed to four women. All four women came west, lived as part of his household, outlived him, and shared in his estate. Three of them bore him children.

Brigham Young chose twenty-year-old Lucy Ann Decker Seeley for his first plural wife, and they were married by Joseph Smith on 17 June 1842. She was the daughter of Isaac Decker, a longtime friend of Brigham Young and his father John Young. She and her two children had been abandoned in Nauvoo by her husband, William Seeley, who according to family tradition was a drunkard and abusive.[14] In many ways, this marriage to Lucy Ann was typical. A significant number of women sealed to Brigham Young were from families with whom he had long-standing friendships; many were either widows or divorcees with children.

His second plural wife was forty-one-year-old Augusta Adams Cobb, who had left her husband and five of her children in Boston when she came to Nauvoo with two children, one of whom died on the way.[15] The same day, Brigham also married Harriet Elizabeth Cook, a nineteen-year-old convert to the church with no relatives in Nauvoo. The fourth wife was sixteen-year-old Clarissa Caroline Decker, Lucy's sister. They were married 8 May 1844, one month before Joseph Smith's death.

All four of these women swore that they were married to Brigham Young on these dates in affidavits signed in 1869 and 1870.[16] Lucy's marriage date and sealing were also recorded in the Nauvoo Temple records, which document confirmed sealings for the other three in the temple in January 1846.

Martha Bowker was born a Quaker, converted to the LDS Church, and married Brigham Young in 1846. She was remembered for her cheerful spirit despite health problems that rendered her an invalid. Used by permission, Utah State Historical Society, all rights reserved.

CLARA CHASE ROSS.

BEFORE THE NAUVOO TEMPLE'S COMPLETION:
September 1844–May 1845

After Joseph Smith's death but before the temple in Nauvoo was completed, Brigham Young was sealed to fifteen women in secret ceremonies. Brigham Young recorded them in code in his diary as "M E" (marriage for eternity) or "M T" (marriage for time), capitalized and underlined at the top of the diary pages when his marriages were performed. For example on 10 September 1844 he wrote, "This day I visited Br. Isac Chace. Br. H. C. Kimball was with me. Br & Sister Chase with their daughter Claricy was at home. We had a good visit. . . ." "M. E." is written on that page. Since Heber C. Kimball was often a witness to those marriages it is instructive to compare his diary entry for the same day. For example, he confirms Brigham Young's marriage to Clarissa Chase on September 10: "went to . . . Br Chaeces. They ware sealled all wright."

Brigham Young's diary records his marriages to all fifteen wives married during this period except Emily Dow Partridge and Mary Elizabeth Rollins Lightner. Emily's family has dated her marriage in September 1844.[17] Her son Edward Partridge Young was born the next year. Brigham Young's diary does not continue into May 1845, but Heber C. Kimball's diary records, "Seald B to Life," meaning to Mary Elizabeth Rollins Lightner on 22 May 1845. Mary Elizabeth affirms in her autobiography: "I was also sealled to B. Young as proxy for Joseph."[18]

Of the fifteen women, four—Emily Dow Partridge, Louisa Beaman, Eliza R. Snow, and Olive Gray Frost—were sealed to Joseph Smith for eternity with Brigham Young standing as proxy for the murdered prophet. A fifth, Margaret Pierce Whitesides, a young widow, was sealed to her first husband for eternity and to Brigham Young for life. Like Margaret, six others had been married before. The previous marital status of Clarissa Blake, five years older than Brigham, is unknown. So is her death date. Three of these fifteen (Elizabeth Fairchild, Diana

Zina D. H. Young, Bathsheba W. Smith, Emily P. Young, Eliza R. Snow (Smith)
Leading Women of Zion

Chase, and Mary Ann Clark) divorced him in the next few years. Three died before they reached Utah. Olive Gray Frost died in October 1845 before the temple was completed. Her sealing is the only one from this period not confirmed after the temple was open. Five of this group bore Brigham children and seven lived in his household in Utah. Thus, at one point in this period, the forty-three-year-old Brigham had twenty wives ranging in age from seventeen to forty-eight and had eight children—two by Miriam Works, six by Mary Ann Angel (daughter Mary Ann died in 1843), and a four-month-old son by Lucy Ann Decker.

Nauvoo Temple Marriages: *January–February 1846*

When the temple was completed, the Saints rushed to perform sealings and endowments before leaving for the West. Often church leaders would spend several consecutive days in the temple. Brigham Young wrote in his diary on 21 January 1846, "I gave myself up entirely to the work of the Lord in the temple almost night & day. I have spent [*sic*] not taking more than 4 hours upon an average out of 24 to sleep & but seldom ever allowing myself the the [*sic*] time & opportunity of going home once in a week. . . ."

In the five-week period between 7 January and 6 February 1846, Brigham Young was married to nineteen women, and his sealings to all of his living wives were reconfirmed. Fourteen of his nineteen new wives had been married before and seven were significantly older, including Phebe Morton Angel, the mother of Mary Ann Angel (then fifty-nine), and Abigail Marks Works (then sixty-nine), the mother of his first wife, Miriam Works.

Above: Amanda Barnes Smith had twice married men named Warren Smith before she married Brigham Young. Her first husband and their second son were both killed in the massacre at Haun's Mill. Used by permission, LDS Church Archives, all rights reserved.

Top: In 1867, three of Brigham Young's wives were noted as among the "leading women of Zion." Left to right, Zina Huntington Young, Bathsheba W. Smith (wife of George A. Smith), Emily Partridge Young, and Eliza R. Snow Smith Young. Used by permission, LDS Church Archives, all rights reserved.

Of this group, only two, Margaret Alley and Zina Huntington, bore him children. Six of these women were sealed to dead husbands for eternity (three to Joseph Smith) with Brigham Young standing proxy. Nine of these women predeceased him, three received divorces, and another two may have either died before reaching Utah or stayed in the East.

ON THE PLAINS:
February 1847–April 1848

Between Brigham Young's departure from Nauvoo and his permanent arrival in the Salt Lake Valley, he was sealed to four women. The first, Jane Terry Young, was a widow with two young children, who requested on her deathbed that she be sealed to Brigham Young. (Her dead husband, George W. Young, was no relation to Brigham Young.) Four days after the sealing, she died.[19] This particular marriage was the shortest of Brigham Young's marriages. (The longest was his union with Mary Ann Angel. They had been married forty-three years when he died in 1877.)

Sixteen-year-old Lucy Bigelow and her nineteen-year-old sister Mary Jane were sealed to him in Winter Quarters on 20 March 1847, just before he left on his first expedition to Utah. According to Lucy's daughter, Susa Young Gates, these sealings were secret even though there were almost no non-Mormons in the area.[20] Brigham Young took his wife Clara Decker to Utah, left her in Salt Lake City, returned to Iowa in the fall of 1847, and, while there, was sealed to Sarah Malin. Mary Jane later left him, marrying four more times. Lucy, however, lived in his Utah household and bore him three children.

SEALINGS IN UTAH:
October 1852–December 1872

On 29 August 1852, Orson Pratt expounded the principle of plural marriage in a general conference session, ending the period of secrecy. At that point, Brigham Young was fifty-one years old. Of his forty-two plural wives, seven had died and six had received divorces. The history of four is unknown. Thirty-one children had been born; three more were conceived that year.

A few days later, Brigham Young married Eliza Burgess. She was twenty-five years old and her father had been a church leader in England. Brigham would marry ten more women before his death in 1877. Eight had been married before, and several brought young children into the family. Five were older women who seem to have been nonconjugal wives. None of the eleven were sealed for eternity to former husbands. Three of the eleven bore him one child each, and two received divorces.

By his death on 23 August 1877, Brigham Young had married fifty-six wives. Nineteen had predeceased him, ten had received divorces, four are unaccounted for, and twenty-four survived him. Seventeen wives received a share of his estate while the remaining seven apparently had nonconjugal roles.

Sixteen women gave birth to Brigham Young's fifty-seven children; Emmeline Free had ten; six wives had only one child. The oldest child, Elizabeth Young Ellsworth, was fifty-two at Brigham's death and the youngest, Fannie

Catherine Reese Clawson married Zepheniah Clawson in 1824 and bore him six children, four of whom were living when she was sealed to Brigham Young in 1855. Several of Brigham's wives were either widowed or divorced and needed support. Used by permission, Utah State Historical Society, all rights reserved.

BRIGHAM YOUNG AND HIS WIVES.

After Brigham Young's death, one of his sons-in-law, Charles Johnson, published this popular print of Brigham with twenty-one of his wives. Used by permission, Utah State Historical Society, all rights reserved.

Young Clayton, was seven. Eleven of these sixteen women survived him. None of the women who bore him children cancelled their sealings or remarried.

DIVORCES

Rather than being the political and domestic despot whose image appeared in the Eastern press, Brigham Young apparently maintained a remarkably open attitude toward divorce. Although the circumstances of all of his divorces are not known, what documentation exists seems to indicate amicable partings. In many cases, these women remarried and remained in Utah, taking an active part in the church for the rest of their lives. This fact tends to dispel the myth of the horrified woman, enslaved against her will, disgusted equally with Brigham Young, the church, and plural marriage.

The first documented divorce was from Mary Woodward on 13 December 1846, his wife of less than a year. In a brief but warm letter that day, he wrote: "In answer to your letter of yesterday, the 12 inst; I will say, you may consider yourself discharged from me and my counsel" and added that he would be glad to help her if she and her children were ever hungry.[21]

Divorce records are sketchy for the emigration period, but two women who had been sealed to him in the Nauvoo Temple left him then to marry other men. Diana Chase married William Montgomery Shaw on 1 January 1849 and raised a large family in the Ogden, Utah, area. The widowed Mary Elza Nelson Greene, who had been sealed to her first husband for eternity and to Brigham Young for this life, was sealed to Bruce Israel Philips on 17 September 1850 by Parley P. Pratt in Salt lake City.

On 18 June 1851 Mary Ann Clark Powers wrote from Kanesville, Iowa: "I wish you to release me from all engagements with you for time and eternity. . . ."[22] The request was granted.

After the church began recording divorces in 1851, Mary Ann Turley and Mary Jane Bigelow obtained divorces in 1851, Eliza Babcock in 1853, and Elizabeth Fairchild in 1855.[23] They were under twenty when they married Brigham Young and had never become part of his household. They all remarried, and Mary Jane, Eliza, and Elizabeth remained in Utah.

Almost twenty years later in 1873, Ann Eliza Webb applied for a civil divorce. The case came to trial in 1875, and the court ordered Brigham to pay $500 per month allowance and $3,000 court costs. When he refused, he was fined $25 and sentenced to a day in prison for contempt of court.[24] There is no record of application for a church divorce, but she was excommunicated 10 October 1874 and devoted much of the rest of her life to publishing her somewhat sensational memoirs and giving anti-Mormon lectures.

Twenty-one of Brigham Young's fifty-six wives had never been married, seven were separated or divorced from their husbands, sixteen were widows, and six had living husbands from whom divorces had apparently not been obtained. Marital information is unavailable for six.

A devout Latter-day Saint, Hannah Tapfield King wanted to be sealed in the temple, but her husband, Thomas Owen King, was not a member of the Church of Jesus Christ of Latter-day Saints. Concerned for her eternal welfare, she asked to be sealed to Brigham Young for eternity, and he agreed. Hannah was the last wife sealed to Brigham Young, but they never lived together, and he never provided a house for her. She remained the wife of Thomas King and was known as Mrs. King on civil and church records and as a writer for the *Women's Exponent*. Used by permission, Utah State Historical Society, all rights reserved.

IN MEMORIAM BRIGHAM YOUNG.
"AND THE PLACE WHICH KNEW HIM ONCE SHALL KNOW HIM NO MORE."

From a current-day perspective, the polyandrous marriages seem most problematic. Three of these women (Mary Ann Clark Powers, Mary Elizabeth Rollins Lightner, and Hannah Tapfield King) were married to non-Mormons, which meant, according to the theological understanding of the times, that their salvation could not be assured. Mary Ann Clark Powers, married to Brigham Young 15 January 1845, later said she had not "bin a wife to" Powers after the sealing and expressed relief when Powers went to California. She received a divorce from Brigham Young in 1851.[25]

Mary Elizabeth Rollins Lightner was an early and fervent member in Kirtland and Missouri. She and her husband, Adam Lightner, gathered with the Saints at Nauvoo and eventually Utah. Joseph Smith prophesied (correctly) that Adam would never join the church and explained to Mary Elizabeth that she needed to be sealed to a worthy priesthood holder for eternity. She was sealed to Joseph before his death and the sealing was confirmed in the Nauvoo Temple, Brigham Young acting as proxy. In the same ceremony, she was sealed to Brigham Young for life, but her relationship to Adam Lightner seems to have remained unchanged. They had ten children and both died in Minersville, Utah, many years later. She was never known as a wife of Brigham Young.

Hannah Tapfield King joined the church in England, came to Utah with her non-Mormon husband, became known as a poet and writer, and was sealed to Brigham Young for eternity in 1872 when she was sixty-five. This sealing did not affect her relationship with her husband, and she never became part of the Brigham Young household.[26]

The remaining three women, however, had living husbands who were Mormons, and it is not clear why they chose not to be sealed to those husbands. Zina Diantha Huntington Jacobs had been sealed to Joseph Smith before his

Even after Brigham Young's death, cartoonists continued to lampoon the man with many wives. Used by permission, Utah State Historical Society, all rights reserved.

death. When that sealing was confirmed in the Nauvoo Temple, Brigham Young acted as proxy. It seems to have been the invariable custom that when a woman was sealed to one man for eternity, she was sealed to his proxy for time. Her husband, Henry Jacobs, was present during the ceremony and apparently agreed to the sealings.[27] Zina and her two sons by Henry became part of Brigham Young's family; she later bore Brigham a daughter. Henry remarried and died years later in Salt Lake City, still a member of the church.

Mary Ellen Woodward applied to the Nauvoo High Council in about 1844 for a divorce from James B. Woodward, her Mormon husband, on grounds of physical cruelty to her and their three children. After she was sealed to Brigham Young, James persuaded her to come back to him; and by her request, Brigham Young granted a divorce. However, her letter to Brigham Young on 25 February 1847 asks, "If I do all I can and after this he treats me bad, will you let me leave him and live with my children?"[28]

The third woman, Lydia Farnsworth Mayhew, had nine children by her Mormon husband, Elijah Mayhew.[29] At sixty-two she was sealed to Brigham Young for eternity on 8 May 1870. This sealing did not change her relationship with Elijah, and they lived together until he died in 1896.

It is clear from the analysis of Brigham Young's sealings that marriage was a more fluid relationship in nineteenth century Mormonism than it is today. It served multiple functions—theological, economic, and social. The pragmatic flexibility Brigham Young brought to these sealings, while the source of considerable confusion, also provides a measure of the significance of the marital relationship as an ordering device in nineteenth century Utah society.

Chapter 2

Brigham Young's Birthplace and New York Residences

Marianne Harding Burgoyne

I was worth a little property when I started to preach; but I was something like Bunyan—it was "life, life, eternal life," with me; everything else was secondary.

Brigham Young[1]

A story reads better if a great man emerges from humble roots. The idea of the self-made man, whose accomplishments set him far above the reach of other men, rising from incapacitating circumstances, is the American dream. We like to think a man can be a Paul Bunyan, endowed with such strength, vision, and cunning to create Puget Sound, the Grand Canyon, and the Black Hills or with his ox to haul an entire forest at one time.[2] This myth allows us the possibility that a little of this life force resides in all of us.

Brigham Young was such a man. Born into the poorest of families in a log home on a hillside in Whitingham, Windham County, Vermont, Young left an indelible mark on the landscape of America.[3] He was a Bunyan. There was nothing he couldn't build: chairs, mantelpieces, homes, ships, temples, cities. He built a religion from the blueprint of Joseph Smith's visions and led his people across the American continent to a land so barren that presumably no one else would want it, so he and his followers could worship without persecution. He peopled his cities. Called by his biographer, Leonard Arrington, "American Moses," Young was a giant among men.[4] His story is epic; his achievement, measured two hundred years after his birth, remarkable for a man of any age.

Once Brigham Young was famous, he received several letters from various sources requesting an account of his birth and early history. One such request is recorded in the Mary Van Sickle Wait monograph, *Brigham Young in Cayuga County: 1813–1829*, perhaps the earliest source for tracking Young's New York years.[5] Wait begins her history: "We have Brigham Young's own word for the fact that he came to Cayuga County in 1813 and settled in Genoa." She then produces the following letter:

Great Salt Lake City, July 23, 1858
To _____:

I received your letter dated Canandaigua, May 5, 1858. I will give you a short sketch of my history. I was born at Whitingham, Windham County, Vermont, June 1, 1801. My father and family moved to Smyrna, Chenango County, New York, when I was about eighteen months old. We lived in the place until 1813.

Shortly after the commencement of the late war with Great Britain, my father and family removed to the town of Genoa, Cayuga County, New York, in which county I lived until 1829, when I moved to Mendon, Monroe County. . . .[6]

The more famous Young became, the more people became interested in the exact location of his birth. In another letter, dated sixteen years later, 16 May 1874, Albert Carrington, at Young's request, wrote to Dr. Oramel Martin, who had inquired (letter of 6 May 1874) concerning the site of Young's birth:

Dr. Humphrey Gould of Rowe, Franklin County, Mass., if I am rightly informed, can direct you to the spot in Whitingham where it was said the house stood in which President Young was born. President Young will be pleased to see you at any time it may suit you to visit this city.

Very Respectfully, Albert Carrington[7]

Today, there is no home standing which marks the exact location of Young's birthplace. There is a stone memorial placed on Stimpson Hill, also known as "Brigham Young Hill." Stimpson Hill Road (Town Road 33) intersects Vermont State Highway 100 in Whitingham just east of Brown's General Store and the U.S. Post Office. A sign at the intersection points to the birthplace southward up the steep hill. The memorial is located precisely one-fifth of a mile southward up Stimpson Hill Road.[8] The inscription on the stone reads, "Brigham Young / Born

Brigham Young's birthplace still resembles the farming area it was when he was born. Photo by Marianne Burgoyne.

on this Spot 1801 / A Man of Much Courage and Superb Equipment."
Postcards of this memorial existed by 1900, and it still stands today.[9]

Although a home is located just to the west of the monument, it is not the original Young dwelling. The view from the back of this current home, owned by Raymond A. Purinton, overlooks the land that Brigham's father, John Young, once owned. With its rolling pine-covered hills and covert lake, the spot of Brigham's birth is one of the most breathtaking in Vermont. The secluded lake is the man-made Lake Whitingham, built in the 1920s, replacing the river that would have flowed through the land in the early 1800s.[10]

Whether or not the stone memorial marks the exact location of Young's birth is no longer known. It is most likely that Young was born on the 51.5 acres John Young purchased from his brother-in-law, Joseph Mosely, on 18 November 1800.[11] (The stone memorial is located within this property.) Clark Jillson, a nineteenth-century local historian whose book *Green Leaves from Whitingham, Vermont* was published in 1894, stated repeatedly that Brigham Young was born on Stimpson Hill.[12] He also said that Hezekiah Murdock, a resident of Whitingham during the early 1800s, also claimed that Young was born on Stimpson Hill.[13] Young's birthplace is also disputed to be on another five-acre tract of land in Fitches Grant, Lot 22, owned by Joseph Mosely and on which John Young may have lived with his family.[14] However, land deeds indicate Mosely owned the five-acre parcel only until 1797. The land did not come back into his possession until after the John Young family moved from Whitingham in 1804.[15]

The important fact is that Brigham Young was born in Whitingham and lived in several residences there as a small child. John Young owned the Stimpson Hill property for a little over a year and ten months. On 24 September 1802, he sold the land back to Joseph Mosely for the original purchase price of $100.[16] He did not purchase land again in Whitingham; rather, he apparently rented from or worked for others during his remaining tenure there.[17] Wait quotes M. R. Werner's *Brigham Young*, which records, "the Young family was the poorest that ever came to Whitingham and at the time of Brigham's birth, John Young did not own a horse, a cow, or any land, but gained a poor living as a basket maker.[18] This is slightly exaggerated. John Young did own land the year of Brigham's birth, and Joseph, an older brother, confirms his father purchased a cow from Caleb Murdock in the spring of 1801.[19]

Brigham recorded that his father remained in Whitingham three years, opening new farms.[20] The older sons helped their father with the farming.[21] Joseph Young wrote in his journal, "We changed places 4 times during our stay on Green Mountains. Our last place of residence was over the pond in the Hemlock woods."[22] This pond is presumed to be in the area of Sadawaga Pond, now renamed Sadawaga Lake.[23]

John Young was an itinerant farmer, always moving in pursuit of better living conditions for his family, yet never able to raise his circumstances above a poverty level. Brigham Young said in 1860, "My father was a poor, honest, hardworking man . . . and his mind seemingly stretched from east to west, from north to south; and to the day of his death he wanted to command worlds; but the

Brigham Young's birthplace is marked by three signs: a metal marker posted by the state of Vermont, a stately stone monument erected by the Church of Jesus Christ of Latter-day Saints, and perhaps the most entertaining, a weathered stone (no indication of the maker given) inscribed, "Brigham Young Born on this Spot 1801, A Man of Much Courage and Superb Equipment." Photo by Marianne Burgoyne.

Lord would never permit him to get rich."[24] This nostalgic glimpse fails to convey the impressive credentials John Young acquired as a young man in the military. At sixteen, he enlisted in the American Revolutionary War, serving under General Washington. He served in three campaigns in Massachusetts (his native state) and in New Jersey. However poor his father may have been, Brigham remembered him as "very circumspect, exemplary, and religious" and noted that he was "from an early period of his life, a member of the Methodist Church."[25]

Brigham's grandfather had impressive military credentials as well. Joseph Young was a physician and surgeon in the French and Indian War.[26] His great-grandfather, William Young, was among the original proprietors of Barrington and Nottingham, New Hampshire. He is first heard of in 1721:

> These towns were settled by men, or the children of men, who had shown faithfulness and bravery in the Indian wars. The lands were given to them by the government in recognition of this service. Wm. Young had a number of freeholds in these towns, and bought several other [*sic*]. . . . He resided in later years in Boston, but died in Hopkinton, Massachusetts. In his will in Middlesex County Record, he leaves about $10,000.00 to his wife and daughter and minor son and names Rev. S. Barrett as the guardian of the latter.[27]

Brigham's ancestry is certainly more impressive than his father's financial status. Whatever once existed of family money or education had disappeared by the time John Young moved from Hopkinton, Massachusetts, to Whitingham, Vermont.

In his biography of Brigham Young, Leonard Arrington speculates that the log home John Young built in Whitingham after his arrival there in January 1801 would have been a single-room dwelling, possibly sixteen feet square. This shelter would have required perhaps sixty poles, eighteen to twenty feet in length. If tradition

Sadawaga Lake was called Sadawaga Pond when the John Young family lived near it in 1803–1804. Photo by Marianne Burgoyne.

were followed, men from the village, participating in a "log raising," would have helped John Young raise the walls of his home in a day. Over the next few days, workers would have completed the roof, the chinking of the mud clay, a stick chimney, and bunk beds made of corn shuck mattresses or balsam fir boughs.[28] Brigham was born into this kind of humble dwelling, the ninth child of John and Abigail Young. It is doubtful any of his family's other rented residences in Whitingham would have been more accommodating than this first log home.

In the spring of 1804, John Young moved his family west to Sherburne, Chenango County, in central New York, where the land was reported to be better than the stony soil of Whitingham.[29] Here, he cleared land and built another log home. His and Abigail's tenth child, Louisa, was born 25 September 1804. Their eleventh and final child, Lorenzo Dow, was born 19 October 1807, in the same dwelling as Louisa;[30] however, by 6 April 1808, the section of the town in which the Youngs resided was renamed Smyrna. Joseph Young recalled, "the town of Sherburn[e] was divided and one part called Smyrna, and here my brother Lorenzo was born, in the same place as sister Louisa, but different name. Here my sister Nabby died in 1807 and the same year we moved to Cold Brook where we lived five years."[31]

The most valuable secondary source for tracking the many moves of the Young family, and later of Brigham himself, through their New York years is the meticulous research of Richard F. Palmer and Carl D. Butler in their monograph, *Brigham Young: The New York Years*. Inspired by and eventually replacing the Wait monograph published in 1964, Palmer spent a decade retracing the family's sojourns through New York.[32] He reports that Joseph's account concurs with local tradition that the Youngs lived near Cold Brook in a rural neighborhood called "Dark Hollow," about three miles southwest of the village of Smyrna. According to Mrs. Vaughn Fargo, a Smyrna town historian, it is

Cole Road, near Dark Hollow, where the John Young family lived, was identified as Cold Brook Road on the 1875 map of the area. Photo by Marianne Burgoyne.

NORWICH — CABIN SITE. Abandoned sawmill in the Town of Plymouth, near Norwich, stands on the site of the log cabin built by Brigham Young and his father back just before the War of 1812. John Young and his son Brigham (who later became the great Morman leader) threw up a windbreak of pine boughs on this site one Autumn evening when they stopped here from sheer exhaustion. The family, father, mother and son—remained in Chenango County for a for a year before moving on to Cayuga County.

The ruined sawmill just off Chenango County Road was identified in the 1960s as standing on the site of the cabin built by John Young and his sons. The Youngs stayed in Cold Brook or Chenango County five years (1807–1813), rather than one as the caption states. From *Campfires in the Forest* by Roy Gallinger, used by permission, Chenango County Historical Society.

believed that their home was a log dwelling on the west side of a road leading from Dark Hollow to nearby "German Hollow."[33]

The rural area where the Youngs lived is west of Sherburne on Highway 80. In the middle of Smyrna, Chenango County Road 20 bears left at the site of the War Memorial. Approximately two miles farther at Four Corners, County Road 21 bears right (southwest) up the hill. The site of Brigham's boyhood home, according to a state historical marker, is just off Chenango County Road 21, one-half mile north on Cole Road. An 1875 map of Smyrna and surrounding area names what is presently Cole Road "Cold Brook" Road.[34] A ruined sawmill still exists. An earlier picture of an abandoned sawmill also exists, taken prior to 1960 and is likely the same site. The log cabin where the Youngs lived stood on this site.[35] German Hollow is actually just a little farther uphill, to the left off Chenango County Road 21. Local tradition records that when the Young family traveled from Whitingham, Vermont, the parents stopped one night in Chenango County, too exhausted to travel farther. John Young and his son Brigham threw up a windbreak of pine boughs for shelter. The tradition records, "No one knows what John Young thought that [fall] night as he watched the big moon sail in the heavens above him. But there is one thing he did not think of. He did not realize that the stalwart son sleeping beside him would one day bring fame to the little family."[36]

John Young's name appears on the highway assessment list of Sherburne, 8th and 9th townships, District 21, for two days' work in 1808. Every able-bodied man in the community was required to work on public roads and highways for a specified number of days each year.[37] His name also appears in the 1810 federal census of Smyrna, Chenango County. Family records indicate that the household at this time included John, his wife Abigail, sons Brigham, Lorenzo Dow, Phinehas, and Joseph, and daughters Louisa, Susannah, Rhoda, and Fanny.[38]

Brigham spent his boyhood in Smyrna (Sherburne), Chenango County, and Cold Brook, where he remained until his thirteenth year. He wrote: "At an early age, I labored with my father, assisting him to clear off new land and cultivate his

farm, passing through many hardships and privations incident to settling a new country."[39] Not only did he help his father and brothers clear their own land for farming, but also, in exchange for needed products and supplies, the land of others in the region as well.[40] Brigham later described the experience: "I had the privilege of cutting down the hemlock, beech, and maple trees and then rolling them together, burning the logs, splitting the rails, and fencing the little fields." He described the tasks of "picking up brush, chopping down trees, rolling logs, and working amongst the roots, and of getting our shins, feet and toes bruised."[41] He used to work in the woods, he said, "logging and driving a team, summer and winter, not half clad, and with insufficient food until my stomach would ache. . . ."[42]

Brigham grew up in such destitute circumstances that, as a boy, he didn't even own a pair of shoes. When he did come by a pair, he used them only for church, carrying them in his hands until he reached the church and taking them off after the service.[43] In his more prosperous years, Young often recalled just how poverty-stricken the family was, and as a result, how economical. He recalled:

> My sisters would make me what was called a Jo Johnson cap for winter, and in the summer I wore a straw hat which I frequently braided for myself. I learned how to make bread, wash the dishes, milk the cows, and make butter. . . . These are about all the advantages I gained in my youth. I know how to economize, for my father had to do it.[44]

Brigham probably did not realize how self-sufficient he was becoming, even as a very young boy. Perhaps braiding his own straw hats taught him he could make much out of little or if something needed doing, he could do it for himself. It is clear from his memories that the entire family was put to work meeting the family's minimal survival needs.

A poignant reference to the Cold Brook home exists. In 1809, Brigham's older sister Rhoda, who had been left behind in Hopkinton, likely with her

Today the sawmill is a pile of rubble beside the road. Photo by Marianne Burgoyne.

mother's parents, returned after an absence of eight years.[45] Brigham's brother Joseph recalled:

> . . . in September of this year she arrived at our humble home on Cold Brook with old deacon Abner Morton, our mother's uncle. The whole family [was] much overcome by the arrival of sister Rhoda, whom we had not seen for 8 years. It was like one rising from the dead! Never did a child seem to appreciate a father's home more—humble as it was, than did sister Rhoda; this was fully reciprocated by the whole family. It seemed as though an Angel had visited our house, and to add to our happiness she had come to abide with us.[46]

Although no physical description of the home exists, the quotation is telling, nevertheless. Two references to its "humble" circumstance seem muted by the abundance of good will and love among family members. Rhoda's homecoming ignites the family like a warm fire. Set against a backdrop of poverty, the moment seems even more important to enjoy.

The next move of the John Young family was to Cayuga County, fifty miles west of Sherburne (Smyrna). Joseph records: "In the winter of 1813, my father moved his family to the town of Genoa, in the county of Cayuga on the shore of the lake of the same name."[47] No deeds have been located to indicate that John Young purchased property in either Cayuga or Tomkins County, nor does John Young's name appear as an early settler in Elliot Storke's "History of Cayuga County."[48] Wait records, "It can be assumed that he never held property in the area, but made a poor living hiring out as a farmer or working at some menial trade."[49] The exact location of the Young home cannot be determined by the evidence available. Palmer proposes that because Genoa is located seven miles east of the lake, the Youngs may have lived about seven miles southwest of Genoa, closer to the lake, near Lansing or Lansingville.[50] Wait explains that Genoa took in a great deal more territory at the time the Youngs lived there than it did later. It embraced the towns of Locke, Summerhill, and Groton in Tompkins County until 1802, and Lansing in Tomkins until 1817. She proposes, based on vague rumors, that the Youngs lived in East Genoa at Lansingville Ridge.[51] Residence at or near Lansingville (North Lansing) is indicated by the fact that Abigail was buried near there, likely in the Old White Settlement Cemetery, located west of Lansingville, on the east side of Lansingville Road.[52]

In one account, *It Happened in Lansing*, Isabelle H. Parish, town of Lansing historian, reports that Brigham Young lived as a boy with his parents on the shore of Cayuga Lake, near Lansing Station. Parish also reports that Brigham's mother, Abigail, is said to have been buried in the White Settlement burying ground.[53] Orrin Drake, a life-long resident of that vicinity, said "he remembered seeing the stone that marked the grave in the southeastern corner of the cemetery."[54] The stone was either removed or, as Parish suggests, "lies beneath a covering of leaves and soil."

A sign has been erected in this cemetery which reads, "White Settlement Cemetery / This Cemetery is the Burying / Place of Abigale [*sic*] Young, the / Mother of Brigham Young, the Second / President of the Church of Jesus Christ of Latter-day Saints / D 1815.[55] The cemetery is small. Most tombstones are broken, the writing on them not discernible. Abigail's original marker does not exist. Only the sign is visible, placed on the southwest corner of the burying ground.[56]

Young Brigham attended the Drake schoolhouse in Lansing.[57] How long he attended the school is not known, although Brigham later admitted he had only eleven days of schooling.[58] His books were rather his natural surroundings. He learned the skills of home and shop and field—enough, as he expressed it, to enable him to be independent. He said, "In my youthful days, instead of going to school, I had to chop logs, to sow and plant, to plow in the midst of roots barefooted, and if I had on a pair of pants that would cover me I did pretty well."[59]

His education was forming in moral ways as well. Brigham said of his upbringing:

> I was brought up so strict, so firm in the faith of the Christian religion by my parents, that if I had said "Devil," I believed I had sworn very wickedly. . . . If I had used the name of Devil, I should have certainly been chastised, and that severely. . . . My mother, while she lived, taught her children all the time to honor the name of the Father and the Son, and to reverence the holy Book. She said, "Read it, observe its precepts, and apply them to your lives as far as you can; do everything that is good; do nothing that is evil; and if you see any person in distress, administer to their wants; never suffer anger to arise in your bosoms; for, if you do, you may be overcome by evil."[60]

Brigham admitted that if he swore, it was "out of sight" of his father and mother.[61] He never credited himself with being a perfect child. He even admitted that his upbringing was at times too strict and vowed to change those circumstances with his own family:

> When I was young, I was kept within very strict bounds, and was not allowed to walk more than half-an-hour on Sunday for exercise. The proper and necessary gambols of youth having been denied me, makes me want active exercise and amusement now. I had not a chance to dance when I was young, and never heard the enchanting tones of the violin, until I was eleven years of age; and then I

Brigham Young's mother, Abigail, is said to be buried in the southeast corner of the White Settlement Cemetery. Photo by Marianne Burgoyne.

thought I was on the high way to hell, if I suffered myself to linger and listen to it. I shall not subject my little children to such a course of unnatural training, but they shall go to the dance, study music, read novels, and do anything else that will tend to expand their frames, add fire to their spirit, improve their minds, and make them free and untrammeled in body and mind.[62]

And Brigham admitted he liked the freedom of deciding for himself. Once, when his father urged him to sign a temperance pledge, he argued: "No, sir, if I sign the temperance pledge I feel that I am bound, and I wish to do just right, without being bound to it: I want my liberty; and I have conceived from my youth up that I could have my liberty and independence just as much in doing right as I could in doing wrong."[63] Thus, his parents' religionist views worked both ways in forming young Brigham's values. Observing God's laws, which he was steered to do, did not mean for him being curtailed and unhappy.

Another biographical entry depicts a happier glimpse of Brigham's upbringing. Susa Young Gates, Brigham's daughter, in her *Life Story of Brigham Young*, writes:

> Brigham Young's childhood was marked by plain living and high thinking. The family diet consisted of baked potatoes, eggs, milk and cheese, Johnnycake and buttermilk, varied by "garden sass" in summer, and gingerbread and squash pie and dried beans put into the brick oven on Saturday night for the Sabbath dinner so that no cooking and work should mar the sacred peace of that day.
>
> All this made for the health and simplicity of the happy home. In it all was cleanliness. Father, mother, children, all loved and made music. The mother was a choir singer in the Methodist Church. All the children inherited easy verbal expression, literary and musical tastes with "genteel" manners. Some were very gay and vivacious. Both parents were affectionate, generous, and cheerful.[64]

Gates reports that Brigham's mother mellowed his father's stern effect with her "tender solicitude," and gave Brigham and the other children what little schooling she could at home.[65] This last insight helps explain why only eleven days of schooling didn't matter in Brigham's case. He was gifted with "verbal expression" and intelligence, exposed to culture and manners—the kind of grace not often found in poor families. A simple explanation of good genes and good upbringing is why Brigham thrived, despite no formal education.

Brigham's memory of his mother indicates respect for her and her lessons:

> Of my mother—she that bore me—I can say, no better woman ever lived in the world than she was. I have the feelings of a son towards her: I should have them—it is right; but I judge the matter pertaining to her from the principles and the spirit of the teaching I received from her.
>
> Would she countenance one of her children in the least act that was wrong according to her traditions? No, not in the least degree.[66]

That Brigham strove throughout his life to live the precepts of the Holy Bible is a tribute to his mother. J. P. Barnum reports that during his mother's life, Brigham was remembered as "a very studious, industrious boy, and very much devoted to his mother. . . . One of his chief characteristics was his great taciturnity. He held himself aloof from the boys his own age and seemed to care for nothing but study and to work for his mother."[67] His mother's death must have come as a blow. Brigham was barely fourteen when his mother died of consumption.

Abigail's death, 11 June 1815, at forty-nine, split the family apart. John Young moved again, leaving his farm and its many improvements. With his older boys, Joseph, eighteen, Phinehas, sixteen, and Brigham, John Young moved thirty-five miles west of Genoa, to the "Sugar Hill" district of Steuben County, near Tyrone, along the Tioga River.[68] His daughters Nancy, Susannah, Rhoda, and Fanny had all married and moved away by 1815, although Fanny had left her husband to return home and take over the care of the family shortly before Abigail's death. John Jr. had married in 1813. Lorenzo went to live with his older sister Rhoda and her husband John P. Greene, near Cayuga Bridge. Louisa most likely went to live either with the Greenes or with Susannah and her husband James Little in Auburn.[69] The family would never again be a core unit.

Lorenzo later wrote that his father "moved to what was then considered the Far West," where the family settled in the midst of a dense wilderness "of about 20 miles in length and breadth." Here, John purchased one hundred acres from General Wordsworth, "on what was called 'Wordsworth Tract,' which had just opened for market."[70] According to the *History of Tioga, Cheming, Tomkins and Schuyler Counties,* the family settled on a farm near Pine Grove, seven miles west of what is now Watkins Glen, on Sugar Hill Road. Members of the Young family also lived for a time on the premises later occupied by "Uncle Dan" Hughey, about a half-mile south of Pine Grove.[71]

John Young's home in the "Sugar Hill" district was remote—at least fifteen miles from any settlement where supplies could be purchased. The nearest Indian and trading establishment at Painted Post was eighteen miles away. According to Jabez Hamner, an early settler who also arrived in 1815 with his family and who lived in the house of John Young until he could build for himself, John Young's only neighbors were his eldest daughter Nancy and her husband Daniel Kent. Kent would have been the only person to help Young and his sons build their small log house.[72]

John Young now made his living tapping maple trees. Lorenzo wrote that his father "had a nice lot of sugar maples on his place. He made troughs and tapped the sugar bush."[73] The "sugaring-off" season was in the early spring. The tapping of the maple sap was as important as haying and corn husking. Not only did maple sugar have household uses, but it was also used as barter to purchase essential items.[74]

Brigham hauled the sugar his father had made from sap—up to fifty or sixty pounds on his back—to the settlement to exchange it for flour, according to Lorenzo, "as all our flour was gone and that was our main living, in those days. Our boys would think it hard fare to sit down to a breakfast of nothing but bread, water and porridge, although that was our living, only as my brother John would once in awhile kill a deer or perhaps a partridge."[75] Lorenzo remembered when Brigham shot a single robin, which fed the two boys while their father was away:

> On this occasion father had been gone two days, and brother Brigham and I had worked very hard to gather the sap, which labor fell entirely on Brigham, but I kept it a-boiling. We had eaten the last flour the day father left, and had not a

bite all day except what sugar we had eaten and we were very faint, but as night drew nigh we started to our house and to our joy a little robin came flying along and lit on a tall tree near the house. Brigham ran to the house and got the gun, and if I ever prayed in my life, I did then that he might kill the poor little robin. The gun cracked and down came the robin. We soon had it dressed and boiling in the pot and when we thought it cooked we then wished for flour enough to thicken the broth. Finally brother Brigham got the flour barrel and told me to set a pan on the floor and he held up the barrel and I thumped it with a stick and the flour came out of the cracks and we got two or three spoonfuls and thickened the broth, and then with thanks to God for his mercy, we ate and seemed to have all we wanted, a full meal for two hungry boys on one little robin and two spoonfuls of flour.[76]

Brigham said of his years living in Tyrone, "I have seen the time that I had not food to satisfy the craving of my nature. I know what it is to be in poverty, and to be destitute of raiment necessary to keep my body warm."[77]

In 1817, John Young remarried the widow Hannah Brown, and the family split apart again.[78] Brigham's older brother Phinehas married. Joseph, Lorenzo, and, for a brief time, Brigham were taken in by their sister Susannah Little. They lived at "Half Acre," near the village of Cayuga in the township of Aurelius about four miles from Auburn.[79] Living here, Brigham's circumstances would not have improved much because the Littles were also poor. However, Susannah's husband farmed and gardened with some ingenuity. He is credited with being the first person in New York to sell packaged seeds and to introduce tomatoes for table use.[80]

It was also in 1817 that Brigham Young struck out on his own. He records: "When I was sixteen years of age, my father said to me, 'You now have your time; go and provide for yourself'; and a year had not passed away before I stopped running, jumping, wrestling and laying out my strength for naught. . . ."[81] At this time, Brigham moved a few miles east to the bustling town of Auburn. Its thousand residents worked clearing land or found employment in the mills or in various shops, stores, and taverns along Genesee Street, where at least thirty shops and six taverns operated.[82] Brigham's shift from the country to the bustling village was an education in itself. He put to use the building skills he had developed clearing out forests. Now, however, his skills were to be noticed and enhanced by apprenticeship training.

Once he went to the village, he was "farmed out" or bound to various families, working for his board and a small amount of pay. An article in *The Antiquarian* about the Grover Street corner home of David M. Dunning validates Young's first work as a "chore boy":

> Here, perhaps, is the oldest asparagus bed in the county, set out in the 20's by Nathan Osborne, the old-time gardener of North Street, assisted by Brigham Young, who was then a chore-boy about the Reed and Wadsworth farms on Aurelius Road and had made up his mind to quit the country life and see what he could find to do in the village. . . .[83]

Brigham worked hard for meager wages. His living conditions may or may not have improved, but he probably had more to eat than when he was in the Sugar Hill district harvesting maple sap with his father. This first work on the Reed and Wadsworth farms was menial; the prospect was not enough to keep him.

Brigham's second job set him on a career path. He was apprenticed to John C. Jeffries, a cabinetmaker, painter, and chair manufacturer, to learn the trades of carpenter, painter, and glazier.[84] He later recalled:

> The first job my boss gave me was to make a bedstead out of an old log that had been on the beach of the Lake for years, water-logged and watersoaked. Said he—"There are tools, you cut that log into right lengths for a bedstead. Hew out the side rails, the end rails and the posts; get a board for a head board, and go to work and make a bedstead." And I went to work and cut up the log, split it up to the best of my ability, and made a bedstead that, I suppose, they used for many years. I would go to work and learn to make a washboard, and make a bench to put the wash tub on, and to make a chair.[85]

Apparently the Jeffries home became Brigham's foster home, although he could have still been living on either the Reed or Wadsworth farms.[86] Jeffries took his young journeyman Brigham with him, to help him paint and finish the Elijah Miller home[87] (later the Seward House) at the same time Young was gardening for Nathan Osborne, who was himself commissioned by Miller to plant trees, bushes, and flowers on the five-acre estate.[88]

Under Jeffries' apprenticeship, Brigham established himself as a skilled artisan who became famous for his stairwell decorations, fanlight doorways, door frames, stair rails, louvered attic windows, and, above all, fireplace mantels. Practically every old home in Auburn claims the distinction of owning one crafted by Brigham.[89] During the slack seasons for building and house painting, a supply of these beautiful hand-wrought mantelpieces, which can be detached from the wall in one piece, was laid in, and these purchased as the need arose by carpenters of lesser skills. There is a variety of patterns, but enough duplication to assume these fireplaces were produced in large quantities.[90] All the

Master carpenter John C. Jeffries, assisted by his journeyman Brigham Young, finished and painted this house for Elijah Miller in Auburn, New York. William H. Seward later married Miller's daughter and moved into the house. It is now preserved as a museum, the Seward House. Photo by Robert Burgoyne, courtesy of the Seward House.

Above: Under Jeffries' tutelage Brigham Young became famous in the Auburn area for his carpentry, mantlepieces, and windows. While numerous places claim to have mantlepieces built by Brigham Young, this one in the Seward House is definitely known to be his. Photo by Marianne Burgoyne, courtesy of the Seward House.

Top: The Wait family has lived in this farmhouse since it was built by John C. Jeffries, assisted by his journeyman, Brigham Young. While he was working on the house, Brigham may have lived on the property. Photo by Marianne Burgoyne.

houses built in the early years between 1800 and 1830 relied on the open fireplace for heat. The best rooms of the house had a decorated mantel to add to their beauty. Brigham may have produced many of these mantelpieces, but unless he were Paul Bunyan himself, could not have made every chair and doorway New Yorkers have credited him personally for building. His later fame added to the myth that every old chair in Cayuga County was made by him.

One fireplace—perhaps the most ornate in the city—is one that Brigham carved for Judge Elijah Miller's home. He surely would have known Elijah's daughter, Frances, while he was helping to construct the home. If he wooed her, he didn't win her. William Seward, later Abraham Lincoln's secretary of state, married Frances Miller, and moved into the Miller home in 1824.[91] William H. Seward and Brigham, both born in 1801 and both governors of their respective states, likely did not meet until 1869, when Seward, having just retired as secretary of state, came west upon completion of the transcontinental railway. In his writings, Seward fails to mention that Brigham Young kept him waiting three days. He recounts the interview:

The meeting with Brigham Young was interesting. Accurately attired in a
    black suit and white cravat as became a religious guide, the President's face
betokened his resolute character, and his manner had the mingled ease and dignity befitting a chief magistrate.
    "Governor Seward," said he, after an exchange of greetings, "who lives in Squire Brown's house in Auburn now?"
    "I bought it from Squire Brown and lived there a year or two," replied Seward, "and since then it has had several owners."
    "I worked on that house as a journeyman carpenter when they were building it," said Young, "about the same time that I was employed at the Theological Seminary."[92]

In this interview, Brigham reduced Seward's rank to governor. Perhaps he held a little animosity for the spoiled young man who seemingly had everything when he himself was a mere carpenter working on two properties, which, unknown to both in 1817, Seward would own one day.

Brigham left his carpentry mark in Auburn. Besides the Miller home, he helped build the first marketplace, the prison, the theological seminary, the home of "Squire" William Brown (later Hutchinson, then Dunning House), the Joseph Wadsworth House (later owned by the parents of David M. Dunning), the Abijah Miller (uncle of Judge Elijah Miller) Mansion, and the magnificent Wait farmhouse.[93] Brigham may have lived for a time on the Wait property while he helped construct the farmhouse and barn.[94] Wait, inspired by the beauty of Young's workmanship to gather information about his life, calls him an "artisan without peer."[95] Samuel Hopkins Adams, who spent seventy-five summers at his boyhood home on the shores of Owasco Lake, wrote in the *Holiday Magazine* in 1951:

> Inspired carpenters who would never have claimed the name architect are responsible for much of what is best in our building. One such carpenter-artist who won greater fame in another field was Brigham Young. Before 1820 he was well content to earn a dollar a day with his hammer and saw. He built the beautiful old Wait farmhouse west of Auburn, and had at least a hand in the Seward mansion in the heart of the city."[96]

David Dunning, who resided in the Brown house (where Brigham had worked as a carpenter, painter, and glazier) until his death in 1940, spoke of Brigham's connection to his family:

> My grandfather [Joseph Wadsworth] always spoke very highly of Brigham as an energetic, active and capable young man. His living there [at the Wadsworth House he helped build] was generally known in the family and often mentioned during our life there.[97]

Top: Nancy Wait, the current owner of the Wait house, says Brigham Young helped build this barn beside it at the same time he worked on the house. Photo by Marianne Burgoyne.

Above: Brigham Young completed the carpentry and the glasswork on this fanlight doorway for the Wait home. Photo by Marianne Burgoyne.

MIRIAM WORKS.

Auburn was a tremendous training ground for Brigham. If he were highly thought of in that village, it was because he sought to ensure the respect he gained. Years later, he said of his early career:

Among various other occupations I have been a carpenter, painter, and glazier, and when I learned my trades and worked, both as a journeyman and master, if I took a job of painting and glazing, say to the amount of one pound sterling, or five dollars, and through my own carelessness in any manner injured the work or material, I considered it my duty to repair the injury at my own expense.[98]

Brigham lived long enough to relish the myths surrounding his carpentry work. In 1876, he responded to word that a chair he had made was receiving recognition:

I felt amused and interested in your statement that a chair made by me would occupy a place in your Centennial supper to be held next Tuesday. I have no doubt that many other pieces of furniture and other specimens of my handiwork can be found scattered about your section of the country, for I have believed all my life that, that which was worth doing was worth doing well, and have considered it as much a part of my religion to do honest, reliable work, such as would endure, for those who employed me, as to attend to the services of God's worship on the Sabbath.[99]

From Auburn, Brigham moved north eight miles to Port Byron (called Bucksville in 1820), then located on the Erie Canal. He moved presumably because he could no longer get enough work to sustain himself in Auburn or because his prospects looked brighter near the canal. In Port Byron, "he got in with an old chair repairer and general tinkerer who gave him a job with $7 a month tenant house and an antique vehicle to collect furniture for repairs."[100] The *Auburn Daily Bulletin* reported in 1877 that Young had worked about any odd jobs he could get: "At Port Byron, in this county, he painted boats."[101] William Hayden, a boy growing up in the area during the 1820s, knew Brigham and later wrote about him. He recounts that Brigham began building boats as well as painting them and eventually was given the charge of other men. Hayden recounts that the proprietors of the boatyard said Brigham "would do more work in a given time and secure more and better work from his help without trouble than any man they have ever employed."[102]

On 26 May 1823, Brigham purchased a one-acre lot in Port Byron from Aholiab Buck for sixty dollars. The deed located the lot "on the west side of the Owasco Creek lying between the Montezuma Turnpike and the Erie Canal."[103] Brigham may have purchased the property thinking he would settle here, but he never made use of it.

Brigham gained employment manufacturing wooden pails in a pail factory, operated by Charles Parks at Haydenville, or Mentz. He worked for fifty cents a day, with the understanding that he "should do such work as might be required of him."[104] Parks, impressed with an invention of Brigham's for mixing paint—a water-powered pigment crusher that used a cannonball as a pestle to an iron pot—promoted him from painter to carpenter. Brigham began turning out chairs, tables, settees, cupboards, and doors.[105]

Above: This photo is often identified as Miriam Works Young; however, Miriam died in 1832, when photography was still in its infancy and certainly not accessible to a poor family in rural New York. Some members of the Young family believe it may be her daughter, Vilate, who was reported to look much like her mother. No one really knows who this lovely lady is, but she cannot be Miriam Works.

While he was working for Parks, he met Miriam Angeline Works, who became his first wife. She was the second child of Asa and Abigail Marks Works, friends of Charles Parks. Her father was a Revolutionary War veteran and had come to Aurelius from Worcester, Massachusetts, not far from Hopkinton where John Young had lived. Miriam, born in Aurelius on 7 June 1806, was eighteen when she met Brigham.[106] She was "a beautiful blonde with blue eyes and wavy hair; gentle and loveable."[107]

Brigham and Miriam likely met through Charles Parks or other mutual acquaintances in Haydenville. They may have met at a dance, or at least enjoyed them together, considering they both lived near Half Acre, an Aurelius crossroads on the Seneca Turnpike which boasted three taverns within a half-acre space. Respectable community dancing parties were periodically held in them. Brigham attended such social gatherings, as did "nice young girls of the township, properly escorted."[108] William Hayden gives an account of that romance:

> . . . while Brigham was employed at the pail factory, a young woman friend of the proprietor's family who was in the custom of visiting there was introduced to him and this was the beginning of Brigham Young's acquaintance with a very worthy young woman, Angeline Works. As their acquaintance ripened, her visits were thought to be a little more frequent, or, at least, they were noticed more. Her long walk home in the evening would have been monotonous, not to say dangerous, if taken alone, therefore, Brigham, with characteristic gallantry, used to accompany her, her home being distant from his boarding place about four miles, or one mile south of Troopsville.
>
> As might have been expected, only a few of these long walks were enjoyed before arrangements for marriage were entered into and on the morning of the wedding day, while we were at our breakfast, a sharp rap called my father to the door. A short conversation ensued, after which father and his visitor went to the barn and soon we saw Brigham drive out of the yard with our horse and wagon. My mother wished to know why father would allow Brigham to take his horse

Maria Axton, current owner of this house just south of Port Byron in Haydenville (formerly Mentz), New York, says Brigham and Miriam Young lived in the bedroom at the far left on the second floor of this house. Photo by Marianne Burgoyne.

when his rule was to refuse it to all young men. His reply was that Brigham was not like most young men, for he knew enough to use a horse and not abuse it and, beside that, he was going to bring home a bride.[109]

Brigham and Miriam were married 5 October 1824. Brigham was twenty-three and Miriam still eighteen. The *Cayuga Patriot* belatedly printed a brief notice of the marriage on 3 November 1824:

On the 5th ult. [October] by Gilbert Weed, Esq. Mr. Brigham Young, to Miss Marian [*sic*] Works, daughter of Mr. Asa Works.[110]

The first home where Brigham brought his new bride is still standing. It is located a mile and a half south of Port Byron on a small hill near the Owasco Outlet, in Haydenville (Mentz). William Hayden described the house as it looked at the time the couple lived there:

The house where Brigham lived . . . was a frame building sixteen feet wide and twenty-four feet in length, a short story and a half high, devoid of paint inside or out, standing with the end toward the road nearly opposite the old factory and directly in front of the old bridge crossing the outlet between Troopsville and Port Byron.

In the east end was an old-fashioned fire place and large chimney, with stairway on one side and a small pantry on the other. Two rooms were partitioned off on the west end for bedrooms, being about seven foot square. The intervening space was parlor, sitting room, dining room and kitchen combined. The lower rooms of the house were roughly plastered; but were without the luxury of a cellar.[111]

The current owner, Maria Axton, says that Brigham Young spent his honeymoon here in the upper left bedroom.[112] A previous owner, Marion Knapp,

validates that the couple spent their honeymoon and first months of marriage here while Brigham worked at the pail factory across the road.[113]

As it stands today, the home has been completely enlarged and remodeled, although the bedroom where Brigham and his wife slept is still visible from the road. Also on the property is the original well Brigham dug. The Axtons have added a rock finish to it, enhancing its looks from Brigham's days when it was serviceable only.[114]

The couple's first daughter, Elizabeth, was born in Port Byron on 26 September 1825.[115] By then, the Youngs were living there. At that time, the Erie Canal flowed directly in back of their home and Brigham reportedly worked for a time on the canal.[116]

The Port Byron home also stands today, enlarged and remodeled. A sign at the four-corners' intersection in Port Byron points east diagonally one hundred yards to the home. Matthew and Genevieve Uglialoro, who have owned the home since 1927, claim the original wood floors still exist. The front door is the original. So, too, are the cellar beams, cabinets with original latches, and fireplace oven. This oven, located in the basement, was deep and at least a foot thick. The Youngs used to bake bread, walk it down to the canal, and sell it to boatsmen and canal workers. Today, the oven is no longer in use.[117]

The Uglialoros have one treasure in their possession, which they found when they repegged the original pegs of the home. They possess an old shoe of early 1800s vintage. Matthew and his son found the shoe in the corner of the upstairs attic behind the pegs. The possibility exists that it could be Miriam's shoe, although there is no way to prove it. The Auburn Historical Society once offered Matthew Uglialoro fifty dollars for the shoe. He said he wouldn't sell it for one hundred fifty. He plans to keep the shoe and the home, proud of the Young history that goes with their place.[118]

The Owasco Outlet runs west of the Axton home. Photo by Marianne Burgoyne.

Brigham and Miriam Young's first daughter, Elizabeth, was born in this house. The current owner, Matthew Uglialoro, has lived in it since 1927. The top photo shows the house in 1949 before it was remodeled. Uglialoro says that every year during the the Hill Cumorah Pageant, "busloads of tourists pile out and snap pictures of this house." *Above:* Photo by Marianne Burgoyne. *Top:* Courtesy of the Uglialoro family.

In 1828, Brigham moved with Miriam and Elizabeth to Oswego, New York, on the shore of Lake Ontario, twenty-eight miles north of Port Byron. In a letter to David B. Smith, 1 June 1853, Brigham stated he "built a large tannery there."[119] Nothing is known of their living conditions. The Youngs remained there for less than a year.

In the spring of 1829, Brigham moved with his family back to Mendon, fifty-seven miles to the southwest. His father's family had already begun to gather there. His sister, Susannah Little, widowed when James Little was killed in a wagon accident, had remarried William B. Stilson and was living in Canandaigua, nine miles southeast of Mendon. Another sister, Rhoda, and her husband John P. Greene moved to Bloomfield, seven miles southwest of Mendon, as early as 1826. His brother Phinehas and family were in Mendon by 1829, and his sister Louisa and her family were there by 1830.[120] Fanny was there also, living with the Heber C. Kimball family. John Jr. was in nearby Hector. Lorenzo may have lived in Mendon for a brief time.[121]

Brigham's father, John Sr., still remarried to Hannah Brown, had moved from Tyrone to Mendon in 1827. Joseph was living with him. There, John Sr. purchased eight acres of land just south of the town.[122] The farmland surrounding Mendon was fertile. Author John Fowler called it "one of the finest farming districts I have yet seen in the State of New York."[123]

After their arrival in Mendon, Brigham and his family likely lived briefly with John Sr. before building his own place on his father's land.[124] John Sr.'s home is still standing, located a few miles south of Mendon on the southeast corner of Cheese Factory and Mendon-Ionia Roads.[125] Eileen Havens, who once lived in the home and whose daughter and grandchildren now live there, says her great-grandfather bought the farm in about 1876. Her father was born in the home in 1897. Her family boasts that six generations of Hutchinsons have lived there. Haven's sister, who did her dissertation on Brigham, says that Brigham helped his father build the T- shaped house. She recalls the story that the front of the original house was moved and placed on a house diagonally across the road. The dimensions of the two fronts are the same, so there may be validity to the move. The second story was then added to the John Sr. house and a room serving as a kitchen built on the east side.[126]

Brigham would not have lived long with his father. He built a combination home, mill, and place of business across the street, located on the southwest corner of the Cheese Factory and Mendon-Ionia Roads. Historian Anah B. Yates reported in the *Honeoye Falls Times* in 1922 that Brigham,

> following his trade at Mendon . . . built the fine old house still standing and occupied on the Hutchinson farm; he and his family occupying a log house farther up the road. He put up a saw mill on the little creek (where now water cress and forget-me-nots grow in profusion and brook trout are very plentiful in the Spring), and when business was dull made up the lumber, felled by his brothers, into chairs and baskets, that they sold from house to house throughout the country during the winter months.[127]

According to John D. Lynn, an old-time Mendon resident, Brigham operated a basketmaking shop in the rear of the house. He stated:

At the eastern end of this farm a large spring pours out of the foot of the hill, forming the source of a beautiful trout stream now frequented by discriminating sportsmen of Rochester. Brigham conveyed this water, through a duct of hollow logs, to an overshot wheel of his own construction, to which he fastened one end of a crosscut saw and, seated on a stump, he held the other end of the saw and watched the waterpower do the work preparing his lumber for the shop.[128]

Brigham's house was once described by George Washington Allen, who remembered that, as a boy, he was sent on an errand there:

> His house and shop stood some 80 rods from the highway, nothing but a footpath led to it. . . . I followed this path which lay along the side of a beautiful little stream of clear water noted for the speckled trout it contained. A dam had been thrown across this stream and a sufficient water power obtained to run a turning lathe in his shop.
>
> On arriving at the house and shop I ascended a rickety outside stair case and was bidden to come in. Pulling a leather string and lifting a wooden latch, enabled me to open the door and I entered.
>
> There was only one room in the house, which served for a bedroom-kitchen-sitting room and parlor. . . . There was a bed in one corner, a cupboard for dishes in another, a table and a few splint bottom chairs.[129]

Havens reports that Brigham's combination home, shop, and mill is no longer standing, although the trout stream still flows through the old site. This area cannot be seen from the road. The beginning of the stream is in the woods above the site.[130]

Heber C. Kimball, who lived in Mendon just southwest of the Young residences,[131] recorded in his history that the Youngs remained very poor:

The John Young home in Mendon, New York, is still standing. His son, Brigham, is credited with building the east wing which houses the kitchen. Photo by Marianne Burgoyne.

They were in low circumstances and seemed to be an afflicted people in consequence of having a great deal of sickness and sorrow to pass through; and of
course were looked down upon by the flourishing church where we lived.[132]

Brigham's investment in the mill apparently did not provide the stability
and permanence he needed. After his second daughter, Vilate, was born on 1
June 1830,[133] (Brigham's twenty-ninth birthday), and Miriam was well enough to
travel, Brigham moved his family to "Number Nine," a rural community a few
miles west of Canandaigua.[134] Brigham said he moved "into a small house
owned by Jonathan Mack, situated on the west side of the road opposite to
where Mr. Mack then lived. I helped to finish his new house, so that he moved
into it before I left the place. I left Canandaigua in 1832 and returned to
Mendon."[135] His house in this ninth township was situated on what is now
Woodhouse Road.[136] The Brigham Young family appears twice in the 1830 U.S.
Census, both in Mendon and in Canandaigua. They must have moved while
the census was in progress.

While in Canandaigua, Miriam contracted tuberculosis. The *Ontario
Republican Times* reported years later that Brigham had been an involved husband and father:

> . . . there could scarcely be a more kind and affectionate husband and father than
> he was, and few men in his circumstances would have provided better for their
> families. Mrs. Young was sick, most of the time unable to do any kind of work,
> but she was a worthy woman, and an exemplary Christian; she was well deserv-
> ing his care and attention, and she had it while she lived in Canandaigua.[137]

Once back in Mendon, Brigham spent less and less time with his work as
his wife became increasingly ill. His daughter records:

> He worked for half a crown a day when he could not get more; got breakfast for
> his wife, himself and the little girls, dressed the children, carried his wife to the
> rocking chair by the fire, left her there until he could return in the evening,
> cooked the family's supper, put her back to bed, and finished up the day's labor.[138]

He continued to accrue debts. The family's lot was as miserable as it had ever
been. George Washington Allen recorded that, as a young boy, he was sent to
the Young home to ask for payment for a debt. He remembered that upon
entering her home, he found Miriam alone,

> poorly and thinly clad, having an old black shawl thrown around her shoulders,
> endeavoring to keep warm over a single stick of wood on the fire in the fireplace.
>   She was evidently in feeble health. The only person about the premises was
> a little red-haired girl five or six years old, with a basket gathering chips and bits
> of wood for fuel. . . .
>   Mrs. Young said her husband had gone to Miller's corners (Ionia) to attend a
> quarterly meeting and she did not know when to expect him home. I made
> known my errand to her. She replied, "I do not know how or when Mr. Young
> can pay Dr. Sheldon, he had been gone two or three days and left us without fuel,
> the last stick is on the fire—we have no flour or meat or anything else in the
> house to eat. As soon as he comes home he will first have to provide fuel and pro-
> vision for his family. Dr. Sheldon will have to be patient a little longer.[139]

The account seems stilted; nevertheless, inferences can be drawn. Miriam may have had her own opinion on how much Brigham helped at home, for the family was extremely poor. Miriam was alone and unhappy, and Brigham had been gone too long, apparently to a church meeting. In short, her lot was destitute.

Brigham continued to do a variety of custom works in the Mendon-Canandaigua area. This included building homes; making and repairing furniture (chairs, tables, desks, chests, baby cribs); putting in windowpanes, doorways, staircases, and fireplace mantels; and other handyman types of work.[140]

Heber Kimball, who was fast becoming Brigham's best friend later recalled:

> Brother Brigham and myself used to work hard, side by side, for fifty cents a day and board ourselves; we had seventy-five cents a day when we worked in the hayfield; we would work from sunrise to sunset, and until nine o'clock at night if there was sign of rain. We would rake and bind after a cradler for a bushel of wheat a day, and chop wood, with snow to our waist for eighteen cents a cord, and take our pay in corn at seventy-five cents a bushel.[141]

Farmers for whom Young worked remembered Brigham as handy with his tools and industrious.[142] One George Hickox reported that Brigham once approached him about borrowing a dollar. "Chop wood with me and earn it," was Hickox's reply. On another occasion Brigham owed Hickox a bill and made a dozen chairs to satisfy the accounts.[143]

Miriam Young continued to fail in health. Brigham moved her to the Heber C. Kimball home, where the Kimballs and he nursed her. She died there 8 September 1832, less than five months after converting to Mormonism.[144] Brigham, his children (Elizabeth, seven, and Vilate, two), and Heber and Vilate Kimball were at her bedside. She was buried in a little cemetery at the top of Boughton Road, where a modern stone marks her grave.[145] At that time, Brigham's daughters went to live with the Kimballs. Brigham, who had also been baptized in April 1832, began to preach and travel.[146] When in Mendon, he stayed with the Kimballs too. His final residence in New York may have been a borrowed room in Kimball's home.

At some point, Brigham abandoned the mill-shop-home he had built in Mendon, either after he returned from Canandaigua "Number Nine" or after Miriam died, when he left his children (as his father had before him) in the care of others. It was at this point Brigham's life changed completely. Life as he had known it halted when he gave up all for his new religion. Many years later, he referred to his young manhood and first marriage as seeming so long ago and far away that is was as if they had been part of the life of a different person.[147]

J. Sheldon Fisher, historian, archaeologist, and owner of the Valentown Museum in Fishers, New York, claims that he has a lathe that Brigham used for making furniture, along with numerous other items found when he excavated the abandoned Young mill. He claims to have found bricks with BY on them, a precision lathe for metalwork, together with a variety of steel-cutting tools, jackknives, drills, reamers, screwdrivers, hammers, axes, punches, awls, files, and screws. He found a forge hammer, together with a number of horse and oxen shoes, suggesting Brigham shod his own animals. He also found a fireplace shovel and tongs, door latches, locks and keys, iron hinges for doors, many sizes

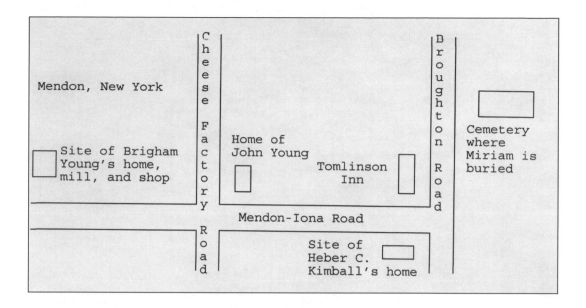

of hand-wrought nails, a flint and steel, called a Strike-o-light, and a garden hoe.[148] He even claims he may have found a wedding ring, presumably belonging to Miriam Young.[149] Fisher's find also indicates what the family ate:

> There were fragments of handmade toys and some marbles, a crushed Easter egg with a painted design, and pits of cherries, peaches, apricots, and wild plums; seeds of apple, pumpkin, melon, squash, and charred corn; chestnuts, butternuts, hickory nuts, pig nuts, black walnuts, and beechnuts. Bones from roast beef and beef steak were plentiful, as well as pork bones, lamb and mutton, passenger pigeon, various game birds, chicken, duck, and goose bones. Brigham's family also ate turtle, fish, and freshwater clams.[150]

If Fisher's find is to some degree reliable, then a concrete picture emerges of how the Youngs lived while in Mendon. Arrington concludes his chapter on Brigham's New York years, "It is clear that while missing a formal education, Brigham had become an expert farmer, gardener, carpenter, glazier, mason, cabinetmaker, painter, and boatbuilder.[151] In short, at thirty-one, he was a practical genius. These skills he would need as he continued to move west with his family.

Upon conversion en masse by the John Young family to the LDS Church, family after family of Youngs moved to Kirtland, Ohio. John Sr. sold forty-five acres of land to Rufus Richardson for $725.30 on 14 May 1833. Later, he filed an affidavit with the War Department stating that he had removed to Kirtland in June 1833.[152]

Brigham followed his family to Kirtland in the fall of 1833.[153] He and his little girls, along with Heber and Vilate Kimball and family, all moved together. Starting over in Kirtland, Brigham said:

> If any man that ever did gather with the Saints was any poorer than I was—it was because he had nothing. I had something and I had nothing; if he had less than I had, I did not know what it could be. I had two children to take care of—that was all. I was a widower. "Brother Brigham, had you any shoes?" No; not a shoe to my foot, except a pair of borrowed boots. I had no winter clothing,

Heber Kimball's and John and Brigham Young's homes were close to the Tomlinson Inn, where Samuel Smith first delivered the Book of Mormon to Heber C. Kimball. Kimball passed the book along to the Young family. Map by Marianne Burgoyne.

except a homemade coat that I had had three or four years. "Any pantaloons?" No. "What did you do? Did you go without?" No; I borrowed a pair to wear till I could get another pair. I had travelled and preached and given away every dollar of my property. I was worth a little property when I started to preach; but I was something like Bunyan . . .[154]

Thus, Brigham Young left New York as poor as his father was when John Sr. first moved his son to Sherburne. Brigham left debts, which he later repaid.[155] Now, he had a calling and a one-track mind. His destiny was set. He would preach the gospel of his newfound religion. As poor as ever as he traveled to Kirtland, he could not then know what level of greatness he would yet achieve.

The cemetery at the top of Broughton Road is the burial place of Miriam Works Young. She shares the ground with several members of the Kimball family. The Heber Kimballs took in her two small daughters after her death. Photo by Marianne Burgoyne.

Chapter 3

A Missionary's Life
Ohio, Missouri, England, and Illinois
Marianne Harding Burgoyne

Once Brigham Young read the Book of Mormon, investigated its worth, and was baptized into the Mormon faith, he embraced the new religion with gusto, dedicating his life to its missionary cause. And once he journeyed to Kirtland, Ohio, to meet its founder, Joseph Smith, he had a mind single in purpose with Smith's. In September 1833, he records in his *Manuscript History*,

> . . . in conformity to the counsel of the Prophet, I made preparations to gather up to Kirtland, and engaged a passage for myself and two children with [B]rother [Heber C.] Kimball, and sent my effects by canal and lake to Fairport. We arrived in Kirtland in safety, travelling by land, where I tarried all winter, and had the privilege of listening to the teachings of the Prophet and enjoying the society of the Saints, working hard at my former trade.[1]

Whatever Joseph Smith requested, Brigham Young executed, so firmly did he believe in Smith and his message.

Smith himself settled in Kirtland because his fledgling church had made notable conversions there in the summer and fall of 1830.[2] By January and February of 1831, he had moved his New York membership of about two hundred to Kirtland.[3] Several hundred new converts a year moved to Ohio from Maine, Vermont, New Hampshire, New York, and Pennsylvania. Also in 1831, Joseph Smith appointed a "central" gathering place for the Saints in Jackson County, Missouri, where twelve hundred Saints, including most of the original Kirtland members, moved by the fall of 1833. He did not move with them. He made Kirtland his residence until 1838.[4]

When Brigham and Heber Kimball arrived in Kirtland, its population was about thirteen hundred.[5] A trading and milling village surrounded by fertile farmland, Kirtland was a place where Brigham quickly found work. His new mission "to sustain the Kingdom of God"[6] was now simplified, aligning with his trade. He built God's kingdom by building homes in Kirtland, Joseph Smith having said, "Never do another day's work to build up a Gentile city."[7] Brigham writes:

I labored for brother Cahoon and finished his house, and although he did not know he could pay me when I commenced, before I finished he had me paid in full. I then went to work for father John Smith, and others, who paid me, and sustained myself in Kirtland, and when the brethren who had gone out to work for the Gentiles returned, I had means, though some of them were scant.

He continues: "I was so directed by a prophet of God and I was not going away to Willoughby, Painsville, Cleveland, nor any where else to build up the Gentiles,"[8] once again demonstrating his zeal to do the prophet's bidding, and thereby be paid for his obedience and labor.

Brigham also built his friend Heber Kimball a home. Kimball purchased seventeen acres on which the new home was located for a sum of $1,200 from Elijah Smith, a prominent landowner.[9] This home was not completed until April 1834. Meanwhile, Kimball rented a small house, where Brigham also lived with his daughters, an arrangement that apparently worked well for both families since cohabitating in Mendon, New York.[10] This rented home was likely located on the property of Elijah Smith.[11] Brigham probably never lived in the new home he built for Heber because he remarried 10 (18) February 1834.[12]

Brigham's second wife, Mary Ann Angell, whom he married seventeen months after Miriam died, had joined the church after reading a Book of Mormon loaned to her by Thomas B. Marsh.[13] A native of Seneca, Ontario County, New

Brigham Young married Mary Ann Angell after his first wife died. When plural marriage was introduced, Mary Ann accepted his subsequent wives, apparently with remarkable grace and kindness. In this painting by William W. Major, begun in Nauvoo in 1845 and completed in Salt Lake City between 1848 and 1851, the Youngs are shown with their children, from left to right: Brigham Young, seated and holding a hymnal, Joseph A. Young, Luna Young, Brigham Young Jr. and his twin, Mary Ann Young, Alice Young, John W. Young, and Mary Ann Angell. The fanciful parlor and scenic outlook doubtless grow from Major's training in the English tradition since they do not represent any of Brigham Young's homes. "Brigham and Mary Ann Angell Young and Their Children," by William W. Major, copyright by Intellectual Reserve, Inc. Courtesy of Museum of Church History and Art, used by permission.

York, she was the daughter of James and Phoebe Morton Angell, born 8 June 1803, two years and seven days after Brigham. When she was very young, her parents moved to Providence, Rhode Island. Of Puritan roots, she became a member of the Free Will Baptists and taught Sunday school. "Her study of the scriptures, especially the prophecies, so engrossed her mind, that she constantly looked for their fulfillment."[14] Years later, she was working in Providence, Rhode Island, when she first heard Mormon missionaries speak. Wishing to learn more, she returned to Ontario County in 1832, to be "on the scene" where Mormonism originated.[15] There she met Brigham's brothers, Joseph, Phinehas, and Lorenzo Young. She was baptized by John P. Greene, a brother-in-law of Brigham's, in Avon, New York, in 1832.[16] Her parents were also baptized. Mary Ann set out alone for Kirtland and was there when Brigham arrived in 1833.[17]

Mary Ann resolved never to marry until she should "'meet a man of God,' one in whom she could confide and with whom her heart could unite in the active duties of a Christian life."[18] She heard Brigham preach and was impressed. Likewise, he heard her "bear testimony" and was equally impressed, in that he proposed.[19] Where Brigham first lived with his second wife is unknown. Given his building skills, he likely soon built her a home of her own. Brigham records only: "In February 1834, I married Mary Ann Angel[l] who took charge of my children, kept my house, and labored faithfully for the interest of my family and the kingdom."[20] Mary Ann Angell was Young's devoted wife for forty-three years. She bore him six children: Joseph Angell, born 13 October 1834; twins, Brigham Jr. and Mary Ann, born 18 December 1836 (Mary Ann died at age six); Alice, born 4 September 1839; Luna, born 20 August 1842; and John Willard, born 1 October 1844.[21] Little did Mary Ann suspect when she gave her consent to marry Brigham that just eight years later she would be asked to accept the enormous burden of giving consent to his plural marriages.

Brigham had been married less than three months when he was called to march with Zion's Camp. This camp was organized to help Mormon Saints in Missouri reclaim their homes, which had been plundered and burned by Missouri mobs.[22] When the Saints complained to Governor Daniel Dunklin, he promised to restore their homes if provided with a posse of assistance. So Joseph Smith quickly raised an army. Always willing to do the bidding of the prophet, Brigham volunteered, leaving his family from May until August. Not only was Mary Ann caring for Elizabeth and Vilate and pregnant with her first child, but her brother Solomon Angell and his friend Lorenzo Booth left their families with Mary Ann while they marched with Joseph Smith as well.[23] This good-bye was the beginning of countless times Brigham would leave his family for the work of the church. Mary Ann's walk through the refiner's fire was just beginning.

Reflecting years later, Brigham claimed the two-thousand-mile march with Zion's Camp was one of the most difficult experiences he ever faced:

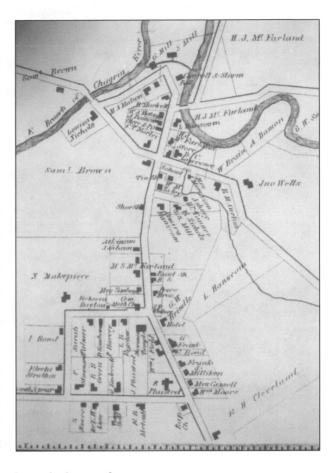

Map of Kirtland, Ohio. Brigham Young may have had at least three residences in Kirtland, two of them within the township (shown here) and one south of the main part of town. Used by permission, Utah State Historical Society, all rights reserved.

The longest journey on foot that ever I took at one time was in the year 1834, when a company of brethren went up to Missouri, the next season after the Saints were driven out of Jackson county. . . . We performed a journey of two thousand miles on foot; we started on the 5th of May, and accomplished that journey inside of three months, carrying our guns on our shoulders, doing our own cooking, etc. And instead of walking along without having to labor, much of the way we had to draw our baggage wagons through mud holes and over sections of bad road. Twenty or thirty men would take hold and draw a wagon up a hill or through a mud hole; and it was seldom that I ever laid down to rest until eleven or twelve o'clock at night, and we always rose very early in the morning. I think the horn was blown at three o'clock to arouse us, to prepare breakfast, etc., and get an early start; and we averaged in the outward trip upwards of forty miles a day. . . .

We laid on the ground every night, and there was scarcely a night that we could sleep, for the air rose from the ground hot enough to suffocate us, and they supplied [musketos] in that country, as they did eggs, by the bushel. . . .[24]

From Brigham's earliest days, moving with his itinerant family, his bed often had been simply where he stopped to rest. Zion's Camp was an unwelcome and more difficult reflection of that past, as well as a dreadful premonition of the future.

On 3 July 1834, after an outbreak of cholera at Rush Creek, the members of the camp were officially discharged; their mission to help the Missouri Saints was never accomplished. The men who had marched and survived had walked through the valley of death. Their endurance powers were honed, their loyalty to their prophet finely defined. Nine of the twelve first apostles of the church were chosen from Zion's Camp on 14 February 1835.[25] Joseph Smith said he knew by the spirit that "it was the will of God" for those who had gone to Zion at the risk of their lives to be the ones to "be ordained to the ministry and go forth to prune the vineyard for the last time."[26] These men had proved their metal; Joseph Smith could count on them.

Construction work on the Kirtland Temple began in 1833, and it was dedicated on 27 March 1836. Brigham Young supervised its painting and finishing. Photo by Marianne Burgoyne, courtesy of Community of Christ.

Brigham returned to his home in August 1834. He worked through the fall and winter for wages building, painting, and glazing. His major effort, however, was his commitment to Kirtland's "public" projects: in his words, "quarrying rock, working on the Temple and finishing off the printing office and schoolroom."[27] He also attended a grammar school that was held for a few weeks. His *Manuscript History* mentions nothing of his home life during this winter.

Brigham began his first appointed mission a year, almost to the day, after he had left with Zion's Camp. (He had served freelance missions before this.) He left 4 May 1835, returning 25 September,[28] after journeying 3,264 miles, or an average of almost twenty miles a day. He records that upon returning home, "we found our fameules [sic] well and [likewise] all the Brothering."[29]

Again, Brigham remained at home—no doubt to Mary Ann's relief—during the fall and winter 1835–1836, occasionally going out and preaching to the neighboring branches.[30] He writes: "In the course of the winter there was a Hebrew school started, which I attended until February 22, 1836, when I was called upon by the Prophet to superintend the painting and finishing of the Temple, upon which I labored until March 27th, when the Temple was so far finished as to be dedicated to the Lord by the Prophet. . . ."[31]

Brigham and his brother Joseph built the frames for the temple's windows, then installed and glazed them.[32] This work included the dramatic Federal-style arched windows that framed the triple-tiered pulpits at each end of the temple, and the unusual Gothic but sectioned side windows with their intricate panes.[33] The brothers were skilled craftsmen. With simple hand planes, they shaped the curved mullions and frames of the Gothic windows, as well as the elliptical shapes in the windows on the facades. These original windows are now stored in a secured location. Next, Brigham supervised the painting of the upper and lower courts or chapels.[34] Finishing the temple was no small feat. It was a $60,000, three-story accomplishment.[35]

Brigham Young and his brother, Joseph, built the framework and glazed the windows for the Kirtland Temple, including these Federalist windows for the priesthood rooms. Photo by Marianne Burgoyne, courtesy of Community of Christ.

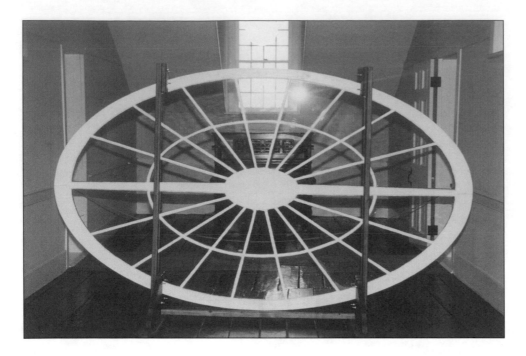

All this while, Brigham took time to provide for the family's survival needs, since he and his family were still coping at poverty level. Joseph Smith told the Twelve that they had a "right by virtue of their offices to call upon the churches to assist them."[36] Brigham claimed, however, that he did not rely on anyone but himself, except in emergencies. "Who supported my family?" he asked. "God and I. Who found clothing? The Lord and myself."[37] Once he complained to Parley P. Pratt, another apostle: "What shall we do? I have nothing to eat & don't know whare to get it. . . ." Pratt suggested they each borrow $25 from a friend, Crosby, who had just arrived in Kirtland. They did.[38]

Brigham was still in debt when Joseph Smith called him and Joseph Young on a mission to New England to preach to their family and friends. Brigham later said, "It has never entered into my heart from the first day I was called to preach the Gospel to this day, when the Lord said, 'Go and leave your family,' to offer the least objection."[39] Again, Brigham left his family in destitute circumstances in the spring of 1836, trusting that God and the church would care for them. He wrote compelling letters to Mary Ann:

3 June 1836
What shal I say to you to comfort your hart. I pray for you and feele that the Lord will bles and keep you from danger and bare you upon the arms of faith. Tell the children that I remember them in my prares. I pray the Lord to give you strength and wisdom in all things.

Let me say to Elizabeth, be a good girl and mind your mother and be good to Vilate and letle Joseph and I [k]now you will be. Vilate be a good girl and mind your mother and studdy your book. . . . Mary, Kiss that lettle son of ours and tell him make hast[e] and groe so he can goe with me. . . . If enny [of] the Brethern inquire about me tell them I am doing as well as I can. So Fair Well. The Lord bless you.[40]

21 July 1836
Once more I take my pen in hand to right to you. I think this is the fo[u]rth time that I have ritten to you sence I left home, but I have not heard a word from

This elliptical window, fashioned by Brigham Young, is now on display inside the Kirtland Temple. Photo by Marianne Burgoyne, courtesy of Community of Christ.

you sence I left. I have some faint hopes that I shall here from you when I get to Boston. . . . I am calculating to return home as so[o]n as Posable after the first of September. I think that I shal be able to return and pay for my house and I want to repare it this fall so that I can feele contented about my famely when I leve them. Mary if you can I wish you wold have Brother A Bonney get som lumber or timber or ston and if you have a chance to b[u]y enny thing for bilding and when I com home I [will] Pay for it I [would like] to say agradel [a great deal] but I will not write with pen and enk but I com[e] and see you and speak to you face to face. I want you should write to me as so[o]n as you rec[e]ive this. . . . My Dear Mary I remember you continuly in my Prayrs. My love to all my little children. Be good to your mother and pray for me when I am away. Fairwell. I remane your hosbon and frend.[41]

This July letter is the first reference in Brigham's writings to confirm that the Youngs had a place of their own in Kirtland, albeit one in need of repairs and financing. Both letters capture a glimpse of the family's poverty and suffering. Not having heard from Mary Ann, Brigham seems expressly lonely for his family. The conjugal sacrifice must have been intense, and Mary Ann had the extra burden of handling the welfare of three young children, ages eleven, seven, and two, as well as being pregnant with twins.

Only one deed exists confirming that Brigham owned property, 0.375 acres, while in Kirtland. This property is located west of Route 306 just across the road and up the hill from the northwest corner of the current LDS Stake Center, 8751 Kirtland Road. (Kirtland Road is Route 306, which turns into Chillicothe Road, midpoint up the steep hill to the Kirtland Temple.) It is not known if the home in which Brigham lived with Mary Ann and his children was once on this property. No house exists at the present time. Brigham sold this property to his brother-in-law, Solomon Angell, 3 July 1837.[42]

Brigham also may have had a farm, located on the east side of Chillicothe Road, two-fifths of a mile north of the Geauga County line. A 29 June 1921 *Willoughby Republican* article by George H. Morse reports, "Brigham's place was

Joseph Smith's office in the Kirtland Temple. The attic with these dormer windows allowed sufficient space for classrooms and offices on the topmost floor of the building. Photo by Marianne Burgoyne, courtesy of Community of Christ.

located at the south part of the farm now owned by N. C. Ferry, close to the Geauga county line, back about one-quarter mile from the Chillicothe Road."[43] N. C. Ferry owned 132.17 acres until 15 August 1921, when he sold the land to his daughters, Blanche Ferry Guild and Madge Ferry Chase, for ten dollars.[44] "Brigham's place" is still standing, located at 10831 Chillicothe Road. The white, two-story house faces west and could be the home Brigham built and lived in with Mary Ann, at least part of the time they resided in Kirtland. Verifying the location of the Ferry property is the best evidence which exists today that Brigham Young lived at this site. Several local traditions point to this site as well.[45]

Today, the home is owned by Charles and Lucy Wellhausen, III, who have lived there since 1975. Lucy Wellhausen says that Mormon missionaries approached her in the early 1980s and told her Brigham Young built the home. Then, two years ago (2000), an official from the LDS Church came inquiring about the home. She is surprised the home's historical significance has gone largely unnoticed until now. She says much of the home, including the basement beams and windows, could be the handicraft of Brigham Young. "The windows have the weeping (wavy)glass similar to the windows of the Kirtland Temple. And I am probably the only person to have glazed those windows since Brigham," she jokes. Lucy says a cemetery is located on the property. When she and her husband planted a garden, they dug up hundreds of pieces of broken dishes. She was astonished to learn that when Mary Ann left her Nauvoo home, she may have been the person to hide dishes in the well located on her property. Now, Lucy speculates that the broken dishes on her own property (which she threw away) may have belonged to Mary Ann Angell Young.[46]

Historian Elwin C. Robison toured the Wellhausen home on two occasions in 2000 and 2001 and believes that much of the original construction is of a very early period and could have been built in the 1830s. He found evidence for this early dating in the original beams supporting the home; doors, door latches, and door frames; and windows. Many of the weathered clapboards are original to the home. He acknowledged that the paneled doors are different from Kirtland houses of the early 1830s,[47] suggesting a different carpenter's hand in its construction.

Just to the east of the Chillicothe home is a red barn, located at 8265 Bridlehurst Trail, and also supposedly built by Brigham. The barn door opens west, facing the back door of the Wellhausen home. The current owners of this barn are James and Andrea Hunziker. The Hunzikers confirm local tradition that Brigham did, in fact, build the barn, but maybe not on this property. Either Brigham or someone else moved it to its current site. A picture of the barn sitting atop its foundation adds validity to the belief that the barn, indeed, may have been moved. However, Elwin Robison dates the barn to the 1890s and speculates that if Brigham built a barn near here, it is one of three earlier barns no longer existing but that once stood on this property.[48]

Brigham may have owned a third piece of property in Kirtland as well. This land is located off Garfield on Timothy Lane. Tradition points to this piece of property, but no other information is known. Today, no home is standing. The land is now part of someone's yard.[49] Because one of Brigham's daughters attended the little red schoolhouse near the temple site, speculation exists that the Young family could have lived within the township of Kirtland at one time.[50]

votes could be relied on" and had them occupy the stand and prominent seats.[57] The conference ensured Smith's presidency.

The disfellowshipments and excommunications, however, had future consequences for Brigham. He writes: "On the morning of December 22, I left Kirtland in consequence of the fury of the mob, and the spirit that prevailed in the apostates, who had threatened to destroy me because I would proclaim, publicly and privately, that I knew by the power of the Holy Ghost, that Joseph Smith was a Prophet of the Most High God, and had not transgressed and fallen as apostates declared."[58]

Brigham fled to Dublin, Indiana, staying with his brother Lorenzo, who had stopped to winter there. Joseph Smith soon joined him, along with Sidney Rigdon and George W. Robinson, having fled Kirtland due to insurrections of the apostates. Smith dropped his heavy burden directly in Brigham's hands. Brigham records that Joseph came to him and said, "Brother Brigham, I am destitute of means to pursue my journey, and as you are one of the Twelve Apostles who hold the keys of the kingdom in all the world, I believe I shall throw myself upon you, and look to you for counsel in this case." Brigham soon was able to secure for Joseph three hundred dollars from a man named Tomlinson, who had just sold his tavern-stand.[59]

One small reference exists in the *Manuscript History* of Brigham's living quarters in Dublin. The day Joseph started once again on his travels, Brigham received visitors, Isaac Seeley and his wife. He mentions, "The house was pretty well littered up. I sat writing to my wife, but I welcomed them to the use of the house and what was left in it."[60] These itinerant leaders were gathered in Lorenzo's home, carrying on church business, living in crowded quarters, making their circumstances do, all the while neglecting proper care of themselves or Lorenzo's property.

The outcome of the church's internal strife was that Joseph Smith shifted church headquarters to Far West, Missouri.[61] Brigham arrived there 14 March 1838 and within two weeks had set up a home: "I purchased a small improvement on Mill Creek [a tributary of Shoal Creek, about eight miles east of Far West], located my family and proceeded to fence in a farm. I bought several pieces of land and obtained deeds for these."[62]

By now, leaving property behind was becoming a habit with Brigham. Years later, Brigham reported to a congregation, "When I left there [Kirtland] for Missouri, I left property worth over five thousand dollars in gold, that I got comparatively nothing for."[63] His Mendon, New York, property had been worth a nice sum as well when he abandoned it to heed the call of the prophet. He also wrote to a friend of his youth, David B. Smith, that when he left Kirtland, he left behind property worth "$3 or $4000."[64] His seemingly nonchalant attitude toward leaving property was, nevertheless, inspired by a higher cause: "I have no heart to look after my own individual advantage, I never have had; my heart is not upon the things of this world."[65] This "high road," however, doesn't explain why he failed to care for the needs of his family.

When Brigham fled Kirtland, he left Mary Ann and the children to fend off the angry mob. By the time he retrieved his family, locating them on Mill Creek, Mary Ann was gravely ill. Her spirit had been wounded back in Kirtland when apostates harassed her and her children. They frequented her property, "pretending to believe" that Brigham was "hid up there." They used "threats and vile language" that weakened her physical and mental health. She told her biographer, "This was undoubtedly the severest trial of my life."[66] Brigham records only, "My wife was taken very sick, so that her life was despaired of for a long time."[67]

Realizing that Brigham's and Mary Ann's situation was desperate, Joseph Smith spared the family by commanding Brigham: "Verily thus saith the Lord, let my servant Brigham Young go unto the place which he has bought, on Mill Creek, and there provide for his family until an effectual door is opened for the support of his family, until I command him to go hence, and not to leave his family until they are amply provided for."[68] This promise was short-lived and the home was less than a year a resting place for the beleaguered couple.

The Missouri mobs were once again attacking the Mormons, this time with the help of the state paying them militia wages.[69] They feared the Mormons, especially their bloc voting powers. Missouri mobs began attacking Mormon settlements and set fire to DeWitt, Carroll County, in October 1838. Brigham, concerned for his family living on the outskirts of Far West, moved them eight miles into town.[70]

In his *Manuscript History*, Brigham records shocking treachery:

> I knew men in the course of the fall to gather up their flocks and herds, and take their families into their wagons, and then burn up their houses and leave for other parts. I afterwards saw their names attached to affidavits, stating that Mormons had driven them from their homes and burned their houses. This was quite effectual in raising prejudice against us. . . . Many Saints were wounded and murdered by the army, and several women were ravished to death.

And by November 1838, he writes, "The brethren were compelled to give away their property by executing a deed of trust at the point of the bayonet."[71]

The violence against the Mormons escalated with Governor Lilburn W. Boggs's "Extermination Order," 27 October 1838: "The Mormons must be treated as enemies and must be exterminated or driven from the state, if necessary for the public good. Their outrages are beyond all description. If you can increase your force, you are authorized to do so, to any extent you may think necessary."[72] This edict culminated three days later in the massacre of men, women, and children at the Mormon settlement of Haun's Mill.[73]

On 14 February 1839, Brigham moved from Far West: "I left Missouri with my family, leaving my landed property and nearly all my household goods, and went to Illinois, to a little town called Atlas, Pike [C]ounty, where I tarried a few weeks; then moved to Quincy."[74] Mary Ann later remembered the journey from Missouri as dangerous and traumatic. As the families made their way east to Illinois, they faced frostbite, illness, and threats to their lives. Several times Brigham left his family in camp or at the house of a friendly family and returned with his teams to help others. During one absence, their infant daughter was thrown from a wagon and run over. She survived. Before arriving at the Mississippi River gathering place in the spring of 1839, Mary Ann had "kept house in eleven different places."[75]

Once in Quincy, Brigham and the other members of the Twelve met to raise money to help move fifty more families from Far West. He writes: "Among the subscribers was widow Warren Smith, whose husband and son had their brains blown

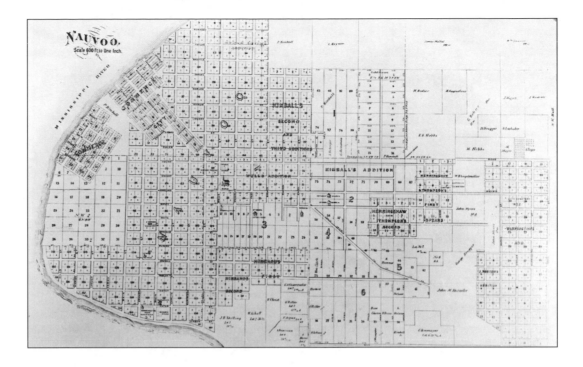

out [and] another son shot to pieces at the massacre at Haun's Mill. She sent her only team on this charitable mission." By April 1839, Brigham records that all the poor Saints had been moved from Far West, excepting Parley P. Pratt and Morris Phelps, who were still in prison and "brother Yokum, who had been so dreadfully mutilated in the Haun's Mill massacre that he could not be moved."[76]

Brigham had one more pressing matter of business in Far West. He, along with the Twelve, wanted to fulfill a revelation announced by Joseph Smith nine months earlier, on 8 July 1838: ". . . and next spring let them depart to go over the great waters, and there promulgate my Gospel, the fulness thereof, and bear record of my name. Let them take leave of my Saints in the city Far West, on the 26th day of April next, on the building spot of my house, saith the Lord." So, at risk of their lives, he and others of the Twelve—Heber C. Kimball, Orson Pratt, John E. Page, John Taylor, and newly chosen Wilford Woodruff and George A. Smith— held a conference at Far West early on the morning of 26 April. They met on land designated for the temple and rolled up a large stone near the southeast corner.[77] Fulfilling Joseph's prophecy, Brigham was primed for his greatest mission effort yet. This was the beginning of the Twelve's extraordinary mission to England.

Before he departed, however, Brigham moved his family one more time. Joseph Smith had recently purchased Iowa lands just across the river from Commerce, where Sidney Rigdon now resided and where the church met for its first conference since being warned not to congregate. Brigham arrived there on 18 May, and on the 23rd recorded, "I crossed the Mississippi with my family, and took up my residence in a room in the old military barracks, in company with brother Woodruff and his family."[78]

These barracks are no longer standing, but their foundations remain. They were located on the West Bank of the Mississippi River, across from Nauvoo on the East Bank.[79] Today, standing at the site, one can see the newly built Nauvoo Temple situated on the same hilltop where the first Nauvoo Temple was destroyed.

Map of Nauvoo, Illinois. The straight streets meeting at ninety degree angles reflect the building pattern that would continue in Mormon settlements throughout the West. Used by permission, Utah State Historical Society, all rights reserved.

These foundations are all that remain of the army barracks on the west banks of the Mississippi across from Nauvoo, where Brigham Young left Mary Ann and their children when he departed on a mission to England. Photo by Marianne Burgoyne.

On 2 July, the Twelve and the Presidency assembled at Brigham's home for missionary instructions. Wilford Woodruff recorded that the First Presidency blessed each apostle and his wife individually, promising, "if we were faithful we had the promise of again returning to the bosom of our families and being blessed on our missions and having many souls as seals of our ministry."[80] The wives seemed especially in need of the blessings. They were once again to be left by their husbands and for a longer time than preceding missions. And now, in temporary barracks, with church persecutions having scattered the fold, more financially desperate than ever before, their circumstances were more critical than any time heretofore.

The apostles' departure was halted by an outbreak of malaria. Every man intending to go to England was stricken by the sickness that swept the temporary Iowa settlements.[81] But Smith challenged them once again "to go forth without purse or scrip, according to the revelations of Jesus Christ."[82] On 14 September, Brigham records, "I started from Montrose on my mission to England. My health was so poor I was unable to go thirty rods to the river without assistance. . . . I left my wife sick, with a babe only ten days old, and all of my children sick and unable to wait upon each other."[83]

It must have seemed unimaginable to Mary Ann for her husband to be leaving her newly delivered and so ill, with only barracks for living quarters, no possessions, little money, and little food. Brigham's response, "I was determined to go to England or to die trying. My firm resolve was that I would do what I was required to do in the Gospel of life and salvation, or I would die trying to do it."[84] Once Brigham started, he had to stop at Heber Kimball's house, too sick to continue. Mary Ann crossed the river by herself and visited him there.[85] This was the last she would see him for twenty-one and a half months.

Brigham's first letter to Mary Ann, written only hours after parting, explained debts that he owed and monies he had left her to pay them with, ending with a balance of $2.72 for herself: "This is allmost rob[b]ing You I [k]now. But I doe not now wht elce to doe. Brother Joseph [Smith] has pledged himself that the wives of the Twelve should have what they wanted. . . . I doe feele as thou the Lord would provide for you and me."[86] Brigham's courage sprang from his message to Mary Ann here. He simply believed that if he put complete trust in the Lord, he would return to find his family well, as the blessing of the First Presidency had promised.

Brigham traveled with the other apostles through the Eastern states for the next five and a half months. They stayed in Mormon homes or in inns or taverns and preached as they went. Traveling without purse or scrip, Brigham records that by the time they reached Kirtland, he still had money, despite having spent so much.

> I had a York shilling left; and on looking over our expenses I found we had paid out over $87,00 out of the $13,50 we had at Pleasant Garden, which is all the money we had to pay our passages, to my certain knowledge, to start on. We had traveled over 400 miles by stage, for which we paid from 8 to 10 cents a mile, and had eaten three meals a day, for each of which we were charged fifty cents, also fifty cents for our lodgings.[87]

The explanation, of course, for their continuing funds is that Mormon Saints refilled their pockets as they journeyed on.

These members helped them with their clothing as well. Brigham writes: "The brethren were very kind to us; brother Benager Moon gave me satinette to make me an overcoat; sister Lucetta Murdock made it for me; this was a great blessing to me, as I had worn a quilt, with a comforter run through it, in lieu of an overcoat, all the way from Nauvoo, which had not much of a ministerial appearance."[88] Traveling without purse or scrip meant depending on anyone who would to help them in whatever way.

Most of the journey, these men were still sick and weak. Early on, Brigham was fitted with a bed in the wagon because he was unable to sit up. At one point, he records that Heber was fed a spoonful of morphine and nearly died. Brigham nursed him through the night, keeping him on his feet so he wouldn't give up, and remarks, "There was not a healthy man among us, and some more fitted for a hospital than a journey."[89]

These missionaries finally set sail for England on 7 March 1840, on board the *Patrick Henry*, a packet ship. Brigham records that they paid "$18 each for a steerage passage, furnished our own provisions and bedding and paid the cook $1 each for cooking." He also explains sleeping arrangements.

> Brother H. C. Kimball and myself occupied a lower berth, brothers Parley and Orson Pratt the one over us, brothers George A. Smith and R. Hedlock an upper berth at their feet; two Englishmen occupied the berth below. The brethren in New York furnished us with an ample supply of provisions by dona-tion; the sisters made us ticks and filled them with straw for beds and filled some bags with straw for pillows.

Of all the sleeping arrangements Brigham had, this came close to being the most uncomfortable. Brigham was sick and confined to his bed for most of the thirty day journey.[90]

The ship arrived in England on 6 April 1840, the tenth anniversary of the organization of the church.[91] The missionaries' journey "to the nations of the earth"[92] had been fraught with circumstances unbelievably difficult. Testimony of this is a letter, which survives from Heber C. Kimball to his wife Vilate: "I will tell you, my Dear, that time will be remembered by me as long as time lasts. Fore no man has ever suffered as much as I did in my feelings. No more do I ever wish to while I live on earth. I think if ever one man did, I have left all for the Caus of Christ."[93] All of the voyagers survived. Young records, "When I landed on the shore [Liverpool] I gave a loud shout of hosannah. . . . I felt that the chains were broken, and the bands that were upon me were burst asunder."[94]

The missionaries procured a room at "No. 8 Union-street" in Liverpool.[95] At once, they were offered hospitality by the British members. Brigham records that he met with the Quorum of the Twelve at Mother Moon's. "She presented a bottle of wine for us to bless and partake of, which she had kept for over forty years, and she said there was something providential in its preservation, for when she was married she designed to use it, but forgot until the event was over, and when her first child was married, it was also forgotten, and so it had passed over several events until she now had the privilege of presenting it to the Quorum of the Twelve Apostles."[96]

The missionaries began by meeting with Mormon members happy to welcome them, including Willard Richards, who had already been laboring in England. He gave the apostles "an account of the condition of the Churches in the British Isles."[97] On 14 April, they held their first meeting with a majority of the Quorum of the Twelve in a foreign nation. Present were Young, Kimball, Parley P. and Orson Pratt, Wilford Woodruff, John Taylor, George A. Smith, and Willard Richards, who was ordained that day. Young was chosen standing president of the Twelve by a unanimous vote. At once, these men began holding general conferences, the first of which was in Preston, Lancashire, England. Brigham records, "There were represented 1,671 members, 34 Elders, 52 Priests, 38 Teachers and 8 Deacons."[98] As they traveled throughout England, they stayed in members' homes. These missionaries' goal was to bring Mormon Saints to Zion.

On his thirty-ninth birthday, 1 June 1840, Brigham records only that "Brother Kimball and I met with the brethren about to sail for America, and organized the company," and on the 6th, "the first company of Saints from England numbering forty-one souls, sailed for the land of Zion; John Moon, President."[99]

John Moon carried a letter and a little gift from Brigham to Mary Ann, dated 2 June 1840:

> To my Dearest Mary Ann Young,
>   You will find a small key in this Letter which will enable you to unlock a little work Box. There you will [find] 2 letters. Read No. one first then No. two. Then look at the little presents. I have no more time to wright to you at present so I sub[s]cribe my self you[r] husben and companion in life. So fare well. Yours in the Bonds of matrimony, Brigham Young.[100]

Brigham's little gift was given with a heavy burden. His family was always on his mind; he obviously worried for their welfare. He inserts a poignant personal note in his journal on 11 June: "We went to the Zoological Gardens. It rained, and I returned, thankful that I had a comfortable lodging-place in my own hired house. . . . I retired to my bed and soon fell asleep, and had a dream about my family being well. They informed me that the church was not able to sustain the families of the Elders on missions."[101]

This prompted Brigham to write Mary Ann a long letter the next day and tell her of his dream, seeing her, shaking her hand, kissing her two or three times, and seeing little Elizabeth. In this dream, he asked about his four other little children, but did not see them.[102] A week later, on 20 June, he added to the letter:

I asteam [esteem] it a grate privelege that I can converce with you with my pen. . . . As to my enjoyments I am as happy in this contry as I could be enny place in the world whare I had got to be deprived of the sociity of my famely. They [the] people of England are as loving a set of people as ever I saw in my life, y[e]a thay are more so in their aperance then the Americans. But my soul says sweet home sweet home, my blesed famely, yea my kind and loving family, how sweet is home. You might think that I am very anxious to get home, but it [is] not so. . . . but when the time has fully com, and the Lord says goe home my hart then will leap for joy. . . . If we get 5000 copes of the Book of Mormon spread in Urop [Europe] and brother Pratt gets his famely here so he can attend to the paper and keep it agoing, I shall feele perty well satesfyde to com home and see you and the chldren and my Brotheren that I love in the Bonds of truth.[103]

Before he sent this letter, he heard some news about Mary Ann from a letter sent to John Taylor by his wife. He wrote a third installment to this letter on 24 June before he sent it, addressing the issue of Mary Ann building a home:

I understand you are agoing to have a house built and som of the rest of the Sisters. I reculect what Br. Joseph said to us, if we would leve our famelies and goe to Englan on our mision that our famelies should want for nothing. This he said in the name of the Lord Jesus Christ. I beleve it. I have felt satesfied and contented about my famely ever sense I left them. And I had rather you would stay there then goe to the east as things are at present. For when I com home I shall want to be with the Brotherin [of] the first Presedency.

If you get a house built have it built whare it will suite you there. I have not anide [an idea] of injoying a house and home long at a time till the ancent of days comes and sets and Judgment and power is given to the saints of the most high God. Then and not till then doe I expect to have peace on the Earth long at a time, I think I shall com home and enjoy a season of [peace] with my family ecaisonly [occasionally].

I think much about you having the c[are o]f such a large famely upon your hands and no one to see to or doe enything for them but your self. Your task must be grate. I shall endevor to Send to your assistence as often as I can. I have sent a little present by sister Moon to you that I think will cheere your hart. You may expect to here from me agan this fall. . . .[104]

After subscribing himself in the "Bonds of love matrimony and the everlasting covenant," he signed off and went to work. Although Brigham longed to be home, he was not unhappy with his responsibilities in England. The letter in fact reveals his enjoyment of the work.

In November, Brigham wrote a concerned letter to Mary Ann. Worried that she had not received his last letters, he expresses sympathy for her hardships:

Once more Mary I wright to you for fere that you have not recived the letters that I have latly sent to you. I sent you one this weak, one weak before last, and now there is som going to America and I feel to say a little more to you. . . . I understand you have had hard worke to get enny thing for your self and and famely to make you comfortable. This I doe not here from you but from others. You may well think that my hart feeles tender toards you, when I relise your patiants and willingness to suffer in poverty and doe everything you can for my children and for me to goe and due the thing the Lord requires of me. I pray the Lord to bless you in all things and my children and help us all to be faithful to him and our Bretherin. This will bring [honor] to the name of our Redemer on the Earth also upon our heds and the best of all is we shall have eternal life.[105]

Brigham was not careless about the burden he had left for Mary Ann. This letter indicates he suffered, thinking of his wife's impoverished state. One wonders if he ever panicked over her predicament, or if he were simply strong enough to believe she and his children would bear their lot without him. He must have felt at times impotent to help them, while being lifted by the budding success of missionary conversions. Certainly, he yearned for her at nights, crawling into an always empty and often strange bed as he proselytized throughout the country.

The last known letter of Brigham Young to his family from England is dated 15 January 1841, from 72 Burlington Street, Liverpool. He writes a long, wistful letter to Mary Ann:

I feel thankful that I can communicate to you my thaughts and feelings, thou[g]h far from you. I am injoying tolarble good he[l]th for me. I have rec[e]ived a long letter from you which was a blesing to mee to have knews from your own hand. I felt sorry to here [hear] that you had ben sick. I am aware that your worke is to[o] hard for you, even if you ware all well; I pray for you and the children continuly. It is all I can due. I can not help you about your daly work. . . .

I feele a grate desire for my famely, but I feele they are in the hands of the Lord God of Isreal. . . . I am aware the time seems longer to you and the children that I am gon then [than] it do[e]s to me for you onley have one seene [scene] of things before you. It is not so with me and the fact is my buisness or mision is so hevey upon me that I have but little time for enny thing elce. If I would give up my mind to think of my famely it would destract me and I should not be fit for the work the Lord has set me about.[106]

In this letter, Brigham responds to Mary Ann's charge that she hoped he would not accuse her of ingratitude:

I due not know that I have. If I have, I have don it ignerently for it has not ben in my hart to due it nether is it now in my hart to due it. I desire to ad[d] to your comfort and hapiness. I have nothing to say to you upon this point, for I think you have . . . [never] had enny thing elce in your hart toards me but to make me happy and comfortable. . . .[107]

Both time and separation were taking their toll on the couple. His words are a testament of endurance and forbearing. Yet always there is in his message an irrepressible optimism. Brigham mentions his children one by one in a showering of affection, and promises his boys a nice little wagon. He melts when he learns his tiny daughter has prayed for him, "Bles the little creater. How I want to see hir." He writes of the money he sent and ends his letter with an eye toward home:

I hope you have got what I sent to you by Br. Turley. He will pay you thirty dallars when ever you want. You said in your letter I might think you was rich know [now] but I did not nether due now think you are. But I think one thing, glory to God in [the] highest for his goodness to me in putting it in to my power to help my poor wife and children to a little to b[u]y them a morsel of bread. It is not me

but the Lord that has don it . . . th[r]ough me. If the Lord bleses me so I can I shall send you a little by Br. Hyram Clark who will get there in Apriel. . . . I should like too have you b[u]y a nother first rate Cow so we can have plenty of milk and butter when I get home so we can feed the poor, for I shall have a grate menny to visit me. (I am your for ever) Brigham Young.

. . . if you get a garden planted this seson I will try to be there to fence it. If you can get your house finished by the time I come home I shall be glad. But due not truble your self if it is not convenent.[108]

The letter that Mary Ann wrote to which Brigham refers in his 15 January 1841 letter is not extant.[109] Only one letter from Mary Ann to Brigham during the English mission exists. It might have been only the second one she wrote and was begun on 15 April and completed on 30 April 1841, directed to a New York address. Mary Ann confesses her difficulties of the past year:

Agreeable to your request I Attempt to communicate a few lines to you. I have red your kind letters. They have been a great comfort to me. . . . I long to see you att home once more. I pray my Heavenly Father in the worthey name of Jesus that he will protect you from all evil and prosper you on your way home. . . . I hope you will forgive me for not writing to you. . . . I feel in hopes I shall be able to get work and fire wood along this Spring. . . .

Saturday the 17th. Br. [Hyram] Clark . . . called the next morning after his arrival and gave me the two letters from you and the litle Box undisturbed as it was from your hand. I feel the Lord is good. I think we have learned quite a lesson since you left home. That is to trust in the Lord. Alas, that is a great thing. . . .

I think you would hardly know the children. They have grown so much larger since you left home. The girls did not recover from their sickness until January. There was four or five months my family was helpless nearly on my hands. But through the mercy of my heavenly Father we are in good health at presant. . . .

This picture of Brigham Young's home in Nauvoo was taken before any restoration was begun. Used by permission, Utah State Historical Society, all rights reserved.

Brigham Young's Nauvoo home still stands today at the corner of Kimball and Granger Streets. Photo by Marianne Burgoyne, courtesy of Nauvoo Restoration, Inc.

I should be glad if I had a better house to receive into. But it has been so difficult to obtain work that what I had done is not done as I wanted itt. But I am thankful for a comfortable shelter from the Storm. . . . The litle Boys talk much about their litle wagon that Father is a going to bring them. Joseph [says] tell Father I send my best love to him. E[lizabeth] says she wants some Light plain silk to make her a Bonnet of, [also a] Belt & Slide. She would like some litle white artificial flowers. . . .

The letter was finished on 30 April with these lines about the children: "Litle Brigham says tell Father to come home. Mary says I want to see Father and Emma says yes. I think she will go to you as you Dreamed when you come home. I Bid you farewell for a litle Season."[110] Apologizing profusely for not writing more often, she tells him she is too fatigued to write in the daytime and "sore eyes" have prevented her from writing by candlelight.[111] Then, too, she might not have been able to bring herself to it until she realized her husband was on his way home. His safe return became her dream.

The log house in which Mary Ann would receive Brigham is no longer standing. It was located on the same property where Brigham's Nauvoo home stands today. Apparently, Mary Ann chose the land and had the small log home built, which was little more than a temporary shelter.

The English mission was a blazing success. Nothing is more telling of this than Brigham's journal entry of 20 April 1841, the day he and six other apostles, along with 130 Saints, set sail at Liverpool aboard the ship *Rochester* for New York. The first night, the ship cast anchor within sight of Liverpool. Brigham writes:

It was with a heart full of thanksgiving and gratitude to God, my heavenly Father, that I reflected upon his dealings with me and my brethren of the Twelve during the past year of my life, which was spent in England. It truly seemed a miracle to look upon the contrast between our landing and departing

from Liverpool. We landed in the spring of 1840, as strangers in a strange land and penniless, but through the mercy of God we have gained many friends, established Churches in almost every noted town and city in the kingdom of Great Britain, baptized between seven and eight thousand, printed 5,000 *Books of Mormon*, 3,000 Hymn books, 2,500 volumes of the *Millennial Star*, and 50,000 tracts, and emigrated to Zion 1,000 souls, established a permanent shipping agency, which will be a blessing to the Saints, and have left sown in the hearts of many thousands the seeds of eternal truth, which will bring forth fruit to the honor and glory of God, and yet we have lacked nothing to eat, drink, or wear; in all these things I acknowledge the hand of God.[112]

The Twelve left behind Orson Hyde and Parley P. Pratt to attend to the British Mission. From these beginning missionary efforts, thirty-eight thousand Britons migrated to Nauvoo and to Salt Lake City by 1870.[113]

Brigham arrived home to Nauvoo on 1 July 1841. His journal entry fails to adequately convey the moment: "We arrived in Nauvoo, and were cordially welcomed by the Prophet Joseph, our families and the Saints." He found Mary Ann and her six children living "in a small unfinished log-cabin, situated on a low wet lot, so swampy that when the first attempt was made to plow it the oxen mired."[114] He had been away from his family nearly twenty-two months. Since joining the church in 1832, he had been away from his family nearly half of that time.

Eight days after his return, Brigham was visited by Joseph Smith, who came to his home. There, Joseph received a revelation: "Dear and well-beloved brother Brigham Young, verily thus saith the Lord unto you, my servant Brigham, it is no more required at your hand to leave your family as in times past, for your offering is acceptable to me; I have seen your labor and toil in journeyings for my name. I therefore command you to send my word abroad, and take special care of your family from this time, henceforth, and for ever. Amen."[115]

Because the ground was so moist, this root cellar was built above ground with an insulating wall several inches from the outer wall all the way around. Photo by Marianne Burgoyne, courtesy of Nauvoo Restoration, Inc.

Joseph Smith's assessment of the mission in England was this: "Perhaps no men ever undertook such an important mission under such peculiarly distressing, forbidding and unpropitious circumstances. . . . Their lives were several times despaired of, and they have taken each other by the hand, expecting it would be the last time they should behold one another in the flesh. . . . They truly, 'went forth weeping, bearing precious seed,' but have 'returned with rejoicing, bearing their sheaves with them.'"[116]

Brigham went to work, taking care of his family. He writes:

Although I had to spend the principal part of my time, at the call of brother Joseph, in the service of the Church, the portion of time left me I spent draining, fencing and cultivating my lot, building a temporary shed for my cow, chinking and otherwise finishing my house; and as the ground was too damp to admit of a cellar underground, I built one with two brick walls about four or six inches apart, arched over with brick. Frost never penetrated it, although in summer articles would mildew in it.[117]

In January 1842, after having been home six months, Brigham wrote an isolated entry in his diary, which stands as a simple testament of his sacrifice: "This evening I am with my wife a lone by my fire side for the first time for years. We enjoi it and feele to prase the Lord."[118]

Their peace was short-lived. The previous spring, 1841, Joseph introduced the doctrine of plural marriage while the Twelve were still in England. Brigham learned about the practice sometime after his return in the summer of 1841. Devastated, he writes: "I was not desirous of shrinking from any duty, nor of failing in the least to do as I was commanded, but it was the first time in my life that I had desired the grave, and I could hardly get over it for a long time. And when I saw a funeral, I felt to envy the corpse its situation, and to regret that I was not in the coffin, knowing the toil and labor that my body would have to undergo; and I have had to examine myself, from that day to this, and watch my faith, and carefully mediate, lest I should be found desiring the grave more than I ought to do."[119]

Whatever his feelings, Brigham married his first plural wife, Lucy Ann Decker Seeley, secretly on 14 June 1842.[120] Joseph Smith performed the ceremony in his office at the Mansion House. The revelation on polygamy was not written until July 1843 and then limited to a few men Joseph selected.[121] Brigham made no entry regarding his third marriage in his Manuscript History. Nor does he mention any reference to polygamy until a 9 July 1843 entry when he rebuts a professor for inquiring if Joseph Smith had more than one wife.[122]

Lucy Ann Decker Seeley was two weeks shy of being twenty-one years younger than Brigham. Born in Phelps, Ontario County, New York, 17 May 1822 to Isaac Perry Decker of Holland and Harriet Page Wheeler Decker of England, Lucy was eleven when she and her family moved to Portage County, Ohio, in 1833. There, the family joined the Mormons and then moved to Kirtland in 1837.[123]

Lucy married William Seeley when she was sixteen.[124] The couple moved to a Mormon settlement in Missouri, where Lucy had her first child, Isaac. Lucy and William were among the Saints driven out of Missouri by anti-Mormon mobs. They then settled in Illinois and had two more children, Harriet and William Jacob, although Jacob died shortly after birth. William Seeley was probably never

Archeologists from local universities found some of these original dishes, probably from the Brigham Young home, in the well. Not all dishes on display are from this property. Photo by Marianne Burgoyne, courtesy of Nauvoo Restoration, Inc.

a member of the Mormon Church; however, he lived with his wife in Mormon communities and is listed on the roster of one of the wards in Nauvoo. No record of his baptism exists. According to Alfa Jean Carter, great-great-granddaughter of Lucy, as Lucy became more interested in the church and its beliefs, William became less interested.[125] Arrington records that William was abusive to Lucy,[126] but Seeley family sources say that William and Lucy's daughter Harriet reported that her mother denied any abuse.[127] At some point, however, William abandoned Lucy. For a time she thought he was dead, although she learned later that he was alive and living in Chicago. Lucy never divorced William and he never remarried. He died in Chicago in 1851, leaving a sizable estate to Isaac and Harriet. They never received the money because a family relative—a lawyer—who went to Chicago to claim the money, disappeared with their inheritance. A city street in Chicago is named after William.[128]

Lucy was living in Nauvoo when she met and married Brigham. She continued to live in the home provided by William, located on city block 121.[129] That land is today a part of a city park. Over the next eighteen years, she bore Brigham seven children: Brigham Heber, 19 June 1845; Fanny, 26 January 1849; Ernest I., 30 April 1851; Shermira, 21 March 1853; Arta de Christa, 16 April 1855; Feramorz, 16 September 1858; and Clarissa H., 23 July 1860.[130]

However dissatisfied Brigham may have been with polygamy, he obeyed the commandment with gusto. By February 1846, when Brigham made final plans for his trek across the Great Plains, he had thirty-eight plural wives, including Lucy.[131] He married Augusta Adams and Harriet Elizabeth Cook in November 1843; Clarisa Decker, Emily Dow Partridge, Clarissa Ross, Louisa Beaman, Eliza Roxcy Snow, Rebecca Holman, Diana Chase, Susannah Snively, and Olive Gray Frost in 1844; Margaret Pierce, Mary Pierce, Emmeline Free, and Mary Elizabeth Rollins in 1845; and twenty-two more women in January and

The original fireplace features several labor-saving devices, including a warming oven on the opposite side of the back wall and a crane to hold pots over the fire. Photo by Marianne Burgoyne, courtesy of Nauvoo Restoration, Inc.

February 1846. By then, he had nine children and several foster children. Eight of Brigham's wives had been married to Joseph Smith.[132]

On 26 November 1842, just over five months after Brigham took his first plural wife, he was suddenly attacked by a slight fit of apoplexy. By evening of the next day, the fever turned deadly. He writes, "I was attacked with the most violent fever I ever experienced." Although he received a blessing from Joseph Smith and Elder Willard Richards, who prophesied that he should live, Brigham lost all of his skin, recording, "and I was skinned all over." He recalls, "I laid in a log-house, which was rather open: it was so very cold during my sickness, that brother Isaac Decker, my attendant, froze his fingers and toes while fanning me, with boots, greatcoat and mittens on, and with a fire in the house from which I was shielded by a blanket."[133] Brigham remembers the event as a near-death or death experience:

> When the fever left me on the 18th day, I was bolstered up in my chair, but was so near gone that I could not close my eyes, which were set in my head—my chin dropped down and my breath stopped. My wife, seeing my situation, threw some cold water in my face; that having no effect, she dashed a handful of strong camphor into my face and eyes, which I did not feel in the least, neither did I move a muscle. She then held my nostrils between her thumb and finger, and placing her mouth directly over mine, blew into my lungs until she filled them with air. This set my lungs in motion, and I again began to breathe. While this was going on I was perfectly conscious of all that was passing around me; my spirit was as vivid as it ever was in my life, but I had no feeling in my body.[134]

It is likely Brigham died and Mary Ann revived him with mouth-to-mouth resuscitation. Brigham probably had been stricken with scarlet fever, along with a secondary infection that prolonged the fever.[135] To date, Brigham had been beset with great sickness, including malaria, but this fever was the most life-threatening. It took him months to recover.

The kitchen is the central room of the house. The door to the right opens into Brigham and Mary Ann's west bedroom. Photo by Marianne Burgoyne, courtesy of Nauvoo Restoration, Inc.

Better days were ahead for him. On 31 May 1843, Brigham writes, "I moved out of my log cabin into my new brick house, which was 22 feet by 16, two stories high, and a good cellar under it, and felt thankful to God for the privilege of having a comfortable, though small habitation."[136] The house is still standing in Nauvoo. It has been restored and is open for tours. Located on the southeast corner of Kimball and Granger Streets, it faces north. When Brigham first built the house, he constructed the two-story center section of somewhat crude, handmade brick.[137] The large downstairs room served as a kitchen–dining room. The fireplace and crane are original, although the wood mantel is not. Upstairs, Brigham built two small bedrooms. Later, he added a one-room wing on each side, one room serving as a bedroom and the other as his office.[138] He had already built a root cellar and a well and cistern in back, also to the west side of the property. The barn is also located in back of the home, also on the west side. At a cost of $400 in labor, it was the nicest house in which Brigham had to date lived.[139] The log home the Youngs moved out of was thought to be a few feet away on the west side of the home. The log home, then, would have been torn down to construct the west wing or additional bedroom to the home. This homestead sat on a one-acre lot, now marked by a wood fence. Miniature bunnies hop around the property.

A few items in the home are original besides the fireplace. The rocking chair and the black mirror in the west main-floor bedroom belonged to the Youngs. Also, some of the dishes on display in two cabinets in the kitchen were found buried in the well located on this property. They could have belonged to Mary Ann and Brigham who may have buried them when they left Nauvoo. If so, presumably, they buried the dishes so that the new tenants would not find them and also possibly hoping they could retrieve them at some future time.[140]

Brigham owned other property in Nauvoo as well. An historic map of Nauvoo shows that Brigham owned the four-acre block, 117, and two acres on block 121, as well as the acre on block 126 where the home stands. He also owned large sections of farmland, including 160 acres and another ten acres in the surrounding area. Certainly, his financial status was finally making a turn. Accumulating years of hard labor, combined with available, cheap lands, helped Brigham establish some stability during his Nauvoo years. The township was prospering as neighbors helped each other and outsiders, for a time, left the citizens alone to build their community.

Brigham lived in his Nauvoo house just one month before he left on a mission to raise money for the Nauvoo Temple and the Nauvoo House.[141] On the same day that Mary Ann writes Brigham, informing him the children are suffering from influenza and cholera morbus,[142] he writes to her, sick also:

> I have ben verry sick with my old complaint. Feele some better to day. . . . When I was so sick I thought if I could only be at home, I should be thankful. There is no place like home to me. I due not value leveing home and all that is deare to me for the sake of the gospel if I could onley injoy my helth. You and I must take some masurs to recover our helth or we shall not last a grate meny years; and I want that we should live meny years yet and due much good on the earth. . . .[143]

Today the bedroom in the west wing addition features a mirror and rocking chair originally owned by Brigham Young. Photo by Marianne Burgoyne, courtesy of Nauvoo Restoration, Inc.

While he was gone, his family took gravely ill, and his daughter, Mary Ann, six-year-old twin of Brigham Jr., died of "dropsy and canker." No record exists of where or when Brigham received the devastating news.[144] Brigham returned home on 22 October 1843, recording only that "H. C. Kimball and Geo. A. Smith [and] I . . . paid Joseph Smith every cent of the means we had collected for the Temple and Nauvoo House.[145]

In the spring of 1844, Brigham undertook a special mission to the East to solicit support for the United States presidential candidacy of Joseph Smith.[146] While waiting for a boat at Fairport, Ohio, on Lake Erie, he started a letter to Mary Ann:

> I feele lonsom. O that I had you with me this somer I think I should be happy. Well I am now because I am in my cauling and duing my duty, but [the] older I grow the more I desire to stay at my own home instead of traveling.[147]

He continued the letter from Albany, New York:

> Last night I felt for somtime as though I had got to get a new const [it]ution or [I would] not last long. How I due want to see you and [the children]. Kiss them for me and kiss Luny [Luna] twice or mor. Tel hir it is for me. Give my love to all the famely. I nead not menshion names. . . . Don't you want for eney thing. You can borrow monney to get what you want. . . . After taking a grate share of my love to your self then deal it out to others as you plese.[148]

The older Brigham became, the longer away from home, the more he longed to be with his family. The above letter is a turning point for Brigham. He was never so sick again until his death thirty-three years later, having the strength to lead the church, as head of the Quorum of the Twelve, upon hearing of the assassination of Joseph Smith. Joseph and his brother Hyrum were gunned down by Warsaw and Carthage militiamen while incarcerated at the Carthage jail the evening of 27 June 1844.[149] Mary Ann, worried for Brigham's safety, wrote him on 30 June 1844:

> I hope you will be careful on your way hom and not expose yourself to those who will endanger your Life. Yours in hast[e]. If we meet no more in this world may we meet where parting is no more. Farewell.[150]

Brigham heard of the prophet's death on 9 July and again on 16 July 1844 in Peterboro, New Hampshire: "The first thing which I thought of was, whether Joseph had taken the keys of the kingdom with him from the earth; brother Orson Pratt sat on my left; we were both leaning back on our chairs. Bringing my hand down on my knee, I said the keys of the kingdom are right here with the Church." Brigham started for Boston, heading home, that day.[151] His next mission was to save the church.

Brigham arrived back in Nauvoo 6 August 1844, just in time to keep Sidney Rigdon from becoming spokesperson for the deceased prophet. Rigdon believed the martyred prophet still to be the head of the church, and he, Rigdon, would now receive revelations from him.[152]

Brigham disagreed: "I do not care who leads the church, even though it were Ann Lee [founder of the Shakers]; but one thing I must know and that is what God says about it. I have the keys and means of obtaining the mind of

The small, one-story east wing contained Brigham Young's office. Photo by Marianne Burgoyne, courtesy of Nauvoo Restoration, Inc.

God on the subject. . . . Joseph conferred upon our heads all the keys and powers belonging to the Apostleship which he himself held before he was taken away, and no man or set of men can get between Joseph and the Twelve in this world or the world to come."[153]

Brigham addressed the gathering of saints on 8 August just after Sidney Rigdon addressed them. One present, Mosiah Hancock, recorded, "Although only a boy, I saw the mantle of the Prophet Joseph rest on Brigham Young; and he arose lion-like to the occasion, and led the people forth."[154] After a meeting with all leaders, Brigham addressed the audience once again in the afternoon. He said, "You cannot appoint a prophet, but if you let the Twelve remain and act in their place, the keys of the kingdom are with them and they can manage the affairs of the church and direct all things aright."[155] Brigham's great speech held his audience, and that day the Quorum of the Twelve was unanimously sustained as the presidency of the church and ratified at the next general conference 6 October 1844.[156] Although Brigham was not sustained as president of the church until 27 December 1847, he became at once the leading official and his *Manuscript History* became the History of the Church.[157]

Brigham acknowledged that the Mormons could not stay where they would continue to be persecuted. Before Smith died, he had begun deliberations with the Council of the Fifty and Quorum of the Twelve on where the Saints could move to avoid persecution.[158] They narrowed their choice to the "Oregon and California country." During the winter of 1844–1845, the Quorum of the Twelve read the journals of fur trappers, the reports of government exploring parties, and newspaper articles about Western travelers. They also talked with people who had spent time in the "Rocky Mountain region." They learned that there were at least two contiguous unsettled areas, both of which they might occupy: the valley of the Great Salt Lake, sometimes referred to as Bear River Valley, and Utah Valley, the

The restored Nauvoo home features furniture and toys from the period when the Young family lived there. Photo by Marianne Burgoyne, courtesy of Nauvoo Restoration, Inc.

valley north and east of Utah Lake and south of Salt Lake Valley. Either or both of these regions would provide the desired isolation, thousands of acres of arable land, and a suitable base for expansion into irrigable patches between the Rockies and the Sierra Nevada.[159] By mid-1845, Brigham and the Twelve had definitely decided on the Salt Lake Valley as the most suitable site for a settlement.

Governor Thomas Ford wrote Brigham Young in April 1845:

> Your religion is new, and it surprises the people as any great novelty in religion generally does. They cannot rise above the prejudices excited by such novelty. . . . If you can get off by yourselves you may enjoy peace, but surrounded by such neighbors I confess I do not foresee the time when you will be permitted to enjoy quiet. . . .
>
> I would suggest a matter in confidence. California now offers a field for the prettiest enterprise that has been undertaken in modern time. It is but sparsely populated by none but the Indian or imbecile Mexican Spaniard. . . . Why would it not be a pretty operation for your people to go out there, take possession of and conquer a portion of the vacant country, and establish an independent government of your own subject only to the laws of nations. You would remain there a long time before you would be disturbed by the proximity of other settlements. If you conclude to do this your design ought not to be known or otherwise it would become the duty of the United States to prevent your emigration. But if you once cross the line of the United States territories you would be in no danger of being interfered with.[160]

This was good advice well taken. Mobs began again burning homes and farms in the outlying areas. More than two hundred houses, barns, shops, and granaries were destroyed in the fall of 1845.[161] Although reports are given that some Mormon men were murdered and their wives and daughters raped, Brigham mentions only one man killed by the mob, Edmund Durfee, 15 November 1845.[162] Brigham made plans to move "all the saints with us, to the extent of our ability."[163]

In an "Epistle to the Church," Brigham declared that the Mormon community faced "a crisis of extraordinary and thrilling interests: the exodus of the

The log home Mary Ann lived in while her husband served as a missionary was reportedly on the west side of the current home, next to the root cellar. Photo by Marianne Burgoyne, courtesy of Nauvoo Restoration, Inc.

nation of the only true Israel from these United States to a far distant region of the west." He called it "a new epoch, not only in the history of the church, but of this nation." Obviously, he had grasped the significance and enormity of the enterprise. He urged the Saints: "Therefore, dispose of your properties and inheritance [land], and interests for available means, such as money, wagons, oxen, cows, mules, and a few good horses adapted to journeying and scanty feed. Also for durable fabrics suitable for apparel and tents."[164]

On 30 November 1845, the Nauvoo Temple was dedicated. The important temple sealings, work Brigham had waited to perform, were carried out in the next few months. Brigham and Heber Kimball assumed the leading roles of this temple work through January and February 1846. The ordinances were administered to more than five thousand people during these two months. Husbands and wives were sealed and, by the ceremony of "adoption," leaders adopted members and families as their own children.[165] Brigham had twenty-two more wives sealed to him. It isn't that he needed twenty-two more wives just then; his purpose was to provide security in crossing the plains, and sealings (eternal bondings), should deaths occur on the great trek.

The evacuation of Saints was originally planned for April 1846, but Brigham, fearing federal intervention, arranged a "safe elopement" as early as 2 February. Brigham and eight other apostles had been indicted for harboring a counterfeit operation and were under threat of being arrested. Also, he had heard rumored a warning from Governor Ford and others that federal troops in St. Louis were planning to intercept the Mormons and destroy them. He thought it prudent to move quickly. On 4 February, the first group of church authorities and their families crossed the Mississippi. In succeeding days several hundred Saints left and assembled in temporary camps in Iowa.[166]

Brigham remained in Nauvoo until 15 February to help administer temple ordinances to more Saints. When he did join the camps, he left a committee of five to dispose of all property and effects left behind, including the temple and

The well that provided water for the family was located on the west side of the house, adjacent to the root cellar, but the cistern by the back door of the kitchen stored water to make access easier for the cook. Photo by Marianne Burgoyne, courtesy of Nauvoo Restoration, Inc.

This barn on the southwest side of the home may date from the period of the Youngs' occupation. Photo by Marianne Burgoyne, courtesy of Nauvoo Restoration, Inc.

the Nauvoo House he had worked so diligently to help build. Of his own property, Brigham once again walked away from it. Years later, he said, "I left my property in Nauvoo, and many know that I left a number of good houses and lots and a farm, and came here [Salt Lake] without one farthing for them, with the exception of a span of horses, harness and carriage, that Almon W. Babbit let me have for my own dwelling-house that my family lived in; and when I arrived here I owed for my horses, cows, oxen and wagons."[167]

By mid-June, Brigham and Heber reached the Missouri River and established temporary headquarters on the lands of the Potawatomi Indians. The east bank camps were at the present location of Council Bluffs, Iowa, or Kanesville; the west bank camps at present-day Florence, near Omaha, Nebraska, or Winter Quarters. By the winter of 1846–1847, sixteen thousand saints were spread out over several hundred miles of prairie. Brigham established an internal mail service, built a gristmill, organized relief teams to bring families who hadn't yet left Nauvoo to the main body, sent several apostles to England to oversee the missionary exodus from that country, and continued to interview people about the geography of the Far West. On 14 January 1847, he announced "the Word and the Will of the Lord" to the Camps of Israel to move west.[168]

By now it was becoming a habit for Brigham to build cities. He lived thirty more years. He is credited with directing the colonization of the West from Fort Bridger to San Bernardino. His greatest accomplishment, however, was the one he was staring this moment head on: leading his persecuted people into untrodden territory where he hoped to separate them from all who pursued them. By now, Brigham must have known the magnitude of his calling and, if he succeeded, the monumental achievement of his life. No man was better equipped than Brigham, with Heber C. Kimball at his side, to move his people west. That he did so—becoming an American Moses—is the monumental credit to his name.

Chapter 4

WIVES IN WAGONS

Winter Quarters and the Trek West

JUDY DYKMAN AND COLLEEN WHITLEY

Although Brigham Young and other church leaders had planned an orderly evacuation for the spring of 1846, in February many of the traumatized Saints began streaming across the frozen Mississippi River. The original plan had been for some of the leaders to cross into Iowa Territory, where they would be immune to arrest on bogus warrants threatened by Illinois officials. Once there, they would establish orderly camps, ready to receive the bulk of the Saints later that spring. However, fears of further persecution from both government agencies and random mobs pushed many to rush toward the emotional security of their leaders, however insecure the physical conditions.[1]

They all knew that during the exodus to the West everyone would live in the same kind of houses: tents and wagons, and that privacy would be practically nonexistent. Nonetheless, plans had been made to make the trip as safe and pleasant as possible. The wagons were nine to ten feet long, their width varying from thirty-eight to forty-eight inches. The wheels themselves were four feet, eight inches in diameter. When handcarts were devised later, the wheels were set at the same distance apart as those on the wagons so that they would fit into the same ruts in the road.[2] Today pioneer wagons or replicas of them can be seen in various places from Iron Mission State Park in Cedar City to the LDS Museum of History and Art in Salt Lake City. The Daughters of Utah Pioneers Museum also contains many wagons and carriages, including, according to their records, the one from which Brigham Young announced, "This is the right place."

Each wagon could carry up to two tons, and a family traveling to the Great Basin needed every ounce they could manage. Each family was advised to have a year to eighteen months' supply of food along with animals, seeds, and materials to set up farming or shops once they reached the Great Basin. They were not merely adventurers but a community moving to a remote and desolate area to start again.

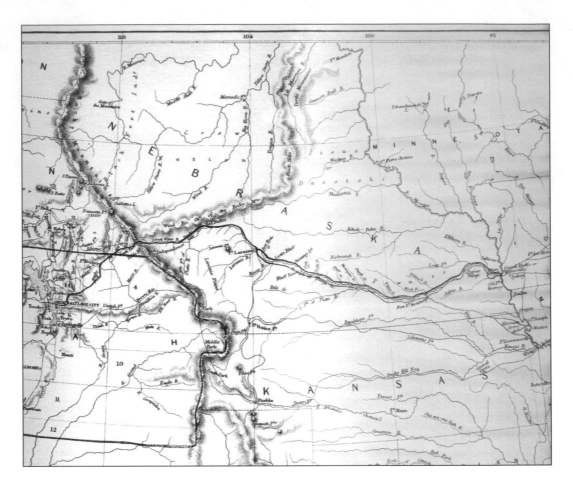

Each family needed two or three yoke of oxen, aged four to ten years, to pull the wagon, and they also had one or two beef cattle, two or three milk cows, and a few sheep. Some had much more; Perrigrine Sessions, for example, took a whole herd of cattle when he came to Utah.[3] Food supplies included a bushel of beans, one hundred pounds of sugar, one thousand pounds of flour in good sacks, one pound of tea and five of coffee, twenty-five pounds of grain, five pounds of dried peaches, ten pounds of apples, and a few pounds of dried beef or bacon. Spices and other condiments were also needed: two pounds of black pepper, some cayenne pepper, five pounds of soda, one pound of cinnamon, and half a pound of cloves. Other necessities included twenty pounds of soap and a gallon of alcohol, primarily for sterilizing wounds. In addition, each family had to carry a few pounds of nails and fifteen pounds of iron and steel for wagon repair and building once they reached the valley. Most also had up to five hundred pounds of clothing and bedding, cooking utensils—pots, pans, kettles, plates, cups, knives, forks, and spoons—as well as goods to trade with Indians along the trail.[4]

Two families might share a tent and some furniture, and each male over twelve was equipped with a good musket or rifle along with a pound of powder and four pounds of lead, and a weighted fish net plus four or five hooks and lines. Hunting and fishing were essential, not recreational. Shared equipment included farming and mechanical tools, saws and gristmill irons. Crossing rivers required two ferry boats for each company and two sets of pulley blocks. Ten extra teams were included for each one hundred people.[5]

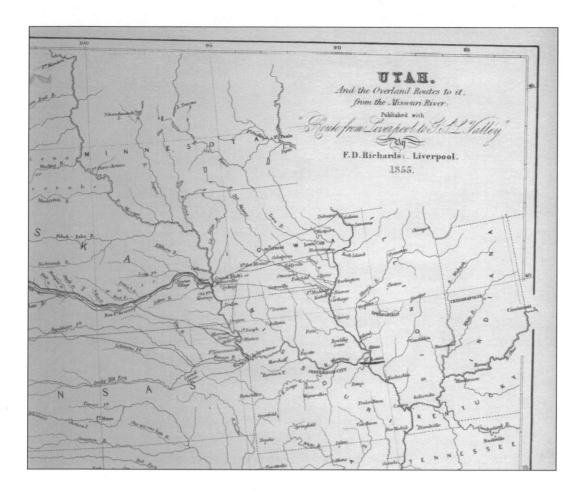

For those who made such preparations, the trail was not particularly unkind. Irene Hascall Pomeroy described her wagon as she left Nauvoo:

> We have [our wagon] fixed expecting to stay until spring. There is two companies on ahead of us. One is stopped 150 miles from here [Au: or was this in the original (*sic*)?] the other has gone on. There is about 800 waggons in this company with brother Brigham Young and brother Weber Brimhall at the head and more adding daily.
>
> Now I shall give you a history of my journey or a sketch of it. We started from Nauvoo the 30th of May. Had as good a waggon as any of them; three yoke of oxen with flour enough to last us one year, ham, sausages, dry fish, lard, two cans hundred pounds of sugar, 16 of coffee, 10 of raisins, rice with all the other items we wish to use in cooking. I will describe our waggons and tent as well as I can. I wish I could make you know exactly how they look. The waggon is long enough for both our beds made on the flour barrels, chests and other things. (Thales [her husband] and I sleep [in] the back end and F and Irene [her children] at the forward end. While we were travelling if we camped too late to pitch our tent.) It is painted red. It has eight bows eighteen inches apart; a hen coop on the end with four hens. We had two webs of thick drilling.[6] We put on one cover of that, then three breadths of stout sheeting over that and then painted it. The heaviest showers and storms does not beat through, only a few drops now and then. Our tent is made of drilling sixteen breadths in the shape of an umbrella. A cord three feet long on the end of every seam and a pin on that to drive into the ground. The pole in the middle that holds it up carries it three feet from the ground, then a breadth of sheeting put on the edge to let down in cool weather and fasten with loops and pins in the ground.[7]

The Mormon pioneers, forced from their homes in Nauvoo, traveled through Iowa, Nebraska, Wyoming, and northern Utah to reach the Salt Lake Valley. Steelplate engraving from Frederick Piercy, *Route from Liverpool to Great Salt Lake Valley.*

Top: Nauvoo, Illinois, as seen from the Mormon refugees' encampments across the Mississippi River. Steelplate engraving from Frederick Piercy, *Route from Liverpool to Great Salt Lake Valley.*

Above: A family says goodbye to a member of the Mormon Battalion. Woodcut by Frederick Piercy, *Route from Liverpool to Great Salt Lake Valley.*

Few people, however, were so well equipped. Under the original removal plan, each family would have disposed of their own property, using the funds from those sales to purchase what they needed for the trek west and to provide seed money to start anew in the West. In desperation, however, some owners traded homes and farms for as little as two yoke of oxen and a wagon.[8] Although Brigham left some agents behind to attempt to sell both church and personal properties, their success was limited.[9] Some unscrupulous local residents, recognizing the desperation of the Mormons' situation, simply took possession of abandoned homes, with very little or no payment at all.[10]

Still other Mormons had been impoverished by mobs before the exodus even began. Elisha and Johanna Keyes lost their home and farm during persecutions in Henderson County, north of Nauvoo, in 1845. Johanna recorded,

There came to our house a man who said he had helped to kill the Saints at Hauns Mill in Missouri. My husband was very sick at the time and light headed. He would say yes to every thing this man made a pretense of buying, everything belonging to the place and giving nothing in return. When I objected to such a sale, he drew a pistol and presented it within 4 inches of my breast saying at the same time "Dam you say another word and I will blow you thru." But to make a long story short we got to camp Creek to a brothers house with the loss of everything.[11]

As a result of such persecutions and the fear of more to follow, many people simply fled across the Mississippi River with whatever they could manage. Brigham was forced to divide precious resources and supplies to make emergency provisions. The temperatures fell below zero.[12] All suffered terribly, some

Entrance to Kanesville

freezing to death. The Keyes family's experience contrasted sharply with Pomeroy's: "The water came up and our camps were filled with water. We had nothing but a sheet stretched over us for shelter."[13] Although those with means shared with their neighbors, food became extremely scarce. People in the "poor camp" in October 1846 were saved only when an event from the Old Testament was repeated: "I was among the people who camped on the bank of the Mississippi River when the quail came so thick around we could pick them up at our feet, when we were out of provisions."[14]

While the Saints continued to move, Brigham directed several attempts to mitigate the situation for the travelers. Jesse Little went to Washington as an envoy from the church to propose that the Mormons be allowed to travel without harassment so that they could build way stations for others immigrating to California and Oregon. The difficulties involved in moving so many people and building settlements along the way exacerbated the already desperate financial situation among the Mormons. As leader of the church, Brigham Young had been assuming some of the organization's debts and paying bills personally. Both financially and pragmatically he could not afford to transport his entire family as a group. His wives and children traveled piecemeal, sometimes living with other families.[15]

In February 1846 Lansford Hastings approached Brigham Young and offered to take some of the Mormons to California as part of his wagon train at the rate of $4,000 for every two hundred people.[17] Brigham, however, opted to lead his people west himself. A camp was established nine miles into Iowa at Sugar Creek, a little north of Montrose. Since Sugar Creek was far too small to accommodate all the people who would be following, Brigham sent people

Kanesville, Iowa, also known as Council Bluffs, on the east bank of the Missouri River, became an important station on the trail west. Steelplate engraving, Frederick Piercy, *Route from Liverpool to Great Salt Lake Valley.*

View of the Missouri River & Council Bluffs from an elevation.

halfway across Iowa to establish Garden Grove and twenty-seven miles further west to establish Mt. Pisgah as part of a corridor of settlements. They built structures, planted gardens, dug wells, and established other necessities for large numbers of people moving west.

The difficulties of settling those towns is reflected by one of Brigham's wives, Zina D. Huntington, who lived in a one-room cabin in Mt. Pisgah with her two little sons by Henry Jacobs. Her father, William Huntington, lived with them. Widowed when his wife had died of exhaustion following the persecutions in Missouri and Illinois, William had been called to preside over the branch at Mt. Pisgah. Despite the small size of her home, Zina invited seven homeless Saints to live with her. In the summer of 1846, the settlement was plagued with sickness, much of it fatal. Coffins could not be built quickly enough for those who died. Some bodies were simply dropped into graves lined and covered by logs and brush. Among the deaths was Zina's father, for whom she mourned greatly. Nonetheless, she continued to care for others in the household who became ill.[17]

The Saints' financial situation was alleviated to some degree when Captain James B. Allen of the United States Army arrived in Mt. Pisgah on 26 June 1846. The Mormons were initially terrified, assuming still more persecutions. Their fears were fueled by a rumor, forwarded by Samuel Brannan, that the United States Army was planning to stop the Mormons from leaving the United States. The army, however, was actually responding to a request from Jesse Little, the emissary Brigham Young had sent to Washington. Little had suggested the government raise an armed force among the Mormons, and President Polk was glad to have their allegiance. He had feared they would react to their previous abuse and unite with the Indians or the British against the United States. That fear had,

View of the Missouri River and Council Bluffs from an elevation. Steelplate engraving, Frederick Piercy, *Route from Liverpool to Great Salt Lake Valley.*

indeed, brought Allen to the camp, but his errand was quite different from what the Mormons expected. Polk had sent orders to Colonel Stephen Kearney to recruit five hundred Mormon men for the army. The plan was to send them to California to insure that area's loyalty in any quarrels with Mexico, Britain, or the Indians. Some also suggested the motivation was to deplete any force the Mormons might send against the country.[18]

Apparently the vagueness of Polk's orders left Kearney and Allen some latitude, which they used in negotiating with the Mormons. The men of the battalion would be allowed to stay together as a unit, have their own officers, and even take along some women as laundresses. In addition, the government would give each man a $42 clothing allotment up front; that money could help support their families as well as purchase their needed clothing. During their term of service, each man would be paid a salary, beginning with $7 per month for a private, the amount increasing with rank. The money went into a general fund for the church to be used for the families of the men and to purchase supplies along the way.[19] Allen further promised on behalf of Polk that the Mormons could stay on Indian lands, providing yet another important outpost for the immigration corridor. The military authorities offered Brigham Young an even more enticing promise: the men of the Mormon Battalion would not be required to fight in the Mexican War.[20]

Council Bluffs Ferry & group of Cotton-wood trees.

Acting on Allen's promise to use Indian lands, Brigham Young and other church leaders approved the establishment of Winter Quarters, near what is now Florence, Nebraska, on 9 August 1846.[21] Winter Quarters was located on a plateau between two bluffs on Indian land. The Omahas welcomed the Mormons as a buffer against their enemies, the Sioux, and because the Mormons offered to help them with food. Brigham's experience in negotiating with the Omahas later influenced his methods of dealing with natives in Utah. There would be no other settlements the size of Winter Quarters on Indian land for many years. Although the Mormons never intended to settle there permanently, Allen's guarantee had promised some security for at least the foreseeable future. Since the Mormons believed they might well stay there for some time, they set about establishing a substantial city, making it the largest settlement along the immigration corridor. The pressure increased for them to move on, however, when Allen died in Fort Leavenworth before he could pass on to federal authorities his promise of Omaha land to induce the Mormons to organize a battalion.[22]

Like Mt. Pisgah and Garden Grove, Winter Quarters was laid out on a grid, patterned after that used in Nauvoo. The same pattern would be repeated throughout the Utah Territory, becoming one of the distinguishing characteristics of Mormon settlements. The two major streets were intersected at right angles by sixteen smaller ones. At the height of its Mormon settlement the long rectangular city contained about 594 lots. Each five-acre block held twenty lots, each lot measuring 72 by 165 feet; five wells were dug for each block. Small homes of various types sat close to the street with outhouses dug eight feet deep at the back. Each block accommodated 150 to 350 people, depending on how many houses could be built and how many people crowded in each house.[23]

Pioneers waiting to cross the Missouri River at Council Bluffs. Steelplate engraving, Frederick Piercy, *Route from Liverpool to Great Salt Lake Valley.*

This view of the Elk Horn River Ferry, in what is now Nebraska, shows something of the living conditions on the trail. Steelplate engraving, Frederick Piercy, *Route from Liverpool to Great Salt Lake Valley*.

Since the Mormons knew they would be moving on, most of the houses were small; some people used temporary dugouts. Some simply remained in their wagons or wagon beds. Still others collected driftwood from the river to build cabins.[24] The quality of homes varied from inadequate shanties without floors, doors, or windows and with only partial roofs, to hundreds of large, sturdy, two-story structures with solid floors and roofs.[25] Those larger homes, however, usually housed several families, often one family per room. Families were located together as much as possible, but settlement was also based, at least in part, on relationships established by the "law of adoption," a doctrine whereby individuals were sealed to non–family members in temple ceremonies. Lots outside the city were larger to allow for more extensive farming. Eventually the Mormons were scattered in more than ninety settlements over an area ninety miles broad.[26]

People lived in their wagon boxes while necessary public works and infrastructures were established: a council house and bowery were built, wells dug, roads laid out, areas fenced off, and land cultivated. In time a hotel was added, along with a carding machine house, a store, and several small schools. A large stockyard was built at the south end of the town.[27]

Most houses were made of cottonwood or lynwood logs with single rooms, rectangles twelve by eighteen feet, seven feet high, with dirt floors. Poles covered by sod, willows, or straw on sod constituted roofs. Chimneys were made of sod or bricks, and doors were made of shakes pinned together and finished with a string latch. Some were forced to move into partially built homes and finish them while they lived there.[28]

The home often cited as Brigham Young's house reflected this basic pattern. Located in the south end of town, it was made of logs, one and one-half stories high, and measured sixteen by thirty-two feet. Like Heber C. Kimball's house

nearby, it had two rooms upstairs and two down, roofed with sod, and boasted
a brick chimney and a plank floor. It housed many people.[29]

Irene Hascall Pomeroy left a housewife's insights into her living quarters.

> We have lived in our log cabin through the winter very comfortably. We have a
> brick chimney and hearth (two thirds of the people have them made of sods
> and they do very well), a window with four lights of glass 10 by 12; gave eight
> cents a light. The furniture consists of sacks, barrels, chests, trunks, and two
> bedsteads with curtains from eaves to floor; my chest for a table."[30]

While he stayed in Winter Quarters, Brigham Young married three women.
The first was Jane Terry, a widow with two small children. Born 21 May 1819, in
St. Louis, Canada, daughter of Parshall and Hannah Terry, Jane first married
George Tarbox when she was seventeen years old. Shortly after the birth of their
son, Elisha Terry Tarbox, the family encountered the Mormon missionaries and
were converted, as were Jane's parents and most of her brothers and sisters.
Together they left Toronto on the steamer *Transit* on 10 July 1838 bound for Far
West, Missouri. That winter George died in Quincy, Illinois.[31] At nineteen, Jane
was a widow with a small son. She subsequently married George Young (no relation to Brigham) and together they had a daughter, Emma Amanda, on 28
February 1841.[32]

Fleeing mob persecution, George and Jane were among those Saints who left
Illinois, crossing the Mississipi River in January 1846 to Sugar Creek, Iowa. That
fall George died during the subsequent trek across Iowa, leaving Jane a widow for
a second time, now with two small children. She was also desperately ill.

In her diary, Jane's sister, Elizabeth Terry Heward, recorded Jane's arrival in
Council Bluffs and their subsequent journey to Winter Quarters, over roads so

A wagon train on the trail. Woodcut,
Frederick Piercy, *Route from Liverpool to Great
Salt Lake Valley.*

Independence Rock

Devil's Gate

Above and facing: Independence Rock, Devil's Gate, and Chimney Rock, landmarks on the trail. Steelplate engravings, Frederick Piercy, *Route from Liverpool to Great Salt Lake Valley.*

bad the fifteen-mile trip required four days' travel. Elizabeth left Jane with a Sister Thompson but took Elisha Tarbox to live with her family. By 5 February when Elizabeth returned with her husband John, Jane's condition was considerably worse. She asked to see President Young and Elizabeth delivered her request. Brigham visited and married her on 10 February 1847. Four days later she was dead.[33] Her daughter Emma was also ill but recovered. Both children lived for a time with the Hewards and then with Jane's parents. Both lived to maturity, married, and had families.[34]

Brigham's next two wives were sisters: Lucy and Mary Jane Bigelow. Their parents, Nahum and Mary Gibbs Bigelow, joined the LDS Church in 1838 and the family moved to Hancock County, Illinois, where they experienced the mobbings and persecutions inflicted on the Mormons there and then traveled west.[35] Their courtship reveals a number of things about Brigham's attitudes toward his many marriages. Lucy, age seventeen, had already received two proposals of marriage, not at all unusual for a girl her age during that time period. Her parents rejected the first, but both approved of the second man, David Ward. He was five years older than Lucy and supported himself, his mother, and a young brother by teaching school. Lucy was in the process of making arrangements to marry him when he died from measles.[36]

Soon afterwards a polygamist named Wicks contacted Lucy and Mary Jane and asked them to marry him. Both of the girls rejected him; they were more interested in younger, single men. Not easily discouraged, Wicks approached Nahum and asked if he could marry Nahum's daughters. Nahum initially said he would need the girls' consent, but became confused and upset because the man was very persistent. He took the matter to his good friend, Brigham Young. He asked what Brigham thought of Wicks, particularly whether he would make his daughters happy. Nahum wanted the matter settled because the girls were in their late teens, an age when most girls married at the time and because movement to the West was imminent. Brigham soberly reported that Wicks was a fine man, but his first wife was very high-strung and advised against him on those grounds. Then Brigham offered to visit the Bigelows and talk to the girls about the matter. As promised, Brigham later visited the family and asked the girls if they wanted to marry Wicks. When both indicated they were not interested, Brigham asked them if they wanted to marry him instead. At the time of the proposal, he had sixteen wives and was nearly thirty years older than the Bigelow girls. Such a casual proposal may have surprised the girls, but he told them to think about it and he would get their answer later. This unemotional and businesslike way of proposing and courting

Chimney Rock

women was typical of Brigham. He didn't have time to woo women and wouldn't chase after young girls. He once commented that he believed in "marry first and spark afterward."[37]

Initially Mary Jane was willing to marry Brigham but Lucy wasn't interested in him or any married man. When he came to visit the Bigelows several times in the following weeks, Lucy avoided him. Finally sometime in early 1846, Brigham visited and finding both girls home asked for an answer. Afraid to hurt his feelings, Lucy agreed to marry, so the three set a date. On 14 March 1846 Brigham, Heber C. Kimball, and two other apostles visited the Bigelow home in Winter Quarters to conduct the ceremony. The wedding was simple and neither girl had a fancy dress or friends in attendance. With only their immediate family and the apostles present, Heber married Brigham to both girls. After the ceremony ended the groom and the apostles left and the brides stayed with their parents. Brigham would, in fact, never live with Mary Jane.[38]

Shortly after she arrived in the Salt Lake Valley in September 1848, Mary Jane asked to be released from her marriage to Brigham and he agreed, as he did in virtually every case where a wife asked to leave a plural marriage. "While not an advocate of divorce, Brigham was nevertheless fairly liberal in granting it, especially in cases of plural marriages." Brigham believed, however, that "It is the woman's place to ask for a divorce and not the man's."[39] Mary Jane subsequently married four more times: to Horace Roberts, John Bair, Daniel Durham Hunt, and Philander Bell, having children with none. She died in Salt Lake City, 26 September 1866. Lucy, however, became Brigham's wife in the traditional sense, although they did not live together until after they had both

Great Salt Lake

moved to Salt Lake City and their marriage had been ratified in temple ceremonies conducted in the upstairs room of the Council House.[40]

In April of 1847 Brigham Young and 147 other pioneers set out from Winter Quarters in seventy-two wagons along with "ninety-three horses, fifty-two mules, sixty-six oxen, nineteen cows, seventeen dogs, and some chickens."[41] Unlike romanticized Hollywood wagon trains, the entire group did not set out in designated order, a wagonmaster shouting, "Wagons ho!" The first six wagons under the direction of Heber C. Kimball led out and were followed by other small groups over the next few days.[42]

That first train set the pattern for the others that would later follow. Subsequent trains were organized into groups of "tens" and "hundreds," each with its own leader, the groups of ten taking turns leading the train.[43] Each train was also to "bear an equal proportion, according to the dividend of their property, in taking the poor, the widows, the fatherless, and the families of those who have gone into the army [the Mormon Battalion]."[44] Only one of Brigham's wives, Clarissa Decker Young, accompanied him on this initial crossing.[45]

When the first wagon train was reasonably settled in the Salt Lake Valley, Brigham and several others returned to Winter Quarters to guide subsequent trains across the plains. Brigham took several of his wives and families to Utah during that first migration season. Many of those who remained in the Midwest worked in the surrounding communities—building homes, planting crops, grading roads, taking whatever jobs they could find—to support themselves and to buy supplies for the trip west. Brigham's wife, Lucy Bigelow, for example, went to St. Louis with her mother and brother. While they were there, they arranged their own housing, and Lucy trained to be a tailor.[46]

The journey ended in the Great Salt Lake Valley. Frederick Piercy, *Route from Liverpool to Great Salt Lake Valley.*

During a crossing the next spring Brigham married Sarah Malin on 18 April 1848. His marriage to Sarah brought to an even thirty the wives known to be alive in 1848 for whom Brigham had to provide houses in Utah.[47] One of those wives was Emily Dow Partridge, pregnant during the crossing, who observed, "We were more comfortable fitted out than we had been at any time before, but on account of ill health the journey was most unpleasant. I do not wish to think of that time." Her memories were still strong forty-nine years later, however. After watching a July 24 Pioneer Day parade she wrote: "The old Pioneer waggons were almost too realistic. They brought back in a forcible manner the horrible journey across the plains. I only sat and cried while they passed."[48] Others remembered the trip more kindly, but all were glad when the journey was over and they could settle, even if settlement meant the deserts of the Great Basin.

Chapter 5

Settling in Salt Lake City

Judy Dykman and Colleen Whitley

For Brigham Young, settlement in the Great Basin brought even more responsibilities than he had carried on the trail. He assumed the secular duties of territorial governor as well as the religious leadership of the church. His obligations now entailed supervising settlements and building structures such as the Salt Lake Temple. On a personal level, it also meant that he would actually provide homes for all of his wives, most of whom had simply stayed with their own families or traveled with others. His Salt Lake City properties are listed here in approximately chronological order of his family's occupation, recognizing that several homes might be built in one year and precise dates for the building or occupation of others are not available. Some houses of close location are grouped despite differences in the times that they were occupied. Only a few of the homes occupied for a short time or rented from someone else for temporary housing are included. Brigham Young's Salt Lake homes are keyed to map 1 and the text includes a brief history of each home and the current occupant(s) or uses of its site.[1]

For Brigham Young's polygamous wives, life in Utah required that they learn to live together, often in very close proximity. Anyone who has spent time in a military barracks or a college dormitory appreciates how difficult it must have been to have several families share a single log cabin, and yet they did it, the wives often showing remarkable grace. Individual wives noted their own decisions not to quarrel, gossip, or backbite. Lucy Bigelow, for example, left some insights into the challenges and limitations polygamy put on marital relationships and privacy. Initially she rarely had her own room and often shared a bed with a sister wife or slept on the floor. Lucy's daughter, Susa, observes that her mother resolved early in her marriage that for her own peace of mind she would not lower herself to backbite or criticize anyone, particularly her husband, if children were around. Susa remembers that her mother rarely said anything negative about anyone in the family.[2]

In addition to adapting to changes in living arrangements, each wife also assumed specific duties in the division of labor necessary to maintain the family in the new environment. Many of their homes were designed or designated for one of those specific tasks, but it took time to build those homes. In the meanwhile,

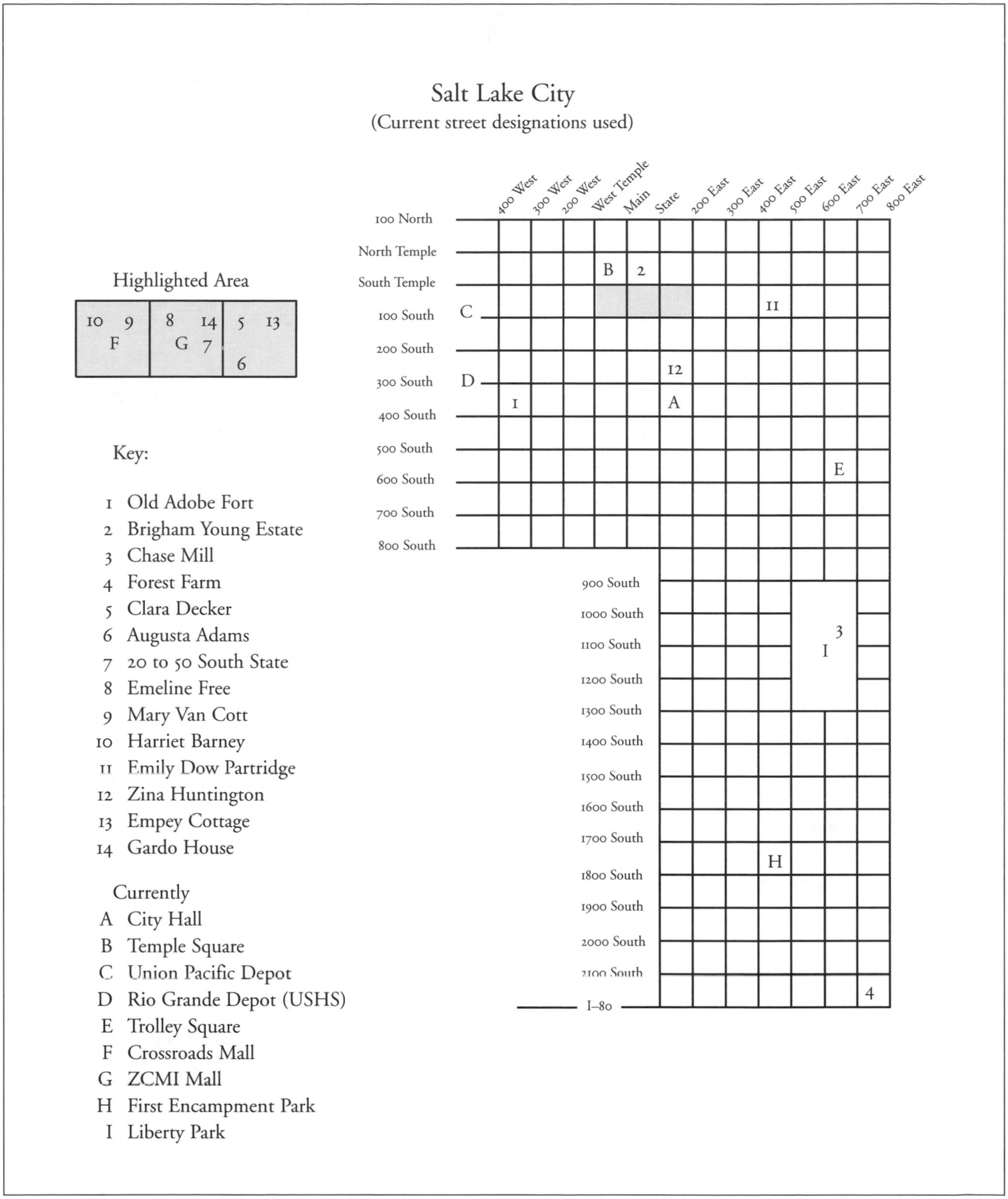

Salt Lake City
(Current street designations used)
400 West
300 West
200 West
West Temple
Main
State
200 East
300 East
400 East
500 East
600 East
700 East
800 East
100 North
North Temple
South Temple
100 South
200 South
300 South
400 South
500 South
600 South
700 South
800 South
900 South
1000 South
1100 South
1200 South
1300 South
1400 South
1500 South
1600 South
1700 South
1800 South
1900 South
2000 South
2100 South
I–80
B
2
C
11
12
D
1
A
E
3
I
H
4
Highlighted Area
10
9
F
8
14
G
7
5
13
6
Key:
1 Old Adobe Fort
2 Brigham Young Estate
3 Chase Mill
4 Forest Farm
5 Clara Decker
6 Augusta Adams
7 20 to 50 South State
8 Emeline Free
9 Mary Van Cott
10 Harriet Barney
11 Emily Dow Partridge
12 Zina Huntington
13 Empey Cottage
14 Gardo House
Currently
A City Hall
B Temple Square
C Union Pacific Depot
D Rio Grande Depot (USHS)
E Trolley Square
F Crossroads Mall
G ZCMI Mall
H First Encampment Park
I Liberty Park

On this street grid of Salt Lake City numbers indicate locations of Brigham Young's homes; letters indicate current structures or parks. Map by Colleen Whitley.

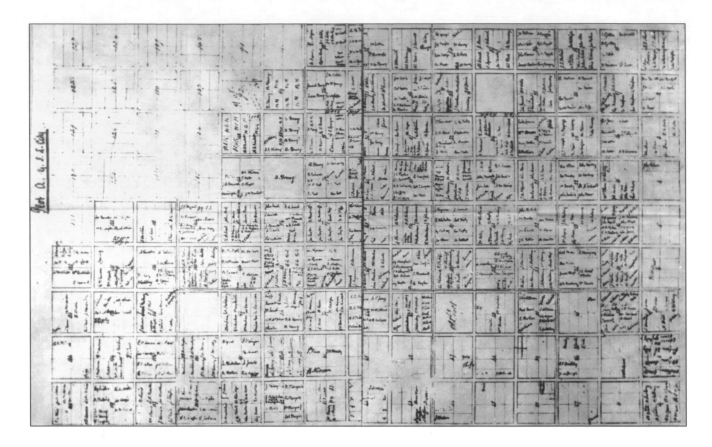

like all of the pioneers, they continued to live in their tents and wagons as they had on the trail.

The first company to enter the valley arrived on 23 July 1847 and camped on present-day 1700 South and 500 East in what is now First Encampment Park. The park was created in 1997 as part of Utah's sesquicentennial celebration by the Wells and Emigration Stakes of the LDS Church and turned over to Salt Lake City.[3] The main camping area, however, developed between the two branches of City Creek, from Third to Fourth South running east of what is now Main Street. A temporary bowery, twenty-eight by forty feet, was built on what is now Temple Square on 31 July 1847. An example of such a bowery stands near This Is the Place Heritage Park in Salt Lake City.[4] Meanwhile, the Saints began laying out their permanent city.

On 3 August Orson Pratt and H. G. Sherwood began surveying the north end of Salt Lake City. By 20 August they had marked out the 135 blocks of Plat A running from 500 West to 300 East and from 500 North to 900 South.[5] The land beyond Ninth South was called simply the "Big Field" which was eventually divided into "five acre lots next to the city to accommodate the mechanics and artisans."[6] Still farther out farming parcels ranged from ten to eighty acres.[7]

In town, streets oriented north-south or east-west were measured at 132 feet wide including twenty-foot sidewalks and space for gutters on each side. The central, ten-acre site was reserved as Temple Square, and Salt Lake City's street numbering system radiated out from the Meridian Marker on the corner of Main and South Temple Streets. Each remaining block was then divided into eight lots of one and one-quarter acres each.[8]

This early map of Salt Lake City shows the streets laid out in straight lines at right angles. Houses on alternate blocks faced north and south or east and west so no street became simply a side street. Used by permission, Utah State Historical Society, all rights reserved.

The sequential numbering of streets makes finding locations in the city very easy; as long as one can count, he or she can locate addresses. Ryan Gibbons, a Salt Lake banker who has also lived in Portland, Seattle, Sacramento, and Boise, observed, "If you get an address in another town, you have to pull out a map to find your way. . . . If you get lost in Salt Lake, you're an idiot."9 Many urban planners have also observed the wisdom of this farsighted design. Harry Truman, who was greatly concerned with metropolitan problems, said, "There isn't a city in the United States that was properly planned to begin with. I know of only one whose streets were laid out in anticipation of the automobile and that is Salt Lake City. The old man that laid out that city really had vision—in more ways than one."10

As more settlers arrived, it quickly became evident that more lots would be needed, and a second plat of sixty-three blocks was surveyed east of Plat A, from South Temple to 900 south and from 300 East to 1000 East. The area of Capitol Hill and the Avenues would eventually be broken into twenty-two smaller blocks going up the hills. Both plats were divided into nineteen wards, and people automatically became members of the wards in which they settled, regardless of their race or place of origin.11

300 to 400 South, 300 to 400 West: The Old Fort

Even with streets laid out, though, the pioneers knew it would be some while before homes could actually be built, so within a week of their arrival, they began work on the first permanent structure for housing in the valley, the Old Fort in what is now Pioneer Park. Builders brought logs from the canyon, prepared mounds to mark boundaries, and made adobe bricks by mixing wet clay or mud with straw or plant fiber and then molding bricks which were dried in the sun. On 9 August 1847, seventy-six volunteers assembled logs and started making

Pioneer Park, shown here in late autumn, remains as a memorial to the Old Fort, first home to nearly all the settlers in the first two years of the state's existence. Photo by Judy Dykman and Colleen Whitley.

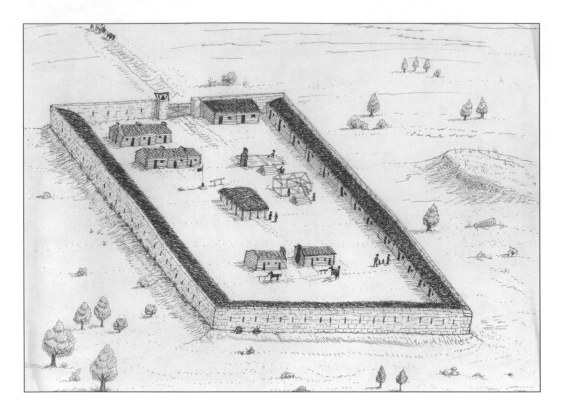

adobe. Construction began the next day on the first fort in Utah, enclosing what is now called Pioneer Park. As more people arrived, the fort was expanded with wooden walls to include the two blocks beside the original structure as well. The fort would be a home for the pioneers while the city was carefully laid out.[12]

Adobe walls eight to nine feet high and twenty-seven inches thick ringed three sides. The east side of the fort was made of wood and had a bell tower and a heavy gate which was locked at night. Many of the nearly seventeen hundred people who arrived in 1847 lived in the fort that first winter; some simply stayed in their wagons, while others had homes built into the fort itself. While the fort as a whole was not completed until December, by 23 August, twenty-nine log houses lined its interior walls. Each was sixteen to seventeen feet long by fourteen feet wide and eight to nine feet high. Each house had doors and windows facing inward; however, since each rear wall was also part of the exterior of the fort itself, it had only a small loophole to accommodate a rifle barrel looking out. The roofs were made of willows, brush, and dirt which sloped inward toward the center of the fort. Apparently the roofs did not slope enough, however, because as winter's heavy snow melted, it soaked through, "descending in drizzling streams upon the miserable inhabitants."[13] That same brush also accommodated a bountiful population of mice and insects, adding to the discomfort of the human inhabitants.[14]

Difficult as living conditions were in the Old Fort, however, life settled into ordinary routines. A bowery of tall vertical poles topped with cross-poles covered with brush stood in the center of the fort; it served as a public gathering place for meetings both ecclesiastical and secular. Hung in the tower on the east side of the fort was the Nauvoo Bell, the only part of the Nauvoo Temple salvaged when the Saints fled Illinois. The bell announced activities ranging from church meetings to a school for the children conducted by Julian Moses and Mary Jane Dilworth.[15]

No photographs remain of the Old Fort, but several descriptions exist, permitting artists to offer reasonable facsimiles. This aerial view of the fort from the west looks toward the main gate. Beside it is the tower holding the Nauvoo Bell. Around the edges are some of the brush-roofed houses incorporated into the exterior wall of the fort. In the center are the bowery and other shelters where meetings and schools were held. Pen and ink drawing by Jana Whitley, used with permission, all rights reserved.

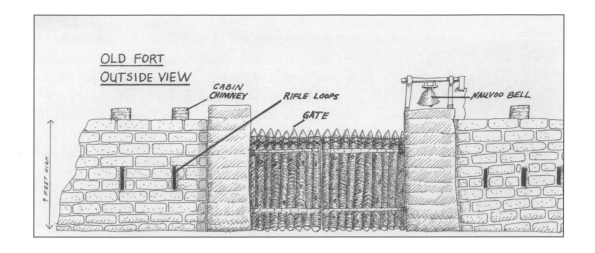

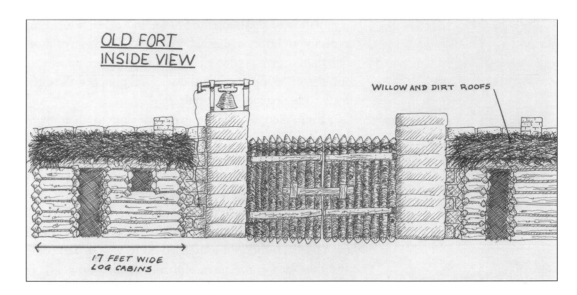

Ironically, a fort in Salt Lake Valley may not have been necessary at all. Native tribes had recognized the value of the resources in the valley, including the salt that all of them needed. Consequently, they held the area as a buffer zone between the Shoshoni on the north and the Utes on the south and pitched no battles in the valley of the Great Salt Lake. The Mormons had landed in the one place regarded as neutral by the indigenous populations. As they expanded into other parts of the territory, however, they would encounter Native Americans protecting their own territory.[16]

That first winter the fort housed Brigham's wives who had crossed the plains during that summer. Eliza Snow shared quarters with Clarissa Decker, and their living arrangements give some insights into conditions in the Old Fort. They had two pieces of furniture: a chest Clarissa brought with her served as a table and a bed was built into one corner. A post put in the ground a few feet out from the corner supported the ends of two horizontal poles set at a ninety degree angle. The other ends of those poles were attached to the walls and along with the walls became the sides of the "mattress"—cords wound tightly around pegs from the poles to the walls.[17]

This pair of elevation studies shows how the wall of the Old Fort functioned as both a line of defense and a part of individual cabins. The shooting slits in the wall also constituted the only windows for each cabin that looked outside the fort. Pen and ink drawing by Jana Whitley, used with permission, all rights reserved.

The next year 2,200 more emigrants arrived.[18] By September 1848 the population of the city had reached 6,000 and the surveyed lots were assigned, usually in ways that kept families reasonably close together. Assignments were made to heads of families, which included married men, widows, and divorced women, but not unmarried men. The land itself was free, but each landholder paid $1.50 for the survey and filing. Thomas Bullock recorded each parcel's location and gave the new owner a receipt, which served as title to the land. Real estate transactions have never been so simple since then.[19]

The new owners were allowed to build one house on each city lot, set back twenty feet from the street. There was room for each landholder to plant a small garden and keep livestock. Some people, however, needed more than one and a quarter acres. Larger agricultural lots in the "Big Field" south of the city were distributed by a drawing of numbered slips of paper, again by heads of families. The amount of farm acreage granted depended upon the size of the family, occupation of the household head, and other mitigating factors. Owners were expected to improve the land and make good use of it or the land could be forfeited. No one was allowed to subdivide or speculate in land to new arrivals. The stipulation to improve the allotted land presaged the distribution of federal land by the Homestead Act of 1862.[20]

Even though residents were moving to their own homes, the fort still housed new arrivals, and it was an important center for public occasions. On 9 December 1848, a meeting was held to organize the provincial State of Deseret. The first Twenty-fourth of July celebration started there in 1849, commemorating the pioneers' arrival in the valley. "Festivities began at Brigham Young's home on the northeast corner of Pioneer Square. Then there was a parade with prancing horses, brass bands, and flags. At 9 a.m. the procession started from the Old Fort, and as it proceeded on its way to Temple Square, cannons roared and the Nauvoo Bell pealed forth its somber notes."[21]

The fort became redundant as people moved on to individual lots. Some even dismantled their log cabins and took them from the fort to their new locations. Neglected, the adobe began to crumble with the weather, although some parts of the wall stood for several decades. When city fathers learned "it had become a trysting place for persons of loose morals," they ordered its destruction, an action stopped cold by irate citizens, who wanted it to remain a commemorative park.[22] On 25 July 1898, the area where the fort once stood was dedicated as Pioneer Square and is now administered and maintained by the Salt Lake City Department of Public Services, but alternatives keep being suggested for its use.[23]

In 1948 the city proposed selling the park for industrial development and using the proceeds to build a golf course. Then Mayor Earl J. Glade reacted to objections from historians and community leaders who maintained the park was a "shrine to Utah."[24] When rumors of a proposed sale surfaced again in 1955, individuals and groups ranging from the Sons of Utah Pioneers to the Greek Orthodox Church protested. The SUP proposed a "Pioneer Village" or a replica of the Salt Lake Theatre be built there, but both the village and the replica were built elsewhere and the park remained a park. Only three years later, the City Council proposed building a ten-thousand-seat civic auditorium and a five-hundred-car parking terrace. In 1971 Governor Calvin Rampton appointed a committee to look into

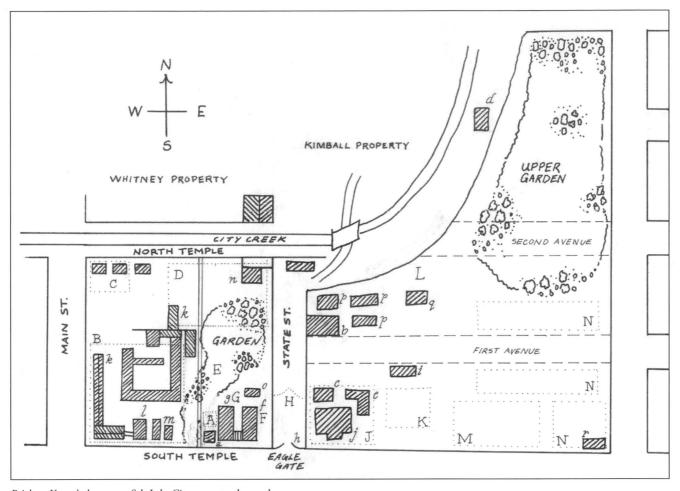

Brigham Young's downtown Salt Lake City property, then and now

a. cabin*
b. Log Row*
c. Zina Huntington's cabin*†
d. Harriet Cook's cabin*
e. White House
f. Beehive House
g. Lion House
h. Eagle Gate
i. cemetery
j. school†
k. tithing office/storehouse
l. Deseret News
m. mint
n. barn and pigpens
o. bunkhouse or cocoonery
p. corral, woodhouse, smokehouse, lamb barn (after Log Row had been removed)
q. swimming pool*
r. Bell's Furniture Shop

A. LDS Church Administration Building
B. Joseph Smith Memorial Building
C. Relief Society Building
D. LDS Church Office Building
E. plaza with fountain
F. Beehive House
G. Lion House
H. Eagle Gate
I. cemetery
J. Eagle Gate Apartments
K. Elks Club Building
L. Brigham Young Park
M. Brigham Young Condos
N. apartments

limits of Brigham Young's property, and outlines of buildings on the property during Brigham's lifetime
division giving the LDS Church title to that part of Brigham Young's original property containing Church buildings
... outlines of current buildings
current boundaries of city streets
* original sizes and locations uncertain
† Judging from photographs and early descriptions, it is possible that Zina's cabin was incorporated as part of the family school; these two buildings may be the same
Map by Jana Whitley. Drawing for the early estate is based on one by Marguerite Cameron; information for the current buildings is determined by measurements (often simply paced off) by the authors.

building a replica of the fort, but nothing came of that effort. In 1992, Mayor Deedee Corradini proposed building a baseball stadium on the site, a proposal which met with considerable opposition, and once again, the park remained a park. More recently Steve Schulkens of the Living Planet Aquarium Foundation has proposed locating an aquarium accompanied by a themed playground in the park. That has been tabled, but new ideas are suggested frequently.[25]

Part of the reason so many alternatives kept being proposed for the park's use is that it has continued to be a "trysting place for persons of loose morals" including vagrants, drunks, and drug dealers. Many citizens were afraid to go there, and surrounding businesses and nearby residents have raised genuine concerns. In the past few years public officials have launched a series of efforts to clean up the park and the surrounding area, encouraging businesses to locate in nearby buildings, persuading prominent chains and motels to bring greater traffic into the area. The city also increased police patrols and sponsored activities that would bring in a greater cross-section of the population. Today some events, like the Easter egg hunt, are designed to serve the increasingly family-centered population at the homeless shelter only a block away. The park has also recently been the site of a Native American Freedom Festival, arts and crafts displays, and a farmer's market through the harvest season. One of the most positive impacts has come through locating the Utah State Historical Society in the main section of the old Rio Grande Depot on 300 South while encouraging other businesses and agencies to make use of the rest of the magnificent old building. That action has both revitalized the area and preserved an historic structure at minimal cost.[26]

BRIGHAM YOUNG'S DOWNTOWN PROPERTY[27]

Because polygamists were allowed one lot for each of their families, Brigham Young initially obtained several town lots and opted to keep them together. In

Brigham Young Historic Park provides green space in downtown Salt Lake City. It contains land from both Brigham Young's and Heber C. Kimball's original land grants and features replicas of the wall around Young's property and a mill wheel typical of the period. Photo by Judy Dykman and Colleen Whitley.

First two adobe homes of Brigham Young
in Salt Lake Valley, north side So. Temple between Main and State
1.— Later residence of Daniel H. Wells- here was born Heber M. Wells,
Utah's first Governor

addition to housing his numerous wives and children, he was both president of the LDS Church and governor of the territory. Consequently he had to provide space for church offices and accommodations for an assortment of visiting dignitaries. During the initial distribution of land, he took two blocks in Plat A, east of Temple Square, running east to what is now A Street, then north up the hill to Fourth Avenue, west a short distance along Fourth Avenue and then following the curve of City Creek down the hill to a little above what is now First Avenue, then west a little south of the current North Temple to Main, and south again to South Temple.[28]

Although he later built homes in other areas both inside and beyond Salt Lake City, Brigham intended this fifty-acre enclosure to be as self-sufficient as possible, so in time it included corrals, barns and other outbuildings, a school, a store, a gristmill, a blacksmith shop, carpentry shops, and a small cemetery. His property initially included some land which was soon assigned to the church and housed public facilities such as the tithing office, and even some entities, such as the *Deseret News*, which would be regarded as secular today. Neither Young nor the Mormon Church made a great distinction between his property as an individual and that which he held as president of the church. The practice of pooling church property in the prophet's name had also prevailed when Joseph Smith led the church and caused a great rift between his widow, Emma, and the church as a whole, and particularly between her and Brigham.[29]

Young's inclination to intertwine his own and church property was exacerbated by U.S. government attempts to confiscate church property. By keeping many properties in his own name, Brigham prevented the government from

The first adobe cabins in Utah temporarily housed several of Brigham Young's families on his downtown property on South Temple between Main and State. Used by permission, Utah State Historical Society, all rights reserved.

appropriating them. The practice, though, led to confusion in the church and divisions in his family after his death.[30] The buildings on his estate are keyed to the map showing both original and present structures.[31]

CABINS

Soon after the division of property occurred, Brigham had two small, low-roofed cabins hastily built somewhere in the vicinity of South Temple and State Streets. In 1847 Lucy Decker Young (and possibly others) lived in a log cabin, and in 1848 Brigham had an adobe cabin built on South Temple near the current location of the LDS Church Administration Building. Charlie and Vilate Decker lived in the front room while Margaret Pierce and Emmeline Free and their children lived in the back rooms. Others of Brigham's wives and children in the valley at that point probably stayed in wagons or tents for a time. Intended as interim shelter, the cabin was eventually torn down as more adequate homes became available.[32] Doubtless the family was grateful for more room, however rustic the facilities.

The location of those cabins may have been dictated by the location of City Creek, a branch of which ran past them, or by the presence of nearby springs, which today feed the fountain in the plaza between the LDS Church Office Building and the Beehive and Lion Houses.[33]

FIRST AVENUE EAST OF STATE STREET: LOG ROW

Young built a long log cabin with seven or eight rooms in a row, in the fall of 1848. Its location was adjacent to City Creek just east of State Street approximately along what is now First Avenue but possibly a little farther south, on the same site later used for the family school. Once it was completed, his wives who had been living in the Old Fort moved in. Several of his children were born there, including Margaret Alley's daughter Evelyn Louisa (Eva); Eliza Burgess's son Alfales, who eventually became the telegraph operator for the *Deseret News*; and three of Lucy Decker's children: daughters Fanny and Shemira (Mira) and son, Ernest. The birth years for those children indicate that the Young family occupied Log Row until at least 1855 or 1856.[34]

While Log Row certainly provided more adequate shelter than wagons, survival still depended on hard labor. Cooking was done on primitive fireplaces in iron ovens and pots. The baking skillet had a rimmed lid that allowed hot coals to be placed on top as well as underneath, much like modern dutch ovens. Candle-dipping, butter-churning, and all of the attendant animal care and gardening needed to support the family meant everyone old enough to manage a tool or a task, especially the wives, had responsibilities to the household.[35]

As more permanent structures, notably the White, Beehive, and Lion Houses were completed, the Youngs moved out of Log Row, and the building was torn down. Because its location is stated unspecifically and road configurations have changed, the current use of the area is uncertain, but the Row probably stood on land now occupied by apartment houses on First Avenue.

Near Log Row

Meanwhile, the practicalities of housing needs and farm maintenance temporarily merged. Mary Ann Angell and her children were housed in a small building that later became the "corn crib"; three wagon boxes on a foundation housed two other wives, and Margaret Pierce lived in what would eventually become the milk house. All of them moved to better, more permanent quarters as quickly as they became available.[36]

Zina Huntington's Cabin

Soon after Log Row was completed, Brigham built a small adobe home for Zina Diantha Huntington Young. It provided housing for Zina and her two children by her marriage to Henry Jacobs, but perhaps even more importantly, it served as the family school until the Lion House was built.[37] Zina's home may well have provided the core for the Brigham Young School, which later provided education not only for Brigham's family but for neighborhood children as well.

Zina served as midwife to the family and was one of several competent nurses among the wives.[38] Susa Young Gates remembers her as a gentle and tenderhearted woman who cared for the sick and suffering.[39] In her later life, Zina was one of the leading women of Utah and of the LDS Church. In 1875 she became president of the Deseret Silk Association. Relief Society sisters raised

The monument for Charles Crismon's Mill, probably also the home of Harriet Cook, stands at approximately 150 North Canyon Road. Nearby flows City Creek, which provided the power to turn the mill wheels. Photo by Judy Dykman and Colleen Whitley.

silkworms, carefully feeding them mulberry leaves, then reeled the silk from the cocoons and wove it into cloth.[40] Zina traveled to the Sandwich Islands in 1879 and in 1881 served as a missionary in New York and other states. She followed her sister wife, Eliza R. Snow, as general president of the Relief Society, serving until her death in 1901.[41]

SOMEWHERE BETWEEN THIRD AVENUE AND CANYON ROAD

While most of the family lived in or at least near the Log Row, Harriet Elizabeth Cook Campbell Young reportedly lived in a log cabin of "one room with fireplace, board floor, bed, chairs, and a table made of logs" north of the Log Row. While some published works indicate that her cabin was on the current site of the State Capitol Building, it was probably down the hill, closer to Third North and Canyon Road, since Heber C. Kimball owned the land on which the capitol now stands. The highest house on the hill was reputed to be that of Colebrook, keeper of the arsenal, near the site of the current McCune Mansion. This location put him in proximity to the arsenal itself, which was located a little south of the present DUP Museum. The State Capitol Building property itself seems to have simply served as grazing land for several years.[42]

The cabin spoken of as Harriet's could well have been the one Charles Crismon built on approximately Third Avenue and Canyon Road in the fall of 1847. There Crismon also built the first gristmill in the city and ground wheat brought across the plains. Brigham Young bought it from him when the land divisions in 1848 gave him the property on which it stood. Today a monument

to Crismon's mill stands at approximately 150 North Canyon Road, in the median where City Creek flows.[43]

Why Harriet lived separately and relatively far from the other early homes may raise some questions, since she apparently meshed reasonably well with the rest of the family. If the cabin was Crismon's or any other that used the stream to power a mill, it could explain her isolation. She would have been following the pattern for Brigham's family in which each wife had a specific duty or stewardship, overseeing a location or function necessary for the common good. Certainly Harriet was capable of managing alone in a difficult situation. Brigham once observed she "would make a good sheriff: if she once decided to get her man, she would get him."[44] Wherever her cabin was, Harriet lived there only a few years. In 1856, she and her son, Oscar Brigham, moved to the Lion House. From then on Harriet contributed to the family by teaching school, initially in one of the rooms on the lower floor of the Lion House and then in the family school when that was built. Her pupils included Brigham's children from his assorted wives and neighborhood children as well.[45] Susa Young Gates recalled Harriet's teaching style:

> Brilliant minded, Aunt Hariet Cook who was a profound student of the scriptures and whose tongue was as a flame of darting fire . . . knew as all her sister wives knew, that there was no corroding acid of hate there, just an outlet for the flashing genius that might have made her a great general or a mighty organizer of human forces, had she been a man. Her sex, her real affection for father, her love of the Gospel, her circumstances, her flashing sharpness of speech kept her from achieving. And so we [the Young children] all watched out for Aunt Harriet whose quick sarcasm whipped us, oftentime, into the love of our duty more effectively than the gentle reproofs of our own mothers.[46]

The fireplace in the White House is reminiscent of some of the mantlepieces Brigham Young built early in his career as a carpenter. Used by permission, Utah State Historical Society, all rights reserved.

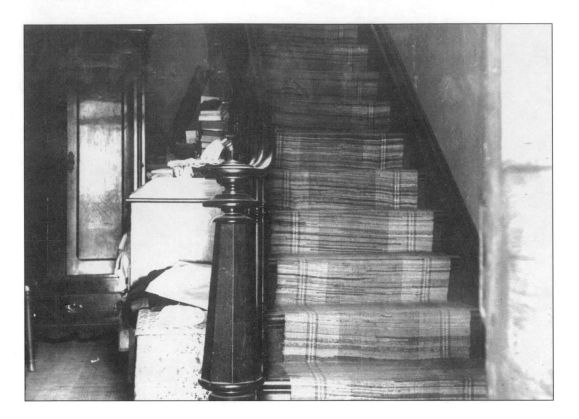

Harriet also worked as a bookkeeper for ZCMI and earned money to buy the books she loved to read. She died in the Lion House in 1898.

119 East South Temple: The Mansion House, Sometimes Called the White House

While he was living in the Log Row, Brigham started work on several other homes. The first to be completed was the White House, immediately south of the old Log Row and ready for occupancy in 1854. Located at the top of a hill a little east of what is now the corner of South Temple and State Street, it commanded a view of the city and was connected with the street by a flight of stairs. Its colonial design included large porches and later a balcony. It was reported to be the first house in the state with a shingled roof. The exterior walls were plastered adobe painted white, from which came its common name, the White House.[47] The more formal name "Mansion House" may have been derived from the name of Joseph Smith's home-hotel–church headquarters in Nauvoo, but it doubtless also came from its elegance and its whitewashed walls, the only whitewashed building in the territory in that early period. Perhaps the name came most of all from the fact that the Mansion House was the official residence for both the government of Utah Territory and the LDS Church until the Beehive House was completed.[48]

The interior easily accommodated such official business. The rooms were regarded as good-sized; the main floor seemed especially spacious since the ceilings were higher than those on the second floor. The interior was also painted white and French doors with plate glass joined its main floor parlors and allowed access to the front porch from a small sitting room. The property also

United States troups entering Salt Lake City in the spring of 1858, passing Brigham Young's residence on Brigham Street, now South Temple Street

had a carriage house, barn, and other outbuildings, as well as a vegetable garden and fruit trees. A row of box elder trees lined the yard on the west and south. The wall around the estate was eight feet tall from the street, but the ground behind it at the White House was only "waist high" for Brigham and Mary Ann's grandson, George Spencer Young.[49]

The Mansion House was built for Mary Ann Angell Young who, because she was the senior wife, was simply called "Mother Young." She moved to the house in 1854 along with her five children, Joseph A., then 20; Brigham Jr., 18; Alice, 15; Luna, 12; and John W., 10. Mary Ann's brother, Truman Osborn Angell, who had designed the house, lived there with her and her children until he married. Susan Snively Young also lived there for a time until she moved to Forest Farm.[50]

On at least one occasion, the White House was sold, along with several other properties, to support the Perpetual Emigrating Fund.[51] Then in 1857 during the Utah War Mary Ann, and most of the other citizens of Salt Lake City, "went south" for safety when the United States Army invaded Utah. Responding to an alleged rebellion against the United States government by the "traitorous" Mormons, President Buchanan sent 2,500 soldiers under Albert Sidney Johnston to Utah to control the populace. To insure U.S. control he appointed Alfred Cumming of Georgia to replace Brigham Young as governor. Initially the Mormons perceived Cumming as a threat, though they later realized he was fairly competent for a federal appointee.[52]

Brigham responded to accounts that the army was coming by mobilizing the Mormons. Men were told to get their weapons ready and to stockpile food. Settlers in outlying valleys were ordered back to the Salt Lake Valley. Scouts sent to Wyoming destroyed the army's supply trains and stole their livestock. Forts

This woodcut shows the troops of Johnston's Army marching down South Temple past the Lion House, Beehive House, the White House, and the family school. Used by permission, Utah State Historical Society, all rights reserved.

Bridger and Supply were burned so the soldiers would have no place to stay and Echo Canyon was filled with dozens of armed men. The army was forced to winter over outside the city. Fortunately, the delaying tactics prevailed long enough for heads to cool. Brigham followed the advice of a friend, Colonel Thomas Kane, who had volunteered to mediate in the dispute. Brigham stepped down as governor and the army agreed to march through the city without stopping. When the army finally entered the city the next June, 1858, they found it deserted, virtually a ghost town. The women and children had moved south to Utah Valley while some men were left in the city to torch the homes rather than surrender them to the invading army.

On 26 June 1858 the soldiers came through Emigration Canyon and down South Temple. They then marched to the Jordan River and across the bridge, where the sight of their campfires reassured the frightened citizens that they were, indeed, honoring their bargain to go on south and west. They established Camp Floyd in Cedar Valley, forty miles southwest of Salt Lake City, where there was adequate water and forage, although some of them found that area less than delightful. A Union soldier described Camp Floyd as "one of the most miserable, disagreeable and uninteresting places that ever disgraced the earth."[53]

In a short while the Salt Lake families returned to their homes and the Mormons actually benefitted from the invasion.[54] Johnston granted contracts to poorer people and low bidders, which Brigham Young condemned, charging that the general was deliberately using federal funds to create dissension among the Saints. Nonetheless, local settlers were paid for providing some foodstuffs and labor to build the camp, and the Mormons profited even more three years later. With the onset of the Civil War, Camp Floyd was decommissioned, and Governor Cumming and the army left.[55] The supplies and materials from the

fort were auctioned at a fraction of their value and the "traitorous" Mormons obtained wagons, food, and even the lumber to build many homes, businesses, and the Salt Lake Theatre at a fraction of their cost. "Goods worth four million dollars, were sold for one hundred thousand."[56] Among the items sold so far below cost was the camp flagpole, which became a symbol of one of the great ironies in Utah history.

General Albert Sidney Johnston had come to Utah specifically to require the "traitorous" Mormons to give due allegiance to the United States, frequently emphasizing his own patriotism. When the Union broke, however, he joined the Confederacy and was killed at Shiloh fighting against the United States. Meanwhile Brigham had placed Johnston's flagpole in the front yard of the White House, and "Old Glory" fluttered from that mast for many years.[57] Brigham and Mary Ann's grandson, George Spencer Young, recalled playing games around "the old flagpole out west of the house."[58]

Mary Ann lived in other places periodically, but for all practical purposes, the White House was her home until she died there in 1882. Her son, John W. Young, inherited the house and sometime before 1890 sold it to Priscilla Jennings, widow of William Jennings, an early convert to the LDS Church who became a wealthy merchant. According to a 1911 newspaper report the house was "taken down, adobe bricks, beams, floors and rafters, and rebuilt in its present location" which was apparently on a lot immediately west of its original site. By about 1918 the original building had become an antique store called simply "My Shop." Its location was reported as both the original site and the lot to the west of it. That confusion may help account for the White House address ranging from 119 to 139 South State in various reports.[59]

In any case, the fate of both properties was the same. Priscilla Jennings built an elegant home on the site which she in turn sold to Philo Farnsworth Sr. by

The Elks built this spacious clubhouse on the site of the White House, but when Lodge Number 78 was closed, Zions Securities purchased the building and now manages it as commercial office space. Photo by Judy Dykman and Colleen Whitley.

Eagle Gate. 1869.

1906. In 1922 the Salt Lake Elks took down both houses to build their clubhouse. When Elks Lodge #78 was closed, the building sold to Zions Securities, which now manages the property as commercial offices.[60]

71 East South Temple: The Beehive House

See chapter 6.

63 East South Temple: The Lion House

See chapter 6.

State Street at South Temple: The Eagle Gate

The Young estate was bounded by a nine-foot wall punctuated by several gates. The most prominent and the one used by the public was Eagle Gate on the north side of what is now State Street at South Temple. The eagle was designed by H. B. Clawson and carved of native wood by Ralph Ramsey and William Bell. The carved wooden eagle stood on a beehive, atop wooden beams

anchored on each side of the street to the cobblestone wall that surrounded Young's property. Beneath the arch was a wooden gate, by which Young controlled access to City Creek Canyon.[61]

Erected 17 February 1859, the gate served for nearly forty years; however, by 1892, it posed a problem for the new streetcars. Spencer Clawson campaigned to keep the old gate, asking Don Carlos Young, LDS Church architect, to look for possibilities to save the eagle. The citizens of Salt Lake City raised $2,700 to move and enlarge the gate to accommodate the trolley lines. The eagle was sent east to be electroplated with copper. The gate was replaced in 1892 and crossed State Street at South Temple until 1960 when the street was widened and the gate removed. The wooden eagle was placed in the Daughters of Utah Pioneers Museum where it can still be seen. George Cannon Young designed a new eagle, sculpted by Grant and Justin Fairbanks. When its twenty-foot wingspan was cast in bronze, it weighed in at two tons. It was erected in 1963 and moved several feet north from the intersection of State and South Temple to facilitate the increased traffic those streets now bear.[62]

The Family Cemetery

Given the certainty of eventual death for all members of the family and the probability of unexpected deaths from diseases and injuries, a cemetery was absolutely necessary. The family cemetery became Brigham Young's final home, 142 East First Avenue.

Brigham Young died on 29 August 1877 and was buried on September first in "the little burying ground, which I have reserved on my lot east of the White House on the hill."[63] The area was originally ten by ten rods but half of the lot was sold, the money from the sale used to provide care for the property. Several

This metal eagle replaced the wooden Eagle Gate in its original location. In 2000, however, this gate was moved half a block north. Behind it are the Eagle Gate Apartments, which occupy the site of the Brigham Young school. Photo by Judy Dykman and Colleen Whitley.

Top: The tithing storehouse contained offices, barns, and storage facilities for food to be distributed to needy citizens and to new arrivals into the Salt Lake Valley. Used by permission, Utah State Historical Society, all rights reserved.

Above: The newly built Hotel Utah, seen across the lawn of the Gardo House, July 1916. It operated as a luxury hotel until 1987 when it was closed and renovated to become the Joseph Smith Memorial Building which now provides space for receptions, dinners, films, and family history research. Used by permission, Utah State Historical Society, all rights reserved.

of Young's wives, including Eliza R. Snow, Mary Ann Angell, and Lucy Decker, are buried there. Across the street is a piece of the original cobblestone wall from Young's estate. It begins at the end of the parking lot and runs north to the Brigham Young Historic Park on the corner of State Street and North Temple. At the entrance to the park itself is a replica of the wall, built in 1995.[64]

109 EAST SOUTH TEMPLE: THE FAMILY SCHOOL

Among the other buildings on the estate was the schoolhouse, built in 1860 when the family school outgrew its room in the Lion House. An adobe building just inside Eagle Gate, the school had a long room with windows and a high ceiling. A small wing on one side provided a private room for the teacher. The brass bell in its spire called for classes at 9 a.m., year-around. All grades and several older students met together until 1868 when the University of Deseret (now the University of Utah) opened.[65]

Harriet Cook continued teaching, as she had in the Lion House, but one of Brigham's daughters, Alice Young Clawson, was noted as the school's first teacher. Most of the other teachers were also family members but other tutors also taught there, including the brilliant Karl G. Maeser who would subsequently found Brigham Young Academy, precursor of today's Brigham Young University. Students included children from the neighborhood as well as Brigham's offspring. Some of his wives even attended classes there.[66]

In 1877 the building became the meeting place for the Eighteenth Ward and was also used as a gymnasium, music studio, and political convention hall. On Brigham's death the building went to George W. Thatcher and in 1902 was sold to Susanna Bransford Holmes, Utah's "Silver Queen," who tore it down to erect the Bransford Apartments. The building cost $150,000 and provided the most

Where printing presses once produced the *Deseret News* and Utah's currency, the LDS Church Administration Building now houses the general authorities of the church. Photo by Judy Dykman and Colleen Whitley.

The twenty-nine-story LDS Church Office Building stands on the site of Brigham Young's barns and pigpens. Photo by Judy Dykman and Colleen Whitley.

elegant apartment lodging in the city, including a formal dining room, and quarters for live-in cooks and servants with every apartment. The Bransford was demolished in 1984 and replaced with the look-alike Eagle Gate Apartments that stand there now.[67]

TITHING OFFICE AND STOREHOUSES, *Deseret News*, AND THE DESERET MINT

The western end of Brigham Young's property eventually became so crowded with LDS Church buildings that he split off what is now the west half of the block between Main and State Streets, giving the church title to that property containing its buildings.

The Tithing Office complex was the largest of those buildings. On 6 April 1850 a large storehouse was proposed to supply the needs of the people. By the end of the year, the three-story building was in place to store and distribute food and other goods. In the General Tithing Office, a long, single-story building north of the storehouse, the presiding bishop or his appointees (Joseph C. Kingsbury was the weighmaster) accepted donations "in kind"—eggs, animals, grain, even, occasionally, money. The job of managing all these contributions and dispensing them to the needy required great skill, as well as a lot of space.

The food and other goods donated were dispensed to both the chronically poor and those with immediate if temporary needs. Andrew Jenson, who later became the assistant church historian, arrived in Utah in 1860 as a young man. Years later he described the exhausted pioneer company being given peaches when they arrived. Famished, they devoured the fruit as the crickets had the early crops. The tithing offices, barns, and storehouses served the community well for over fifty years.[68]

Like food, money and communications were as important to the Great Basin kingdom as they are to every other empire. Inititially a room in the Tithing Offces housed the *Deseret News*, but soon a small, one-story adobe building, "almost as easy to get on top of as into" was built to accommodate both the newspaper and the mint, located on South Temple, a few rods east of Main Street.[69] A replica of the original building now stands in This Is the Place Heritage Park.[70]

By 1909 the community's needs had changed and the LDS Church donated the land on which the *Deseret News* and the Tithing Office had stood to a joint venture by church and business leaders. They planned to build a truly elegant hotel to serve the increasing number of visitors to the city. Two years and $2 million later, the ten-story Hotel Utah opened on 9 June 1911. Over the next seventy-six years the white brick building "hosted legislators, Latter-day Saint conference goers, conventioneers, visitors, skiers, and every U.S. president since William Howard Taft." At the same time, it provided more than 260 guest rooms and facilities for community activities ranging from big band dances to wedding receptions. In the process, the hotel gained an international reputation for excellence and was named a National Historic Site.[71]

Over those years the LDS Church bought out other investors to become the sole owner, and in 1987 the hotel was closed. To increase earthquake safety, the

Brigham Young's final home is the family cemetery, which he shares with several of his wives. Originally a quiet corner of the family farm, the cemetery today is backed by the Brigham Young Condominiums and closely flanked by apartment buildings. Photo by Judy Dykman and Colleen Whitley.

A recent addition to the cemetery is the statue of Brigham Young reading to two children. His grave can be seen in the background, surrounded by a wrought-iron fence.

building was literally jacked up and a new foundation built under it. It reopened in 1993 after extensive renovation as the Joseph Smith Memorial Building, housing a range of facilities. A theatre shows films such as the pioneer epic *Legacy* and the scriptural comparison *Testaments*. In the Family Search Center two hundred volunteers and 130 computers help visitors locate their genealogies. The Roof Cafe and Garden Restaurant provide magnificent views of Temple Square along with their meals, and several rooms of various sizes can be rented for private dinners, receptions, and parties.[72]

The Deseret Mint initially shared quarters with the *Deseret News* but later had its own building, "a small adobe building on South Temple, a little east of where the palatial Hotel Utah now [1916] stands."[73] The first item printed there was a one dollar bill. The first money in the territory was issued from the Deseret Mint on 2 January 1849, while the government of Deseret was still being organized and the territory was governed by the Municipal Council. While a state or a territory printing its own money may seem odd today, it was commonplace in the 1840s. The United States did not have a standard national currency until the Civil War. Before that, paper and coins circulating in the country came from private mints.[74]

Today part of the site of the old mint is occupied by the LDS Church Administration Building, which provides offices for the General Authorities of the church: the First Presidency, Quorum of the Twelve, presidents of the Seventies, and others.[75]

Barns and Pigpens

Along with housing Brigham's extensive family, there was an obvious need for buildings to house animals. The number of animals on the farm and the configuration of their housing and corrals varied according to the needs of the family. At least one rock barn was located on what is now First Avenue. The cows

This view of Salt Lake City from the west in approximately 1900 shows several of Brigham Young's homes as well as the properties of the LDS Church on what was originally the west end of his downtown property. The long rambling building at the bottom is the tithing barns and storehouse. To its right, along South Temple, is the building for the Deseret News. Behind the tithing storehouse is the Lion House with its distinctive dormer windows. Behind that can be seen the roof of the Beehive House. Across the street is the Gardo, surrounded by trees. To the right of the Gardo is the roof of the Salt Lake Theatre.

were let out to pasture every morning and driven back each evening to the barn where some of Brigham's grandchildren eventually helped to milk them.[76]

Today apartment houses have replaced the barns along First Avenue on the east of Main Street, and on the west side of Main the LDS Church Office Building occupies their space as well as much of the area formerly used for some of the Tithing Office storehouses and the family garden. The Church Office Building provides nearly a million square feet of office space and parking. The twenty-nine-story central tower is flanked by two wings of four stories each and houses twenty-two departments, including Audio Visual, Auditing and Budget, Curriculum (which includes church publications such as the *Ensign, New Era,* and *Friend*), Church Education, Security, Correlation, History, Human Resources, Information Systems (computers and telephones), Missionary, Translation, and Materials Management, which sees to food services, postal, travel, and assorted other physical needs.[77] There are also administrative offices for Welfare Services and Family History, although the bulk of those departments are housed in their own buildings. The building also contains offices for the Presiding Bishopric, military oversight, music, Relief Society, Young Women, and Primary.[78]

BUNKHOUSE OR COCOONERY

Behind the Beehive and Lion Houses was a small two-story building used to store wood and coal on the lower level. The upper level was sometimes used for sleeping, but that area is best remembered as the home of Utah's silkworms. Fifteen-year-old George D. Pyper, son of Brigham's business manager, reportedly helped Zina Huntington Young master the care and feeding of silkworms

While Brigham Young owned the Chase House, his wife Margaret Pierce lived there and managed the operations in the mill. Photo c. 1851, used by permission, LDS Church Archives, all rights reserved.

imported from France. The area today is the plaza between the LDS Church Office Building and the Beehive and Lion Houses.[79]

110 EAST NORTH TEMPLE: SWIMMING POOL

North of the school and near the smokehouse was a swimming pool about twenty feet square and four to five feet deep which occasionally doubled as a baptismal font. Supplied by water from City Creek, it afforded bathing for the family—in modest costume, of course. The area of the pool is now covered by apartment buildings.[80]

CORRAL, WOODHOUSE, SMOKEHOUSE, LAMB BARN

Corrals, a woodhouse, smokehouse, and lamb barn were essential outbuildings for a farm. Like most of the area along First Avenue, the land that formerly housed animals now houses humans in various apartment buildings.

1100 SOUTH 600 EAST: THE CHASE MILL

As his family grew and the city expanded, Brigham Young built or purchased many more homes. One of the first was the Chase Mill. New York native Isaac Chase, a miller by trade, brought three wagons across the plains in 1847, containing "mill irons, four burrs, two sets of chisels, five shafts, a smutter, an elevator pipe, a fan, a roll of bolting for sifting purposes, some wheat and grains, a sack of black locust seed, and a small upright saw." His "inheritance" in the land drawing included both a city lot and a five-acre farming lot in the "Big Field." When he moved onto the five acres in 1851, he found a clear spring, suitable to

The Chase House is one of the few adobe homes left standing in Utah. Now open to the public, it houses the State Folk Art Collection and Utah Folklife Archives, which regularly display traditional arts by modern artists in four areas: Native American, rural, occupational, and ethnic. Photo by Colleen Whitley.

turn a mill, so he bought the adjoining fifteen acres and later acquired more land, a total of 110 acres.[81]

He first built a small sawmill, and then in 1849 or 1850 began improving it by creating a large millpond and millrace, using water from streams as distant as Red Butte, Parleys, and Emigration Canyons. Next he built a flour mill with a stone foundation. That is now the buried basement of the present structure. The machinery was probably close to the Oliver Evans type, and the mill became an important producer of flour in a survival economy.[82] Using the rough boards the original sawmill produced, Chase built a small house, little more than a shack where he and his wife, Phoebe, stayed for a time. Later they moved up in class to an adobe home and finally in 1853–1854 to an eight-room adobe home with windowpanes made of glass that had been freighted across the plains. In 1852 the gristmill itself was built. Like the house, the mill was made of adobes produced on a church farm at 2375 South Ninth East, the current site of the Forest Hills Golf Course. Chase himself became a leader in the community. When the plague of crickets attacked the crops in 1848, it was Chase who offered the prayer for relief at the public meeting. Relief came in the form of seagulls that devoured the crickets faster than they could devour the crops.[83]

Isaac Chase became Brigham Young's partner in 1854, having already become his father-in-law in 1844 in Nauvoo. Young had married Chase's step-daughter, Clarissa Ross, often called Chase after her stepfather who raised her.[84] Brigham and Clarissa had four children, Mary Eliza, Clarissa Maria, Willard, and Phoebe Louise. When Clarissa died in 1858, her sister wife Zina Huntington took the responsibility for her children and raised all four.[85]

Chase and Young maintained a loose partnership for several years; during that time Young helped bring in new machinery. While the mill provided a living for its owners, it also served the community; in 1856–1857 needy families

Brigham Young's initials and the date, "1852," were added to the south gable of the Chase Mill in 1896 following a campaign by Chase descendants to preserve the building. Photo by Judy Dykman and Colleen Whitley.

Chase Home Timeline
© 2001 by Carol Edison, Utah Arts Council

1847

In October the Isaac Chase family arrives in Utah and Chase is given permission to build a sawmill. By December the Chase family had moved from living in wagon boxes into the Old Fort and Chase's sawmill had begun producing rough lumber.

1848

In the spring Chase begins work on a second mill, a gristmill, and builds a rough lumber shanty for his family nearby. By fall the gristmill is operational in time to provide food during the famine of 1848–1849. Chase is allotted four five-acres plots—three located about 1500 South between 300 and 600 East, and Lot 3, Section 19 adjacent to his mills.

1849

Young begins building mills for carding, threshing, and other processes near Chase's mills, developing an important industrial complex.

1850

Chase begins work on the foundation of a third mill, a flourmill that still stands south of the Chase Home.

1851

Young assigns a crew to assist with work on the flourmill.

1852

The flourmill is substantially completed under the direction of mill builder Frederick Kesler. Today Young's initials and the year 1852 are still on the mill indicating his participation in this enterprise.

1853

During the winter of 1853–1854 construction of the Chase Home begins with help from a crew assigned by Young.

1854

The Chase family moves into the partially completed Chase Home.

1855

By 1855, through gaining ownership of the other nineteen lots in Section 19, Young had created the Mill Farm, or Old Locust Patch, that ultimately became Liberty Park.

1856

The Chase Home is completed and many people are fed with bread baked by Phoebe Chase in her sixteen-loaf Dutch oven, located, and still visible, at the rear of the Chase Home. The Chase Home becomes a popular out-of-town destination for afternoon teas and evening dances.

1859

By the end of the year, Brigham Young Jr. had taken over supervision of the flourmill; Chase's son, polygamous wives, and their families had moved to Centerville; and ultimately Chase, his first wife, daughter, and grandson had moved to a downtown property he bought from Young.

1861

Chase dies on 2 May at the age of sixty-nine. Members of the Young family and other millers continue to oversee repairs and operation of the flourmill.

1879

By the end of the decade the flourmill had ceased to be profitable and was closed down.

1881

The 110-acre Mill Farm, including the Chase Home and the 1852 flourmill, is purchased from the Young estate by Salt Lake City Corporation for $27,000.

1883

Liberty Park opens to the public. For the next eight decades the Chase Home is a residence for the park superintendent and other city employees.

1896

Chase's granddaughter Kate leads a successful campaign to save the flourmill from demolition. In the process the initials "B.Y." and date "1852" are added to its south gable.

1920s

The shed porch on the Chase Home is replaced with a two-story portico allowing passengers in buggies and cars to drive up to the front door.

1934

With another attempt to demolish the flourmill, the Daughters of Utah Pioneers take it over, using it for offices and as a relic hall to display pioneer artifacts.

1964

The Chase Home becomes the Daughters of Utah Pioneer Relic Hall filled with pioneer era furnishings and open to the public for tours.

1983

Through a partnership between Salt Lake City and a state agency, the Utah Arts Council, the interior of the Chase Home is turned into a gallery featuring contemporary designer crafts. For the next few years the Visual Arts Program of the council displays paintings from the State Fine Art Collection.

1986

The Folk Arts Program of the council moves into the Chase Home, exhibiting traditional crafts from the State Folk Art Collection and offering free summer concerts outside.

2000

Through a financial partnership between Salt Lake City and the State of Utah and with assistance from the LDS Church, a major renovation of the Chase Home is undertaken.

2001

The Chase Home reopens to the public as a home for the State Folk Art Collection and the Utah Folklife Archives and offers an expanded summer concert series.

AUGUSTA ADAMS.

Top: Clarissa Decker was a quiet woman who seldom took a public role, but she was noted as well read and aware of current events. Used by permission, Utah State Historical Society, all rights reserved.

Above: Augusta Adams, a member of the politically active Adams family of Massachusetts, was noted for her strong beliefs in both religion and politics. Used by permission, Utah State Historical Society, all rights reserved.

were given flour at no cost. Young and Chase's personal association doubtless outweighed their business arrangements, and formal agreements between the men have not been found. In 1859 Isaac Chase purchased a house from Brigham Young near Augusta Adams's home, while some of his family lived on a farm in Centerville.[86]

When the mill and the home became Brigham Young's, his wife, Margaret Pierce Young, moved into the house and managed the mill.[87] Margaret was born 19 April 1823 in Delaware County, Pennsylvania. With her parents, she accepted the Mormon faith and emigrated to Nauvoo in 1841. She was a childless widow when she married Brigham Young in 1845, her first husband Morris Whitesides having died shortly after their marriage in 1844. Susa Young Gates called her "an Israelite in whom there was no guile. She bore her trials so quietly that none knew she suffered. And she did suffer, for she loved children, and bore but one son, Brigham Morris, when she would gladly have mothered a dozen."[88] Susa also notes Margaret's ability to weave cloth and carpets. She also learned to weave when some looms arrived in the valley and for some time she raised silkworms, while also managing the gristmill and cooking and caring for the mill hands.[89]

In 1881 Salt Lake City purchased the mill, the home, and virtually all of the original 110 acres from the Young estate to create Liberty Park, a forward-looking creation of green space. The park opened on 17 June 1882 with a procession of federal, territorial, and military dignitaries led by William Jennings, Salt Lake City's mayor. The park housed an animal menagerie until Hogle Zoo was built and the animals were moved to Sunnyside Avenue. In the 1930s a movement to tear down the old mill was thwarted by the Daughters of Utah Pioneers and descendants of Isaac Chase. The DUP used it as a relic hall, housing several historic items. On 15 June 1970, the significance of the Chase Mill was recognized, and it was placed on the National Register of Historic Places.[90]

Today the Chase Home is administered by the Utah Arts Council and the house and mill by Salt Lake City. Both stand beside the duck pond and the aviary, not far from the playgrounds and the picnic tables, all of which are encircled by one of the most popular running tracks in the city. The park draws individuals and groups, dog walkers and family reunions, joggers and church picnics from throughout the city and even around the state.[91]

ASHTON AVENUE, EAST OF 700 EAST: THE FOREST FARM HOUSE

See chapter 7.

29 SOUTH STATE

Brigham Young bought Bishop Edwin D. Woolley's house north of the Social Hall (39 South State) and moved in Clarissa Decker Young, mother of five of his children: Jeanette R., Nabbie Howe, Jedediah Grant, Albert Jeddie, and

Charlotte Talula. Her parents, Isaac Perry and Harriet Page Wheeler Decker, had joined the LDS Church when Clara was a child and the family gathered with the Latter-day Saints in Ohio, then Missouri and Illinois, where Clarissa married Brigham 8 May 1844 in Nauvoo. In doing so, she joined her sister, Lucy Ann, as a plural wife to Brigham.[92]

Clarissa was a quiet woman who took a far less public role than did some of Brigham's other wives. Nonetheless, she was well read and known to keep abreast of important topics. Susa Young Gates says she never heard Clarissa "utter an unkind word or slurring thought." Susa's experience with her doubtless came because her mother, Lucy Bigelow, and Clarissa Decker became especially close. The two of them were frequently Brigham's nurses during his occasional "bilious attacks." On each thirty-first of December, they "sat the Old Year out and the New Year in" in Clarissa's sitting room until Lucy moved to St. George.[93] Clarissa apparently lived in the house on South State for the rest of her life, dying there on 5 January 1889, the last of the three original pioneer women.[94]

Today the Belvedere Apartments occupy the site of her home. When the LDS Church built the nine-story, U-shaped building in 1919, "it was advertised as the city's first 'ultramodern' fireproof hotel." Its colorful terra-cotta reliefs of fruits and flowers provide a marked contrast to the modern buildings that now surround it.[95]

Top: The Belvedere Apartments, on the site of Clara Decker's home, features bas reliefs of fruits and flowers, a form of decoration common when the building was built, though few examples now remain. Photo by Judy Dykman and Colleen Whitley.

Above: The LDS Church built the nine-story Belvedere Apartments on the site of Clara Decker's house in 1919. Used by permission, Utah State Historical Society, all rights reserved.

55 SOUTH STATE

Immediately south of the Social Hall was the home of Augusta Adams Cobb, Brigham's fourth wife.[96] A native of Boston, Augusta converted to the LDS Church, left her husband, Henry Cobb, packed up two of their seven children,

and came to Nauvoo.[97] Her oldest son later came to Utah and joined the LDS Church, but to much of the family in Boston, she remained a pariah.[98] She was sealed to Brigham in Nauvoo on 2 November 1843, one of his unions that proved to be childless and was, in all probability, a caretaker marriage.[99]

Augusta was a distant cousin of the politically active Adams family of Massachusetts. John, Abigail, and Samuel were leaders in the American Revolution; John was the second president of the United States and his son, John Quincy, the sixth. Augusta has been credited with suggesting women's suffrage to Brigham.[100] Apparently a woman of strong opinions, she was noted as a particularly firm defender of her faith until her death in 1886.[101] One critic of Mormonism described her as "a large, fine-looking worman [who] has dark hair, gray eyes and a clear, bright complexion. She is very stylish in her appearance, dresses with excellent taste, and is dignified in her manners. If you did not know she was a Mormon, she is just such a woman as you would think it impossible to convert to the doctrines of Mormonism."[102]

Today 55 South State is home to a commercial office building. Zions Securities acquired the property from the LDS Church in 1922 and rents space to several companies, including Deseret Book.[103]

Above: Emmeline Free was the mother of ten of Brigham Young's children. While her children lived with her, she had a spacious home on Main Street. After they were grown, she moved to a small house directly through the block on State Street. Used by permission, Utah State Historical Society, all rights reserved.

Top: Emmeline Free's home was replaced by the ZCMI department store. Although under new management, the building retains its pioneer facade. Photo by Judy Dykman and Colleen Whitley.

ABOUT 25 SOUTH MAIN

Daniel Wells lived on the southeast corner of Main Street and South Temple. To the south was the home of Emmeline Free Young, said to have been Brigham's favorite wife, indicated in part by her ten children: Ella Elizabeth, Marinda Hyde, Hyrum Smith, Emmeline Amanda, Louise Nelle, Lorenzo

This portion of a drawing from *Frank Leslie's Illustrated Newspaper* identifies some of Brigham Young's homes and some of the significant buildings around them.

1. not shown in this drawing
2. the new residence (not yet named the Gardo House)
3. Emmeline Free's house, the one she occupied after most of her children were grown
4. Amelia Folsom's house, where she lived while the Gardo was being built
5. Augusta Adams Cobb's house
6. the Social Hall
7. the Metropolitan School House

Dow, Alonzo, Ruth, Daniel Wells, and Ardelle Elwin, all of whom lived to maturity. Obviously Emmeline needed space. Brigham purchased a large home built by Jedediah M. Grant, his friend and counselor in the First Presidency of the LDS Church, and moved in Emmeline and her children.

Emmeline had joined the LDS Church along with her parents, Absalom and Betsy Strait Free, and the rest of her siblings. They moved to Nauvoo, where she married Brigham Young on 30 April 1845.[104] While her suspected status as a favorite wife could have caused jealousy, Susa Young Gates reports that in fact she held the respect and affection of the sister wives. "Beautiful as a dream, magnetic, with dark brown hair, regular features, sparkling eyes, a certain vivacity of manner which instantly won and held the pleased attention of her listeners . . ."[105] Emmeline lived on Main Street until about 1873 when she moved to the small house beside the Gardo, where she stayed until her death, 17 July 1875.

Emmeline's house was replaced by Zions Cooperative Mercantile Institution, ZCMI, one of the first department stores in America. The store started as early as 1868. Brigham was aware that the arrival of the railroad and the influx of settlers who did not share their LDS faith would end their isolation in the Utah desert. So he instructed a group of merchants to form a cooperative that would allow the Saints to obtain their needs without patronizing

Top: Harriet Barney Young stands by the bay window of her house at 61 West South Temple. Picture courtesy of the Brigham Young Family Organization.

Above: In 1847 Mary Van Cott was a three-year-old pioneer. She was later divorced from her first husband and had a young daughter to raise when she married Brigham Young. Used by permission, Utah State Historical Society, all rights reserved.

"gentile" establishments, "for so long as we buy of them, we are in a degree dependent upon them." He told the merchants to sell goods "as low as they can possibly be sold, and let the profits be divided among the people at large."[106]

In March 1868 they opened the first store in Salt Lake City, its offerings ranging from candy to cloth and nuts to nails. In addition, ZCMI's goods were available in many of the Mormon settlements through a system of 146 co-ops, owned and operated locally, at the same prices as they were in Salt Lake City. In the first four years of operation, dividends of half a million dollars were declared. Among its remarkable innovations was the employment of women; some worked as sales clerks and others managed whole stores. ZCMI had its own delivery system and its own clothing and boot manufacturers. In 1876 many of the separate departments moved into the three-story brick and iron building with a full basement that still stands on the corner of Main Street and South Temple.[107]

In January 2000, the directors of ZCMI voted to sell the stores to the May Corporation of St. Louis, ending a long tradition of local ownership. Today the chain of stores is owned by Meier and Frank, which now operates the department store on the site of Emmeline's house.

APPROXIMATELY 20 TO 50 SOUTH STATE

Brigham Young owned a home at 50 State Street, immediately behind the Salt Lake Theatre. Originally built by George Grant, Brigham purchased it early in the city's settlement and it is consistently listed as his property on plat maps. Several family members lived there temporarily, as did a number of other people.

It appears to have been a useful home, but is not specifically connected with any of the wives. Today the Beneficial Tower Parking Terrace occupies the site.

A house just to the north was built by Dr. Sprague. He either sold or rented it to Brigham, since Emeline Free lived there for a time, but the Sprague family also returned to it later. North of that, a small home for Emmeline Free was built in a side yard south of the Gardo in about 1872, by which time her older children were grown and her youngest, Ardelle, would have been eight or nine. Today that location, like that of her home directly through the block at 25 South Main, houses the ZCMI Mall.

53 WEST SOUTH TEMPLE

Mary Van Cott, Brigham's fifty-second wife, was the daughter of John and Lucy Sackett Van Cott. They joined the LDS Church and emigrated first to Nauvoo and then in 1847 to Salt Lake City. Mary initially married James Kirby, but divorced him while she was pregnant with their daughter, Luella. She married Brigham Young in 1865 and by him had a second daughter, Fannie, in 1870. Her first home had once belonged to Parley P. Pratt, opposite the south gate of Temple Square. At his death, Brigham willed her that property, through her father, John Van Cott.[108]

The site of her house today is the Crossroads Mall, built in 1979 by developers Sidney Folger and Jack Oakland following an agreement with the LDS Church which owns the land. Crossroads opened in 1980 and is now home to over 150 businesses including large department stores, movie theaters, food chains, banks, travel agencies, and beauty salons. It also provides downtown parking on several covered levels, each named for a local ski area.[109]

Despite its inception by Mormon builders and the fact that it stands on land owned by the LDS Church, Crossroads Mall was generally perceived as

Crossroads Plaza, seen through the south gates of Temple Square, now occupies the sites of Mary Van Cott and Harriet Barney's homes. Photo by Judy Dykman and Colleen Whitley.

the "gentile" mall, in contrast to the ZCMI Mall across the street, which carried the pioneer association with the LDS Church and which also stands on church-owned land. While the exact lease arrangments between the malls and the LDS Church are confidential, they are not unusual. The church still owns much of the property in downtown Salt Lake City; the Salt Palace, for example, is built on church-owned property which Salt Lake County leases for one dollar per year.[110]

61 WEST SOUTH TEMPLE

Next door to Mary Van Cott's house was the home of Harriet Barney Young. When Harriet married Brigham in 1856, she already had three living children from her marriage to William Henry Harrison Sagers: Royal, age five; Joseph, three; and Sarah, one; another daughter having died in infancy. Her first marriage was reportedly unhappy; Sagers was described as "unworthy" of her. She was an artistic woman, expressing her talent, as did so many women, in needlework, some of which is displayed at the Daughters of Utah Pioneers Museum. Her home had belonged to Orson Pratt, and she apparently lived there until her death on 14 February 1911.[111]

The Beneficial Life Insurance Company had a building on that location for a time and the site is now occupied by the Temple View Center containing offices and shops.

Emily Dow Partridge was born in Painsville, Ohio, 28 February 1824, the daughter of Lydia and Edward Partridge, first bishop of the LDS Church. As a leader of the church, Edward was often singled out for persecution by anti-Mormon mobs. One of Emily's most vivid memories was of an incident in Missouri when she was nine years old. She had been drawing water from the spring with her sister, Eliza, and returned to see a mob forcing her father to go into town. When he returned later that day, she ran and hid in terror: he had been tarred and feathered, the tar having been mixed with acid. Partridge appeared to his daughter as a grotesque monster. A few days later another mob set fire to the family's haystack.[112]

The family moved to Illinois in 1839 and when Edward died on 27 May 1840, Lydia kept the small children with her but Eliza, then twenty, and Emily, then sixteen, found refuge with Joseph and Emma Smith. When polygamy was introduced, Emily became a plural wife of Joseph Smith in 1843, marrying Brigham Young after Joseph's death.[113]

Emily left Nauvoo in 1846 and spent one winter at Mt. Pisgah, Iowa, and another at Winter Quarters, Nebraska, finally leaving for Great Salt Lake City in the spring of 1848. Along the way she suffered many of the privations of the trail, once sitting for several hours on a log in a blinding snowstorm holding her three-month-old baby.[114] She must have learned to endure well, for years later Susa Young Gates described her as a "sainted heroine. . . . If she had ever had an irritable mood, or entertained an ignoble thought, it must have passed too quickly for utterance; for the calm serenity of her life was unmarred by humanity's usual explosions. Her room, her home atmosphere, was that of peace and motherly solicitude for all who came near."[115]

When Emily arrived in Salt Lake City, she stayed initially in the Old Fort, then in the Log Row and the Lion House. Brigham eventually gave her a two-story house on Fifth East where she lived with their seven children: Edward, Emily Augusta, Caroline, Joseph Don Carlos, Miriam, Josephine, and Lura. The 1890 City Directory lists an Emily B (widow of Brigham) as boarding on Park Boulevard, another name for Fifth East.[116] She died in December 1899.[117] Today the site of Emily's home is the Picadilly Apartments.

300 South and State

In her later life, Zina Huntington Young lived in a house on the northeast corner of Third South and State. Like most of downtown Salt Lake City, it became commercial property by the turn of the century. For many years, that was the location of the Center Theater, torn down in the late 1980s. Today on that site is the Broadway Center, a fourteen-story office building opened in 1991. In addition to class A offices, the building features a six-screen cinema and various retail shops.[118]

180 East South Temple: The Empey House

About 1871–1872, Brigham Young had a buff adobe cottage built just up the street from his original property. It was octagonal in shape with two or three chimneys

Ann Eliza Webb married Brigham Young, but on becoming disenchanted with both her husband and his religion, she went to the East Coast and for several years made a living by writing and delivering lectures on the horrors of Mormonism and polygamy.

and had a mansard portico bay window. It appeared taller than it was because the Gothic design was accentuated by second-story windows that lent height.[119]

The building was intended as a home for Ann Eliza Webb Dee. Her parents, Eliza Churchill and Chauncey W. Webb, a teacher in Nauvoo, Illinois, brought the family to Utah in 1848 and helped settle the Cottonwood area. Ann Eliza first married James L. Dee on 10 April 1863 and with him had two children, James E. and Lorenzo. She later divorced Dee, charging neglect and cruelty. Her mother bore testimony to Dee's abuse in a letter to Brigham Young saying he had a violent temper and choked and kicked his wife. Brigham responded with a letter to the judge recommending Ann Eliza be allowed to end her marriage. Following the divorce she married Brigham Young on 6 April 1868.[120]

Ann Eliza lived in the house for less than two years before she became disenchanted with Brigham and with Mormonism in general, and left the territory. In 1873 she applied for civil divorce and sued Young for maintenance—$1,000 per month pending trial—claiming his income was $40,000 per month and his estate worth $8 million. "In February 1875, Judge McKean ordered Brigham to pay Ann Eliza $500 per month and $3,000 to defray the cost of the trial." Knowing the "gentile" judge would not believe Brigham's claims of a lower income level, his lawyers argued the marriage was invalid since not only did Brigham have a legal wife living (a fact which would not impede a polygamist) but Ann Eliza, unknown to Brigham, was also still married.[121]

McKean would have none of it. He ordered Brigham to pay and when he would not, the judge charged him with contempt and placed him under house arrest. The case was eventually settled, after assorted rulings by various judges,

Brigham Young originally built this house for Ann Eliza Webb, but when she left him, the Mormon Church, and the state, he gave it to his daughter Ella and her husband, Bishop Nelson Adam Empey. The house became known as the Empey Cottage after Ella's husband, Bishop Empey. Used by permission, Utah State Historical Society, all rights reserved.

and Ann Eliza left the state, continuing to file petitions and suits claiming Brigham owed her vast amounts of alimony. She married again, to Moses R. Deming, but that marriage lasted only three years. She published a book, *Wife Number 19,* describing the horrors of polygamy. Her book caused public outcry and became one of the catalysts for antipolygamy legislation. After a period of popularity lecturing across the United States, Ann Eliza dropped from public life and nothing is now known of her final years.[122]

Her house gained its name from its next occupant, Bishop Nelson P. Empey, who had married a daughter of Brigham and Emmeline Free, Ella Elizabeth, to whom Brigham left the property in his will.[123] When Ella died, Empey married Emma Adams and remained in the home until his death. Empey held significant civic as well as ecclesiastical positions, including service on the Territorial Committee for the Chicago World's Fair in 1893.

In 1894 he remodeled the house, but maintained the spirit of the original design. The porch on the northeast corner was converted into a room, and a stair was added from the north entrance, replacing the one from the parlor. One of the significant additions was a diamond-shaped window in the north facade. The window's stained glass beehive was made under the supervision of James Ferguson, another of Brigham's sons-in-law, and had been used in the Utah building at the Chicago World's Fair.[124]

The Empey Cottage was still standing at Christmastime in 1952 when its owner, Heber C. Egbert, gave the deed to the building itself (but not the property on which it stood) to the Sugar House Chapter of the Sons of Utah Pioneers and received a standing ovation for his generosity. The house was scheduled to be moved to a "Pioneer Memorial Village planned at the former site of the Utah State prison . . . [and] restored to its original condition. It is the

A branch of Grandma's Tires now occupies the site of the Empey house. Photo by Colleen Whitley.

first of some thirty homes, blacksmith shops, grist mills and other structures which will be moved to the proposed park."[125]

The site of the old prison became Sugarhouse Park, leaving no room for the proposed village. Consequently, Horace Sorenson, owner of Southeast Furniture Company, allowed the SUP to relocate many old homes to his property at 3000 Connor Street. Just before Sorenson died, the SUP sold the entire village to Lagoon Corporation. Today, the Pioneer Village at Lagoon in Davis County delights thousands of visitors every year who enjoy seeing the beautiful restorations of historic buildings.

Unfortunately, the Empey Cottage is not one of them. The home was dismantled in 1953 and the carefully marked pieces were taken to the Connor Street property. However, lack of time and money prevented its eventual reassembly, and the separate pieces were left behind when the rest of the village moved north. The Empey Cottage ended as a pile of rubble in Horace Sorenson's backyard.[126] The property on which it originally stood is now occupied by a branch of Grandma's Tires.[127]

SOUTHWEST CORNER, SOUTH TEMPLE AND STATE STREETS:
THE GARDO HOUSE OR AMELIA PALACE

See chapter 8.

HOUSES OF UNCERTAIN OWNERSHIP AND OCCASIONAL MYTH

Conflicts in sources, questions arising from Brigham Young's will, and mythology surrounding some houses create several cases of uncertain ownership. One example is a home on 2100 South near 1900 East.[128] It has been noted as Brigham Young's, and it is located in the area included in the Forest Farm. Several buildings were on the property; however, the only homes in which Brigham or any of his family are actually known to have lived were a small cabin and the Forest Farm House now located in This Is the Place Heritage Park (see chapter 7). In all probability, the 1900 East home was built later, although it may have been built by one of Brigham's descendants.

An even more common misconception persists that Brigham had a home at 205 East First Avenue, the site of what is now Rowland Hall. That area was part of Brigham's property, usually called the upper garden, but no building there ever housed Brigham Young or any of his bountiful clan. For years, however, students insisted that not only was it Brigham's house, but that some of his wives are buried there. Those tales were told with such vigor to Marianne Harding Burgoyne, when she was a boarding student there, that she responded by writing a poem, "Waking Up at Rowland Hall," which begins

> The other girls told me
> Brigham Young's wives were buried
> under the floorboards of my room.
> I didn't believe them. . . .
> That didn't prevent the nightmares.

Nightmares or not, the story itself is a dream. Brigham Young used the area as a garden and grazing area until he sold it to his secretary, George Watt. Watt had emigrated to Utah from Nauvoo, Illinois, served an LDS mission to England in 1850, and worked for some time at the *Deseret News*. Watt built the adobe house in 1862 then some time around 1869 sold it to Warren Hussey, a banker by trade and an Episcopalian by creed. Hussey was one of a group who persuaded the Right Reverend Daniel S. Tuttle to establish Christian missions in this "godless wilderness." Tuttle eventually became bishop of the Episcopal Missionary District of Utah, Idaho, and Montana.[129]

One of his early missionaries, Thomas W. Haskins, principal of the school which met in St. Mark's Church on 100 South, lived in the Watt/Hussey house. Haskins put a truncated roof on the house and a large addition on the back. By 1880, the property was turned over to a Reverend Kirby who "received title on behalf of his mother-in-law, Mrs. Rowland." Mrs. Rowland and her daughter gave the lot and building in memory of their husband and father, Benjamin Rowland of Philadelphia. In 1881, it was opened as a boarding school. Half a dozen more additions were made to the building over the years, making it large enough to house the many female boarding students. As fewer and fewer students actually lived at the school, the boardinghouse was torn down and new classrooms built on its site.[130]

Other homes in Salt Lake City have been reputed to be built or owned by Brigham Young, but city maps, directories, and property guides do not support their claims. The bulk of his original properties became commercial areas fairly early in the city's existence. As his children grew, much of the rest of his property was passed along to sons and daughters who built their own homes. Of his original Salt Lake City homes, only four are standing today: the Beehive and Lion Houses, Forest Farm, and the Chase Mill and house in Liberty Park.

Chapter 6

The Beehive and Lion Houses

W. Randall Dixon

Brigham Young's principal residence from 1854 until his death in 1877 was the Beehive House on South Temple Street in Salt Lake City. West of this was the President's Office, and next to the office was the Lion House which housed many of his wives and children. These buildings are all that survive of his original enclosure which included other houses, barns, gardens, orchards, a school-house, and other structures.

Beehive House

The Beehive House replaced the White House as Brigham Young's principal residence, while the Lion House replaced the Log Row as the main home for his family. The plan to build what would become the Beehive House was first noted in February 1852 when Truman O. Angell mentioned that he was working on plans for what he called the Governor's House.[1] A lot had been purchased from Lorenzo Dow Young, the president's brother. Lorenzo had erected a log cabin on this lot in the fall of 1847, and the President's Office had been built there in 1852.[2] Construction was delayed until the following year when Angell recorded: "Laid out the President's house or found the corners and as the wind blew too much to proceed farther, I left the work and went to my office. Made ready the bills of timber and joists of said house and made the bill for cut stone for the same house."[3] By then it was called the President's House, and was connected to the existing office by an enclosed passageway.

By the fall of 1853 the adobe walls had been erected and the roof shingled.[4] Construction resumed in the spring of 1854 and by late in that year Brigham Young and his family had moved into the home, although finishing work continued through 1855.[5]

Architecturally, the building is best described as a traditional Georgian style house with Greek revival features, including a boxed cornice and a roof parapet. The roof contained an observatory with a cupola topped by a beehive, giving the house its name. Another feature was a one-story Tuscan-columned porch on the south and east sides of the building. The house was designed on a central hall plan with a staircase in the hall leading to the second floor. The main floor had two parlors. The west parlor connected by a short hallway to the President's Office and this parlor was often used as a bedroom by President Young. A larger parlor in the southeast corner of the house was used by Brigham Young for his daily family breakfast; while he lived in the house, he took his breakfast there, but he usually ate his other meals in the Lion House. The main floor also included a bathroom, sewing room, pantry, and other storage rooms.[6]

The second floor contained what was called the "Long Hall" on the east. The coved-ceiling room served for entertaining and in the summer as a bedroom for Brigham Young. Horace Greeley, who visited Salt Lake City in 1859, described his reception in the Long Hall. "We were very cordially welcomed at the door by the President, who led us into the second-story parlour of the largest of his houses (he has three), where I was introduced to Heber C. Kimball, Gen. Wells, Gen. Ferguson, Albert Carrington, Elias Smith, and several other leading men in the Church, with two full-grown sons of the President."[7]

A rear wing of a story and a half extended to the north. The main floor contained a large kitchen and the dining room where workmen who boarded ate their meals. The half-story above was used for storage and occasionally for temporary housing. A barn was originally attached to the end of the house.[8]

When Brigham Young first moved into the house he was joined by his wife, Mary Ann Angell, and their children. They lived in the house until 1860 when she moved back to the White House where she felt more comfortable. Lucy Ann Decker and her family moved into the Beehive House. Lucy Ann lived there throughout the remainder of Brigham Young's life. She managed the house and cooked the meals for the workmen who came to the house for lunch. Young women were hired to help Lucy cook for the men. Susa Young Gates observed that the members of the family were never to call the hired help "servants."[9]

The house functioned as a center for social events. As Clarissa Young Spence remembered, "The Beehive House was built with the purpose in view of having a place large enough for the entertainment of Father's visitations and friends and held spacious parlors both upstairs and down that were well suited to its purpose for that day."[10] Probably the biggest use of the house was for his family: wedding receptions, parties, and a number of funerals were held in the house.[11] Two of Brigham's daughters held wedding receptions in the Beehive House. Clarissa particularly remembered her own reception following her wedding to John D. Spencer. When one of her sisters married, Brigham informed one of his sons, "Yesterday your sister Nabbie was married, Bro. Spencer Clawson being the happy bridegroom. In the evening there was quite a brilliant assemblage of the friends of the young couple who gathered at the Beehive House to wish them much joy."[12] Clarissa and John Spencer lived in the house with her mother for several years and their first child was born there.[13] It's important to think of the house as being a busy place, full of activity.

Over Brigham Young's lifetime several changes were made to the house. In the early 1860s the barn at the rear of the house was transformed into a family store, where his families could obtain needed supplies. The one-story porch on the south and east sides was replaced by a two-story Italianate porch in the late 1860s.[14]

More changes were made after Brigham Young's death. In 1878 the high stone wall in front of the house was removed and replaced by a cast-iron fence, but there were few other changes made to the house. Lucy Decker Young received the Beehive House in the estate settlement and continued to live there until 1888 when she sold the house to Mary Ann Angell's son, John W. Young.

Beginning in 1889 John W. greatly expanded the house. He removed the rear wing and made a large Victorian addition that increased—probably doubled—the size of the house. He also heavily remodeled the rest of the house. Then John W., who was involved in a great many businesses, had some reversals and the bank foreclosed on the Beehive House. John Beck, another prominent Utah businessman, purchased the house from the bank at a public auction. He lived there for a short time, but he also had financial problems and the house again reverted to the bank.[15]

In 1899 the church purchased the Beehive House from the Zions Savings Bank and renovated it as a residence for President Lorenzo Snow.[16] President Joseph F. Smith occupied the home after Snow's death. During that period there was a major exterior remodeling. The original beehive was replaced by a new one. The roof parapet was removed and the railing around the observatory replaced by a metal fence.[17]

After Joseph F. Smith's death in 1918, the house remained vacant for a time. The new church president, Heber J. Grant, preferred to live in his own home on Eighth Avenue, so in 1920 the house was given to the Young Ladies' Mutual Improvement Association, which announced,

> The committee of the general board of the Y.L.M.I.A., who have been working for some time with the Social Advisory committee of the L.D.S. church toward establishing a home for working girls and those of moderate means who can not find suitable homes, announce that the Beehive House on east South Temple Street has been turned over to them for this purpose. . . . The spacious pioneer

The Lion House, President's Office, and the Beehive House, in the early 1860s. The wall around the property was complete along South Temple Street, which was still unpaved. Note the trees in front of the wall were only a few years old. Photo by Savage and Ottinger. Used by permission, Utah State Historical Society, all rights reserved.

residence is to be renovated and refurnished and will be used until a larger and a permanent home can be established.[18]

Young women, usually from smaller towns, who came to Salt Lake City seeking work, could stay at the Beehive economically and safely. The house was adapted for that use by dividing many of the rooms into smaller bedrooms, adding restroom facilities and making other practical changes. It served a great many young women until it was closed in 1959.[19]

Later that year it was decided to renovate the house as a museum, and the Beehive House Restoration Committee was organized for that purpose. The committee had a difficult time deciding how to treat the house because of the many changes that had been made to the building. Eventually they compromised, choosing to restore certain parts of the house to Brigham Young's time but not to remove the additions made by John W. Young. Therefore the house now represents a mixture of periods from Brigham Young's to the next generation. One example of this is the room currently called Brigham Young's bedroom. John W. Young had incorporated it into a larger space: a wall had been taken out and new moldings had been added, along with a Victorian fireplace. When it came time to restore the house, the missing wall was put back and the Victorian fireplace replaced with one based on surviving fireplaces in the Lion House, yet the John W. Young molding remains. Such a mixture is common throughout the house. Some of the doorways were widened while others were not.[20]

The Restoration Committee also decided to display historic artifacts in the house to make it useful for people touring the house. That is why the pantry and the bathroom were created as museum exhibits, not true restorations of the house as it was when Brigham Young lived there.

The biggest problem was dealing with the John W. Young addition at the rear. Since the original kitchen, men's dining room, and store had been demolished, the

By the late 1860s or early 1870s when this picture of the Lion House, President's Office, and the Beehive House was taken, the second story porch had been roofed on the Beehive House, but South Temple Street was still unpaved. Used by permission, Utah State Historical Society, all rights reserved.

committee decided to furnish the existing rooms to represent the earlier rooms that had previously existed but were no longer there. One room was designated as a schoolroom and other rooms adapted to symbolize the Brigham Young era, although the actual rooms dated only from the 1890s. As a result visitors might be confused about how much of the present structure dates from Brigham Young's lifetime.

The renovation was completed and the house opened to the public in 1961. Among those involved in the renovation were some of Brigham Young's grandsons, George Cannon Young, George Y. Cannon, and other family members. Today the house is open year-around and is one of the most popular sites for visitors to Salt Lake City.[21]

THE LION HOUSE

By 1878, the long porch on the west side of the Lion House had been replaced by individual gables over each of the three doors. The trees in front of the Lion House, President's Office, and Beehive House had grown tall enough to provide shade, but South Temple Street remained unpaved. Used by permission, Utah State Historical Society, all rights reserved.

In 1854, while work was continuing on the Beehive House, construction began on the adjacent Lion House. Truman O. Angell mentioned in his diary plans for the family house or the "Big House."[22] Within a year George A. Smith was reporting, "The President has put up the rafters for his new large house . . . which is built for three stories high to look like a one-story Gothic building. It stands a little west of the Governor's office and on the same lot."[23] By October 1855 the house was complete enough to mount the lion statue over the front porch. "President B. Young's large dwelling house is progressing rapidly. The walls, chimneys and roof timbers are all up, and the very tasteful granite and polished sandstone portico at the south end is ready for the handsomely carved stone lion that is to surmount it."[24] The installation of the lion was not without incident, however. "This morning the workmen mounted the lion in front of President Young's new house. Weighs twelve Cwt. strap broke and nearly let it down."[25]

Late in the year some of the wives and families started moving into the house, although finishing work continued for a number of months. By 1856 the

house was completed and occupied by many of the wives and families who had been living in the Log Row or other homes in the area.[26]

As opposed to the Beehive House, the Lion House is Gothic revival, another popular style of the period. The building consisted of three main levels. The basement contained the dining room, kitchen and washing facilities, a schoolroom, and a storage room for milk, fruit, and other materials. Most family meals were held in the basement dining room. The main floor featured a large parlor or prayer room where the family would gather each evening. Also on the main floor were bedrooms for the various wives who had children. The top floor was divided into twenty small rooms, one for each peaked gable window. These rooms were generally occupied by wives who had no children or older children or others who were living in or helping in the house. In addition there was an attic at the top of the house used for storage.[27]

One of the remarkable features of the house was its bathroom facilities. Indoor plumbing was, of course, unavailable at the time, so a two-story outhouse was constructed behind the building, connected to the rear of the house. From the north end of the basement, half of which was actually above ground, ran a corridor back to the lower level of the privy; this lower level was used only by men and boys.[28] Built above that was another passageway, leading from the narrow hallway at the north end of the house to the upper level of the outhouse, used by the women and girls. Apparently a false wall at the back of the lower level restricted the passage of material from the top level in much the same way that pipes run through the walls in modern plumbing. Brigham Young "knew the dangers bred by careless sanitation, and the stone-floored vaults which led, by long passage ways from the north end of the Lion House, were covered with lime daily.[29]

There were a few changes to the house during Brigham Young's lifetime. The major change was the addition of a large porch that ran along the west side of the house in the 1860s. This served various purposes. Children used it as a

By the 1920s the wall in front of the Lion House, President's Office, and Beehive House had been replaced by a fence, the Lion House had been faced with faux stone, and South Temple Street had been paved with trolley tracks running up the middle of the street. Used by permission, Utah State Historical Society, all rights reserved.

gymnasium of sorts. On top was a sleeping porch that could be reached through any of the dormer windows on the top floor. A year after Brigham Young's death, that porch was removed and replaced by three smaller two-story porches that enclosed the windows and doors.[30]

Over the years a large number of Brigham Young's wives and children lived in the Lion House. As the families grew larger, some of them moved to separate houses, so occupancy of the Lion House was never static. People moved from one room to another and the use of rooms altered as needs changed. For example, when Brigham Young built a new schoolhouse on his property, the schoolroom was used for other purposes, such as taffy pulls, theatrical presentations, and classes for small children.

The wives had various assignments in the house. Some of the wives did the washing or mending or other chores to run that large household, but Naamah Carter, usually known as Aunt Twiss, was in charge of the meals.

> Aunt Twiss . . . took over the entire management of the kitchens and food problems. And she was a most competent and reliable manager of these difficult labors. She had four young helpers hired to assist in the cooking and serving of the meals. These "hired girls"—as they were called—were newly arrived emigrants and converts, who mingled with the family on equal terms. Few of them remained long . . . for the girls married and settled in homes of their own.[31]

Shortly before his death Brigham Young moved into the Lion House, where he died in 1877. On Brigham Young's death, the house was deeded to the Brigham Young Trust Company, which handled his wives' property. After his death, his wives and family continued to live in the house. As time went on there were fewer and fewer who lived there as children became adults and went out on their own and some wives passed away. The Lion House, however, continued to be visited by wives who lived in other places and would come to stay. It wasn't until 1900 that the house was sold to the LDS Church. At that point there were only two wives left who were living there: Aunt Twiss and Margaret Pierce. They moved to other residences in the city when the house was sold.[32]

In acquiring the Lion House, the church originally intended it to become a church office building. However, LDS University was in the process of building a new campus nearby, and the Lion House was occupied by the university for its classes during the school year of 1900–1901. Over the next thirty years the house continued to be used for various university functions, while other parts of the house were used for church offices.[33]

In order to meet the needs of both the university and the church, the house was heavily remodeled. The partitions in the upstairs dormer floor were removed to make larger rooms. Facilities for teaching home economics were installed on that floor as well. The basement rooms were altered to create a cafeteria. One of the few rooms in the house to maintain its original configuration was the prayer room parlor on the main floor, although its uses varied greatly over the years. Some of the rooms served as a dormitory for female students. Other facilities were used as a carpenter shop for industrial education. One room was set aside as a relic room where artifacts of Brigham Young's life were displayed.[34] The exterior of the house was also altered. Windows were redesigned to reflect a more modern style and the shutters were removed. A faux stone covering was applied to the exterior walls.[35]

When LDS University closed in 1932, it no longer needed the Lion House;[36] therefore the church gave the house to the Young Ladies' Mutual Improvement Association, which had been running the Beehive House as a girls' home since 1920. The YLMIA transformed the house into a social center where young women could entertain and hold social activities.[37]

In December 1932 the building opened as the Lion House Social Center. During this period the room in which Brigham Young died was set aside as a memorial in his honor. For many years it held artifacts of his life. The cafeteria that had served students was adapted to provide meals for LDS Church leaders, Church Administration Building employees, and missionaries staying in the Missionary Home. Since the building was operated by the YLMIA, all female members of the LDS Church were eligible for Social Center memberships for a yearly fee of one dollar, or a monthly fee of ten cents. This was particularly appealing to out-of-towners who might be in Salt Lake City for only a short period. Membership privileges included: "Use of lunch room accommodations where you may bring your lunch and rest during the noon period. Use of rest room accommodations. Use of reading room. Use of a sewing machine. Participation in weekly events such as book reviews; community singing; story-telling hour; social games."[38]

The Social Center served until 31 March 1964, when it was closed. Major remodeling resulted in a great many changes to the house. The exterior was restored to replicate its original state by removing the faux stone and restoring the plaster.[39]

The Lion House reopened as a social center in 1968. The cafeteria on the basement floor became a restaurant called the Lion House Pantry. Other rooms in the building were reconfigured to accommodate more social functions such as wedding receptions, dinners, and similar social events. To meet those needs, large modern kitchens were added. The Brigham Young Memorial Room was replaced by a staircase leading up to the second floor to facilitate movement through the building.[40]

The Lion House continues to be open to the public. The restaurant in the basement serves many meals, and the rest of the building is heavily used for social activities, parties, receptions, luncheons, and dinners, but it is not open for tours, as is the Beehive House.

The Lion and Beehive Houses today, even in their heavily altered state, still give us a connection with Brigham Young, the nineteenth century LDS Church, and early Utah history.

The Beehive House

Top: This picture of the Beehive House was taken in the late 1860s or 1870s after the second story porch was added, but before the wall was taken down. The first Eagle Gate stands as it was originally installed. Used by permission, Utah State Historical Society, all rights reserved.

Right: Lucy Decker Young and her children lived in the Beehive House, where she managed the meals, directed workmen, and arranged social functions. Photo courtesy of the Brigham Young Family Organization.

Top: By the turn of the twentieth century, the wall in front of the Beehive House had been removed. In the 1890s John W. Young added the section at the back of the house. Used by permission, Utah State Historical Society, all rights reserved.

Above: Painting crews stripped old paint and prepared the exterior wood on the Beehive House during the restoration of the old home. Used by permission, Utah State Historical Society, all rights reserved.

Top: The room representing the kitchen in the restored Beehive House features furniture and equipment typical of the period when it was the Young family home. Used by permission, LDS Church Archives, all rights reserved.

Above: The "Long Hall" upstairs features lovely furniture typical of the period when the family occupied the home. The carpet used in the Beehive House is patterned after one used during Brigham Young's lifetime. Photo by Colleen Whitley.

Top: The dining room in the restored Beehive House is in the section added after Brigham Young's death by his son, John W. Young. Used by permission, LDS Church Archives, all rights reserved.

Above: A desk typical of the period occupies a corner of Brigham Young's restored bedroom. Originally that wall space contained a door to a built-in closet. Photo by Colleen Whitley.

The Lion House

One of the distinctive features of the Lion House is the row of ten dormer windows on each side of the top floor. In most cases, each window opened into a single, small bedroom. Since the picture was taken before the building boom of the 1960s, the Utah State Capitol can be seen in the background. Used by permission, Utah State Historical Society, all rights reserved.

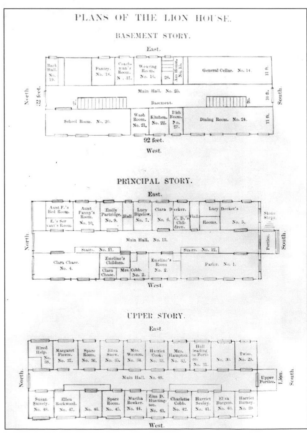

Top: Where solid walls once divided the top floor of the Lion House into many small, separate rooms, folding doors, like those to the right of the archway and at the far back, can now allow variable spaces for large groups or intimate parties. Photo by Colleen Whitley.

Right: The floor plan of the Lion House indicated the location of each wife's room. Some of the designations shown here changed as various wives moved to other houses. Wives with children had larger rooms or separate rooms for the children. Several rooms are marked as spare rooms, since many people stayed at the Lion House temporarily. This floor plan originally appeared in Catherine V. Waite's *The Mormon Prophet and His Harem* (Chicago: J. S. Goodman, 1867). Used by permission, Utah State Historical Society, all rights reserved.

Top: During the period when the Lion House was used as LDS University, later known as LDS Business College, the upper floor was converted to be used for cooking classes. A row of aprons hangs neatly from the pegs on the wall at the left, and the stovepipe in the rear corner enters into the original chimney flue. Shipler Collection, 20 March 1907. Used by permission, Utah State Historical Society, all rights reserved.

Above: Today the same space is used for serving meals. Preparation is done in the kitchens downstairs and at the rear of the house. Photo by Colleen Whitley.

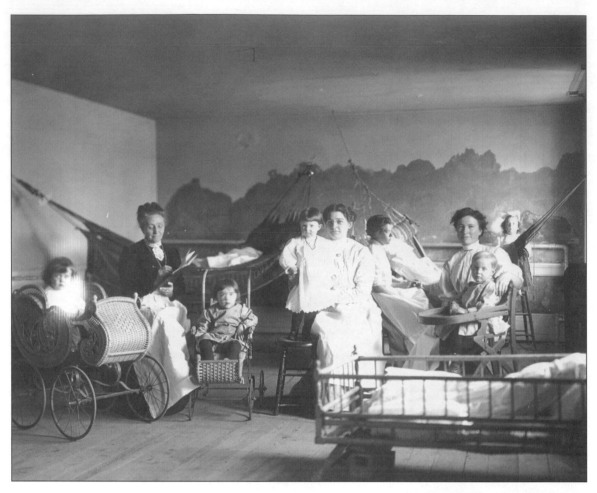

Top: While the Lion House functioned as a school, a nursery provided child care. Shipler Collection, 26 March 1907. Used by permission, Utah State Historical Society, all rights reserved.

Far Right: Eliza R. Snow lived in the Lion House, but she spent much of her time traveling all over the territory organizing auxiliaries, attending conferences, and performing charitable services. Used by permission, Utah State Historical Society, all rights reserved.

Right: Naamah Kendel Jenkins Carter, affectionately known as "Aunt Twiss," managed the kitchen in the Lion House. Assisted by family members and hired help, she provided meals for all those currently residing in the house, workers on the property, guests, and other friends and family members who dropped by. Used by permission, Utah State Historical Society, all rights reserved.

Top: The Lion House parlor has been changed many times in the last century. In 1905, it was a schoolroom for young children. The cabinet at the left seems to have survived all the changes. Used by permission, Utah State Historical Society, all rights reserved.

Above: By the 1920s the parlor was furnished to resemble the kind of sitting room it may have been during the Young family's tenure. At about the same time a second door was added into the next room. Used by permission, Utah State Historical Society, all rights reserved.

Top: About 1940, the Brigham Young Granddaughters' Association met in the Lion House parlor, then a room often used for social gatherings. Seated, left to right, are Jean S. Farr, Gene Rampton, Marjorie Y. Ray, Lutie Y. Lynch, and Gladys Y. Orlob; standing are Cathie D. Platt, Hazel B. Kimball, Carol C. Cannon, Naomi Y. James, Claire D. Bergstrom, Geneva Y. Young, and Kate Y. May. Photo courtesy of the Brigham Young Family Organization.

Above: Today that same parlor is furnished with modern pieces in the style known during Brigham Young's lifetime. It is one of a long series of rooms available for receptions and parties. Photo by Colleen Whitley.

ONE OF THE 20 DISTINCTIVE DORMER WINDOWS

Top: In the 1930s the room in which Brigham Young died was converted to a relic room which displayed some of the Young family mementos. Today the space that room occupied has been divided between the main staircase to the second floor and a small hallway leading to a ladies' rest room. Used by permission, Utah State Historical Society, all rights reserved.

Above: When the Lion House was turned into a social center, some of the upstairs partitions were removed to allow larger spaces for groups to gather for music, performances, or simply conversing. Used by permission, Utah State Historical Society, all rights reserved.

Opposite, top: Brigham Young's children in front of the Lion House. Front row, left to right: Emily Y. Clawson, Susa Y. Gates, Phoebe Y. Beatie, and Brigham Morris Young; center: Colonel Willard Young, Maria Y. Dougall, Zina Y. Card, Clarissa Y. Spencer, Brigham Heber Young, and Mabel Y. Sanborn; back row: Jeannette Y. Easton and Don Carlos Young. The photograph is undated, but was taken before 1928, the year Brigham Heber Young died. Used by permission, Utah State Historical Society, all rights reserved.

Opposite, bottom: Sarah Harmer and Nellie M. Durham, two guides in the Lion House, look at materials in the Pioneer Room in 1951. Photo from Tribune-Telegram Corporation, used by permission, LDS Church Archives, all rights reserved.

Above: In the early twentieth century a faux stone facade was added to the Lion House. In 1964 it was replaced by a stucco more like its original surface. Used by permission, Utah State Historical Society, all rights reserved.

Top: Kim Hill, a member of the Lion House staff, carefully arranges a table for one of the many meals served in the Lion House every year. Photo by Colleen Whitley.

Above: The Lion House can provide a variety in seating styles as well as in space available. Photo by Colleen Whitley.

Chapter 7

THE BRIGHAM YOUNG FARM HOUSE

ELINOR G. HYDE

Forest Farm holds a place in Utah's history. Its clay soil was used for making adobe bricks. The farm became known for its experiments in the silk industry, the sugar beet industry, and the first alfalfa farming in the area. Several wives of Brigham Young lived at Forest Farm at different times, and the produce and dairy products provided for his family and needy people in the Salt Lake area.

LOCATION OF THE FARM

Within a few years after the Mormon settlers arrived in the Salt Lake Valley, Cornelius Lott, who had established a church farm in Nauvoo, started a similar farm near the eastern foothills in part of what was originally known as the Big Field south of Salt Lake City. Listed in historical records as "the President's Farm," it became President Brigham Young's farm and was later called the Forest Farm, or often simply "the Farm House."[1] There food could be grown for the common good. It was located approximately four miles out of town, and was evidently large. Some sources say the farm encompassed about nine hundred acres, but other estimates say the farm covered a square mile.[2] It eventually included up to 11,005 acres of the Big Field, which extended from Ninth South into the south part of the valley.[3]

Property fencing was begun in 1848. Since fencing material was scarce, the city council in 1849 proposed fencing be done in common, with the farmlands allotted into five-acre lots for mechanics and artisans, and ten-acre lots next, with the larger ones beyond that. However, all were to be close to the city for protection. These were fenced into the Big Field, similar to what had been done in previous settlements for the Saints, and communal crops were grown there.

Forest Farm initially bordered the five-acre lots of the Big Field, and the boundaries of the Forest Farm were set as a plat from Ninth South (now Twenty-first South) on the north to what is now Twenty-seventh South on the south, from Third East on the west to about Thirteenth East.[4] However, since boundaries were loosely set and subsequent sales or changes were made, this

description is approximate at best. A natural spring, known later as the Fairmont Springs, was included on the Farm House property.[5] In time, the property of President John Taylor lay to the north of the farm, while on the west and along Park Boulevard (now Fifth East) was the farm of Wilford Woodruff.

While most of the area south of Ninth South was originally fields, settlers arrived in the vicinity on a regular basis until there were enough to be considered a ward. On 16 February 1849 the entire area encompassed in the original five-acre survey was declared to be Canyon Creek Ward; however, the few Saints living in the area attended meetings in Salt Lake City, so no ward was actually organized. On 23 April 1854 the Saints who lived on Canyon Creek were organized into the Sugar House Ward, named after the Sugar House, a factory for refining sugar from the beets grown in the area. Abraham O. Smoot became the first bishop of the new ward, which extended from Fifth East, west to the Jordan River, and south past Twenty-seventh South.[6]

EXPERIMENTS AT FOREST FARM

Pioneers used the resources they found in that vicinity, but they brought in new items as well. One of the naturally occurring resources was the adobe clay on the land just south of Forest Farm. As early as 1852 adobe bricks were being made on the farm. The adobe clay was taken from the area now known as the Forest Dale Golf Club, south of 2700 South. The large adobes were made by having ox teams tramp the clay and mud, then workers shaped the blocks by

Black walnut and black locust trees lined the drive to the Forest Farm when the Young family lived there. Used by permission, Utah State Historical Society, all rights reserved.

hand on tables. By adding a binder of dried wire grass or preferably cowhide hair to the adobe mud, a permanent brick was made. Without the binder, the adobes crumbled in wet weather. The finished adobes were fastened together with clay mortar.[7] It is not known how long adobes were made from the church farm clay, but among the buildings for which the adobe bricks were used was the Chase Mill in what is now Liberty Park.

Forest Farm became famous as an experimental farm for new crops. Since the valley of the Great Salt Lake was a new settlement, what would and would not grow there was an unknown factor. As emigrants set sail from their native lands they were encouraged to bring any kind of seeds or plants that might thrive in the Western desert. Missionaries who traveled throughout the world also sought cuttings or seeds of trees, shrubs, and plants. The results proved interesting. Soon a large number of fruit and nut trees were thriving. Black walnut trees did especially well. Ash, locust, plum, apple, peach, pear, and cherry trees all grew in abundance, black locust trees growing well enough to provide wood for furniture. The buildings were surrounded by acres of meadows, fields of grain, alfalfa, corn, potatoes, and lots of trees.[8] Soon Forest Farm became a showpiece for the territory. Guests were hosted there, and the wonderful assortment of trees and crops were shown off with great delight.

Some plants did better than others. At the 1860 fair sponsored by the Deseret Agricultural and Manufacturing Society, Brigham Young won more prizes than anyone. His apples and strawberries took four awards. It is notable that other prizes were for Chinese sugar and chufa

Top: The "big ten" were Brigham Young's eldest daughters by his polygamous marriages. From left to right, front row: Miranda, Carlie, Ella, Emily, and Fanny; back row: Zina, Evalyn, Jeanette, Mary, and Maria ("Ry"). Photo taken about 1867. Used by permission, Utah State Historical Society, all rights reserved.

Above: Susan Snively Young lived in the Forest Farm House and managed the farm for many years. Used by permission, Utah State Historical Society, all rights reserved.

Today Brigham Young's restored farmhouse sits in This Is the Place Heritage Park in Salt Lake City. It is open to visitors with seasonal programs presented to demonstrate some of the activities that were common to the home, from how the harvest was handled to how Christmas was celebrated. Photo by Alan Hyde.

nut, an edible African root.[9] One account lists a "sunflower, raised at Forest Farm [that] measured 51 inches across the head, exclusive of petals, and weighed twelve pounds."[10] In addition to apples and strawberries, and the regular crops at the farm, many vegetables were grown there and were used by the farm employees and the Young family. Farm workers also raised new crops such as alfalfa and sugar beets. An early attempt to produce sugar from sugar beets took much longer than most experimental crops. Although very heavy and expensive equipment was brought from France in 1852 for making "a good sugar," it wasn't until 1891 that a very frail President Wilford Woodruff finally saw white sugar coming from black molasses.[11]

Another experiment did better—the introduction of alfalfa—under the direction of Hamilton G. Park, a Scotch convert of 1840 who came to Utah in September 1854. He became business manager for Brigham Young until 1869 when he was called on a mission for the LDS Church. Park described the first handling of the hay: "President advertized for someone who knew how to cure hay. He secured no one and the task fell to me. After cutting the lucern it was put into the barn. Inside, it began to smolder and smoke and I was obliged to take it out of the stable for fear the barn would burn down."[12]

Forest Farm eventually became an important element in the silk industry as well. Zina D. H. Young began the silk culture in the Beehive House in 1868, but it was soon apparent more room was needed, so the operation was moved to the Forest Farm, where mulberry trees were planted. In the mid 1860s Octave Ursenbach, a native of Switzerland, imported some silkworm eggs from France and established a small cocoonery in the Sixteenth Ward. President Brigham Young became deeply interested. Because the silkworms ate mulberry leaves, 11,340 mulberry seedlings were imported in 1866, resulting in twenty-five to

thirty acres of trees. Saints were also encouraged to grow mulberry trees, imported from Europe. French immigrant Louis Bertrand, who had a knowledge of the silk industry, brought trees and more cocoons. Bertrand was placed in charge, but the following year or so was replaced by Robert Wimmer. Neither man succeeded at Forest Farm, despite eight hundred thousand worms, because moisture retained by the adobe walls of the cocoonery building damaged the product. One of the farm workers described the process.

> William Buttle, William Hart and I planted the seed from which the old mulberry grove grew. President Young came to the farm with the seeds and said, "Hamilton, I want about an acre of good ground prepared. It must be put in good shape because this is precious seed, all the way from France."
>
> He handed us a package containing between two and three pounds of what looked like mustard seed. We prepared the ground carefully, plowed, and harrowed it five or six times. President Young then came down to see us plant it. He asked me to plant the seed thick because some of it might not germinate. We did so and the young seed came up as thick as the hair on a dog's back. The trees grew rapidly and then a cocoonery was built 18 November 1868.[13]

Another worker observed, "When the little worms hatched out and went to work on the fresh green leaves we thought the question of producing silk in Utah was solved. We soon discovered, however, that it took a great deal of patience, skill, and expert work before the silk fabric was produced, but its production was finally accomplished."[14]

The caterpillars consumed large quantities of the mulberry leaves before spinning their cocoons. Great care was necessary to insure the cocoons were neither too warm nor too cold. A cocoonery was built for the silkworms that had to be kept at certain temperatures or the precious worms would die.[15] The cocoons were then dipped into boiling water to quickly kill the worms inside

The original site of the farmhouse is now a parking lot a little east of 700 East flanked on the south by Interstate 80. Photo by Judy Dykman and Colleen Whitley.

Top: The stairway from the kitchen led up to the boys' bedroom on the second floor. It is steep and narrow and Ann Eliza Webb complained bitterly about how hard it was to climb. Photo by Colleen Whitley.

Above: The barn near the house at This Is the Place Heritage Park is a replica of one kind of outbuilding often used on pioneer farms. Photo by Colleen Whitley.

Top: The animals at This Is The Place are the result of several generations of back-breeding to achieve a closer resemblance to pioneer livestock and eliminate the refinements bred into today's animals. Photo by Colleen Whitley.

Left: Volunteer tour guides Marian Bolto and Jack Ewing greet visitors at the front door of the restored Forest Farm House. Volunteers are trained to explain how the building was used and how its equipment worked. Photo by Elinor Hyde.

before they hatched, so as not to destroy the precious silk strands as the moth emerged. It was not a pleasant task, but the women learned to endure their dislike of handling the silkworms. Patiently the silk strands were unwound, and then made into cloth.

Zina took her own experience and shared it throughout the territory with others called to the "Silk Mission." She was the president of the Deseret Silk Association. Her trials and errors helped others avoid many pitfalls, and the silk produced was triumphantly displayed in the various products such as silk flags, silk dresses, and other ornamental items. The girls of the family, however, did not have Zina's enthusiasm for the work.[16]

In 1875 Mrs. Dunyan, wife of Dr. Dunyan, had succeeded in her own venture in sericulture, and she took charge of the silk industry at Forest Farm. Using the whole building for worms, she was successful, and in six weeks raised seven hundred pounds of cocoons which at that time were worth two dollars per pound in France.[17] From this beginning mulberry trees were planted all over the territory wherever the soil and climate allowed. Such items as handkerchiefs, scarfs, elegant silk fringe, and a few dresses were the result. The mulberry trees were still growing in 1901 when the Woolley family moved to the area. One of them remembers "the stained sidewalks [from the fallen berries] on the way to school."[18] Eventually the silk industry was returned to individual homes, and especially to the cocoonery behind the Beehive and Lion Houses. Although the silk industry was not a great success the results were sufficient to make it an interesting chapter in Utah history.

DAIRY PRODUCTS FROM FOREST FARM

While many crops were raised on Forest Farm, it was primarily a dairy farm in the 1860s. The agricultural census for 1869 listed forty-five dairy cows and 2,900 pounds of butter that year, with eighty-four cattle for breeding purposes, a few pigs, sheep, and chickens, and some farm crops. A separate milk house and a spring cellar were built to care for the milk, butter, and cheese. The cows were milked in the morning and in the evening, and Brigham never would allow the men to milk the cows until they had washed their hands. It had good results. Clarissa Young Spencer said, "I supposed that is one of the reasons why there was so little sickness among us."[19]

After the cows had been milked, the milk was stored in flat pans and kept in a cool place to allow the cream to rise. The cream was then skimmed off and put into a churn. Usually the night milk had the cream and was used for churning, and the morning milk was used fresh, still slightly warm for breakfast. Churning the butter took about twenty minutes and some good, steady arm work to make the butter come.[20] Once the butter formed, the buttermilk was drained off and the butter was rinsed in clear water. The butter maker used a wooden paddle and gathered it. Salt was added, and the butter then put into a butter mold. It was then stored in the cool cellar until ready for use on the farm or to be taken into the city for Brigham's large family there.

Keeping dairy products from becoming tainted required special care to utensils and milk buckets. It was second nature to scald anything out that had

held milk, or any milk subsequently put in those utensils would sour. Sometimes, even with such care, it soured anyway. Sour milk made a good cottage cheese, when left on the back of the coal stove. It was sometimes known as curds and whey, a dish that was either very much appreciated or equally distasteful, depending on the individual's taste.

BUILDINGS ON THE FARM

One of the first buildings at the Forest Farm was a sixty-nine by eighteen foot log cabin with a red pine foundation built in 1857. By 1862, according to Susa Young Gates,

The farm had two log houses, one the cook house and dining room, separated by a roofed-in passage way from the milk and cheese house, and there was a chamber above which was Mother's [Lucy Bigelow's] bedroom. . . . Mother was a splendid milker and milked all the cows of the family in the first days in the Log Row and in the Lion House. That might have been one reason why father arranged for her to go to the farm. [Y]et by then [the time Lucy lived on the farm] men did the milking. She loved churning and cheese-making."[21]

The new Farm House, commenced in 1861 and completed in 1863, had a rock foundation with wood frame walls, covered with plaster or stucco, although most other buildings on the property were adobe. It was the first example of "balloon framing" used in Utah. Balloon framing required thinner two-by-four framing lumber instead of heavy timber. Both stories were erected together and built on simultaneously, rather than the first story being built and then the second, as was customary. The new Farm House was built near a spring, with a

The kitchen was the center of activity, with its own door to the outside to facilitate bringing in water, meats, and vegetables and taking out scraps and waste. Photo by Colleen Whitley.

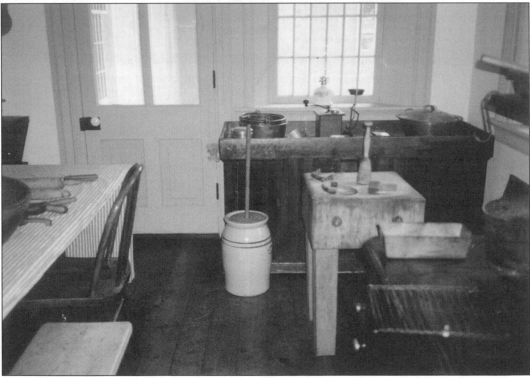

Top: Marion Bolto demonstrates some of the equipment used in the farmhouse kitchen. Photo by Colleen Whitley.

Above: The restored Forest Farm kitchen features much of the equipment typical of pioneer homes. Photo by Elinor Hyde.

door leading down to the cellar where a well tapped into that spring. The cellar was divided into two parts, one for the well and the other part serving as a storage place for the dairy products and other foods. Later the water from the spring was pumped into the kitchen.[22]

The spacious building was located near the center of the farm. It was approached from the north by a broad avenue of lofty black walnut and locust trees planted on either side in double rows. One description of the house calls it "a Double-tee, with one end of the tee facing north and the other south, and joined in the middle." Another described it as a "double cross." The original cost was $25,000.[23] It was was built in the "cottage Gothic" style, and described in 1864 by a visitor who wrote about Brigham Young: "His farm house is 87 x 18 feet, four L's to it, completely surrounded by verandah—balloon frame." He adds, "Visitors were served roast turkey, strawberries and cream and fresh peas."[24] The Forest Farm House was considered the best farmhouse on the best farm in the valley.[25] "The house was a homey place. . . . Hollyhocks and roses bordered the porch, and a great profusion of other flowers grew in odd nooks and corners of the lawn."[26]

The front entrance led into the dining room, which also was the kitchen. On the left was Brigham's small office, where farm accounts were kept. It also had an outside door, which allowed farmhands and visitors who needed a private interview with him to come and go without disturbing the rest of the house. Brass-lined gas lamps, attractive fireplaces and, later, stylish cast-iron stoves provided light and heat. The whitewashed cellar was a sort of summer hideaway, a place to be cool, and, most importantly, a place to store food.

There were two stairways, one on each side of the house. The boys had a bedroom, with Spartan furnishings. It was thought healthy for them to sleep in

Top: The kitchen was the work center of the home. Besides cooking, other chores such as spinning and quilting were done there. Photo by Elinor Hyde.

Above: The woodburning stove provided heat for the kitchen, made cooking possible, and gave the boys in the family a constant job cutting wood. Photo by Judy Dykman.

an unheated room. The girls also had a large bedroom. A wardrobe or chiffonier held their spare clothes. In the Farm House the room at the top of the stairs was known as a servant's room. The person who had this room was likely the one who was up early, getting the fires built.[27] Susa Young Gates recalled: "Upstairs the long hall which spread across the south end of the house had many uses, one of which was dancing, with a band of musicians in one end playing to the caller's 'Balance to the Corner' and 'All Promenade.'"[28]

The house, like all pioneer homes, had no indoor plumbing. Each bedroom, therefore, had a chamber pot under the bed for emergency nighttime use. An outhouse, or privy, was located outside, far enough from the house for privacy and to prevent odors from disturbing the household, although pioneers learned early not to be overly sensitive to farm smells. It simply was an accepted part of life—corrals and barns were odorous, as were animals and even people. It was something everyone just tried to ignore, although most were as careful as possible not to offend. It wasn't considered appropriate to comment on odors. Of course, anyone with "something on their shoes" was invited to step outside and clean it off. One was expected to wipe one's feet before entering, not only for politeness, but also as a sanitary measure. In addition to places of residence, the farm also had barns, a chicken coop, pigpens, and sheep and cattle pastures.

FARM DUTIES AND CHORES

Meals at the farm were important, and the wife in residence was responsible for seeing to their preparation. Breakfast was a hearty meal, since a lot of work was to be done during the day, and by breakfast time, much had already been accomplished. Usually the milking and feeding of the stock was done early, and vegetables were brought from the garden early, to allow for preparation for the noon meal, the biggest of the day, called dinner. Supper in the evening was a much lighter meal. Brigham was well known for his preference of bread and milk, cornmeal mush or cornbread with buttermilk for supper, and his children shared in this choice of an evening meal, whether or not that was their first desire. The children used correct table manners for even such a simple treat. Meal preparations took much time and required large amounts of food, since food was needed for as many as twenty hungry farmhands as well as the family. In addition to daily preparation, of course, the farm residents had to prepare many foods for winter use. Corn and meats were dried. Squash, pumpkins, potatoes, carrots, and apples and other fruits were stored in underground cellars. Nothing was wasted. All pioneer children grew up on the adage, "Waste not, want not."

Water had to be carried from the well or spring in the cellar by one of the hired hands or the older children. A water bench held the water for drinking and washing. Later a pump brought the water right upstairs from the cool spring. Always there would be a teakettle on the stove for hot water to wash with or to use in cooking. A washstand held a basin for washing up, both for the family and hired hands. Soap used was homemade.[29]

Storage is essential in any kitchen. Forest Farm had a small cupboard near the stairway that held dried foods, spices, and other items out of the way but still allowed easy access by the cooks. Photo by Colleen Whitley.

Caring for the laundry was another major task. Water was carried to the stove and heated. Large tubs with a scrubboard were placed on benches in the back room used as a laundry room. Hands were rubbed raw with the friction of the clothes on the board, plus the strong homemade soap made from lye and wood ashes. Heavily soiled clothes were often soaked overnight, and whites and other light clothing boiled in large boilers, stirred with a wooden paddle stick. Whites also had a rinse in blueing to prevent yellowing. A description of the laundry process in the Lion House downtown gives an insight into what washday would have been like at the Farm House.

Water was heated in huge brass caldrons. Two large barrels stood along the wall. In one was stored the water for the washing which was softened with wood ashes in lieu of lye or other commercial softeners. The other was used for washing blankets and quilts, and the work was done with a wooden pounder, or *dolly* as we called it in that day. There were high shelves for such aids to superior laundering as homemade indigo blueing and homemade potato starch. . . . There were always plenty of men around to lift the clothes, bring in the water and assist in every way possible. Father was most considerate of his womenfolk and would not allow them to do any work that could be done just as easily by hired help. The large baskets, which held the piles of snowy clothes, had mostly been made by the Indians and traded to us for food. There was an excellent drainage system for the disposal of waste water, for Father [Brigham Young] was very particular about sanitation.[30]

All items were wrung as dry as possible, both to save the wash water and to hasten the drying. Many things were starched, and then all the clothes were hung

Top: Barrels of flour, tins of spices, and cupboards of various sizes were tucked into any available corner of the kitchen. Photo by Elinor Hyde.

Above: The white china in the kitchen cupboard was ordered by Brigham Young, but he never used it himself. Photo by Elinor Hyde.

The dining room was in the center of the house, next to the kitchen for easy access. The chairs were turned out from the table so everyone could kneel for prayer before each meal. Photo by Elinor Hyde.

out to dry. In the beginning clothes were placed on bushes and on the fences but later clotheslines replaced them. It was heavy work, carrying the wet clothing outside, and a tedious process to bring the dried clothing inside and get it dampened and folded or rolled, ready for ironing the next day. Often hired girls helped with the laundry. After the washing was finished, the wash water was usually used to mop the floors. In the Farm House likely a good stiff brush was used to make the boards look new, as the grime of everyday living was scrubbed away.

In the winter the clothes were washed only when necessary, and hung around the kitchen stoves on the backs of chairs. Some pioneers later told of being "sewn into their underwear in the winter, as children, and unstitched come spring."[31] It was thought unhealthy to bathe too often, especially in the winter. Baths were taken in front of a warm fire whenever possible, in a big tin tub that probably doubled as a washtub on laundry day. However, daily washing was done in a washbasin. Every home had one or more washstands and bedrooms had china basins for private cleansing. Hair was brushed daily but not washed often. A good one hundred strokes with the hairbrush was part of every girl's bedtime preparations. Clothes were carefully brushed and spotted, and aprons worn to help keep them as clean as possible.

Wood gathering was a regular chore, usually for the younger boys, who learned to pick up a bucket of wood chips at the woodpile, and then chop slender sticks of kindling to get the fires going quickly. The larger logs were cut into lengths that would fit into the stoves, and then split into just the right size for longer burning. Hardwoods burned better than the rest, but the pioneers made do with what was available. A wood-gathering excursion was part of the preparation for winter, with several large loads brought from the nearby canyons. Every young man knew how to use an axe, as did most women, if the need arose.

The mirrored hutch or sideboard in the dining room provided space for serving utensils. *Top:* Photo by Elinor Hyde. *Above:* Photo by Colleen Whitley.

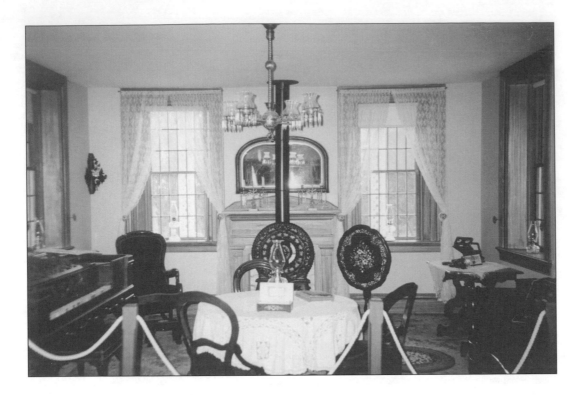

In addition to all other chores, farm residents faced constant cleaning. In pioneer times it was customary for thorough spring and fall housecleaning. The rugs were carried out to be beaten, curtains laundered and rehung, and walls cleaned, usually with a fresh coat of calcimine or whitewash. The constant use of candles and wood- or coal-burning stoves left a grimy film on walls and windows. New straw was put in the ticks or mattresses after harvest and often a layer was put under the rugs as well.

While family members did much of the work, Brigham Young also hired men to do the heavy or specialized chores. After serving a mission for the LDS Church, James Jensen, an immigrant from Denmark, was hired in 1870 to help put up the hay and care for the stock. Later he and George Reese ran the Forest Farm on shares, paying for the use of Brigham Young's team, which proved to be a profitable venture. "Brigham Young was well satisfied."[32] Twice weekly Brother Jensen's wife walked to downtown Salt Lake City with eggs and butter.

The Young children, however, often remembered the fun mixed in with the chores. Chariton Jacobs, son of Zina D. Young and her first husband Henry Jacobs, lived on the farm during the summer and was known for his constant practical jokes and his wit. Susa Young Gates reports:

> Mother [Lucy Bigelow Young] used to make me small turnovers when she made a batch of pies. Chariton would ask the child for a bite of her turnover and return it with nothing left but the outer rim of the crust. How on earth he swallowed the rest of the pie in one gulp was an ever fascinating mystery to [me]. Sometimes when I'd ask him for a piece of his pie or bread and butter he would tell me with that mischievous gleam in his eyes, that I wouldn't want it because he had spit on it.
>
> One day he came up to the house, half-grown boy that he was, without anything on, apparently, but his shirt, making frantic efforts to pull his shirt tail

The parlor occupied one wing of the main floor and was furnished more formally than the rest of the house. Photo by Colleen Whitley.

down to cover the upper part of his bare legs. He ran about in great apparent distress while Mother scolded him for his indecency and insisted upon his going and putting on his pants. Of course his pants were on and rolled up under his shirt, as she subsequently learned when he chose to pull them down.

One unhappy day he [Chariton] came as near the house as he dared and called to Mother to throw out his Sunday shirt and breeches–and oh! The smell of him! He had been a little too familiar with an angry skunk and his clothes had to be buried out of sight for the earth to disinfect them.

One of the men working there was good old Charlie Crabtee and he was kind to [me] a spindling fragile child, who crept upon his knee in the evenings by the fireside to listen to his unmusical but fatherly crooning lullaby. One dull Sabbath day, Chariton "married" me to Charlie Crabtree as [I] sat upon Charlie's stolid patient knee and for years after Chariton used to call [me] Sister Crabtree.[33]

RECREATION AT FOREST FARM

Hard though farm work was, Forest Farm became a wonderful place for the Young family to gather for entertainment and festivities. In the summer the family enjoyed picnics. They arrived in spring wagons and private carriages. Various small remembrances of these outings give a glimpse of the delight of all. In the winter the family arrived from the city in sleighs, sheltered from the cold by buffalo robes. New Year's Day at the farm was a favorite celebration, especially for the "big ten" girls who were in their courting years.[34] The coats were quickly taken upstairs, and all warmed around the cast-iron stoves. Brigham Young liked taking his friends there. It is said he courted the actress Julia Dean, and although she wasn't interested in becoming his wife, nor a Mormon, she did enjoy the attention. He named the big sleigh after her, *The Julia Dean*. This little bit of history was always a source of amusement to the children and grandchildren.[35]

Entertainment was usually social. The piano in the parlor provided a musical center for family singing. Photo by Alan Hyde.

The newly gathered hay, the piles of straw, the shade from the trees, and Parleys Creek running through the property provided an idyllic setting for a pleasant summer outing. Activities for pioneer children included joyfully hunting for birds' eggs or spotting nests in the trees. They played games to see who could collect the most or biggest leaves or pick the loveliest bouquet of wild flowers. Boys climbed trees, showing off by hanging by their knees on lower branches, with an adventurous girl occasionally breaking all the rules to join them. Making willow whistles was a common pastime that excited everyone momentarily, as the high-pitched sound echoed through the air. Whistles were also made from joint grass found near the stream. Butterflies and dragonflies hovering just out of reach, with birds and squirrels or even wild rabbits adding just the right country touch, made pleasant memories. If a harmless snake happened to make an appearance, boys tried to catch it, with the girls squealing in protest.

Since shoes were scarce in the new territory for many years, most children, and especially the boys, were barefoot. That meant wading in the creeks or streams was acceptable, if the cold mountain water could be endured. However, if they encountered "pains in their joints" it was their just dues. Mothers reminded the girls to keep their bonnets or hats on to avoid the sun, since no respectable girl left her complexion unprotected.[36] A visit to Forest Farm by Brigham Young's children was a special outing, no doubt including all of these activities. [37]

Visiting the farm was a pleasant outing for the mothers as well, with the children allowed to run in the wide spacious area, babies tucked cosily away inside or on a blanket in the shade for naps. A rag bee or quilt piecing occupied their spare time or perhaps fancy handwork, since busy hands were considered a sign of a goodly woman. Clarissa Young Spencer remembered how Harriet Cook, who was their schoolteacher, kept her and others busy cutting carpet rags.[38] The spinning wheel was an important part of the Farm House. Wool was

Bedrooms occupied the upper floor of the farmhouse. Today it is furnished with sofas and beds typical of the pioneer period. Photo by Colleen Whitley.

gathered, washed, and then carded and spun. Young girls were expected to know this art at an early age, and they also learned to knit and make samplers.

Chores needed doing, of course, including setting food on the table. Much of the food for these outings was prepared ahead and carried along in baskets. Aunt Susan Snively Young was known as the best cook among Brigham's wives.[39] Any family gathering included some of her well-prepared recipes, but she welcomed help in the final preparations and then with the clearing up and washing of dishes. A bit of secret sharing, light boasting of children's accomplishments, and news of friends and other family added to the festivity. Aunt Margaret Pierce Young taught the children songs, dances, and poems which they presented to the family on special occasions, some with shyness, and others with confidence.[40]

As evening approached, the sight of the cows moving from the pasture to the barn to be milked, and the clanking of the milk buckets by the milking hands would have signaled time for chores. Chickens needed to be given grain, eggs gathered, pigs and calves fed, water poured into troughs, and the horses harnessed ready for the return home, unless the families were spending the night. Susa Young Gates gives a glimpse of the excitement at those occasions.

Top: Displays at the restored farmhouse include furniture, clothing, and accessories from the pioneer period. Some are antiques and some are replicas. Photo by Colleen Whitley.

Above: Pioneer clothing, as well as furniture and equipment, is displayed at the restored farmhouse. Photo by Colleen Whitley.

Sometimes father would have a party for us all when we stayed the night, making beds on the floor, girls sleeping with mothers and the boys up in the hay loft. The mammoth long sleigh with its high driver's seat, its green painted sides outspringing in graceful curves, and holding in its capacious hay- and buffalo-robe-filled box [carried] a bevy of nearly fifty children of various ages all cuddled down under the buffalo robes on hay and all bubbling with laughter and

Top: Volunteers Marion Bolto and Jack Ewing play checkers with a replica of a handmade wooden set. Photo by Colleen Whitley.

Above: This pump organ is typical of the kind used in pioneer homes and churches. Photo by Elinor Hyde.

excitement over the expected festivities of the holiday season. Drawn by six spirited horses all jingling and jangling with the most musical of sleigh bells, the driver's long whip used skillfully and delicately on the glossy sides of the prancing teams, the brilliant stars overhead saw no merrier sight than this sleigh full of unalloyed happiness just behind the Leader's cutter, and followed by the more dignified sleighs holding the mothers of these children on their way for a gala house party at the farm.[41]

Susa continues with a description of the delight of the delicious odors from roast beef, mince pies, stewing chickens, and squash pies. It didn't take long for them to race upstairs and shed their neck comforters and cloaks and the heavy outer woollen stockings, which she says served as both leggings and overshoes.

Nor were the sounds ignored. "A wonderful music box whose exquisite selections from *Il Trovatore* and *The Swiss Echo Song* trilled and pealed along its curved and pin-pointed rollers in the most mysterious and uncanny fashion. The usual band of musicians sat in the end of the [long dancing] hall was sufficient for eager couples to 'Chassè to the right' and 'Balance on the corner' and 'All promenade.'"[42] The dances were called by Jim Currie with Hiram Clawson as grand master at floor managing and also master of ceremonies as the big ten girls and their beaus enjoyed the evening. Other guests were often members of the First Presidency.

Music wasn't the only entertainment. If the dancers tired, there were places to rest, and storytellers and singers to entertain. At intermissions stirring patriotic and "apt remarks" appropriate for the time and place were given by Brigham or his associates. "Here, too, were the winged rocking chairs of home manufacture, rush bottomed, feather cushioned and antimacassared in the latest pioneer

Top: A stereopticon allowed a viewer to see two slightly different pictures at the same time, creating an illusion of three dimensions. Photo by Elinor Hyde.

Above: One popular craft in pioneer times was creating flowers and wreaths from human hair. Photo by Elinor Hyde.

Top: Beside the restored Forest Farm House is a line of Lombardy poplars, "Mormon trees," commonly planted along farms and fields to act as a windbreak. Photo by Colleen Whitley.

Above: Family pictures, including the large one of Mary Ann Angell on the left, decorate the walls of the restored Forest Farm House. Photo by Colleen Whitley.

fashion."[43] A final near poetic description terms the Farm House as "a beacon light and shining example to all Israel" of the realization of a domestic ideal, an example to the church where family could associate in ideal circumstances.[44]

WIVES AT FOREST FARM

Everything that went on at Forest Farm, from chores to parties, was supervised by the wife in residence. Lucy Bigelow Young lived there from 1861 to 1863, then went to St. George, where she stayed for several years.

Ann Eliza Webb also lived at Forest Farm. She complained that the walls of the Farm House were not thick enough to keep out the winter chill nor the summer heat and the stairs too narrow and hard to climb. "The setting for the house, was lovely, but not a desirable place to live because it was away from the center of activity," she wrote. Ann Eliza discusses in detail her life at the farm, charging that Brigham Young only sent wives there who were in disfavor and then he worked them to exhaustion. Her credibility is questionable, though, since she wrote these statements while earning her living by lecturing against Mormonism. Before Ann Eliza and her mother Mrs. Webb moved to Forest Farm, six others of Brigham's wives had lived there and more followed. Some simply accepted the difficulties of farm life, while others appear to have thrived. Emily Dow Partridge, however, appears to confirm of Ann Eliza's charge that "every one of the wives who had been compelled to live there had become confirmed invalids before they left the place, broken down by overwork." Emily said, "I have not been well since I went to the farm to live about five years ago. Nobody knows my feelings while there but myself. There was nothing pleasant in connection with that place."[45] The wife's physical condition was not entirely ignored, however. Susa Young Gates said her family lived there until her mother (Lucy Bigelow) was expecting a child; then they moved because the heavy work required at the farm would have been burdensome for her delicate condition.

Susan Snively, also called Susannah, the wife who lived longest at Forest Farm, seemed to adapt very well. She was skilled with the dairy, making cheese and butter and caring for the many items in the dairy that required cleaning twice each day. She also cared for the poultry.[46] She seems to have learned the art of making cheese and butter and caring for the milk from her parents and grandparents.

Susan was of Swiss heritage, born in Woodstock, Shenandoah County, Virginia, 30 October 1815. She was the daughter of Henry and Mary Heavenor or Havenor Snively, the youngest of ten children.[47] Her father kept a dry goods store in Washington, D.C., and her grandmother often took her knitting to sit with George Washington's mother, Mary Ball Washington.[48] Susan and her older sister, Hannahetta (or Hannahette) Snively, born 22 October 1812, joined the LDS Church in 1836 and moved to

Springfield, Illinois, where they lived together for five years, then moved to Nauvoo, Illinois.[49] The sisters lived in their own brick home, which they paid for from their own earnings.[50] The home was furnished with family heirlooms and keepsakes.[51]

Susan was described as "a little above medium height and of dark complexion. She was energetic and industrious, and ever ready to render aid in every way possible to the needy, or to those in distress. . . . She was a women of strong will power, positive and determined in her general bearing, yet kind and accommodating."[52] The sisters' wholehearted generosity, assisting the ill and any in need, together with their thrift, industry, and cleanliness appealed to Brigham Young, and he later asked Susan to become his wife.[53] Both Susan and her sister Hannahetta were married on the same day in Nauvoo, 2 November 1844, Hannahetta to Parley P. Pratt and Susan to Brigham Young. Parley P. Pratt officiated for Brigham and Susan and vice versa.[54] Later, when the temple was dedicated, Susan was sealed to Brigham Young 22 January 1846.[55]

Susan was reluctant to enter into plural marriage, but Hannahetta reassured her by saying, "Think of it as an eternal marriage." The double wedding took place in the Nauvoo Temple, before the roof was on: "The winter sun shown down on them".[56] When Hannahetta had a child a year later, Susan said to herself, "Eternal marriage, aye?"[57] Whether or not her own union with Brigham Young was strictly an "eternal" one is not known. Her only child was Julia, her foster or adopted daughter, born 3 June 1853 in Salt Lake. Susa Young Gates recorded that "Susan reached between her legs to take the child" from the unnamed birth mother, symbolic of having given birth. Susa added, "Aunt Susan was just as good a woman as any woman who could be but she was childless, until she adopted the charming baby Julia and her motherly solicitude over her fledgling sometimes gave a touch of sharpness to her speech and certainly made her watchful that Julia should share equally with all the other girls. But who cared? Everybody loved and petted Julia and mother [Lucy Bigelow] was very tender over dear Aunt Susan."[58] Julia was raised by Susan and sealed to Brigham Young after his death.[59] There is no record of who Julia's birth parents might have been. Julia grew up not knowing she was adopted and is said to "have fainted when this knowledge came to her as a teenager at a dance."[60]

Julia's pictures show a pretty young lady, hair pulled away from her face in curls. She is well dressed. Brigham Young encouraged his daughters to get an education so they had means to provide a livelihood. At the age of eighteen Julia was commended for ability and training that allowed her to take down records in shorthand. In June 1878 she married Charles Samuel Burton.[61] They had no children and Julia suffered from poor health, dying in 1889.[62] This was a very sorrowful time for Susan, now seventy-four years of age. She was in failing health and had been residing in the Lion House, a member of the Eighteenth Ward for some years, as apparently so were Julia and Charles, since ward records indicate both paid fast offerings there.[63]

Susan herself died a few years later, 20 November 1892, and was laid to rest in Brigham Young's cemetery on First Avenue in Salt Lake. A Daughters of Utah

A school desk occupies a corner of one of the upstairs bedrooms. Photo by Colleen Whitley.

Volunteer guide Jack Ewing writes at one of several desks in the farmhouse. Photo by Colleen Whitley.

Pioneers publication lists her grave as near Brigham's, "marked with a scroll design" and her name, "Susannah Snively Young 1817–1892," but that marker is no longer there.[64] The DUP account mentions "she left no issue," which is technically correct, since Julia was already deceased. When Susan died, she left more than one thousand dollars to be distributed to the poor. This seems to have been divided among the wards in Salt Lake.[65]

FOREST FARM AND THE HOUSE SINCE BRIGHAM YOUNG'S DEATH

After Brigham Young's death the Farm House was used for Sunday School, and later, the first meetings in the newly created Forest Dale Ward were held there. Still later it was used as a residence. "After the death of Brigham Young his son Apostle Brigham Young, Jr. became the owner."[66] From him ownership was conveyed to another son, John W. Young, and then John sold to George M. Cannon in 1889.[67]

Parts of the land had already been disposed of before Brigham's death with sales in 1867 and 1868 to members of the Pratt family. These purchases were on the south end of the farm, approximately south of Driggs Avenue on the west side of Seventh East, and south of the Forest Farm House between Seventh and Eighth East. "Hyrum J. Jensen, a carpenter by trade, according to family tradition, was given his home site on the east side of Seventh East, north of Simpson Avenue in payment for his services in helping to build the Farm House and other aids."[68]

In 1877 the Farmer's Ward was divided from the Sugar House Ward, and the meeting for this important change was held in the Farm House, then occupied by Brigham Young's brother Phinehas Young. Ward meetings and Sunday School continued to be held there until 1878 when the district schoolhouse was rented for Sunday use.

Other transactions of land also transferred ownership of parts of the Forest Farm to other members of the Young family. Still later a section known as the Hansen addition became the Forest Dale development. George M. Cannon divided the land into building lots in 1888 and 1890, making Forest Dale official. The farmland was divided into small building lots until houses, city streets, and a freeway encroached. However, local residents took pride in knowing their settlement was originally Brigham Young's historical experimental farm.[69] Some of the green space has been preserved in Fairmont Park, with the swimming pool a reminder of the natural springs that made it such a desirable place to live and farm.

As the Farm House changed hands, remodeling altered the structure, with the large porches and the rear of the house, including the long hall, removed. Only a portion of the original house remained, now on a small lot. Gwen and Frank Wilcox purchased it in 1954 and lived there for fifteen years. In 1969, they proposed giving their equity in the house to the LDS Church, provided that it would be restored. Approval was given, the remaining mortgage paid, and the physical restoration commenced.[70]

In 1969 the Brigham Young Farm House was turned over to the state of Utah for restoration.[71] That was completed in 1970, in time for April conference. In 1975 it was moved from what is now Seventh East and Twenty-third South (Ashton Street) to its present location, Old Deseret Village at This Is the Place Heritage Park at the mouth of Emigration Canyon.

The Gothic revival–style house has been restored to its former status as "a modern cottage of generous proportions."[72] The porches have been rebuilt and the interior furnished with some original items from Brigham Young's time, and other furnishings typical of the period when the Farm House was used by the family. It is now staffed by volunteer docents rather than busy wives, family, and farmhands.

Florence Jacobsen said of the project: "Restoration meant a lot of paint scraping, and a careful consideration of what the home was like. The small pane windows, the wood painted to look like hardwood on the doors, the floors restored to their original wood, and of course, furnishings that either were original to the Farm House, or from that period must all be considered."[73] Every effort was made to do it correctly. This included using many original cane-bottom chairs, a set of white china ordered by Brigham, although never actually used in his lifetime, and even utensils that would have been in use then. Various other items such as a clock that was Susan Snively's are also displayed. An interesting item in the restored Farm House is a framed wreath made of hair. Making ornaments and wreaths from hair was a popular pastime, and Brigham was presented with this large wreath that contained hair from each member of his family.

Fabrics for curtains, carefully selected, give the feeling of stepping back in time upon entering the restored Farm House. Authentic items such as flatirons, which were heated on the stove, a tin bread box, a large flour bin, handmade braided rugs on the floor, a cradle for a baby, plus quilts on the lounge in the kitchen and on the beds all add to the atmosphere. The mattress on the servant's bed is lumpy, as it likely was when in use.

Susan Snively's clock is one of the few furniture pieces in the restored farmhouse that belonged to one of the wives who lived in the house. Photo by Elinor Hyde.

Restoration has continued outside the house. Animals on the premises have been "back- bred" to achieve animals that represent the pioneer era. Back-breeding means the runts of litters are picked for reproduction purposes, instead of the best of the litters. The results are a gradual change in character, color, and smaller size of the animals, and although not 100 percent accurate, give a feel for how pioneer animals looked.[74] The Farm House is still surrounded by a large tract of land, unique in the sparsity of other buildings. However, with the expansion of Old Deseret Village, the area is quickly filling in with additional restored historical buildings and replicas of early Salt Lake architecture. It is a fitting showplace for a unique residence of Brigham Young.

Chapter 8

THE GARDO HOUSE

SANDRA DAWN BRIMHALL AND MARK D. CURTIS

On 26 November 1921, a crowd gathered at 70 East South Temple Street in downtown Salt Lake City to watch the demolition of a Victorian mansion. One onlooker was ninety-year-old John Brown. In spite of the November chill and the fact it was his birthday, Brown had come to pay his last respects to the doomed building; he had been the construction foreman for the house when it was built almost fifty years earlier. But even for those Utahns without personal ties, the mansion was special. It was the Gardo House.[1]

The Gardo House, or Amelia's Palace, has always been the object of great curiosity and controversy. At one time, the mansion was heralded as one of the finest homes between Chicago and the West Coast. Its unusual architecture and exquisite interior are legendary. The Gardo House was unique among Brigham Young's homes because it was designed from the beginning to serve as an official church residence.

During the last years of his life, Brigham Young perceived a need for a place where he could receive official callers and entertain dignitaries who traveled great distances to see him.[2] The idea for such a residence was not without precedent. Joseph Smith built the Nauvoo House in compliance with a revelation that instructed him to "build a house unto my name . . . a house for boarding, a house that strangers may come from afar to lodge therein; therefore let it be a good house, worthy of all acceptation. . . ."[3]

President Young began building his official residence in 1873.[4] The lot he selected for the new home was located on the corner directly south of the Beehive House. The Mormon prophet was fond of naming his homes and borrowed the name "Gardo" from a favorite Spanish novel.[5]

Joseph Ridges and William Harrison Folsom worked together to draw the plans and superintend the mansion's construction.[6] Both men were highly respected in their chosen professions. Ridges was the designer and builder of the famous tabernacle organ on Temple Square. Folsom, who was Young's father-in-law, served as church architect from 1861 to 1867. He played a vital role in the design and construction of the Salt Lake Theatre, Salt Lake Tabernacle, St.

George Tabernacle, the Salt Lake, Manti, and St. George Temples, and many private residences.[7]

There were widespread rumors the Gardo House was being built for Folsom's daughter, Harriet Amelia Folsom Young, who was allegedly Brigham Young's favorite wife. Amelia first became acquainted with President Young on 3 October 1860, when he welcomed the Folsoms, and others of their wagon company, to Salt Lake City. Their courtship began almost immediately and they announced their engagement in August 1862. Amelia made a favorable impression on others besides Young. Tall and graceful, with blue eyes and light brown hair, she was intelligent, charming, and a gifted conversationalist. She was also an accomplished pianist and vocalist. The couple were married 24 January 1863, and three weeks later Amelia moved to the second floor of the Lion House. She remained there throughout her marriage, except for a short period when she lived at the Beehive House.[8]

Most of the gossip concerning Amelia appears to have originated with Ann Eliza Webb Young, who divorced Brigham Young in 1876.[9] Ann Eliza claimed Amelia demanded to be "first wife," insisted on her own home, and that she was pampered, ill-tempered, and despised.[10] The other wives and children in the family defended Amelia's character and denied any blatant partiality by Young as a husband and father. Amelia also denied she had ever received a favored position in the family, claiming her husband was "equally kind and attentive to all in his lifetime" and that he left "each surviving wife an equal legacy."[11]

In his will, Brigham Young provided both Mary Ann Angell Young and Harriet Amelia Folsom Young a life tenancy in the Gardo House.[12] It was his intent that Amelia would serve there as his official hostess. Family members agreed that Amelia, who was young, childless, refined, and talented, was the ideal wife to assume such large social responsibilities.[13]

Progress on the mansion was slow. There were numerous delays in obtaining the necessary lumber, plaster, granite, and glass.[14] President Young, who was often away on church business, was seldom available to sign requisitions or make important decisions. On one occasion, after returning to Salt Lake City from a visit to St. George, he expressed displeasure with the style of the home, calling it his "tabernacle organ."[15]

After three years' construction, the Gardo House was nearing completion when an unfortunate accident occurred near Arsenal Hill. Arsenal Hill, now Capitol Hill, was a repository for gunpowder and explosives sold by local businessmen. On the evening of 5 April 1876, two young men, Charles Richardson and Frank Hill, were hunting wild chickens and fired their guns into one of the powder magazines.

The resulting explosion, and subsequent concussions of two other magazines, showered the city with five hundred tons of boulders, concrete, and pebbles. The debris crashed through roofs, shattered windows, and plowed through gardens and streets. Many persons were injured and some, including Richardson and Hill, were killed.[16]

Several of the glass windows in the Gardo House were broken and new glass had to be ordered from the East. By 20 May 1876 the windows were reinstalled

WILLIAM HARRISON FOLSOM
Born March 25, 1815, Portsmouth, N. H.
Came to Utah Oct. 3, 1860, Joseph W.
Young Company.

and construction resumed.[17] However, Brigham Young never lived to see the completed mansion. He died on 29 August 1877.

The settlement of Brigham Young's estate divided it into three parts: church properties in Young's name, properties belonging to his private estate, and properties where legal ownership was unknown. Although the Gardo House was classified in the last category, the mansion was credited to Young's heirs, instead of the church, at the highly inflated figure of $120,000. This allowed for a sum of approximately $20,000 to be paid to Mary Ann Angell Young and Harriet Amelia Folsom Young for their interest in the Gardo House. The two women occupied the mansion for a short period, to secure their claims, while it was still under construction.[18]

In 1879, Amelia moved to a new home located on the southwest corner of 100 West South Temple Street. The residence, nicknamed the "Junior Gardo," was designed and built by William Harrison Folsom. Amelia's father, aware of the problems involving her husband's estate, insisted Amelia have a home with an unclouded title. Folsom made a trade for the lot with the Young family, giving them a large block of Southern Utah Railroad stock.[19]

PRESIDENT JOHN TAYLOR'S STAY AT THE GARDO HOUSE

John Taylor succeeded Brigham Young as church president. George Q. Cannon and other church leaders suggested he occupy the Gardo House when it was completed, but he repeatedly refused the offer. When church members unanimously voted, during their semiannual general conference on 9 April 1879, to make the Gardo House the official parsonage for LDS Church presidents, President Taylor reluctantly accepted their decision.[20]

Left: William Folsom had helped to design homes, temples and tabernacles before he was asked to work on the design for the Gardo House. The house's nickname, Amelia's Palace, came from his daughter, Amelia Folsom Young. Used by permission, Utah State Historical Society, all rights reserved.

Right: Brigham Young expected the Gardo House to be as much a public building as a home. His fifty-first wife, Amelia Folsom, would manage the receptions and parties held there and care for guests who might stay. The building is sometimes called Amelia's Palace after her. Used by permission, Utah State Historical Society, all rights reserved.

Moses Thatcher, William Jennings, and Angus M. Cannon were appointed as a committee to oversee the completion of the mansion.[21] It was estimated the church expended from $30,000 to $50,000 to finish the building and furnish its interior.[22] The finished home was four stories high, including the basement, with a tower on the northwest corner. All of the foundation and basement were made of granite. The exterior walls were constructed of studding, lined with adobes, and covered with lath and plaster. The interior woodwork, which included a spiral staircase, paneling, and decorative trim, was carved in black walnut by Ralph Ramsey. Ramsey, a famous local wood-carver, had previously carved the eagle mounted on Eagle Gate. Elegant furnishings and mirrors, imported from Europe, and paintings by local artists graced all the rooms.[23]

The Gardo House was designed in the French Second Empire Victorian style, although it had numerous additional elements besides this narrow description such as a mansard roof, arched dormer, elaborate bay window, tower, and veranda. It resembled many of the homes being built in Chicago around the same time period, yet it would have been equally in style in San Francisco. The opulence and spaciousness of the home lent an air of elegance both outside and inside the structure. The exterior decorations were redesigned several times throughout the years, subject to the owners and their preferences. The Gardo House was known for its many windows and splendid views. One local newspaper reported that there were over 150 windows with a different view from each window. The mansion provided a spectacular view of Salt Lake City's center, its historical buildings, and the ever-expanding population throughout the valley.

With over forty-five rooms in its four stories, the home commanded a distinctive presence in the downtown area. The main floor contained a room called the "fountain house" that functioned mostly as a parlor for guests. The dining area spread from one side of the house to the other and could easily seat thirty to thirty-five people. A sweeping grand staircase extended to the second floor, which consisted mostly of bedrooms and bathrooms. The third floor contained bedrooms and bathrooms as well, but one unique aspect was an office located on each floor. A self-supporting circular staircase led from the third floor to the tower room on the fourth floor. This room had a set of doors that opened out onto the roof allowing a magnificent view of the area.

On 27 December 1881 the *Deseret News* published a letter from John Taylor announcing a public reception and tour of the Gardo House on 2 January 1882 from 11:00 a.m. until 3:00 p.m.[24] Over two thousand persons attended the reception and toured the home. President Taylor greeted all the visitors, who were entertained by two bands and several renditions by the Tabernacle Choir. Moses Thatcher, William Jennings, and Angus M. Cannon and their wives were among the guests as well as other notables such as Joseph F. Smith, Franklin D. Richards, Francis M. Lyman, John H. Smith, and Daniel H. Wells.[25] A year later, on 22 February 1883, the mansion was dedicated as a house unto the Lord in a prayer offered by apostle Franklin D. Richards.[26]

John Taylor's move to the Gardo House was regarded by Mormons as the literal fulfillment of a prophecy. Some years before, when Taylor's circumstances had been the poorest, Heber C. Kimball had boldly prophesied Taylor would someday live in the largest and finest mansion in Salt Lake City.[27]

There were some Mormons, and many nonmembers, who were not pleased with the reception or Taylor's occupancy of the home. Rachel Emma Woolley Simmons recorded in her journal: "Brother John Taylor gives a reception in the Gardo House. . . . I have no fault to find with him for moving into that house, but I think it would have been more becoming if he had stayed in his own home. It was a great expense to furnish it in the style it had to be. . . . I don't believe he is enjoying it much. I heard that his wives were not pleased with the move."[28]

The *Daily Tribune* was extremely critical of the affair and of the church in general. In an editorial published the day before the reception, the newspaper wrote,

> The favored saints have received an invitation to call upon President John Taylor at the Amelia Palace tomorrow. . . . We want the poor Mormons . . . to mark the carpets, mirrors, the curtains and the rest, and then to go home and look at the squalor of their own homes, their unkempt wives, their miserable children growing up in despair and ignorance, and then to reflect how much better it would have been for them, instead of working hard for wages . . . if they had only started out as did Uncle John, determined to serve God for nothing but hash.

The *Tribune* accused the church of attempting "to build up an aristocracy in Utah, where the few are to rule in luxury, while the many, to support the luxury, are to toil and suffer."[29]

During John Taylor's administration as president of the LDS Church, he moved into the Gardo House only after much urging. He was uncomfortable with the opulent image of the building. Used by permission, Utah State Historical Society, all rights reserved.

On 5 January 1882 the *Deseret News* published a rebuttal to the *Tribune*'s scathing editorial. The newspaper pointed out Taylor had taken up his residence in the Gardo House in response to the vote of the Mormon people and that he, as church president, should "be at least as well housed and cared for as prominent men in Church or State here or elsewhere." The *Deseret News* further stated, "We are pleased to see that one of the veterans of the latter-day work, who has traveled from land to land and from sea to sea, who has suffered with the exiles and bled with the martyrs, forsaken all things for the truth . . . is now surrounded with comfort, and has a place to lay his head and to receive his friends."[30]

John Taylor wrote a letter, published in the *Deseret News*, expressing his feelings about the situation. He reminded critics of his initial reluctance to move to the Gardo House and his concern that his occupancy of the mansion would place an intolerable barrier between him and church members. Taylor acknowledged his family had also been opposed to the move, preferring their own homes and familiar surroundings. He explained he was eventually persuaded that "Zion should become the praise of the whole earth, and that we in this land should take a prominent and leading part in the arts, sciences, architecture, literature, and in everything that would tend to . . . exalt and ennoble Zion." Taylor concluded that as church president, it was his duty "to take the lead in everything that is calculated to . . . place Zion where she ought to be, first and foremost among the peoples."[31]

The *Daily Tribune* was right in its assertion Taylor had moved into the Gardo House during a period of economic hardship. In the 1880s, overpopulation in Utah resulted in a scarcity of farmland, unemployment and poverty.[32] And both newspapers were correct in their analysis that the issue of the Gardo House was much broader than the mere occupation of the mansion by a Mormon leader. To Mormons, who had celebrated their church's jubilee in April 1880, the house was a symbol of achievement. It was tangible proof that the persecutions and hardships they had endured over the past fifty years were not in vain.[33] On the other hand, many non- Mormons viewed Taylor's installation in the home as a threat in the continuing struggle for economic and political supremacy.

In 1882 there was another important event that intensified suspicions and ill feelings between Mormons and non-Mormons. In March that year, Congress passed the Edmunds Act, which amended the Morrill Antibigamy Act of 1862. The Morrill Act had outlawed polygamy, disincorporated the church, and prohibited it from owning more than $50,000 worth of property not directly used for religious purposes.[34] The Edmunds Act declared polygamy a felony with up to five years' imprisonment and/or a $500 fine, disfranchised polygamists, and declared them ineligible for jury duty or public office.[35]

John Taylor held a meeting in the Gardo House with sixteen general authorities of the church to discuss the Edmunds law and its threat to their religious practices. According to Wilford Woodruff, "President Taylor with the rest of us came to the conclusion that we could not swap off the Kingdom of God or any of its Laws or Principles for a state government."[36]

The Mormon leader endeavored to conduct church business as usual within the Gardo House, despite persecution. Every morning at 8:30, George Reynolds, secretary to the First Presidency, reported for work at the mansion. Reynolds recorded at least two important revelations that Taylor received in the Gardo House. The first of these revelations was received on 13 October 1882. George Teasdale and Heber J. Grant were called to fill two vacancies in the Quorum of the Twelve Apostles and Seymour B. Young was asked to serve as one of the first seven presidents of the Seventies. The revelation also called for increased missionary work among the various Indian tribes in the West and for a general reformation among priesthood bearers and church members. The second revelation, received six months later in April 1883, reorganized the Seventies quorums throughout the church.[37]

President Taylor eventually decided, in his private life, to outwardly conform as much as possible to the requirements of the antipolygamy laws. He told his wives, "We are living in this building [Gardo House] together . . . under the circumstances it will be better for me or for you to leave this place; you can take your choice. . . ."[38] Taylor's wives opted to return to their own homes and his sister, Agnes Schwartz, became matron of the home.[39]

Mormons began to feel "the teeth" of the Edmunds Act when federal officers arrived in Utah to replace existing lawmen and enforce the new law. Federal marshals made raids on Mormon households, searching for lawbreakers and witnesses. Fear and distrust were everywhere. Children were instructed not to talk with strangers or divulge their names, their parents' names, or where they lived. Polygamists developed a variety of ingenious methods to avoid arrest and many went on the "underground."[40] The "underground" included hide-outs in homes, barns, fields, ditches, and nearby canyons. Some polygamists even left the territory, serving overseas missions or moving to Mexico or Canada.[41]

The Gardo House also served as a meeting and hiding place for those fleeing from federal marshals. Joseph F. Smith, who later served as fifth president of the Mormon Church, met one of his plural wives, Mary Schwartz, at the mansion.[42]

According to John Whitaker, son-in-law of John Taylor, "The Gardo House was a rendezvous where the brethren and sisters on the underground would often come in the night to meet their loved ones . . . Samuel Sudbury, a mysterious man, was custodian of the Gardo House and was ever on the alert for the approach of marshals and deputies searching for polygamists. It was the rule that the Gardo House was to be closed at 10 p.m. without exception, and no stranger was permitted to enter after that hour."[43]

Church leaders were considered prime catches by federal lawmen. Taylor's homes, the church offices, and the Gardo House were always under the surveillance of spies and deputy marshals.[44] As persecution mounted, President Taylor also decided to go "underground." His last public appearance was in the Salt Lake Tabernacle on 1 February 1885.[45]

A few weeks later, on 13 March 1885, a massive raid was made on the Gardo House to capture Taylor. The raid was unsuccessful but other raids soon followed. Taylor's tough-minded sister, Agnes Schwartz, often held raiding marshals and deputies at bay at the front door of the mansion. No one was admitted inside the home unless they presented papers, properly signed by a federal judge.[46]

On another occasion, deputies searched the house for Charles W. Penrose, editor of the *Deseret News*, who was hiding under the name of Dr. Williams. The deputies combed the house from top to bottom but could not find Penrose who was hiding in a specially built closet on the top floor. At one point, the lawmen stood within a foot of him. Penrose later recalled, "I had such a cold and wanted to cough so badly I held my breath until I almost burst, and was thankful Mr. Frank Dyer, the U. S. Marshal, left so I could relieve myself coughing."[47]

In his journal, Wilford Woodruff recorded the details of another raid he regarded as one of the most important events of his life. On 8 February 1886 he and other apostles held a meeting in the church historian's office. During the meeting, approximately twenty federal marshals surrounded the church historian's office and the Gardo House. Woodruff believed that he and Erastus Snow were the only two persons liable to be arrested and so the two men locked themselves in a small bedroom. They waited over an hour while marshals made a thorough search of the Gardo House, Lion House, Beehive House, the president's office and the tithing office. When the marshals turned their attention to the historian's office, Woodruff prayed to the Lord to direct him. When Woodruff finished his prayer

> Brother Jenson stept in to the Room with his glasses on. I put my Glasses on. I said to Brother Jenson I will walk with you across the street to the other Office. We walked out the door to the gate together. There was a Marshal [on] each side of the Gate & a Dozen more on each side of the side walk leading to the Gardo. . . . And the Eyes of all the Marshals was Closed By the power of God. . . . The saints knew me. The Marshals did not. . . . I recognized No one nor paid attention to any one. The dangerous feature of the operation was the Eyes of all the Brethren in the Streets followed me from [the] time I left the Historian's office until I Entered the Presidet's office. . . . When I shut the door of the Clerks office Behind me I felt to shout Glory Halluluhuh though I said Nothing ownly thank God.

Erastus Snow also eluded the lawmen.[48]

On 1 November 1886 John Taylor's family assembled in the Gardo House to celebrate his seventy-eighth birthday. Taylor, who remained in hiding, dared not

attend but sent a letter expressing his love and concern for his wives and children. He deeply mourned that he was unable to comfort two of his wives, Jane and Sophia, who were dangerously ill. Taylor closed his letter, "Some of you have written that you 'would like to have a peep at me.' I heartily reciprocate that feeling, and would like to have a 'peep' at you on this occasion, but in my bodily absence my spirit and peace shall be with you."[49]

A few months later, on 19 February 1887, church leaders' worst fears were realized when Congress passed the Edmunds-Tucker Act. The new law dissolved the Corporation of the Church of Jesus Christ of Latter-day Saints, abolished Utah women suffrage, disinherited children of plural marriages, took control of Utah's Mormon-dominated public schools, dissolved the Perpetual Emigrating Company, abolished the territorial militia, and confiscated virtually all church property.[50]

The crusade against polygamy took a heavy toll on the church and its followers. John Taylor died, while still in hiding, in Kaysville, Utah, on 25 July 1887. Many church members believed he was a martyr for the principles of his faith. On 28 July 1887 Wilford Woodruff went to the Gardo House to view Taylor's remains that were lying in state at the mansion.[51] The next morning, at 6 a.m., the Taylor family assembled at the Gardo House to pay their last respects to their husband and father before his body was removed to the Tabernacle for the funeral.[52]

The day after the funeral, a lawsuit was brought against the church in the Utah Supreme Court by the United States district attorney for Utah to enforce the escheatment provisions of the Edmunds-Tucker Act.[53] Frank H. Dyer, United States marshal in Utah, was appointed by the court as receiver to hold and administer church property. Dyer first seized the general tithing office, Gardo House, church historian's office, and then other church properties such as buildings, farms, mines, livestock, and stock in various corporations.[54] The Mormons were forced to pay the government high rental fees to retain the use of their property. Rent for the Gardo House was initially set at $75 per month but later skyrocketed to $450 per month.[55]

In this view of Salt Lake City, looking northeast from approximately Second South and Main, the Beehive House is on the far left. Next right, the Gardo can be seen dominating the street. The large building at right center is the Salt Lake Theatre. Used by permission, Utah State Historical Society, all rights reserved.

Today the site of the Gardo House is part of the ZCMI Center. Photo by Judy Dykman and Colleen Whitley.

PRESIDENT WILFORD WOODRUFF OCCUPIES THE GARDO HOUSE

Wilford Woodruff succeeded John Taylor as fourth president of the church. He kept an office in the Gardo House, where he frequently held public and private gatherings and occasionally spent the night. Woodruff, who was indignant at the loss of church property, recorded in his journal, "This Law of Congress to take all the Property of the Church of Jesus Christ of latter Day Saints is the most Ungodly and unconstitutional Law Ever Enacted by any Congress since the foundation of the American Government."[56]

The new prophet spent part of each day at the Gardo House attending to correspondence, conducting interviews, and signing temple recommends. On Thursdays and Saturdays, the First Presidency and other church leaders held prayer meetings in the mansion.[57] They also met regularly to discuss the completion of the Salt Lake Temple, the operation of Zions Cooperative Mercantile Institution (ZCMI), the selection of delegates to Congress and the ordination of new apostles. On 7 October 1889 Woodruff, his counselors, and the other apostles ordained M. W. Merrill, A. H. Lund, and Abram H. Cannon to fill vacancies in the Quorum of the Twelve Apostles.[58]

In August and September of 1890, Wilford Woodruff took a 2,400-mile journey, visiting the principal Mormon settlements throughout Wyoming, Colorado, Arizona, and New Mexico. After returning home for a brief stay, he traveled to California in company with George Q. Cannon, H. B. Clawson, and other church leaders. In San Francisco, Woodruff met with business and political leaders Isaac Trumbo, Judge Morrill Estee, Senator Leland Stanford, and Henry Biglow to discuss the past difficulties and future prospects of the Mormon people.[59]

President Woodruff returned to Salt Lake City on 21 September 1890, convinced by what he had seen and heard that the very existence of the church was in jeopardy. The government was threatening to confiscate church temples, halting all ordinances for the living and dead, imprison the First Presidency and Twelve Apostles, and confiscate the personal property of the Saints. The beleaguered prophet arrived at the conclusion that he, as president of the Church of Jesus Christ of Latter-day Saints, must act for the temporal salvation of the church by advising members not to enter into plural marriages. Woodruff sought, and received, divine confirmation for this decision on 23 September 1890 in the upper parlor of the Gardo House. The next day, Woodruff's counselors and the apostles sustained the revelation to abandon polygamy and drafted what later became known as the Manifesto.[60]

On 5 October 1890 church leaders held a special meeting in the Gardo House to discuss a recent telegram sent from Washington, D.C., by Utah delegate John T. Caine. Caine had learned that the government would not accept the Manifesto unless all church members officially affirmed it. The next day, at general conference, Mormons unanimously voted in favor of the document.[61]

The Manifesto eased some of the tensions between Mormons and non-Mormons. Church leaders were cautiously optimistic the government would eventually return their stolen property and reinstate their rights as citizens.[62] Meetings were held in the Gardo House to discuss local, state, and national politics as well as religion. There were frequent debates whether Utahns should align themselves with the national Democratic and Republican Parties. In the past, the political parties in Utah had been the Mormon People's Party versus the non-Mormon Liberal Party.[63]

Church leaders eventually came to the conclusion that the Mormons' political solidarity had been a factor in creating gentile opposition to the church.[64] In May or June of 1891, a special political meeting was held in the Gardo House. According to James Henry Moyle, who was present at the meeting,

> We were there for some time, but little if anything was done until we were advised that George Q. Cannon, then on the underground, was to be present. We had not seen any member of the First Presidency of the Church for some time. . . . I can only remember the gist of what he said, but it was to this effect . . . "Our people think they are Democrats, but they as a rule have not studied the difference between the two parties. If they go into the Democratic Party the Gentiles will go into the Republican Party . . . and we will have the same old fight over again under new names. So, as many as possible of our people must go into the Republican Party."[65]

Moyle told Cannon he had always had a strong preference for the Democratic Party and Cannon reassured him that he, and others like him, should feel free to follow their conscience. Church leaders later published a statement encouraging Mormons to join the national parties and elders were sent to various stake conferences to instruct the people along the same lines.[66]

THE KEELEY INSTITUTE

In November 1891, Bishop J. B. Winder served notice on the federal receiver, Frank H. Dyer, that Wilford Woodruff would vacate the Gardo House by the

Walford Woodruff 1895

The main floor parlor became a focal point for parties and receptions. Its walls were decorated in a rich rose satin brocade and woodwork of ivory enamel. The carpet was reseda green and covered in places with Persian silk rugs and some beautiful skins. Much of the furniture was from France's Louis XVI period, mixed with a few locally purchased pieces. Used by permission, Utah State Historical Society, all rights reserved.

first of December. From 1887 to 1891, the church had paid the government over $28,000 in rental fees for the use of its own property. Church leaders had hoped the Gardo House would be judicially declared an official church parsonage, exempt from escheatment under the laws of the land. When no exemption materialized, Woodruff decided he would rather move than continue to pay the $450 per month rent that was required.[67] Upon learning of the church's intent to leave the mansion, the receiver immediately advertised for a new tenant. The Gardo House was eventually leased to the Keeley Institute in January 1892 for $200 per month, much less than the church had been forced to pay.[68]

The Keeley Institute was an organization established for the treatment of alcohol and drug addiction. Its founder, Leslie Enraught Keeley, was born in Ireland 4 May 1834. His parents moved to Quebec, Canada, in 1835 and when he was a young man Keeley moved to Beardstown, Illinois, where he studied medicine with a physician.[69]

During the Civil War, he served as an assistant surgeon with an Illinois regiment, participated in Sherman's march to the sea, and was captured by the Confederates. Keeley completed his medical degree in Chicago in 1864, while on leave from the army. He eventually settled in Dwight, Illinois, where he engaged in the general practice of medicine.[70]

In 1879 Keeley announced he had discovered a cure for alcohol and drug addiction. The following year, he established the first Keeley Institute in Dwight, Illinois. The cure was allegedly made from "double chloride of gold," but was actually a composition of atropine, strychnine, arsenic, cinchona, and glycerine. Patients, who were gradually weaned from their habits, received periodic injections and ingested a dram of Keeley's formula every two hours. They were also required to follow a healthful regime of diet, fresh air, exercise, and sleep. Keeley

carefully avoided the appearance of quackery by employing only physicians at his establishments and keeping the cost of treatment as low as possible. The program was one of the first in the nation to recognize alcoholism as a disease and offer rehabilitation instead of punishment. Keeley's activities attracted little attention until 1891, when the *Chicago Tribune* published a number of articles praising his work and launching a wave of popularity for the treatment.[71]

The "gold cure" was the most controversial alcohol treatment of its time. Opponents argued there was no such substance as "double chloride of gold" and warned of possible side effects such as rashes, fatigue, weight loss, mental confusion, and even blindness. Despite such warnings, over 400,000 individuals enrolled in the program, which was endorsed by churches and temperance workers. Franchises, using Keeley's name, sprang up across the United States, Canada, Mexico, and England.[72]

The franchise that rented the Gardo House was the only Keeley Institute in Utah and was considered the "most thoroughly equipped institute in the West." Patrons were predominantly middle-class men, although "ladies" visiting the institute for treatment were assured of seclusion and privacy.[73]

The Keeley Institute occupied the Gardo House for a little over one year. On 4 January 1893 President Benjamin Harrison signed a proclamation granting limited amnesty and pardons to Mormons who had abstained from the practice of plural marriage since the issuance of the Manifesto.[74] One year later, President Grover Cleveland pardoned all polygamists, restoring their civil rights, and signed an enabling act to permit the people of Utah to prepare a state government.[75] Church property, including the Gardo House, was eventually

Top: The main parlor opened onto a series of other rooms to provide easy access for entertaining large groups of people. Used by permission, Utah State Historical Society, all rights reserved.

Above: From his study, Colonel Edwin Holmes planned civic improvements and worked on his investments. Used by permission, Utah State Historical Society, all rights reserved.

Top: The dining room had a Gothic decor, with ceiling, woodwork, and furniture in a richly carved Belgian oak. The walls had a dull gold glaze with bronze, dull greens, red, and silver in Gothic designs. The ceiling had a fresco painted above the table and the carpet was a rich red. The draperies were red with appliques of cloth of gold. Used by permission, Utah State Historical Society, all rights reserved.

Above: The dining table could seat sixteen people comfortably. Brigham Young designed the chairs with their extremely high, exquisitely carved backs. Used by permission, Utah State Historical Society, all rights reserved.

returned to the First Presidency.[76] On 15 August 1894 Wilford Woodruff recorded in his journal, "I went to the Gardo with Cannon & Smith Clawson and Trumbo. The Building was badly damaged by the Keeley Institute."[77]

MR. AND MRS. ISAAC TRUMBO'S STAY AT THE GARDO HOUSE

The church expended over $2,000 to clean and repair damages to the mansion.[78] Church leaders then decided to discontinue the practice of using the Gardo House as an official church parsonage and made arrangements to rent the mansion to Mr. and Mrs. Isaac Trumbo.

Isaac Trumbo was born in 1858 at Carson Valley, located in the Nevada section of the Utah Territory. Although his grandfather, Colonel John Reese, was a Mormon, Trumbo's mother married out of the church and he grew up without ever affiliating with Mormonism. During his childhood, his family moved to Salt Lake City where one of their neighbors was Hiram B. Clawson, a cousin of Trumbo's mother. Clawson, a Mormon, was one of the city's most prominent men.

As a young man, Trumbo moved to California where he made his fortune through successful mining and business ventures. In California, he joined the national guard where he achieved the rank of colonel, a title he used throughout his life.[79]

In 1887, he and Alexander Badlam, another California businessman with a Mormon heritage, visited Washington, D.C., and met with Utah congressional delegate John T. Caine. They expressed sympathy for the Mormons and the hardships they were experiencing as a result

of the newly passed Edmunds-Tucker Act.[80] The two men visited Utah on their return trip to California to explore mining and railroad properties and to visit church leaders. Trumbo's interest in Utah was probably renewed by his relationship with Hiram B. Clawson, who was also involved with mining interests in Eureka, Utah. At the time of their visit, Utah was fighting its sixth battle for statehood. Trumbo soon laid his business ventures aside and began an eight-year crusade for Utah statehood.[81]

He masterminded a successful public relations campaign that promoted favorable newspaper coverage and lobbied in Washington, D.C., for the repeal of anti-Mormon legislation and for statehood. The Trumbos, expecting Isaac would be rewarded for his efforts by a senatorship, decided to leave California and establish their residency in Utah.[82]

The couple decided to move into the Gardo House as a favor to church leaders and agreed to act as hosts for dignitaries when they visited Salt Lake City. Emma Trumbo, along with her interior decorators, came to Utah ahead of her husband to prepare the mansion for occupancy.[83] Her arrival caused a flutter of excitement among local society leaders who anticipated lavish socials at the Gardo House on a San Francisco scale.[84] The Trumbos spent months, and great sums of money, to redecorate the home and transport many of their beautiful furnishings from their stately San Francisco residence.[85]

An assortment of people, including church leaders and members of the Mormon underground, took an interest in the project and came to view the restoration. One of the visitors toured the mansion with Emma and pointed out various places of concealment, such as hollowed walls and mattresses, where

Top: The kitchen in the basement had two outstanding features. One was the dumbwaiter at the back left in this picture that carried food directly from the kitchen to the dining room. The other was the light fixture, designed to operate on both gas and electricity. Used by permission, Utah State Historical Society, all rights reserved.

Above: The hallway by the second floor stairway featured a gallery of Native Americans. Used by permission, Utah State Historical Society, all rights reserved.

polygamists hid from federal lawmen. He also called her attention to a crack in the boarded ceiling of the Gardo House's tower where fugitives watched their pursuers.[86]

Utah finally achieved statehood on 4 January 1896, nearly fifty years after the first Mormon pioneers entered the Salt Lake Valley. Trumbo wrote a letter to church leaders, reminding them of his great sacrifices and his desire to become one of Utah's first senators.[87] He arrived in Salt Lake City on a Sunday, hoping to avoid a brass band or crowd at the railway station. When no such fanfare materialized, the Trumbos were chagrined and somewhat bitter. Emma later recalled, "He might as well have chosen a week day, for all the difference it would have made. What the Mormons wanted was Statehood. Gratitude? That had flown to the mountain tops, and frozen there."[88]

His lukewarm reception at the railway station was a harbinger of things to come. Trumbo never became a senator due to a variety of reasons. He had tried to curry the favor of both Mormons and non-Mormons and was distrusted by all. Many Utahns regarded him as a California interloper, motivated entirely by self-interest. Church leaders denied having made any promises made to Trumbo for his services and George Q. Cannon questioned his character. "He is not a person whose manners and characteristics we would desire to represent us," he wrote, "for he is very ignorant, and then he would be, no doubt, a boodler, accepting bribes for services which he would render." Cannon was referring to the fact that Trumbo, and some of his associates, had been suspected in some circles of buying newspaper and delegate support.[89]

According to B. H. Roberts, there had always been a general understanding that Utah's senatorships would be divided between Mormons and non-Mormons. It had also been assumed that territorial delegate Frank J. Cannon, son of church leader George Q. Cannon, would be elected as one of Utah's first senators. Non-Mormons, believing if Trumbo became a senator it would mean too much Mormon influence, supported another candidate.[90]

There is some evidence that Trumbo's wife, who later wrote bitter and outrageous falsehoods about Utah, was also one of the causes of his unpopularity. Emma once acknowledged, "My husband said I always gave the Mormons much uneasiness; they never felt quite sure of me."[91]

When their political dreams were unrealized, the Trumbos moved out of the Gardo House and returned to San Francisco. After their departure, William B. Preston, a member of the church's presiding bishopric, sent them a bill for rent due on the mansion. The Trumbos, who claimed they had spent $17,000 on the home, were incensed.

The problem was compounded when a San Francisco newspaper reported Trumbo had been the church's financial agent, using church money and property to further church goals. Wilford Woodruff immediately wrote an apology to the Trumbos and the church promptly made a $10,000 settlement with them concerning the Gardo House.[92] The First Presidency subsequently, at Trumbo's request, issued a written statement that was published in the *Deseret News* on 5 February 1898. The statement defended both Trumbo and the church, denying the allegations he had ever acted as church agent or used church funds for any purpose. The First Presidency concluded, "In the time of our deep distress, when bitterness and hatred were manifested against us in almost every quarter, Colonel Isaac Trumbo came to Utah, and showed an interest in our affairs. . . . [I]t is sufficient to say that probably no single agency contributed so much to making Utah a State as the labors of Colonel Isaac Trumbo and his immediate friends."[93]

In spite of his disappointments and misunderstandings with the people of Utah, Trumbo remained on friendly terms with Wilford Woodruff. The aged prophet visited Trumbo several times in his San Francisco home and during one such visit, he became ill and died on 2 September 1898.[94]

MRS. A. W. McCUNE.
Her beautiful home in the celebrated Gardo House is the repository of a superb and beautiful collection of rare pieces of Carrara marble, gathered from all parts of the world. The most noticeable being a life size statue of Cleopatra.

THE McCUNES OCCUPY THE GARDO HOUSE

Soon after the Trumbos vacated the Gardo House, Bishop J. R. Winder and Alfred William McCune called at church headquarters and visited with members of the First Presidency. McCune told them that he and his wife, Elizabeth, were building a new home and wished to rent the mansion for a term of two or three years. Church leaders, who were relieved to find a suitable new tenant, accepted his offer and rent was set at $150 per month.[95]

Top: Alfred McCune rented the Gardo House while he and his wife were having their mansion built just below the state capitol.

Above: This photo of Elizabeth McCune appeared in a national publication in May 1901 highlighting Utah and its prominent citizens. Used by permission, Utah State Historical Society, all rights reserved.

Alfred William McCune was born 11 July 1849 at Fort Dum Dum, near Calcutta, India. His parents, Sergeant Matthew McCune and Sarah Elizabeth Caroline Scott McCune, were British transplants to India, where Matthew served in the Bengal Artillery of the East India Company. The McCunes were introduced to Mormonism by two English sailors and were baptized in India in 1851.[96]

The family emigrated to America in 1856 and eventually made their way to Utah. McCune spent his boyhood years in Nephi where he and his family, who had lived an aristocratic lifestyle in India, were compelled to become farmers. When the Union Pacific branch of the transcontinental railroad came to Utah in the late 1860s, McCune and his brothers found profitable employment as freighters and graders for the railroad. On 1 July 1872 he married his childhood sweetheart, Elizabeth Ann Claridge.[97]

McCune initially made his fortune as a railroad contractor but later branched out into the timber and mining industries. He owned business interests throughout Utah and in parts of Montana, British Columbia, and South America. McCune was respected by his contemporaries for his integrity, pleasing personality, and for his generous donations to worthy causes. He was civically minded and, like Trumbo, was politically ambitious. In 1899, he ran for the Senate as the Democratic candidate against Republican, and incumbent, Frank J. Cannon. When both candidates and a third, George Q. Cannon, failed to get the majority of votes necessary for a victory, the election of 1899 went down in history as a time when Utah was unable to select a senator. McCune later tried again for the Senate, but was unsuccessful.[98]

Elizabeth McCune had as many diversified interests as her husband. She served in many prominent church positions and became close friends with Susa Young Gates, one of Brigham Young's daughters. Elizabeth was an active

supporter of women's rights. In 1899, she attended the International Congress of Women in London. After being voted patron of the organization, Elizabeth was entertained by Queen Victoria at Windsor Castle.[99]

The McCunes repainted the interior of the Gardo House, added many beautiful touches to its furnishings and fittings, and decorated the parlors and halls with marble statuary from Italy.[100] While the family was living in the mansion, several of the children, little entrepreneurs like their father, set up a lemonade stand in front of the newly constructed Alta Club on South Temple. McCune was surprised and embarrassed when he discovered the stand on his way into the Alta Club with several business associates. He shut down the budding business and sent his children home.[101]

When they moved to their new "McCune Mansion," at 200 North Main, the McCunes brought with them all their furnishings, decorations, and personal belongings from the Gardo House.[102] The church, heavily in debt from the Edmunds-Tucker Act and weary of maintaining the mansion, decided to sell the home to Colonel Edwin F. Holmes at the sacrificial price of $46,000. When the transaction was completed in May 1901, it was the beginning of a new era for the Gardo House.[103]

AMELIA'S PALACE

The mansion achieved its height of glory during the time it was occupied by Holmes and his wife, Susanna Bransford Emery-Holmes, who was famous as Utah's "silver queen." Susanna, or "Susie" as she was known by friends, was born 6 May 1859 in Richmond, Missouri. She crossed the plains when she was five years old and spent her youth in Plumas County, California. In 1884, she made an extended visit to Park City, Utah, to visit friends. It was there she met, and married, her first husband, Albion B. Emery.[104]

Brigham Young ordered this richly carved bedroom set when he first commissioned the construction of the Gardo House. The Holmeses purchased it from his estate. Used by permission, Utah State Historical Society, all rights reserved.

Emery, who was originally from Maine, emigrated to the West in search of gold in 1869. He eventually moved to Tooele, Utah, where he was elected by the Liberal Party as Tooele's first non-Mormon county clerk and deputy recorder. He moved to Park City in 1880, where he worked at a variety of jobs, eventually becoming one of the town's leading citizens.

The couple, and their business partners, became wealthy from investments in Park City's Mayflower and Silver King mines. When Emery died prematurely on 16 June 1894 from heart and liver disease, Susie and their adopted daughter, Louise Grace, became heirs to his estate. Susie proved to be an astute and tough-minded businesswoman, managing her modest legacy into a vast fortune estimated by newspapers at over $50 million.[105]

In the summer of 1895, one of Susie's business partners, Thomas Kearns, introduced her to Colonel Edwin F. Holmes. Holmes, a widower, was a wealthy businessman who had made his fortune in the lumber and mining industries. Born 8 August 1843 in Orleans, New York, he was largely a self-educated and self-made man. During the Civil War, Holmes had enlisted as a private in the Union Army and was eventually promoted to the rank of captain. Like Trumbo, he preferred to be addressed as "colonel," an honorary title, throughout his life. Although Susie was sixteen years his junior, the two discovered they had much in common and they began a lengthy courtship.[106]

Susie and Holmes were married in New York City on 12 October 1899. After a two-year honeymoon in Europe, the couple returned to Utah. Holmes purchased the Gardo House as a birthday present for his new bride. There were widespread rumors at the time of purchase that the couple planned to raze the mansion to make way for a more magnificent palatial residence. The rumors

were quickly laid to rest when they spent over $75,000 to renovate and refurbish their new home.[107]

During their travels in Europe, the Holmeses had purchased beautiful furniture, carpets, draperies, paintings, and bric-a-brac. The couple hired William J. Sinclair, an interior decorator with Chicago's Marshall Field & Company, to organize and install their acquisitions and to supplement whatever else was required. Sinclair and his associates searched European and American cities for additional furniture, fabrics, and light fixtures for the mansion. Susie renamed her new residence Amelia's Palace, reviving the name of its first occupant.[108]

On 26 December 1901 the Holmeses threw a lavish party to celebrate the completed renovation of their new home. The event was hailed by local newspapers as the most brilliant reception in the history of Salt Lake City. *Elite*, a society magazine published in Chicago, described several of the mansion's forty-three rooms in detail.

> The walls here [in the salon] are of old rose satin brocade and the woodwork of ivory enamel. A reseda green carpet covers the floors as background for rugs of priceless value in Persian silk and some skins of great beauty. . . . A second interior is of the dining room where the design is Gothic. The ceiling, woodwork and all the furniture are in Belgian oak. . . . At present the side walls are in dull gold glaze with bronze, dull greens, red and silver in Gothic design. . . . The carpet is of rich red, and the draperies are of red with application of cloth of gold. . . . Midway between the two rooms a Tiffany electric fountain is placed and the tables so arranged that upon feasting occasions the tables may be extended and united with the lovely fountain as a centerpiece. . . . In artistic equipment the house is magnificently magnificent."[109]

The Gardo House soon became the gathering place for an elite, predominantly non-Mormon society that included Senator Thomas Kearns, Governor

Edmund Holmes bought the Gardo House for his wife, Susanna Bransford, and gave it to her as a birthday present. She renovated and furnished the home to make it a true showplace.

Heber M. Wells, financier D. H. Peery, and Perry S. Heath, owner of the *Salt Lake Tribune.* Fort Douglas military officers, clergyman, politicians, businessmen, educators, and the Holmeses' relatives were also regulars at the mansion.[110]

Now it was the Mormons' turn to gaze at the Gardo House and wonder what went on inside. The children of Joseph F. Smith, who resided across the street in the Beehive House, wistfully watched the comings and goings at the Holmeses' residence. There were endless dinners, luncheons, receptions, teas, dances, card parties, and other events for them to observe. On some nights, the Holmeses put out a beautiful red carpet from their door to the end of the sidewalk to greet their expected visitors. The guests, men with big black capes and women in furs, always arrived in elegant horse-drawn carriages.[111]

Susie employed local musicians such as the Deseret Mandolin Orchestra, the Niles Mandolin Orchestra, chamber music groups, and popular vocalists to entertain at her social gatherings. She decorated the rooms of the mansion with a wide variety of carnations, roses, lilies, azaleas, chrysanthemums, tulips, palms, and syringas. The floral centerpieces and trimmings were provided by Huddart Floral. Peter T. Huddart, the premier florist of the period, had apprenticed under the head floral director for the prince of Wales.[112]

The Holmeses, like other wealthy socialites of their time, set aside a day or two each week when they would be "at home" for friends and acquaintances to call. They often received two to three hundred visitors a week. Newspapers and magazines had a field day reporting social events at the Gardo House and chronicling the couple's activities. They were soon widely acknowledged as the reigning king and queen of Salt Lake City society.[113]

The couple actively supported local social and cultural events. When famous entertainers visited the state, the Holmeses often held box office parties at the Salt Lake Theatre or arranged for private performances in their home. On 17 May 1902 a local newspaper announced Susie had engaged the services of a pianist celebrated worldwide, Alberto Jonas, for a musicale at the Gardo House. Jonas had received rave reviews for his performances at Carnegie Hall and with the Boston Symphony Orchestra. He was the founder and director of the renowned Michigan Conservatory of Music, located in Detroit. The Holmeses invited over two hundred guests to the concert and arranged for Jonas to give another recital at the Salt Lake Theatre for the general public. His musicale was considered to be one of the outstanding cultural events of the year.[114]

The couple did not spend all their time socializing or entertaining, though. They were also occupied with civic affairs, real estate ventures, and frequent travel. The Gardo House was often closed to visitors when they were out of town. The Holmeses traveled extensively throughout the United States, Europe, and Asia. During the course of their wanderings, they visited numerous museums and art galleries and acquired many priceless pieces of art. The couple decided they needed a suitable place to display their acquisitions and so, in 1903, they began planning a two-story structure to be added on to the west end of the Gardo House. The new addition, which cost approximately $10,000, was completed in 1904. The ground floor was used as a garage and the second floor as an art gallery, ballroom, and theater. On 20 February 1904 over four hundred guests were invited to the Gardo House to attend the art gallery's grand opening.[115]

The night of the event, an immense flag in electric red, white, and blue lamps was placed above the entrance to the mansion. The guests were welcomed in the drawing room by a receiving party that included the Holmeses, Governor

The "Aida piano," decorated with scenes from Verdi's opera, is shown here in the art gallery. When the furnishings were sold, the "Aida piano" became the emblem of the Steinway company. Used by permission, Utah State Historical Society, all rights reserved.

and Mrs. Heber M. Wells, Mayor and Mrs. Richard P. Morris, Colonel and Mrs. John W. Bubb, and Mr. and Mrs. Fisher Harris. According to one newspaper account, "From 9 o'clock until midnight . . . the entire house was thrown open for the entertainment of the guests and the already beautiful rooms were made more beautiful by the use of many palms and cut flowers." The Holmeses engaged a quartet and orchestra for the occasion, and they performed for guests in the drawing room and art gallery.[116]

The art gallery, considered by many to be the finest in the West, was "filled with the best works of old-world masters, as well as some of the finest examples of local artists' productions." The Holmeses also displayed porcelain sculptures, vases, Japanese embroidery, and an endless array of curios from all parts of the world. One of the their most prized possessions was a $4,000 Steinway piano they purchased in 1903. The piano, nicknamed the "Aida," was the most exquisite and expensive piano ever manufactured by the Steinways and was second only to art pianos made for celebrated Europeans. The instrument's lid and sides were painted with the principal scenes from Verdi's greatest opera *Aida*.[117]

After the grand opening, the couple made the art gallery available to the general public two days each week. They enjoyed their position as local society leaders for well over a decade. During the years immediately preceding World War I, they began spending more and more of their time at their California home, El Roble, near Pasadena. On 6 June 1917 a local newspaper announced the Holmeses had decided to sell the Gardo House and move their treasures to California. The couple sent a California architect, whom they had previously hired to design a new residence on Wilshire Boulevard, to Utah to examine the mansion. The purpose of his visit was to determine the feasibility of also removing the Belgian glass

Originally, the exterior of the Gardo was painted in natural colors, beige with a white trim. Susanna Bransford had it repainted in the heavy colors favored during the Gilded Age: the walls were a deep Victorian red, and the window frames were white with blue accents. The awnings were red, white, and blue.

windows, black walnut interior finishing, and spiral stair casement from the Gardo House. The Holmeses were disappointed when the architect rendered the verdict they would have to leave the fixtures behind.[118]

There was widespread speculation concerning the future of the Gardo House. Local newspapers published rumors that the mansion would soon be demolished to make way for apartments or an office building. There were also reports the Holmeses were negotiating with Mormon Church representative Charles W. Nibley for the church to repurchase the property.

RED CROSS HEADQUARTERS

The fate of the Gardo House was temporarily postponed when the couple unexpectedly offered the mansion to the Red Cross until the end of the war. According to the *Salt Lake Tribune*, "Amelia's Palace . . . was yesterday dedicated to the service of humanity and is to become the headquarters of the Red Cross and auxiliary workers of Salt Lake County—an army of volunteers that is expected to reach a total of 10,000 within the next few weeks." Red Cross leaders, who had been in desperate need of a place where they could centralize their operations, regarded the mansion as "ideal" for the needs of their organization.[119]

On 1 December 1917, the Red Cross moved into the Gardo House and celebrated with a reception that included speeches and a brass band that played a variety of patriotic songs. William Spry, former governor of Utah, gave a tribute to the Holmeses and praised them for their long record of kindnesses and manifestations of unselfish spirit. Over two thousand persons attended the event and it was estimated that between six hundred and seven hundred young women from Salt Lake City eventually volunteered for service.[120]

Red Cross workers were surprised, and undoubtedly pleased, to find carpets, curtains, desks, tables, and telephones in the mansion in shipshape condition, ready for immediate use. The *Salt Lake Tribune* described the Gardo House's transformation:

> The first floor is devoted to the executive and supply departments. The second floor has offices. . . . The large room to the east is the instruction room, where classes will be held . . . to the south and west is located what is to be known as the "transient room." This is regarded as one of the most important of facilities, it being planned that any transient or visitor who desires to do Red Cross work and who has not time to attend classes regularly may be supplied with materials and given the opportunity for work as desired. The art gallery and ball room have been transformed into the department of surgical dressings.

Classes on elementary hygiene, home care for the sick, dietetics, first aid, knitting, and making surgical dressings were soon regularly held in the mansion.[121]

After World War I came to an end, in November 1918, the Holmeses resumed their efforts to find a buyer for their home. On 20 March 1920, the couple resold the Gardo House to the Mormon Church for $100,000. Two months after the transaction, the Red Cross vacated the mansion and moved its headquarters to the Utah State Capitol.[122]

The church repurchased the mansion with the intent of using it to house the LDS School of Music, "one of the greatest schools of music in the West."[123]

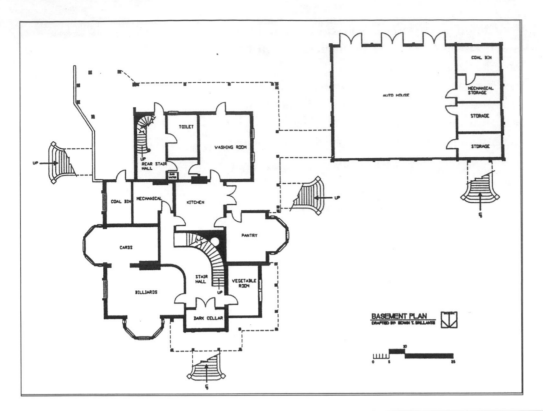

BASEMENT PLAN
DRAFTED BY: EDWIN T. BRILLANTE

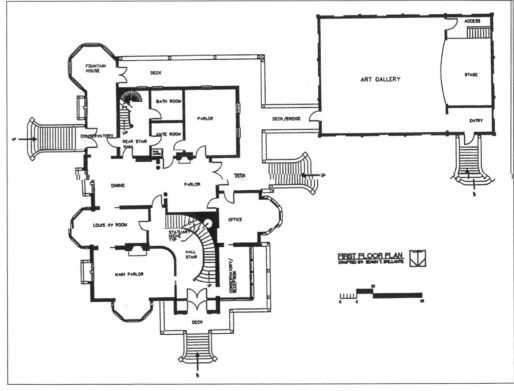

FIRST FLOOR PLAN
DRAFTED BY: EDWIN T. BRILLANTE

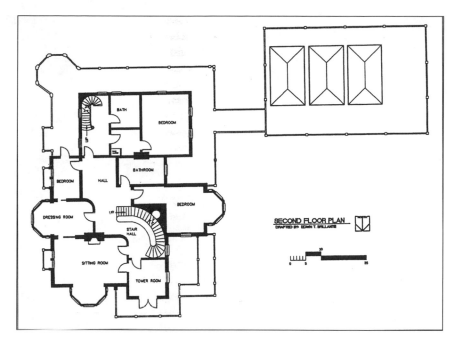

SECOND FLOOR PLAN
DRAFTED BY: EDWIN T. BRILLANTE

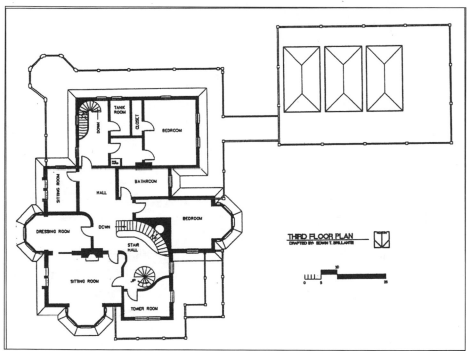

THIRD FLOOR PLAN
DRAFTED BY: EDWIN T. BRILLANTE

Mark Curtis recreated the floor plans for the Gardo House during the period the Holmeses owned it. They demonstrate several of the useful features of the house, such as the rear stairway for family and servants to move from floor to floor without encountering guests. From Curtis's plans and elevation studies, Steve Bennion and Bill Nelson, architects with MHTN Architects of Salt Lake City, along with Judy Dykman and miniaturists Joyce Johnson, JoEllen Sweat, and Ralph and Margene Sweat, have created a large model of the house, now on display at the Daughters of Utah Pioneer Museum in Salt Lake City.

The school, which included piano, vocal, and wind departments, was also intended to serve as a training ground for the Tabernacle Choir. On 2 October 1920 the *Deseret News* reported that the church was reopening the art galley as a permanent exhibition hall for local artists.[124]

During the next few months, the church received an offer from the Federal Reserve Bank to purchase the Gardo House property. The bank, which was quickly outgrowing its quarters in the Deseret Bank Building, was seeking a new building site in the downtown area. On 26 February 1921 local newspapers reported that the church, through its trustee-in-trust, Heber J. Grant, had sold the Gardo House to the bank for $115,000. Church leaders issued a statement assuring the public that the LDS School of Music would continue to function in a new locality and announcing there were tentative plans to place the Gardo House upon piles and rollers and move it to one of several sites that were under consideration.[125]

An article in the *Deseret News* a few weeks later gave further details concerning the plans to relocate the mansion.

> The moving of one of Salt Lake's old landmarks . . . may be one of the most spectacular events staged in the city, if the moving is found to be feasible. President Heber J. Grant said this morning he is having several streets of Salt Lake measured to see if there would be adequate passage way for the moving of the old Gardo House from its location on South Temple and State streets. When in San Francisco last week President Grant consulted one of the best known engineering experts in the country in regard to the moving of the building. This authority said it could be done easily provided five carloads of the necessary equipment could be shipped from San Francisco for the removal.[126]

The Red Cross occupied the Gardo House during World War I. At the opening ceremony, Governor Spry delivered an address from the front porch. The building in the background is the Alta Club. Used by permission, Utah State Historical Society, all rights reserved.

There was widespread speculation on how and where the Gardo House would be relocated. All rumors came to an end on 8 April 1921, when newspapers announced the mansion would not be moved and that it would soon be torn down. After researching and discussing the issue, church leaders came to the reluctant conclusion that the moving expenses, estimated at over $20,000, were more than the church could afford and that the aging Gardo House, with its high ceilings, winding stairways, and outdated bathrooms, was too expensive to maintain.[127]

On 17 November 1921 the *Salt Lake Telegram* reported the Federal Reserve Bank had signed a contract with the Ketchum Builder Supply Company to raze the Gardo House. Nine days later, on 26 November, the Ketchum crew demolished the home. Efforts were made at the time of demolition to salvage doors, windows, mirrors, fixtures, and other valuable items from the mansion. The souvenirs were later sold at auction and many of them were scattered throughout Utah.[128]

A local newspaper, commenting several years earlier on the demolition of Brigham Young's schoolhouse, summed up the mood of the times. "The old Salt Lake is going. Slowly but surely the landmarks that bind the Salt Lake of history to the growing metropolis of the intermountain west are being torn down to the ground, and on the nude earth where they once stood are being erected modern structures, beautiful enough in design, but bare of historical interest."[129]

The Gardo House, and its occupants, played an unforgettable role in Utah's architectural, economic, political, and social history. Although the mansion has been gone for almost eighty years, the memory of it will endure.

Chapter 9

Beyond Salt Lake City

Judy Dykman, Colleen Whitley, and Kari K. Robinson

When Brigham Young moved the Latter-day Saints into Mexico's Great Basin in 1847, he protected them from mob violence and corrupt politics but didn't end their worries. Now isolated from major communities and sources of supply, cut off from affordable and dependable freight and mail service until 1869, the settlers tried to "make do."[1] They imported and exported goods and mail through the Brigham Young Express and Carrying Company and made use of local materials. During the early years companies were formed to grow beets for sugar, to turn wood pulp and rags into paper, and to make pottery from local clay deposits. In 1862 a large mill was built on Parleys Creek in the Salt Lake Valley to process sheep fleece into wool.[2]

Events in the 1850s created crises for the Mormons and increased their distrust of outsiders and gentiles. Although the neutrality of the Salt Lake Valley kept local natives from attacking, settlers in other parts of the state found some stiff resistance from the indigenous occupants. In 1853–1854, Chief Walker led his Utes against settlers in central Utah. During that same period there were constant food shortages because of crop disasters. Then in the next two years, tens of millions of grasshoppers infested many communities and attacked the precious crops. Then in 1857 President Buchanan decided to send 2,500 soldiers to Utah to put down an alleged rebellion against the United States government, an action called the Utah War. No such rebellion existed, of course, but the federal government intended to establish a presence and replace Brigham Young as governor.[3]

General Patrick Connor, decidedly no fan of the Mormons, established his headquarters at Fort Douglas, overlooking Salt Lake City. Creating more than a military presence, Connor encouraged his soldiers to explore for gold and silver, hoping to generate a gold rush that would bring in crowds of gentiles to alter the population balance in Utah. He anticipated an influx of outsiders could destroy the Mormons' communal lifestyle and threaten their practices of polygamy and theocratic government. Connor also pushed for investigations into the Mountain Meadows Massacre, which had occurred during the Utah War of 1857, hoping to at least embarrass Brigham Young and

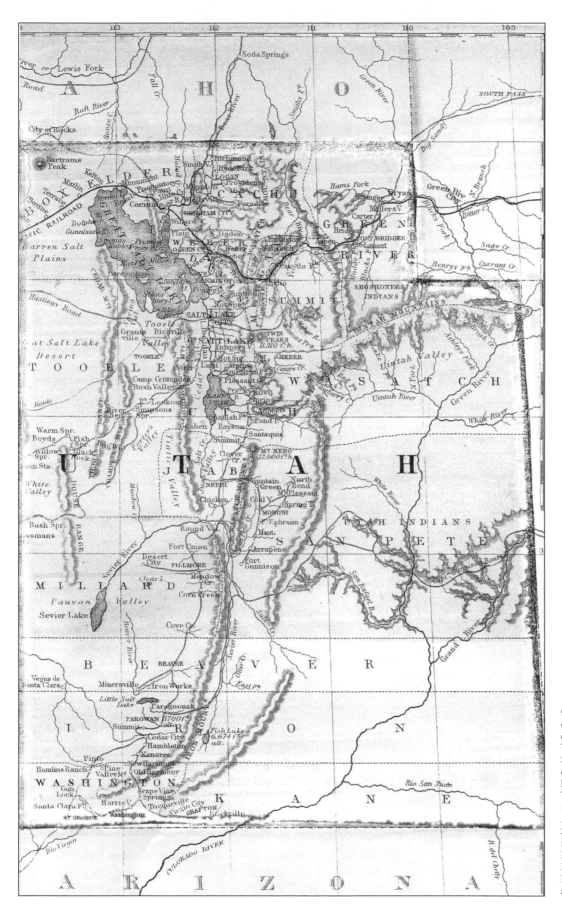

Over time Utah Territory covered varied parts of several states. Since Brigham Young needed to visit the Saints in many areas, some of his wives maintained homes in several cities. William H. Gamble, *County map of Utah and Nevada, 1870* (Philadelphia: S. Augustus Mitchell, 1871). Courtesy of L. Tom Perry Special Collections, Harold B. Lee Library, Brigham Young University, all rights reserved.

Brigham Young
alt. 1868–70 or even 1873

Top: As Brigham Young grew older and developed some of the infirmities of age, he escaped the harsh Salt Lake City winters by living in St. George, becoming the state's first snowbird. Used by permission, Utah State Historical Society, all rights reserved.

Above: Lucy Bigelow lived in several of her husband's homes, but she is most remembered for her lengthy stay in St. George. Used by permission, Utah State Historical Society, all rights reserved.

at most implicate him directly in the horrible crime.[4] As the transcontinental railroad moved closer, Brigham stated his and his followers' fears of contamination:

Our outside friends say they want to civilize us here. What do they mean by civilization? Why, they mean by that, to establish gambling holes—they are gambling hells—grog shops and houses of ill fame on every corner of every block in the city; also swearing, drinking, shooting and debauching each other. Then they would send their missionaries here with faces as long as jack asses' ears, who would go crying and groaning through the streets, "Oh, what a poor, miserable, sinful world!" That is what is meant by civilization. That is what priests and deacons want to introduce here; tradesmen want it, lawyers and doctors want it, and all hell wants it. But the Saints do not want it, and we will not have it.[5]

It was reported that the congregation said, "Amen!"

Brigham had always pushed for self-sufficiency among the settlements in Utah, but these crises and the fears they raised reinforced the Mormons' belief that they needed to take care of themselves. Almost from the beginning of the Utah settlement Brigham had assigned men to find and refine useful minerals, and their explorations spread far beyond the boundaries of Salt Lake City. Las Vegas was settled to mine lead and men were sent to California to mine gold for currency to trade with the outside world. In 1850 Brigham sent a group of people to settle Parowan to mine iron and coal and smelt iron. In 1854, 1856, and 1861 many converts from the southern states and several European countries were assigned to grow cotton along the banks of the Santa Clara and Virgin Rivers in what is now southwestern Utah. In the process they established the communities of Santa Clara, Washington, and St. George. Over the next three decades, Brigham Young and his apostles made annual trips throughout the far-flung settlements to check on the people's well-being and the progress of these projects. Each year these settlers warmly welcomed their leaders as they dispensed religious instruction, encouragement, praise or criticism, along with day-to-day advice on how to survive in this new environment. During each visit, the church leaders stayed with the people they visited, so the church hierarchy and the members became well acquainted.[6] Between visits the Mormon leaders kept their scattered members informed and unified through letters, general conferences, newspapers, and later the telegraph and the railroad.[7] Eventually Brigham recognized the need to establish his own homes with some of his families in a variety of areas.

St. George

By the mid 1860s, the years of hard work and stress and the infirmities of old age began to take their toll on Brigham. Rheumatism was crippling him, making it more difficult and painful to travel every year. Late in 1866, he sent word

to the St. George leaders that he would like to winter there but couldn't until the telegraph line from Salt Lake City to St. George was finished. It is no coincidence that the telegraph line was ready the following year. However, Brigham didn't actually live in St. George until three years later. On 25 November 1870 he and two of his families left for St. George and stayed the winter. Apostle George A. Smith traveled south with the Youngs and mailed a letter 10 January 1871 to Salt Lake City that explains Brigham's departure. "It is clearly apparent that President Young did not seek a temporary retirement from the pressure of his ministry and business any too soon. He has been confined to his room most of the time since we arrived."[8] Brigham hoped that southern Utah's mild winters and the skillful care of his wives there would relieve his suffering so he could continue his many duties as spiritual leader.

The two wives he asked to live in St. George, Lucy Bigelow and Eliza Burgess, had many things in common. Unlike some of Brigham's wives who were well-known public personalities, Lucy and Eliza seemed content to live in the background. Each woman was in her early forties and both had teenaged children when they went to St. George. Eliza's seventeen-year-old son, Alfales, probably stayed in Salt Lake City where he worked for the *Deseret News* as a telegraph operator.[9]

Lucy's difficulties with her three daughters—Dora, Susa, and Mabel, and a foster daughter Ina, who was Mabel's age—may have provided one reason for

Lucy Bigelow's St. George home was on the corner of 100 North and 100 West. While she lived there, she cared for her husband during his winter sojourns and served as president of the female workers in the St. George Temple of the Church of Jesus Christ of Latter-day Saints. Used by permission, Utah State Historical Society, all rights reserved.

her move to St. George. Lucy was upset when her oldest daughter, Dora, became engaged at age fifteen to Morley Dunford because the boy had an alcohol problem. His family had converted to Mormonism and moved to Utah, but Brigham felt the drinking problem would not go away as Morley grew older. Nothing Lucy or Brigham said or did during the next two years could convince Dora that marrying Morley would be disastrous. Finally on 3 October 1970, a month before they were all supposed to move to St. George, Susa helped Dora to elope. Morley and Dora were married by a Presbyterian minister that evening while Lucy celebrated her fortieth birthday. By this time Susa was thirteen and had been enrolled in the University of Deseret because she was more mature than many girls her age, very bright and well read. She might even have been allowed to remain in Salt Lake City with one of Lucy's sister wives, but after the episode with Morley, Brigham was determined that Susa must live in St. George and withdrew her from the University of Deseret. Susa, Mabel, and Ina were initially unhappy in quiet, rural St. George and would have preferred to live in Salt Lake City with one of the "aunts," as the plural wives were often called.[10]

The major reason for Lucy's moving to St. George, however, was probably based on her gift for healing. Since Brigham planned to spend winters in St. George in large part to help his illnesses, he would need a patient, faithful nurse, and Lucy was certainly that. Eventually she became widely known for her ability to treat many ills with herbs and blessings, including blessings using consecrated oil. Many women who were childless or maimed sought her out for a blessing and some were able to have children after the experience.[11]

100 North 100 West

Lucy's St. George home was on the southwest corner of 100 North and 100 West. Brigham obtained Lucy's home from Joseph Birch, who owed Brigham some money. The two-story white colonial had stuccoed adobe walls, large windows, at least four bedrooms, a parlor, a big front porch, and several other rooms. A white picket fence enclosed a large, spacious yard with trees.

Today the site of Lucy Bigelow's home is occupied by a motel and a small shop. Photo by Ann Best.

When the St. George Temple was dedicated in 1877, Lucy was appointed president of the female ordinance workers. She and her girls spent many years working there. In 1888 when the Manti Temple was dedicated, she filled the same position there. Her pattern of temple and genealogical work continued after Brigham's death. She cared for her daughters and her mother wherever she was needed, even watching over a granddaughter while she studied voice in Germany. She served several missions to the Hawaiian Islands with family members. Lucy died of pneumonia in 1905 in Salt Lake City and her funeral was attended by many who remembered her kindnesses and her healing powers.[12]

Her St. George house was eventually torn down and was subsequently replaced by the El Paso Motel and a small shop that has housed a variety of businesses, from souvenir shops to cell phone distributors. A plaque on the building while it was the Trading Post identified the site as that of Lucy Bigelow Young's home.[13]

100 North 200 West

Just a block down the street from Lucy's house was Eliza Burgess's home on the northwest corner of 100 North and 200 West. When Brigham came to St. George, he divided his time between the two houses. Eliza, born in 1827 in Lancashire, England, later kept a house for Brigham in Provo. Whether her home in St. George belonged to Eliza or a relative is hard to determine since the 1861 plat map shows that Malancter Burgess owned the land.[14]

One Hundred North has now become St. George Boulevard, the major thoroughfare for the city and a prosperous commercial area. The site of Eliza's home is now Gates Auto Sales. One of the employees recently observed that someone was found digging behind the store looking for evidence of one of the

While Eliza Burgess stayed in St. George, she lived in a home on the corner of 100 North and 200 West, listed as belonging to Malanthem Wheeler Burgess. It was completed in 1862 and may have been the first home erected in St. George. Used by permission, Utah State Historical Society, all rights reserved.

oldest houses in town, but the only house still standing in that area was built in the mid twentieth century.[15]

100 West 200 North

In early 1870 Brigham purchased the Chesney residence, begun the year before, deciding to remodel it into a larger home. Like the Beehive and Gardo Houses in Salt Lake City, it would be a reception center and office for the church in the St. George area as well as a place where he could stay for several months each winter. As hostess for this large home, Brigham named his youngest wife, Amelia Folsom, who was also scheduled to become the hostess for the Gardo once it was finished.

So extensive was the remodeling needed for the house that it took a year to complete. When it was finished, the house had a large two-story addition on the north-facing front of the house with a large front porch. Builders also added a two-room basement of red sandstone atop a lava rock foundation. In the new part of the house there were a formal entry, a big parlor on the main floor, and another parlor, a bedroom, and several porches upstairs. The house had four fireplaces, one on each of the north and south gables, a third at the junction of the home's two wings and a fourth in the kitchen used for both cooking and heating. There were two stairways, high ceilings, and deep casement windows. Pine woodwork was hand-grained to resemble oak, a style architects now call "Brigham oak." Wood shingles covered the gabled roofs while the cornices were bracketed. The yellow adobe brick exterior was stuccoed and painted white to

Of Brigham Young's three St. George homes, this one on the corner of 100 West and 200 North is the only one still standing. It has been furnished with period articles and is open to the public as a visitors' center for the Church of Jesus Christ of Latter-day Saints. The one-room building beside it was the first LDS Church office building in the state.

protect it from the elements. Although it was smaller than the Beehive House, town residents remember the home being just as nicely furnished with store-bought carpets and fine, sturdy furniture. In 1873 Brigham built a small one-room adobe brick office, roughly eighteen by twenty-two feet, just east of the house. The office was connected to the telegraph line so that when Brigham was in residence he could remain in touch with other church leaders in Salt Lake City.

Miles Romney, the architect for the project, was busy rushing from the house to the St. George Tabernacle, also under construction. Romney was further challenged when Brigham added a new project to his list: a temple in St. George. Since work on the Salt Lake Temple was stalled by assorted federal interferences, including threatened confiscations under the Edmunds- Tucker Act, Brigham decided to have a temple built far from the center of conflict, and St. George was about as far away as possible. Romney saw all of his projects through: in 1877 the St. George Temple became the first dedicated in Utah; the St. George Tabernacle still serves the people of Washington County, and the home welcomes tourists every day as an LDS Church visitors' center.[16]

PROVO
Address unknown

During the exodus from the Utah War in 1857, thousands of Saints moving south from Salt Lake City impacted Provo, so buildings not originally intended as homes were pressed into service. Consequently, Brigham's first home in Provo was described quite simply as an empty stable. Lucy Bigelow found an outbuilding that had once housed a tame bear. Some of the wives, directed by Zina Huntington (known for her organizational skills), cleaned it adequately and moved some of Brigham's family into it for several weeks before they returned to the Salt Lake Valley.[17]

42 North 200 East

No pictures or descriptions of this house remain. There is some suspicion that it may be the same as the stable discussed above. Today the site is occupied by the parking lot for one of Provo's ubiquitous apartment complexes.[18]

124 South University Avenue

In the mid 1870s Eliza Burgess maintained a house in Provo which Brigham used when he visited the Brigham Young Academy, now Brigham Young University. Eliza, born in England, is unique among Brigham's wives in that she worked for the family for a time as a hired girl before she married him. The two-story brick home was probably one of the finest in the city and was located across the street from the Provo Tabernacle. It was torn down in 1968 and today

Eliza Burgess lived in several of her husband's homes, but she is most closely associated with his Provo home on the corner of First South and University Avenue, across the street from the Provo Tabernacle. Used by permission, Utah State Historical Society, all rights reserved.

Top: Brigham Young stayed in this home on University Avenue when he toured the territory and later when he visited the Brigham Young Academy, now Brigham Young University. Used by permission, Utah State Historical Society, all rights reserved.

Above: In 1968 Brigham Young's Provo home was demolished and the Travelodge that still stands in its place was built. Across the street is the Provo Tabernacle. Photo by Colleen Whitley.

the property is home to a Travelodge featuring fifty-nine rooms, a pool, and an exercise room.[19]

SODA SPRINGS, IDAHO
Second South and First East

The area around Soda Springs had been known as Tosoiba, Land of Sparkling Waters, to the local Shoshone and Bannock tribes long before any white men arrived. As those white men passed through the area on their way to Oregon, the "Oasis of Soda Springs" was a major place of rest after leaving Fort Laramie. In 1863 Colonel Patrick Edward Connor established a military post on the east end of the town and modestly named it Fort Connor. The fort was abandoned three years later when the Indian threat appeared to be over and when the soldiers' terms of service were up.[20]

On 10 June 1870, Wilford Woodruff, Brigham Young, and a number of visitors from Salt Lake City were welcomed to the area by Charles C. Rich, leader of the Paris, Idaho, branch of the LDS Church, and about fifty members, including the Paris Brass Band. When Young and Woodruff returned to Salt Lake, they met with other church leaders, called missionaries, and soon the Mormon settlement of Soda Springs was under way. Evidence of the early Mormon settlement pattern still exists in the straight streets laid out at right angles, originally in ten-acre blocks.

By 1874, John Codman, traveling through Idaho, described Soda Springs as "merely a sort of Mormon outpost beyond the confines of Utah, with scarcely fifty inhabitants."[21] Brigham Young was not one of those inhabitants, although he reportedly had a home built on the corner of Second South and First East.[22] Brigham Young visited the town again and probably used the cabin, but so far as can reasonably be determined, he never lived there himself, nor did any of his wives. The house was, instead, a place for emissaries of the LDS leader to stay while visiting Soda Springs: in effect, a motel.

Appropriately, a motel is exactly what occupies that area today. The original cabin, twenty-two by eighteen feet with a good floor and a shingle roof, stood until 1944. That year the owner, Harry Richards, tried to move it to the back of the lot to make room to expand his tourist motel next door. When the roof caved in and the place collapsed, he completed his expansion and then lined the driveways with logs from the fallen cabin. Like the cabin before, the Brigham Young Motor Lodge now temporarily houses visitors to the Soda Springs area.[23]

Although neither Brigham Young nor any of his family ever lived in this cabin, it was locally called Brigham Young's house. It was actually used by visiting officials of the LDS Church when they traveled through the area. Today its site houses a motel. Used by permission, Utah State Historical Society, all rights reserved.

PRESERVING THE PAST

Visiting a house in text and print can be enlightening, and seeing a piece of farm equipment or an item of furniture in a museum is likewise valuable. An adult in a museum or a child on a field trip can learn a great deal in a few minutes by walking through the material culture of the past. But visiting an original or restored building in person carries an impact unattainable in any other way. Observing equipment in the context of a barn or a room in which it could have been used increases our understanding of the past exponentially.

In the case of Brigham Young's homes, only a few such experiences are possible. The home in Nauvoo gives a glimpse of life in that early settlement. The Forest Farm home in This Is the Place Heritage Park helps tourists and school children understand early Utah farm life. His winter home in St. George has recently been renovated and is open regularly. The Beehive House in Salt Lake City is toured by thousands of visitors every year, and the Lion House hosts weddings, dinners, and parties in elegance and charm.

Most of Brigham Young's homes, however, like so many historic buildings, have been lost to weather, neglect, and various forces of progress. Some, of course, were never intended to last very long; renovated wagons and log cabins were needed only to survive a winter or two while better accommodations were being built. Other homes, however, like the Gardo and the White House were magnificent mansions designed to house visiting dignitaries and accommodate large social gatherings. Solidly built, they were constructed to last for many lifetimes, but are accessible to us now only in aging photographs that testify to their lost elegance. Their absence in our cityscape deprives us of significant elements of our communal identity.

As a society we are diminished by the loss of historic structures, though we often do not realize what that loss will be until after the building is gone. An excellent example of that phenomenon is the Salt Lake Theatre, originally located on the northwest corner of First South and State Street. Patterned after the Drury Lane Theatre in London, it was known for the excellence of its productions and became one of the significant social centers of the community. Home to local companies, it also hosted virtually every major artist of the

American stage: Maud Adams, P. T. Barnum, Sarah Bernhardt, Edwin Booth, Billie Burke, "Buffalo Bill" Cody, Al Jolson, Lillian Russell, all four of the first theatrical generation of Barrymores: Drew, Ethel, John, and Lionel, and many more. Despite its significance to the city, the theater was demolished in 1928 to make way for a gas station; the telephone company building currently occupies its place. Although taking it down seemed to make sense at the time, the theater's loss was keenly and immediately felt. Within a year of its destruction, the LDS Church helped finance a replica, the Daughters of Utah Pioneers Museum at 300 North Main, designed by church architect Harold Burton. A second copy was erected in 1963: the Pioneer Memorial Theatre on the University of Utah campus duplicates the old building's front facade. The fact that citizens of Salt Lake City have recreated the same building twice tells us that we need to hold on to buildings that represent important elements of our common past.[2]

As a nation, we treasure Mount Vernon, Independence Hall, and the pueblos of Mesa Verde National Park. Public money initially transformed Biltmore, George Washington Vanderbilt's palatial estate, into a state park for North Carolina; now tourists are happy to pay for its upkeep with admission fees. San Simeon, William Randolph Hearst's great mansion, more than pays its own way, it produces profits for a private corporation.[2] In the 1950s United States citizens recognized the value of the White House. Congress responded to calls to save the historic home with a large appropriation to guarantee it will be available for many more years for presidents to live in and citizens to visit.

Locally, vigilant citizens and organizations have preserved many historic buildings, often led by the Utah State Historical Society and the Utah Heritage Foundation. The Capitol Theatre is used for ballets, plays, and concerts, and part of the joy of attending a performance is entering that magnificent lobby and climbing the baroque staircase (which everyone seems to enjoy climbing, even if their seats are on the main floor). The Karl Maeser building on Brigham Young University campus still hosts classes as it always did, but now it also houses the undergraduate and honors programs.

Not every building can be used for its original purpose, of course. Some may be structurally unsound or damaged too greatly by fires or natural forces. Some may no longer be suitable for their original purposes but can be adapted for other uses. Fortunately visionary people have saved and adapted several such buildings, including many in Utah. The Rio Grande Railway Station in Salt Lake City now houses the Utah State Historical Society, preserving important documents and artifacts while also providing space for meetings and displays. The LDS Church has converted the Vernal Tabernacle into a temple, and Provo City renovated the Brigham Young Academy to make it a public library. Ogden's Union Station houses a museum for recalling the great days of railroading plus theaters, galleries, banquet halls, and similar venues needed for public interaction. Recently they have even added a fully equipped mail car, a sort of post office on wheels, commemorating a once essential occupation that no longer exists. All of these buildings and many similar communal treasures connect us with the past while providing daily, necessary services.

Recognizing which structures are publicly significant is a genuine problem. When that recognition is established, raising funds or finding uses for the buildings becomes the next hurdle, requiring the time, energy, and efforts of many dedicated people. Nonetheless, such buildings need to be preserved.

As a community and as a nation, we are fortunate to have a few of Brigham Young's homes available to us, if not in person at least in pictures. They serve as reminders of great people who persevered under desperately difficult circumstances, and they tell us that we are capable of far more than we might imagine in our current comfortable society. Preserving old buildings, both public and private, lets us look into our past, and examining our past helps us see where we have been and, often, where we are going. Preservation is expensive, but losing our connections with our history costs far more.

Brigham Young's Houses

This list of houses built, owned, and/or occupied by Brigham Young and his family is grouped first by location and then arranged chronologically by the Young family's dates of occupation, followed by whatever information is available about the style, architect, and current use of the house or property.

Whitingham, Vermont

Stimpson Hill, west side of Town Road 33
Occupied by John and Abigail Young family, 1801
Known as Brigham Young's birthplace, the home was destroyed before 1900 and is now marked by a stone memorial.

Sadawaga Pond (now Sadawaga Lake)
The Youngs lived at three other locations in Whitingham, although they did not own land. Their last location was likely on Sadawaga Pond.

New York

Sherburne (Smyrna), Chenango County
Occupied by John and Abigail Young family, 1804–1807
Two children were born in this same house, but because the town was divided, one child was listed as having been born in Sherburne and the other in Smyrna.

Cold Brook (now Cole Road), on the road leading from Dark Hollow to German Hollow, right off Chenango County Road 21
Occupied by John and Abigail Young family, 1807–1813
An abandoned sawmill still exists.

Genoa (Lansing)
Occupied by John and Abigail Young family, 1813–1815
This location is uncertain; possibly more than one residence.

Tyrone, near Pine Grove, seven miles west of what is now Watkins Glenn on Sugar Hill Road
Occupied by John Young and his older sons Joseph, Phinehas, and Brigham, 1815

Half Acre, near Cayuga
Occupied by James and Susannah Young Little, their children, and Susannah's brothers Joseph, Lorenzo, and Brigham Young

Auburn, Reed and Wadsworth farms
Brigham worked as a "chore boy" on these farms and boarded with the families.

Auburn, home of John C. Jeffries
Brigham probably lived with Jeffries while apprenticing under him, although he could still have been living on the Reed or Wadsworth farms.

Auburn, the Wait farmhouse
Brigham likely lived at the Wait farmhouse while he was constructing it and the barn. Mary Van Sickle Wait and current Wait owners of the farmhouse (James and Nancy) believe he lived for a time on the Wait property.

Haydenville, one and a half miles south of Port Byron near the Owasco Outlet
Occupied by Brigham and Miriam Young as roomers
This home is still standing and privately occupied, although enlarged and remodeled.

Port Byron, one hundred yards diagonally east from the four-corners intersection in Port Byron
Occupied by Brigham, Miriam, and Elizabeth Young
This home is still standing and privately occupied.

Oswego
Location unknown.

Mendon, southeast corner of the Cheese Factory and Mendon-Ionia Roads

Occupied by Brigham, Miriam, Elizabeth, and Vilate Young who were living for a time with John, Sr.

Owned by John Young and family

Mendon, northeast corner of the Cheese Factory and Mendon-Ionia Roads

Occupied by Brigham, Miriam, Elizabeth, and Vilate Young

This home also contained Brigham's carpenter shop and mill; it is no longer standing.

"Number Nine," a rural community west of Canandaigua

Occupied by Brigham, Miriam, Elizabeth, and Vilate Young, 1830–1832

Owned by Jonathan Mack

Mendon, Heber C. Kimball home, southwest of John Young, Senior's home on Mendon-Ionia Road

Occupied by Brigham and his family before Miriam died and by Brigham as a boarder after Miriam died

Owned by Heber C. Kimball

KIRTLAND, OHIO

Rented home, likely on property of Elijah Smith

Occupied by Brigham Young and his two daughters, Elizabeth and Vilate, and the Heber C. Kimball family

West off Route 306, across the street from the LDS Stake Center, 8751 Kirtland Road

Occupied by Brigham Young and second wife, Mary Ann Angell Young, and Elizabeth and Vilate

Owned by Brigham Young, .375 acres

No home is currently standing.

10831 Chillicothe Road

Occupied by Brigham and Mary Ann, Elizabeth and Vilate, and children by Brigham and Mary Ann

Likely built and owned by Brigham Young

The red barn in back of the Chillicothe home is located at 8265 Bridlehurst Trail and is still standing and privately occupied.

Garfield and Timothy Lane

Land possibly owned by Brigham Young

No home is currently standing.

DUBLIN, INDIANA

Home of brother Lorenzo Young

Occupied by Joseph Young family, Brigham, Joseph Smith, Sidney Rigdon, and George W. Robinson

Brigham Young fled to Dublin in December 1837.

FAR WEST, MISSOURI

Mill Creek, a tributary of Shoal Creek, eight miles east of Far West

Occupied by Brigham and Mary Ann Young and children for about a year

Farm owned and built by Brigham Young

This home was abandoned when persecutions forced the family to move into the town.

Far West

Temporary residence in town occupied by Brigham Young and family

ILLINOIS

Atlas, Pike County

Temporary residence occupied by Brigham Young and family for a few weeks

Quincy

Temporary residence occupied by Brigham Young and family

Mary Ann observed that during this period they moved eleven times.

MONTROSE, IOWA

Abandoned barracks of Fort Des Moines

Occupied by Brigham, Mary Ann, Elizabeth, Vilate, Joseph A., Brigham Jr., Mary Ann, Alice Emma, Eunice Caroline, and John Willard Young, along with other families forced to leave Missouri

NAUVOO, ILLINOIS

Log cabin, on corner of Kimball and Granger Streets

Occupied by Mary Ann and her children while Brigham was on mission

Owned by Mary Ann, who had a place built while Brigham was in England

Two-story brick home, located on corner of Kimball and Granger Streets

Occupied by Brigham, Mary Ann, Elizabeth, Vilate, Joseph A., Brigham Jr., Mary Ann, Alice Emma, Eunice Caroline, and John Willard

Owned and built by Brigham Young

Other property in Nauvoo

City block 117

Lots 2 and 3 of block 121

Lot 2 of block 126 (Nauvoo home)

Lots 67, 68, 69 of Kim First

Occupied by Brigham's other families

WINTER QUARTERS, NEBRASKA

One-and-a-half story home at the top of one of the two main streets, likely Second Main.

Occupied by a succession of family members and many others as well. Exact records are unclear. Several of his wives stayed with their own families in Winter Quarters.

There was probably a second home, but the location and occupants are unknown.

SALT LAKE CITY, UTAH

300 South, 300 West

Occupied by virtually every pioneer who arrived in 1847 and 1848

Known as Old Fort, it was built in 1847 and demolished in 1849–1851; this location is now Pioneer Park.

Approximately 45 East South Temple

Occupied by Lucy Decker, possibly other family members

Built in 1847, it is now approximately the site of the LDS Church Administration Building.

Approximately 45 East South Temple

Occupied by Charles and Vilate Decker, Emmeline Free and her children, Margaret Pierce, and possibly other members of Brigham's family until the Log Row was completed

Built in 1848 and demolished a few years later, it is now the site of the LDS Church Administration Building.

First Avenue east of State Street

Occupied by nearly all of Brigham's families

Known as Log Row and built in 1848, it was demolished around 1856 and the location is now apartment buildings.

Between South Temple and First Avenue, east of State Street

Occupied by Zina Diantha Huntington and her children

Built in 1848, it was possibly demolished around 1855, or it may have been incorporated into Brigham Young's Family School; the location is now apartment buildings.

Between Third Avenue and Canyon Road

Occupied by Harriet Cook

Built c. 1847–1848, it has since been demolished, possibly hit by the arsenal explosion in 1876; the location is probably now the marker for Crismon's Mill in City Creek Park.

119 East South Temple

Occupied primarily by Mary Ann Angell and her children, although Susan Snively and other family members stayed there for short periods

Known as the Mansion House, its architect was Truman O. Angell. It was completed in 1854, demolished in 1922; the location now is the site of the Salt Lake City Elks' Club Building.

71 East South Temple

Occupied by many of Brigham Young's wives and children

Known as the Beehive House, its architects was Truman O. Angell. It was built in 1853–1855 and is currently an LDS Church museum.

63 East South Temple

Occupied by many of Brigham Young's wives and children

Known as the Lion House, its architect was Truman O. Angell. It was built in 1854–1856 and is currently an LDS Church social center.

140 East First Avenue

Occupied by Brigham Young, Eliza R. Snow, Mary Ann Angell, and Lucy Decker

Established in 1848, the site is currently the Brigham Young cemetery.

1100 South 600 East

Occupied by Isaac and Phebe Chase family, Margaret Pierce, and her son

Known as Chase Mill, this home was built in 1852–1854. Both house and mill are still standing, administered by the Utah Arts Council; the farm became Liberty Park in 1882.

700 East 2100 South

Occupied by Lucy Bigelow and two daughters, plus various hired hands and assistants

Known as Experimental Farm, this home was built about 1857.

It was demolished when Forest Farm House was built; the site now consists of homes, a parking lot, and part of I-80.

700 to 800 East Ashton Avenue

Occupied by Susan Snively and her adopted daughter

Known as Forest Farm, the home was built in 1861–1863. In 1969 Frank and Gwen Wilcox donated the house to the LDS Church; the house itself was subsequently moved to Old Deseret Village, and the property is now a parking lot.

29 South State

Occupied by Clarissa Decker and her children

Built in the 1850s, this home was originally owned by John D. Woolley. Demolished by 1919, the site is now the location of the Belvedere Apartments.

55 South State

Occupied by Augusta Adams

Built in the 1850s, this site is currently an office building owned by Zion Securities.

Main Street near South Temple

Occupied by Emmeline Free and her children

Built in the 1850s, this home was originally owned by Jedediah M. Grant. It is currently the site of the ZCMI Center.

Approximately 53 West South Temple

Occupied by Mary Van Cott and her daughter

The house was demolished in the nineteenth century, the location now occupied by Crossroads Plaza.

Approximately 61 West South Temple

Occupied by Harriet Barney

The house was demolished in the nineteenth century, the location now occupied by Temple View Center.

32 South 500 East

Occupied by Emily Dow Partridge and her children

Picadilly Apartments now occupies the site.

300 South State, northeast corner
    Occupied by Zina Huntington
    The house was demolished early in the twentieth century; site of the Center Theater until the late 1990s, it is now the Broadway Center offices.

180 East South Temple
    Occupied by Ann Eliza Webb, Nelson P. Empey, and his wives Ella Elizabeth Young and Emma Adams
    Known as the Empey cottage, this home was built around 1871–1872. Demolished in 1953, the location is now occupied by ZCMI Tire Company.

70 East South Temple
    Occupied by Amelia Folsom, Mary Ann Angell, John Taylor, Alfred and Elizabeth McCune, Isaac Trumbo, Edwin and Susanna Bransford Holmes, and the American Red Cross
    Known as the Gardo House or the Amelia Palace, its architects were Joseph Ridges and William H. Folsom. Built in 1873–1881, the home was demolished in 1926, the space subsequently occupied by a parking lot, a Federal Reserve Bank, and currently by the ZCMI Center.

Provo, Utah

42 North 200 East
    Current an apartment house and parking lot.

124 South University
    Occupied by Lucy Burgess
    Built in the 1870s, the house was demolished in 1968 and is now the site of Provo Travelodge.

St. George, Utah

100 West 100 North (St. George Boulevard), southwest corner
    Occupied by Lucy Bigelow
    Purchased about 1870, the home was originally owned by Joseph Birch. The house was torn down early in this century. Currently the site houses the El Paso Motel and a small shop which has changed occupants several times in the past few years.

100 North 200 West
    Occupied by Eliza Burgess
    Built about 1870, Gates Auto Sales now occupies this property.

100 West 200 North
    Occupied by Amelia Folsom
    Built beginning in 1873, it is now an LDS Church museum, open for tours.

WIVES OF BRIGHAM YOUNG

Each of Brigham Young's wives who was married and/or sealed to him during his lifetime is listed here in the order of her marriage to him, along with any other marriages and her children by each marriage. The second section of this appendix contains the sources for the information given, but also additional works on that individual woman that may be of use to researchers. Unless otherwise indicated, all manuscript materials are in the Archives of the LDS Church. Microfilms and other materials available through the LDS Church Family History Library are indicated by FHL. All of these names have been checked in the LDS Family History Library Archives and patrons' files, Ancestral File, and similar genealogical repositories. While most of these names are found in many places, some are accessible only through the FHL where files are submitted by individuals; hence, their accuracy is dependent on the work of those submitting records.

1. MIRIAM WORKS
Born: 6 or 7 June 1806, Aurelius Township, New York
Died: 8 September 1832, Mendon, New York
Married: Brigham Young, 5 or 8 October 1824, James Pine's Tavern, between Auburn and Bucksville, New York
    1) Elizabeth, 1825–1903
    2) Vilate, 1830–1902

2. MARY ANN ANGELL
Born: 8 June 1803, Seneca, New York
Died: 27 June 1882, Salt Lake City, Utah
Married: Brigham Young, 10 February 1834, Kirtland, Ohio
    1) Joseph A., 1834–1875
    2) Brigham Jr., 1836–1903
    3) Mary Ann, 1836–1843
    4) Alice Emma, 1839–1874
    5) Eunice Caroline (Luna), 1842–1922
    6) John Willard, 1844–1924

Married as plural wives during Joseph Smith's life:

3. LUCY ANN DECKER
Born: 17 May 1822, Phelps, New York
Died: 24 January 1890, Salt Lake City, Utah
Married: William Seeley, abt. 1835
    1) Isaac Joseph, 1837–1902
    2) Harriet, abt. 1839
    3) infant (possibly William), 1840–1841
Married: Brigham Young, 17 June 1842, Nauvoo, Illinois
    1) Brigham Heber, 1845–1928
    2) Sally (adopted, 1847)
    3) Fanny Decker (Caroline), 1849–1892
    4) Ernest Irving, 1851–1879
    5) Shermira, 1853–1915
    6) Arta De Christa, 1855–1916
    7) Feramorz Little, 1858–1881
    8) Clarissa Hamilton, 1860–1939

4. AUGUSTA ADAMS
Born: 7 December 1802, Lynn Massachusetts
Died: 3 February 1886, Salt Lake City, Utah
Married: Henry Cobb, 22 December 1822, Charlestown, Massachusetts
    1) Mary Elizabeth
    2) Ellen
    3) Henry
    4) Albert
    5) James Thornton, 1833–1910
    6) Charlotte Ives, 1836–1908
    7) Brigham, 1838–1838
Married: Brigham Young, 2 November 1843, Nauvoo, Illinois

5. HARRIET ELIZABETH COOK
Born: 7 November 1824, Whitesboro, New York
Died: 5 November 1898, Salt Lake City, Utah

Married: Brigham Young, 2 November 1843, Nauvoo, Illinois
1) Oscar Brigham, 1846–1910

6. CLARISSA CAROLINE DECKER
Born: 22 July 1828, Phelps (Freedom), New York
Died: 5 January 1889, Salt Lake City, Utah
Married: Brigham Young, 8 May 1844, Nauvoo, Illinois
1) Jeanette Richards, 1849–1930
2) Nabbie Howe, 1852–1894
3) Jedediah Grant, 1855–1856
4) Albert Jeddie, 1858–1864
5) Charlotte Talula, 1861–1892

Married after Joseph Smith's death but before completion of Nauvoo Temple:

7. EMILY DOW PARTRIDGE
Born: 28 February 1824, Painesville, Ohio
Died: 9 December 1899, Salt Lake City, Utah
Married: Joseph Smith, 11 May 1843, Nauvoo, Illinois
Married: Brigham Young, September 1844, Nauvoo, Illinois
1) Edward Partridge, 1845–1852
2) Emily Augusta, 1849–1926
3) Caroline, 1851–1903
4) Joseph Don Carlos, 1855–1938
5) Miriam, 1857–1919
6) Josephine, 1860–1912
7) Lura, 1862–1862

8. CLARISSA ROSS (CHASE)
Born: 16 June 1814, Genoa, New York
Died: 20 March 1858, Salt Lake City, Utah
Married: Brigham Young, 10 September 1844, Nauvoo, Illinois
1) Mary Eliza, 1847–1871
2) Clarissa Maria, 1849–1935
3) Willard, 1852–1936
4) Phoebe Louisa, 1854–1931

9. LOUISA BEAMAN
Born: 7 February 1815, Livonia, New York
Died: 15 May 1850, Salt Lake City, Utah
Married: Joseph Smith, 5 April 1841, Nauvoo, Illinois
Married: Brigham Young, 19 September 1844, Nauvoo, Illinois
1) Joseph, 1846–1846
2) Hyrum, 1846–1846
3) Moroni, 1847–1847
4) Alvah, 1848–1848
5) Alma, 1848–1848

10. ELIZA ROXCY SNOW
Born: 21 January 1804, Becket, Massachusetts
Died: 5 December 1887, Salt Lake City, Utah
Married: Joseph Smith, 29 June 1842, Nauvoo, Illinois
Married: Brigham Young, 3 October 1844, Nauvoo, Illinois

11. ELIZABETH (BETSY) FAIRCHILD
Born: 6 March 1828, Marion, Ohio
Died: 10 June 1910, Grantsville, Utah
Married: Brigham Young, 3 October 1844, Nauvoo, Illinois (divorced)
Married: James Davis Lyman
1) James Acy, 1851–1942
Married: Joseph McMurray, 16 August 1853
1) Elizabeth, 1856–
2) Joseph, 1858–1907
Married: James Matthews
Married: William Lowery Chastain, 1868
1) William Matthew, 1866–1942
2) Junius Franklin, 1869–1927

12. CLARISSA BLAKE
Born: 26 October 1796
Died: unknown
Married: Brigham Young, 8 October 1844, Nauvoo, Illinois

13. REBECCA GREENLEAF HOLMAN
Born: 20 February 1824
Died: 11 July 1849, Kanesville (Council Bluffs), Iowa
Married: Brigham Young, 8 October 1844, Nauvoo, Illinois

14. DIANA SEVERANCE CHASE
Born: 25 July 1827, Bristol, Vermont
Died: 6 September 1886, Ogden, Utah
Married: Brigham Young, 10 October 1844, Nauvoo, Illinois (divorced)
Married: William Montgomery Shaw, 1 January 1849, Ogden, Utah
1) Rosebell, 1849–1914
2) Manly, 1851–1853
3) Geneva, 1854–1920
4) William Dudley, 1855–1913
5) Ambrose "E", 1857–1927
6) Romania, 1859–1939
7) Annis, 1861–1957
8) Ina, 1862–1938
9) Frank, 1865–1922
10) Tirzah, 1867–1948
11) Clarence, 1870–1918

15. SUSANNAH SNIVELY
Born: October 1815, Woodstock, Virginia
Died: 20 November 1892, Salt Lake City, Utah
Married: Brigham Young, 31 October 1844, Nauvoo, Illinois
1) Julia (adopted), 1853–1918

16: OLIVE GRAY FROST
Born: 24 July 1816, Livermore, Maine
Died: 6 October 1845, Nauvoo, Illinois
Married: Joseph Smith, Nauvoo, Illinois
Married: Brigham Young, 7 November 1844, Nauvoo, Illinois

17. MARY ANN CLARK

Born: 28 December 1816
Died: unknown
Married: Mr. Powers
Married: Brigham Young, 15 January 1845, Nauvoo, Illinois
(divorced)

18. MARGARET PIERCE

Born: 12 April 1823, Ashton, Pennsylvania
Died: 16 January 1907, Salt Lake City, Utah
Married: Morris Whitesides, 23 July 1844, Nauvoo, Illinois
Married: Brigham Young, 16 January 1845, Nauvoo, Illinois
    1) Brigham Morris, 1845–1931

19. MARY HARVEY PIERCE

Born: 29 November 1821, Willistown, Pennsylvania
Died: 17 March 1847, Winter Quarters, Nebraska
Married: Brigham Young, 16 January 1845, Nauvoo, Illinois

20. EMELINE FREE

Born: 28 April 1826, Belleville, Illinois
Died: 16 July 1875, Salt Lake City, Utah
Married: Brigham Young, 30 April 1845, Nauvoo, Illinois
    1) Ella Elizabeth, 1847–1890
    2) Marinda Hyde, 1849–1883
    3) Hyrum Smith, 1851–1925
    4) Emmeline Amanda, 1853–1895
    5) Louisa Wells (Nelle), 1854–1908
    6) Lorenzo Dow, 1856–1905
    7) Alonzo, 1858–1918
    8) Ruth, 1861–1944
    9) Daniel Wells, 1863–1863
    10) Ardelle Elwin, 1864–1900

21. MARY ELIZABETH ROLLINS

Born: 9 April 1818, Lima, New York
Died: 17 December 1913, Minersville, Utah
Married: Adam Lightner, 11 August 1835, Lancaster, Pennsylvania
    1) Miles Henry, 1836–1847
    2) Caroline Keziah, 1840–1910
    3) George Algernon, 1842–1843 or 1844
    4) Florentine Mattheas, 1844–1847
    5) John Horace, 1847–1923
    6) Elizabeth, 1849–1927
    7) Mary Rollins, 1850–1928
    8) Algernon Sidney, 1853–1853
    9) Charles Washington, 1857–1932
    10) Adam Jr., 1861–1890
Married: Joseph Smith, 17 January 1842, Nauvoo, Illinois
Married: Brigham Young, 22 May 1845, Nauvoo, Illinois

Married in Nauvoo after completion of the Nauvoo Temple but before the exodus to the Salt Lake Valley:

22. MARGARET MARIA ALLEY

Born: 19 December 1825, Lynn, Massachusetts
Died: 5 November 1852, Salt Lake City, Utah
Married: Brigham Young, 14 January 1846, Nauvoo, Illinois
    1) Evelyn Louisa, 1850–1917
    2) Mahonri Moriancumer, 1852–1884

23. OLIVE ANDREWS

Born: 24 September 1818, Livermore, Maine
Died: unknown
Married: Joseph Smith, Nauvoo, Illinois
Married: Brigham Young, 15 January 1846, Nauvoo, Illinois

24. EMILY HAWS

Born: 22 July 1823
Died: unknown
Married: Brigham Young, 15 January 1846, Nauvoo, Illinois
(divorced)
Married: William Whitmarsh

25. MARTHA BOWKER

Born: 24 January 1822, Mount Holley, New Jersey
Died: 26 September 1890, Salt Lake City, Utah
Married: Brigham Young, 21 January 1846, Nauvoo, Illinois
    1) Ida Ames (adopted), 1860–1927

26. ELLEN ACKLAND ROCKWOOD

Born: 23 March 1829, Holliston, Massachusetts
Died: 6 January 1866, Salt Lake City, Utah
Married: Brigham Young, 21 January 1846, Nauvoo, Illinois

27. JEMIMA ANGELL

Born: 5 October 1809, North Providence, Rhode Island
Died: 13 July 1869, Wanship, Utah
Married: Valentine Young, 21 March 1824, Providence, Rhode Island
    1) Nathan, 1826–1900
    2) James Valentine, 1832–1908
    3) Rachel Maxfield, 1835–1904
Married: William Bryant Stringham, 17 July 1844, Nauvoo, Illinois
Married: Brigham Young, 28 January 1846, Nauvoo, Illinois

28. ABIGAIL MARKS

Born: 6 November 1781, Wilmington, Vermont
Died: 15 July 1846, Nauvoo, Illinois
Married: Asa Works, 1800/01, Leicester, Massachusetts
    1) Abigail, 1804–1843
    2) Miriam Angeline, 1806–1832 (Brigham's first wife)
    3) Adeline, 1808–1859
    4) Perthenia, 1811–1893
    5) Angeline Eliza, 1814–1880
    6) Asa Jr., abt. 1817

7) Joseph Tuncliff, 1819–
9) James Marks, 1822–1889
10) Jerusha (adopted), 1822–1880
Married: Brigham Young, 28 January 1846, Nauvoo, Illinois

29. Phebe Ann Morton

Born: 28 March 1786, Utica, New York
Died: 15 November 1854, Salt Lake City, Utah
Married: James William Angell, 21 March 1824, Camden,
New York
    1) Solomon, 1806–1881
    2) Hiram, 1807–1830
    3) Mary Ann, 1808–1882 (Brigham's second wife)
    4) Jemima, 1804–1869 (Brigham's twenty-sixth wife)
    5) Truman Osborn, 1810–1887
    6) Washington M., 1812–1830
    7) Phebe Ann, 1813–
    8) James, 1821–1829
    9) Abigail, 1823– (died as an infant)
    10) Caroline Frances, 1825–1908
Married: Brigham Young, 28 January 1846, Nauvoo,
Illinois

30. Cynthia Porter

Born: 2 February 1783
Died: 4 January 1861, Salt Lake City, Utah
Married: Mr. Weston
Married: Brigham Young, 28 January 1846, Nauvoo, Illinois

31. Mary Eliza Nelson

Born: 24 November 1812, New York
Died: 28 December 1886
Married: Rev. John Portineus Greene, 6 December 1841,
Nauvoo, Illinois
    1) Mary Emma, 1843–1907
Married: Brigham Young, 31 January 1846, Nauvoo, Illinois
(divorced)
Married: Bruce I. Philips, 17 September 1850, Salt Lake City,
Utah

32. Rhoda Richards

Born: 8 August 1784, Framingham, Massachusetts
Died: 17 January 1879, Salt Lake City, Utah
Married: Joseph Smith, 12 June 1843, Nauvoo, Illinois
Married: Brigham Young, 31 January 1846, Nauvoo, Illinois

33. Zina Diantha Huntington

Born: 31 January 1821, Watertown, New York
Died: 28 August 1901, Salt Lake City, Utah
Married: Henry Bailey Jacobs, 7 March 1841, Manchester,
Ohio
    1) Zebulon William, 1842–1914
    2) Henry Chariton, 1846–1915

Married: Joseph Smith, 27 October 1841, Nauvoo, Illinois
Married: Brigham Young, 2 February 1846, Nauvoo, Illinois
    1) Zina Prescinda, 1850–1931

34. Amy Cecelia Cooper

Born: 30 June 1804
Died: unknown
Married: Joseph Aldrich, 9 March 1825, Sutton,
Massachusetts
Married: Brigham Young, 3 February 1846, Nauvoo, Illinois

35. Mary Ellen de la Montague

Born: 25 May 1805
Died: unknown
Married: James B. Woodward before 1846
Married: Brigham Young, 3 February 1846, Nauvoo, Illinois
(divorced)

36. Julia Foster

Born: 18 November 1811, Vienna, Maine
Died: 17 January 1891, Salt Lake City, Utah
Married: Jonathan Hampton Jr., 4 September 1833, Lyons,
New York
    1) Nephi, 1834–1865
    2) Brigham Young, 1836–1902
    3) Sarah Cerena, 1837–1838
    4) Edaly Foster, 1840–1906
    5) Julia Anna, 1844–1867
Married: Brigham Young, 3 February 1846, Nauvoo, Illinois
Married: Thomas Cole, 6 September 1847

37. Abigail Harbach

Born: 20 September 1790, Sutton, Massachusetts
Died: 25 March 1849
Married: Calvin Hall, 25 August 1812
Married: Brigham Young, 3 February 1846, Nauvoo, Illinois

38. Mary Ann Turley

Born: 13 July 1827, Toronto, Ontario, Canada
Died: 24 December 1904, Utah
Married: Brigham Young, 3 February 1846, Nauvoo, Illinois
(divorced)
Married: John James Cook, 8 September 1851
    1) Sarah Ann Cook, 1860–1933

39. Naamah Kendel Jenkins Carter (Aunt Twiss)

Born: 21 March 1821, Wilmington, Massachusetts
Died: 5 August 1909, Salt Lake City, Utah
Married: John Saunders Twiss, 30 May 1845, Nauvoo, Illinois
Married: Brigham Young, 26 January 1846, Nauvoo, Illinois

40. Nancy Cressy (Crissie)

Born: 20 January 1780, New Brunswick, New Jersey
Died: 17 December 1871, Minersville, Utah

Married: Oliver Walker, 8 February 1803
    1) John R., 1804–1813
    2) Hannah, 1805–1813
    3) William Cressy, 1807
    4) Mary Ann, 1808
    5) Alfred, 1810–1813
    6) Sarah, 1812–1813
    7) Julian, 1814–1814
    8) Diontha, 1816–1896
    9) Nancy Reeder, 1817–1847
    10) Evaline, 1823–1912
Married: Brigham Young, 6 February 1846, Nauvoo, Illinois

Married while crossing the plains:

41. Jane Terry

Born: 21 May 1810, Short Hills, Niagara, Canada
Died: 14 February 1847, Winter Quarters, Nebraska
Married: George Tarbox, 1836, Niagara, Canada
1) Elisha Terry, 1837
Married: George W. Young, abt. 1840, Niagara, Canada
    1) Emma Amanda, 1841–1926
Married: Brigham Young, 10 February 1847, Winter Quarters

42. Lucy Bigelow

Born: 3 October 1830, Charleston, Illinois
Died: 3 February 1905, Salt Lake City, Utah
Married: Brigham Young, 20 March 1847, Winter Quarters,
  Nebraska
    1) Eudora Lovinia, 1852–1922
    2) Susan Amelia (Susa), 1856–1933
    3) Rhoda Mabel, 1863–1950

43. Mary Jane Bigelow

Born: 15 October 1827, Lawrenceville, Illinois
Died: 26 September 1868, Salt Lake City, Utah
Married: Brigham Young, 20 March 1847, Winter Quarters,
  Nebraska (divorced)
Married: Horace Roberts, 29 September 1852, Provo, Utah
Married: John Bair, 8 April 1856
Married: Daniel Durham Hunt, 14 February 1859
Married: Philander Bell, 9 April 1868

44. Sarah Malin

Born: 10 January 1804, Vincent Township, Pennsylvania
Died: 20 March 1858, Salt Lake City, Utah
Married: Brigham Young, 18 April 1848, on the plains

Married in Utah, 1850s:

45. Amanda Barnes

Born: 22 February 1809, Becket, Massachusetts
Died: 30 June 1886, Richmond, Utah
Married: Warren Smith, 20 March 1826, Amherst, Ohio
    1) Willard Gilbert, 1827–1903
    2) Sardis Washington, 1828–1838

    3) Alma Lamoni (twin), 1831–1887
    4) Alvira Lavonna (twin), 1831–1921
    5) Ortencia, 1834–1908
Married: Warren Smith, May 1840, Nauvoo, Illinois (divorced)
    1) Amanda Melvina, 1842–1843
    2) Warren Barnes, 1844–1935
    3) Sarah Marinda, 1846–1925
Married: Brigham Young, 19 January 1852, Salt Lake City, Utah

46. Eliza Burgess

Born: 8 Dec 1827, Lancashire, England
Died: 20 August 1915, Salt Lake City, Utah
Married: Brigham Young, 3 October 1852, Salt Lake City, Utah
    1) Alfales, 1853–1920

47. Mary Oldfield

Born: 28 June 1791, Minisick, New York
Died: 24 September 1875
Married: Eli Kelsey, 7 December 1805
    1) Edson Shepherd, 1810–1866
    2) Fitch Woodruff, 1812–1845
    3) Mary Jane, 1815–1870
    4) Catherine, 1817–1824
    5) Eli Brazee, 1819–1885
    6) George William, 1821–1827
Married: John Pearce, November 1844
Married: John Gribble
Married: Brigham Young, 16 December 1852, Utah

48. Eliza Babcock

Born: 8 October 1828, Mina, New York
Died: 1874
Married: Brigham Young, before 1853 (divorced)
Married: Dominicus Carter
Married: John Groves

49. Catherine Reese

Born: 26 January 1804, New York, New York
Died: 7 November 1860, Salt Lake City, Utah
Married: Zepheniah Clawson, 8 January 1824, Buffalo, New
  York
    1) Susannah, 1825–1826
    2) Hiram Bradley, 1826–1912
    3) John Reese, 1828–1872
    4) Louisa P., 1831–1832
    5) Helen Cordelia, 1835–1884
    6) Harriet Cornelia, 1839–1912
Married: Howard Egan, 1844, Nauvoo, Illinois
Married: Brigham Young, 10 June 1855, Salt Lake City, Utah

50. Harriet Emeline Barney

Born: 13 October 1830, Amherst, Ohio
Died: 14 February 1911, Salt Lake City, Utah
Married: William Henry Harrison Sagers, March 1846, Leroy
  Township, New York (divorced)

1) Mary Maria, 1847–1849
2) Royal Barney, 1851–1929
3) Joseph Ormal, 1853–1917
4) Sarah E., 1855–
Married: Brigham Young, 14 March 1856, Salt Lake City, Utah
1) Phineas Howe, 1863–1903

Married in Utah, 1860s:

51. Harriet Amelia Folsom
Born: 23 August 1838, Buffalo, New York
Died: 11 December 1910, Salt Lake City, Utah
Married: Brigham Young, 24 January 1863, Salt Lake City, Utah

52. Mary Van Cott
Born: 2 February 1844, Canaan (Elmira), New York
Died: 15 January 1884, Salt Lake City, Utah
Married: James Thornton Cobb, abt. 1851
1) Luella, 1860–1920
Married: Brigham Young, 8 January 1868, Salt Lake City, Utah
1) Fannie, 1870–1950

53. Ann Eliza Webb
Born: 13 September 1844, Nauvoo, Illinois
Died: unknown
Married: James Leech Dee, 10 April 1863, Salt Lake City, Utah (Div.divorced)
1) James Edward (Edward Wesley), 1864
2) Leonard Lorenzo, 1865
Married: Brigham Young, 7 April 1868, Salt Lake City, Utah (divorced)
Married: Moses R. Deming, after 1868

54. Elizabeth Jones
Born: 5 April 1813, Caddy, South Wales, Great Britain
Died: 6 May 1895, Salt Lake City, Utah
Married: David Thomas Lewis, 1833, South Wales, Great Britain
1) Thomas, 1834–1854
2) Eliza, 1836–1885
3) John, 1838
4) Canaan, 1841–1908
5) Sarah Elizabeth, 1844
6) Lewis, 1846–1920
Married: Captain Dan Jones, 8 November 1849
1) Ruth, 1850–
2) Brigham, 1852–
Married: Brigham Young, 3 July 1869, Salt Lake City, Utah

Married in Utah, 1870s:

55. Lydia Farnsworth
Born: 5 February 1808, Dorset, Vermont
Died: 5 February 1897, Pleasant Grove, Utah
Married: Elijah Mayhew, 2 October 1832, Shelbyville, Indiana

1) Lucinda, 1833–1833
2) Laurana, 1834–1835
3) Otto Lyman, 1836–1917
4) Austin Ship, 1838–1910
5) Elijah (twin), 1841–1841
6) Elisah (twin), 1841–1841
7) Caroline Abigail, 1842–1924
8) Elijah Warren, 1844–1845
9) Walter Franklin, 1848–1914
Married: Brigham Young, 8 May 1870, Salt Lake City, Utah

56. Hannah Tapfield
Born: 16 March 1807, Sawston, Devon, England
Died: 25 September 1886, Salt Lake City, Utah
Married: Thomas Owen King, 6 April 1824, Dernford-Dale, Cambridge, England
1) son, 1825–1825
2) Margaret, 1827–1828
3) Charlotte, 1829–1829
4) Georgiana, 1830–1852
5) Owen, 1831–1840
6) Louisa, 1833–1912
7) Bertha Mary, 1835–1912
8) Peter Tapfield, 1837–1838
9) Thomas Owen Jr., 1840–1921
10) Andrew Crookson, 1841–1842
Married: Brigham Young, 8 December 1872, Salt Lake City, Utah

For Further Reference
1. *Miriam Works.* "History of Brigham Young," *Deseret News,* 10 February 1858, 385; "Nauvoo Sealings and Adoptions," 577, 581, FHL; *Documentary History of the Church,* vol. 1, (n.p., n.d.), 297; Leonard J. Arrington, *Brigham Young: American Moses* (New York: Alfred A. Knopf, 1985), 15–17, 20, 26, 30, 33–34; Kate B. Carter, ed., *Brigham Young: His Wives and Family* (Salt Lake City: Daughters of Utah Pioneers, 1990), 11; Journal History of the Church of Jesus Christ of Latter-day Saints (Liverpool and London: LDS Booksellers, 1855–1886), 15 February 1845 (hereafter cited as JH).
2. *Mary Ann Angell.* "History of Brigham Young," *Deseret News* 10 February 1848, 385; "Nauvoo Sealings and Adoptions," 577, FHL; Record of Members, Eighteenth Ward, Salt Lake Stake, Salt Lake City, Utah, 1; Death records, no. 184801864, Salt Lake City, Utah, 271; Carter, *Brigham Young: His Wives and Family,* 12; Obituary, *Deseret Evening News,* 28 June 1882, 3, 11; Obituary, *Woman's Exponent* 11, no. 4 (15 July 1882): 28–29.
3. *Lucy Ann Decker.* "Nauvoo Sealings and Adoptions," 577, FHL; Record of Members, Eighteenth Ward, Salt Lake Stake, Salt Lake City, Utah, 1; Joseph F. Smith, *Plural Marriage Affidavit Books,* 2 vol., Archives of the Church of Jesus Christ of Latter-day Saints (hereafter LDS Church Archives), Salt Lake City, Utah, 1:48; "Death of Lucy D. Young," *Deseret Evening News,* 24 January 1891, 8; Arrington, 210; "Death of Lucy D. Young," *Woman's Exponent* 1 (March 1891); Carter, *Brigham Young: His Wives and Family,* 15; Orson F. Whitney,

History of Utah, 4 vols. (Salt Lake City: George Q. Cannon & Sons, 1904), 63. Sally came into the family as a teenager in 1847. She and another teen, a boy, were captured in a raid led by Wanship against another band of Utes led by Little Wolf. Another Ute, Batiste, offered to sell both youngsters to the Mormons, threatening to kill them if he could not sell them. When the Mormons refused, Batiste killed the boy. Charles Decker then bought the girl and gave her to his sister, Lucy, to raise as one of her own children.

4. *Augusta Adams.* "Nauvoo Sealings and Adoptions," 577, FHL; Record of Members, Eighteenth Ward, Salt Lake Stake, Salt Lake City, Utah, 1; Smith, *Plural Marriage Affidavit Books*, 1:50; Obituary, *Deseret Evening News*, 3 February 1886, 2; Mary Cable, "She Who Shall Be Nameless," *American Heritage* 16 (16 Feburary 1965): 50–55; Mary Cable, telephone interview with Judy Dykman, July 2000; Carter, *Brigham Young: His Wives and Family*, 15; photo collection, Utah State Historical Society, Salt Lake City. Sequence of her children is uncertain.

5. *Harriet Cook.* "Nauvoo Sealings and Adoptions," 577, FHL; Smith, *Plural Marriage Affidavit Books*, 1:50; Obituary, JH, 5 November 1898, 2; Edith Harriett Young Booth, "A Biographical Sketch of the Life of Oscar S. Young," typescript; "How One Wife Outwitted Brigham," *The Utah Magazine* (June 1947), 22. Brigham Young Family Organization lists her birthplace as Utica, New York, a neighboring city to Whitesboro and county seat of Ontario County.

6. *Clarissa Decker.* "Nauvoo Sealings and Adoptions," 577, FHL; Smith, *Plural Marriage Affidavit Books*, 2:16; Obituary, *Deseret Evening News*, 7 January 1889, 2; Clara Decker Young, "A Young Women's Experience with the Pioneer Band," 1884, Bancroft Library, University of California, Berkeley; Orson F. Whitney, "The Three Pioneer Women," in *History of Utah*, 4:63–67; "Death of Clara D. Young," *Woman's Exponent*, 15 January 1889; Carter, *Brigham Young: His Wives and Family*, 15.

7. *Emily Dow Partridge.* "Nauvoo Sealings and Adoptions," 503, 577, FHL; Record of Members, Eighteenth Ward, Salt Lake Stake, Salt Lake City, Utah, not paginated; Susa Young Gates and Mabel Young Sanborn, "Brigham Young Genealogy," *Utah Genealogical and Historical Magazine* 11 (April 1920): 127; Emily Down Partridge Young, "What I Remember," typescript, 1884; Obituary, *Deseret Evening News*, 9 December 1899, 7; Carter, *Brigham Young: His Wives and Family*, 18; Linda King Newell and Valeen Tippetts Avery, *Mormon Enigma: Emma Hale Smith* (New York: Doubleday, 1984), 49, 89, 137–38, 144–45, 170–71, 309; *Woman's Exponent* (October 1908); Todd Compton, *In Sacred Loneliness* (Salt Lake City: Signature Books, 2000), 396–456; news article from *Kansas City Journal*, 12 December 1899, microfilm, LDS Church Archives, Salt Lake City, Utah.

8. *Clarissa Ross.* "Nauvoo Sealings and Adoptions," 577, FHL; Brigham Young, Journal, 10 September 1844, 10 October 1857; Heber C. Kimball, Journal, 10 September 1844; Phoebe McLaughlin Welling, "History of Isaac Chase," typescript, 1964; JH, 10 October 1857, 1; Carter, *Brigham Young: His Wives and Family*, 17. Clarissa is sometimes called "Chase" after her stepfather. Her birthplace is also given as Northville, Cayuga County, New York.

9. *Louisa Beaman.* "Nauvoo Sealings and Adoptions," 503, 577, FHL; Historian's Office, Journal, 16 May 1850; Brigham Young, Journal, 19 September 1844; Kimball, Journal, 19 September 1844; Smith, *Plural Marriage Affidavit Books*, 1:3, 38–39; Compton, 55–70.

10. *Eliza Roxcy Snow.* "Nauvoo Proxy Sealings, 1846," 67, FHL; "Nauvoo Sealings and Adoptions," 513–14, FHL; Record of Members, Eighteenth Ward, Salt Lake Stake, Salt Lake City,

Utah, 1; Obituary, *Deseret News*, 36: (7 December 1887): 744; Brigham Young, Journal, 3 October 1844; Kimball, Journal, 3 October 1844; Allen Kent Powell, ed., "Eliza Roxcy Snow," in *Utah History Encyclopedia* (Salt Lake City: University of Utah Press, 1994), 509; Carter, *Brigham Young: His Wives and Family*, 26; Whitney, 573; Newell and Avery, 60–61, 68, 106–7, 119–20, 122, 129, 131–34, 136–37, 155, 165, 207, 211. Brigham Young Family Organization lists marriage date as 29 June 1849; Compton, 306–41; biographical sketch in Lucy Marie Canfield Margetts's account of travel from New York to Utah, microfilm, LDS Archives Salt Lake City, Utah.

11. *Elizabeth Fairchild.* "Nauvoo Sealings and Adoptions," 577, FHL; Brigham Young, Journal, 3 October 1844; Kimball, Journal, 3 October 1844; Divorce certificate, 2 June 1855, Brigham Young Papers, LDS Church Archives, Salt Lake City, Utah; Family group sheet of William Lowery Chastain and Elizabeth Fairchild. Elizabeth was sealed to Brigham Young on 30 January 1846.

12. *Clarissa Blake.* "Nauvoo Sealings and Adoptions," 577, FHL; Brigham Young, Journal, 8 October 1844.

13. *Rebecca Holman.* "Nauvoo Sealings and Adoptions," 577, FHL; Brigham Young, Journal, 9 October 1844; Elsie M. Williams, "Biography of Joshua Sawyer Holman," typescript, n.d.; Cutlers Park (Nebraska), Death and burial records, 1846–1849. Rebecca was sealed to Brigham Young on 6 February 1846.

14. *Diana Chase.* "Nauvoo Sealings and Adoptions," 577, FHL; Brigham Young, Journal, 10 October 1844; Kimball, Journal, 27 May 1845; Olive Virginia Grey Madsen, "Diana Chase Shaw," typescript, n.d.

15. *Susannah Snively.* "Nauvoo Sealings and Adoptions," 577, FHL; Record of Members, Eighteenth Ward, Salt Lake Stake, Salt Lake City, Utah, not paginated; Obituary, *Deseret Evening News*, 21 November 1892, 5; Brigham Young, Journal, 31 October 1844.

16. *Olive Gray Frost.* Mary Ann Frost Pratt, "Biographical Sketch of Olive Gray Frost," *Historical Record* 6 (January 1887): 234–35; Brigham Young, Journal, 7 November 1844; Carter, *Brigham Young: His Wives and Family*, 16; Compton, 586–92.

17. *Mary Ann Clark.* "Nauvoo Sealings and Adoptions," 31, 577, FHL; Brigham Young, Journal, 15 January 1845; Mary Ann Clark Powers, letter to Brigham Young, Brigham Young Papers, LDS Church Archives, Salt Lake City, Utah.

18. *Margaret Pierce.* "Nauvoo Sealings and Adoptions," 31, 577, FHL; Record of Members, Eighteenth Ward, Salt Lake Stake, Salt Lake, City, Utah, 1; "Widow of President Brigham Young Who Died Last Night . . ." *Deseret Evening News*, 17 January 1907, 10; "Autobiography of Margarette P. W. Young," holograph, n.d.; "One of the Pioneers," *Young Woman's Journal* 15 (1 April 1904): 162–66; *Improvement Era* 10:400.

19. *Mary Pierce.* "Nauvoo Sealings and Adoptions," 31, 577, FHL; Eliza R. Snow, Diary, 17 March 1847; JH, 17 March 1847, 1.

20. *Emeline Free.* "Nauvoo Sealings and Adoptions," 577, FHL; Death records, no. 6867, Salt Lake City, Utah, 172; Obituary, *Deseret Evening News*, 19 July 1875, 1, 3; Susa Young Gates and Mabel Young Sanborn, "Brigham Young Genealogy," *Utah Genealogical and Historical Magazine* 11 (April 1920): 129; Arrington, 371; Carter, *Brigham Young: His Wives and Family*, 19; Obituary, *Woman's Exponent* 4, no. 5 (1 August 1875): 37.

21. *Mary Elizabeth Rollins Lightener.* "Nauvoo Sealings and Adoptions," 505, 577, FHL; Mary Elizabeth Rollins Lightner, Autobiography and Diary, Special Collections, Harold B. Lee Library, Brigham Young University, Provo, Utah, n.d.; "Mary Elizabeth Rollins Lightner," *Utah Genealogical and Historical Magazine* 17 (July 1926): 193–205, 250–60; Kimball, Journal,

May 1845; Kate B. Carter, "Mary Elizabeth Rollins Lightner," *Our Pioneer Heritage* 5 (1962): 305–24; Obituary, *Woman's Exponent* 41 (January 1914): 95; Compton, 205–27.

22. *Margaret Alley.* "Nauvoo Sealings and Adoptions," 577, FHL; Historian's Office, Journal, 6 November 1852; Carter, *Brigham Young: His Wives and Family*, 20.

23. *Olive Andrews.* "Nauvoo Proxy Sealings, 1846," 4, FHL; "Nauvoo Sealings and Adoptions," 153, 577, FHL.

24. *Emily Haws.* "Nauvoo Sealings and Adoptions," 577, FHL; Kimball, Journal, 15 January 1846.

25. *Martha Bowker.* "Nauvoo Sealings and Adoptions," 577, FHL; Record of Members, Eighteenth Ward, Salt Lake Stake, Salt Lake City, Utah, 1; Obituary, *Deseret Evening News*, 26 September 1890, 3; Kimball, Journal, 19 December 1845; *Woman's Exponent*, 1 November 1890 and 26 September 1890; Carter, *Brigham Young: His Wives and Family*, 22.

26. *Ellen Rockwood.* "Nauvoo Sealings and Adoptions," 577, FHL.

27. *Jemima Angell.* "Nauvoo Sealings and Adoptions," 577, FHL; Marjorie McCandless and Utahna Frantz, "History of Jemima Angell Young," typescript, n.d.

28. *Abigail Marks.* "Nauvoo Sealings and Adoptions," 577, FHL; Family group sheet of Asa Works and Abigail Marks, FHL; Kimball, Journal, 7 January 1846.

29. *Phebe Morton.* "Nauvoo Sealings and Adoptions," 577, FHL; Family group sheet of Asa Works and Abigail Marks, FHL; Kimball, Journal, 7 January 1846; Ancestral File.

30. *Cynthia Porter.* "Nauvoo Sealings and Adoptions," 577, FHL; Salt Lake City Cemetery records, no. 1273, 4 January 1861.

31. *Mary Eliza Nelson.* "Nauvoo Sealings and Adoptions," 299, 581, 701; Obituary, *Deseret Evening News*, 29 December 1885, 2; Brigham Young Family Organization; Ancestral File.

32. *Rhoda Richards.* "Nauvoo Sealings and Adoptions," 511–12, 581, FHL; Obituary, *Deseret Evening News*, 18 January 1879, 3; Edward W. Tullidge, *Women of Mormondom* (New York: Tullidge and Crandall, 1877), 421–22.

33. *Zina Huntington.* "Nauvoo Proxy Sealings, 1846," 61, FHL; "Nauvoo Sealings and Adoptions," 511–12, 581, FHL; "Passed into the Repose of Death," *Deseret Evening News,* 28 August 1901, 8; Emmeline B. Wells, "Zina D. H. Young—A Character Sketch," *Improvement Era* 5 (November 1901): 43–48; "Zina D. H. Young: A Brief Sketch of Her Life and Labors," *Deseret Evening News*, 25 January 1896, 5; Whitney, 576; Carter, *Brigham Young: His Wives and Family*, 23; Compton, 71–113; Martha Sonntag Bradley and Mary Brown Firmage Woodward, *Four Zinas: A Story of Mothers and Daughters on the Mormon Frontier* (Salt Lake City: Signature Press, n.d.), 2001.

34. *Amy Cecelia Cooper.* "Nauvoo Sealings and Adoptions," 577, FHL.

35. *Mary de la Montague.* "Nauvoo Sealings and Adoptions, 577, FHL; Brigham Young, letter to Mary Woodward, 13 December 1846, Brigham Young Papers, LDS Church Archives, Salt Lake City, Utah.

36. *Julia Foster.* "Nauvoo Proxy Sealings, 1846," 66–67, FHL; "Nauvoo Sealings and Adoptions," 327–28, 581, FHL; Brigham Young Hampton, Diary, holograph; Obituary, *Deseret Evening News*, 17 January 1891, 8.

37. *Abigail Harbach.* "Nauvoo Sealings and Adoptions," 577, FHL.

38. *Mary Ann Turley.* "Nauvoo Sealings and Adoptions," 577, FHL; Kimball, Journal, 20 December 1845; Divorce certificate, 14 January 1851, Brigham Young Papers, LDS Church Archives, Salt Lake City, Utah.

39. *Naamah Carter.* "Nauvoo Sealings and Adoptions," 533–34, 581, FHL; Record of Members, Eighteenth Ward, Salt lake Stake, Salt Lake City, Utah, 1; Obituary, *Deseret Evening News*, 6 August 1909, 1; "A Pioneer Speaks," *Improvement Era* 42 (July 1940): 404; Carter, *Brigham Young: His Wives and Family*, 24.

40. *Nancy Cressy.* "Nauvoo Sealings and Adoptions," 559, FHL; "Index to Nauvoo Endowments, FHL.

41. *Jane Terry.* "Nauvoo Sealings and Adoptions," 799, FHL; "Pre-Endowment House and Endowment House Sealings," book E, 321; Elizabeth Terry Heward, "Autobiography," in *Parshall Terry Family History* (Salt Lake City: Mr. and Mrs. Terry Lund, 1956), 68–78; Nora Lund, "History of Jane Terry Young," (unpublished, n.d.), typescript, microfilm, LDS Church Archives, Salt Lake City, Utah. George Tarbox is sometimes listed as Turbox or Tarbor. Jane's birth place is also given as Short Hills, Niagara, Canada.

42. *Lucy Bigelow.* "Nauvoo Sealings and Adoptions," 783, FHL; Record of Members, Eighteenth Ward, Salt Lake Stake, Salt Lake City, Utah, 1; Obituary, *Deseret Evening News*, 3 February 1905, 1, and 4 February 1905, 3; *Improvement Era* 8:396; Susa Young Gates, "Lucy Bigelow Young," Utah State Historical Society, Salt Lake City (hereafter cited as Gates, "Lucy Bigelow"); Emmeline B. Wells, "Lucy Bigelow Young," *Young Woman's Journal* 3 (January 1892): 145–47; Miriam Murphy, "From Impulsive Girl to Patient Wife: Lucy Bigelow Young," *Utah Historical Quarterly* 45, no. 3 (summer 1977): 283; Lucy Bigelow Young, autobiography, unpublished, Brigham Young Family Organization. Lucy's autobiography gives her marriage date as 14 March 1847.

43. *Mary Jane Bigelow.* "Nauvoo Sealings and Adoptions," 783, FHL; Gates, "Lucy Bigelow"; Divorce certificate, 3 September 1851, Brigham Young Papers, LDS Church Archives, Salt Lake City, Utah; Lucy Bigelow Young, autobiography, unpublished, Brigham Young Family Organization.

44. *Sarah Malin.* "Nauvoo Sealings and Adoptions," 783, FHL; Death records, 22, no. 863, Salt Lake City, Utah, 22.

45. *Amanda Barnes.* Endowment House Sealing Records, 19 January 1852; Nauvoo Temple Endowment Register, 40 (20 December 1845); correspondence and divorce papers, Brigham Young Papers, LDS Church Archives, Salt Lake City, Utah; "Death of a Veteran Lady," *Deseret Evening News,* vol. 35 (12 July 1886), 403; Frank E. Esshom, *Pioneers and Prominent Men of Utah* (Salt Lake City: Utah Pioneers Book Publishing Co., 1912), 1170; Warren Smith (1794–1838) family group sheet and Warren Smith (1808–1885) family group sheet, FHL. An interesting fictionalized view of Amanda is contained in Paul W. Hodson, *Never Forsake: The Story of Amanda Barnes Smith, Legacy of the Haun's Mill Massacre* (Salt Lake City: Keeban Publications, 1996).

46. *Eliza Burgess.* Record of Members, Eighteenth Ward, Salt Lake Stake, Salt Lake City, Utah, 1; "Pre-Endowment House and Endowment House Sealings," book A, no. 806; "Eliza B. Young Dies at Son's Home," *Deseret Evening News*, 21 August 1915, 16; Carter, *Brigham Young: His Wives and Family*, 27.

47. *Mary Oldfield.* "Pre-Endowment House and Endowment House Sealings," book A, no. 953; and book D, 93, no. 4947, 93.

48. *Eliza Babcock.* Nauvoo Temple Endowment Register, 10 January 1846, FHL; Divorce certificate, 4 September 1853, Brigham Young Papers, LDS Church Archives, Salt Lake City, Utah; Family group sheet of Adolphus Babcock and Jerusha Rowley, FHL. The sequence of these marriages is uncertain as reliable dates and places are not available on all of them.

49. *Catherine Reese.* "Nauvoo Sealings and Adoptions," 49, FHL; Family group sheet for Zepheniah Clawson and Catherine Reese, FHL.

50. *Harriet Barney.* "Pre-Endowment House and Endowment House Sealings," book B, 49, FHL; Obituary, *Deseret Evening*

News, 11 February 1911, 2; *Improvement Era* 14:563; Wayne D. Stout, "William Henry Harrison Sagers," in *History of Tooele County* (Tooele County: Daughter of the Utah Pioneers, 1961), 570; Ray Moss, interview with Judy Dykman, 2000; Carter, *Brigham Young: His Wives and Family*, 28.

51. *Amelia Folsom.* "Salt Lake Endowment House Records," 2 March 1861, FHL; Obituary, *Deseret Evening News*, 12 December 1910, 1,; and 15 December 1910, 2; "Death Beckons to Mrs. Young," *Salt Lake Tribune*, 12 December 1910; *Improvement Era* 14 (1910):280; Carter, *Brigham Young: His Wives and Family*, 29.

52. *Mary Van Cott.* "Salt Lake Endowment House Records," 18 April 1856, FHL; "Death of Mary V. Young," *Deseret Evening News*, 5 January 1884, 5; Death records 1848–1884, Salt Lake City, Utah, 297.

53. *Ann Eliza Webb.* "Salt Lake Endowment House Records," book E, 126; Ann Eliza Webb Young, *Wife Number 19; or, The Story of a Life in Bondage, Being a Complete ExposÈ of Mormonism and Revealing the Sorrows, Sacrifices, and Sufferings of a Woman in Polygamy* (Hartford, Connecticut: Dustin Gilman & Co., 1876); Irving Wallace, *The Twenty-seventh Wife* (New York: Simon & Schuster, 1961); Arrington, 333–34, 373, 389; Carter, *Brigham Young: His Wives and Family*, 31.

54. *Elizabeth Jones.* "Salt Lake Endowment House Records," book E, 308; "Death of Sister Jones," *Deseret Evening News*, 6 May 1895, 1, 5; Tullidge, *Women of Mormondom*, 460; Rex LeRoy Christensen, "The Life and Contributions of Captain Dan Jones," (master's thesis, Logan, Utah: Utah State University, 1977); life history of Elizabeth Jones Lewis Jones Young by her granddaughter, Josephine Lewis Andersen, unpublished; Alice Cloward, great-granddaughter of Elizabeth Jones, telephone interview with Colleen Whitley, 20 June 2000.

55. *Lydia Farnsworth.* "Salt Lake Endowment House Records," book F, 172; Obituary, *Deseret Evening News*, 6 February 1897, 8; Family group sheet of Elijah Mayhew and Lydia Farnsworth, FHL.

56. *Hannah Tapfield.* "Salt Lake Endowment House Records," book H, 353; *Deseret Evening News*, 27 September 1886, 3; Kate B. Carter, ed., "My Story—Hannah T. King," *Treasures of Pioneer History* 3 (1954): 45–48; Family group sheet of Thomas Owen King and Hannah Tapfield; Kenneth L. Holmes, et al., *Covered Wagon Women*, vol. 6 (Lincoln: University of Nebraska, 1997); Hannah Tapfield Young, "Autobiography," LDS Church Historical Department, Salt Lake City, Utah, circa 1864–1872; Alfene Page, *Woman's Exponent: Cradle of Literary Culture among Early Mormon Women*, (master's thesis, Logan, Utah: Utah State University Press, 1988).

Women Sometimes Named as Young's Wives

Various women have been listed in published accounts as wives of Brigham Young. Some could possibly have been wives, but have not been conclusively established as such. Other claims have been disproven altogether. Still others were simply allegations stated so vaguely as to defy identification. Some are downright silly.

A few of those claimants are listed here alphabetically by their surnames or by the nicknames attributed to them. In some cases, only allegations about their marriages exist and no records of the women themselves have been found. In other cases a good deal of factual information can reasonably be determined. This list is certainly not conclusive; it simply contains names listed in widely circulated, published accounts. Obviously the status of any of these women could change with the discovery of heretofore unknown records. The second section of this appendix list records relating to each woman.

Nancy Chamberlain

Ann Eliza Young claimed that Nancy was

a very old, half-crazed woman, known, I fancy, to every Mormon in the Territory, who solemnly declares that she was sealed to Brigham in Nauvoo, and that she had the promise of being promoted to the place of first wife. She lived with his family for a long time, but she grew old, and infirm, and useless, and he turned her out of the house some years ago; and now she lives as best she may, going about from house to house, and performing light work to pay for her support.

She considers it her duty every little while to go and "free her mind," as she calls it, to Brigham's wives, telling them that they may usurp her place and defraud her of her rights in this world, but she shall be Brigham's queen in heaven. She is an eccentric old woman, but there is no doubt, I think, about her having been sealed to the Prophet.

While Ann Eliza may have had no doubts, others do. No record of a sealing between Brigham Young and Nancy Chamberlain has been found to date. Nancy Chamberlain is not mentioned in the 1860 census. Many people, however, lived in the Lion House at various times, and any individual's being there does not necessarily indicate marriage to any member of the family.

Moreover, Ann Eliza's accusation that Brigham turned Nancy out when she became old and infirm runs counter to his behavior in every other known case of wives, children, relatives, and assorted other folks not related at all. Most importantly, the statement was made at the time when Ann Eliza was earning her livelihood by writing and lecturing against the evils of Mormonism, making her word suspect at best.

Charlotte Cobb

Charlotte Cobb accompanied her mother Augusta Adams Cobb to Nauvoo in 1843. Augusta became Brigham's fourth wife, but no record has been found of a marriage between him and Charlotte. Brigham, in fact, sealed her to William S. Godbe on 7 April 1869 in the Endowment House in Salt Lake City. Brigham officiated in his capacity as prophet of the LDS Church, but also as Godbe's friend and a "father of the bride," having adopted Charlotte when he married her mother. Charlotte, an accomplished pianist and excellent conversationalist, was called the "belle of Salt Lake City," and even territorial governor Benjamin Ferris, not one to lightly accord praise to any Mormon, described her as "handsome in face."

Charlotte's marriage to Godbe lasted until 1879. She apparently remained faithful to him through his excommunication from the LDS Church and his ventures into other forms of worship. Eventually, however, describing herself as having "wobbled around in the faith," she returned to the fold and henceforward defended it valiantly. Like her New England forebears, she sought social change. With Godbe's other wives, she had enrolled in the National Woman Suffrage Association during the 1870s and spoke and wrote publicly about women's rights, the evils of drink, and other significant issues. She's an interesting woman, but not one of Brigham's wives.

MINA A. COOK, SUSAN TAFFINDOR, AND ELIZA Y. YOUNG

Stanley P. Hirshorn claims that in the 1860 census, Brigham Young listed Mina (37), Susan (16), and Eliza Y. Young (19) as wives. They are, indeed, included in the census with Brigham's household. However, the 1860 Utah census simply lists the people living in the house, their ages, genders, and usually but not always, place of origin; the heads of households are identified by occupation. Few relationships are given; in the Young listings, even known wives like Mary Ann A[ngell] are simply entered by name, age, and birthplace. No other records have been found to date indicating marriages to Mina, Susan, or Eliza, so the allegation appears to be based simply on an erroneous assumption about a census record. Why these women were named as wives presents an additional mystery, however, since the Young household in 1860 included several other women who could equally have been assumed to be wives but whom Hirshorn does not name.

MARGARET G——

Samuel Hawthornthwaite, an apostate Mormon, described Margaret G—— as a convert from Manchester, England. He says she was "decoyed" to Utah by Elder Moses Martin, who "disgraced" her on the way. He reported that she then joined Brigham Young's household, then subsequently married James Ferguson and John Cook. Given the lack of a surname for Margaret, investigation into this case becomes problematic at best. The Ancestral File lists many James Fergusons (with, of course, variant spellings) and dozens of John Cooks (and Cookes, Cokes, et al.); among all of those born between 1820 and 1860, one James Ferguson married a Margaret, but they were from New York, and one John Cook married a Margarutte Gratrix, listed simply of Utah, with whom he apparently remained married. This story appears to be another example of bashing by a disgruntled anti-Mormon.

TALULA GIBSON

Talula Gibson was the daughter of Walter Murray Gibson, one of the more colorful characters in early LDS history. Talula traveled with him as he opened a mission in the Sandwich Islands (Hawaii), although Brigham Young had sent him to Japan. When Gibson landed in Hawaii on 4 July 1861, he showed the natives Young's authorization, an impressive-looking parchment, which Gibson had embellished with ribbons and seals. His mission operated a little differently from most in the Church of Jesus Christ of Latter-day Saints: he sold church offices, required the natives to enter his home on all fours, and put the Book of Mormon in a hollow stone and announced that touching it meant instant death. Not surprisingly, he was excommunicated in 1865. Release from the Mormon Church, however, did little to slow Gibson. He entered the Hawaiian legislature, eventually becoming prime minister. During a revolution in 1887 he escaped with Talula and her husband Fred H. Hayselden. Gibson died penniless in San Francisco the next year.

Reports of Talula's marriage to Brigham Young come from comments made by Richard Burton in *City of the Saints* and from reports that the 1860 census lists a seventeen-year-old "Toledah" Gibson of Georgia as a wife. However, as noted in the discussion of Mina A. Cook, the 1860 census does not list relationships. The fact that a woman named Toledah Gibson was staying with the Young household does not mean she was a wife. She may well be Walter Murray Gibson's daughter, since he was serving a mission and missionaries' families often stayed with others while the family breadwinner was away. No record has been found of a marriage between Talula and Brigham or of a divorce from either him or Hayselden.

MARIA LAWRENCE

Maria Lawrence, born 18 December 1823 in Pickering Township, Ontario, Canada, has probably been listed as Brigham's wife in more publications than any other in this appendix. Even Leonard Arrington called her a wife, though he later expressed regret at having done so. She was certainly a member of the LDS Church, joining with her parents and traveling with her sister, Sarah, from Canada to Nauvoo in 1838 where they lived for a time with Joseph and Emma Smith. Emily Partridge reported in her diary that both Maria and Sarah were sealed to Joseph Smith. Maria was married to Almon W. Babbit in January 1846 and had one child by him. Some secondary sources say she was sealed to Brigham Young at about the same time, but no records have been found of such a sealing or of a cancellation of her sealing to Babbit. Benjamin F. Johnson, a longtime friend, on hearing of reports that Maria had been sealed to Brigham Young, wrote a letter to the *Deseret News* in 1897 stating that no such sealing had ever taken place and that Maria died in Nauvoo in 1847.

ELEANOR JANE MCCOMB MCLEAN

Described as "tall," "handsome," and "queenly," Eleanor Jane McComb was born 29 December 1817, in Wheeling, West Virginia. She married Hector Hugh McLean of Wheeling, West Virginia, and they had three children, Fitzroy (1839), Albert (1841), and Ann Blanche (1847). At the time Eleanor came into LDS history, McLean was a customs house official in San Francisco. She was converted to the LDS Church and married Parley Parker Pratt, the missionary who had converted her, on 14 November 1855. She later returned to New Orleans, reclaimed her children, and was attempting to travel with Pratt to Utah when McLean shot and killed him near Van Buren, Arkansas, in May 1857.

The only evidence offered for Eleanor's alleged alliance with Brigham Young is that she lived for a time at the Lion House, which, in fact, she probably did—as did a great many other people who were also not married to Brigham. For the bulk of her later life she lived in a one-story adobe house on Pratt's land, an indication by itself that she was his widow. Eleanor died in Salt Lake City on 24 October 1874.

SARAH ANN MCDONAL

Sarah Ann McDonal was born 3 March 1856 in Springville, Utah, and died 21 June 1925 in Heber, Utah. She did, indeed, marry Brigham Young—Brigham Jonathan Young, born in England, the son of Jonathan Young and Sarah Toomer. He appears to be no relation to Brigham Young the prophet. The couple married on 11 April 1875 and apparently remained together for the rest of their lives, producing fifteen children. This allegation probably results simply from confusing two men with similar names.

SUSAN TAFFINDOR

See Mina A. Cook.

TWO SIOUX INDIANS

In an anti-Mormon polemic in 1852 William Hall said Brigham Young had married two Sioux women in mid January 1847 at Winter Quarters. Hall also reports Young "dressed his two new brides in large gold chains, elegant slippers, and various ornaments. . . ." Given the financial state of the Saints at the time, such elaborate gifts are highly improbable. Moreover, while the Mormons encountered many Native Americans while traveling west and settling in Utah, they had little to do with the Sioux. The Omaha tribe, in fact, allowed the Saints to settle in their territory at Winter Quarters in large part to serve as a buffer against the Sioux. The Sioux, then, is not a likely tribe from which Mormons might have garnered wives. One reason for such an allegation from an anti-Mormon source may be the alignment of two separate bigotries. The common American attitude toward Native Americans at the time was extremely negative, casting doubt on their intelligence, honesty, even their humanity. To accuse a white man of an alliance with Native women would be more than an insult, in this case, just further proof of the Mormons' fundamental indecency. Since no names are given for these women and since no other report corroborates Hall's story, it is impossible to verify and is probably just another anit-Mormon story.

JANE WATT

Jane Brown was reported to have married both Brigham Young and her half-brother, George Watt. No evidence has been found of a marriage to Brigham; she did, however, marry George. The LDS Church Archives contains a letter from George to Brigham asking permission for the two of them to marry. They had five children before Jane divorced George, married a soldier, and moved to the Midwest.

ELIZA Y. YOUNG

See Mina A. Cook.

FOR FURTHER REFERENCE

Nancy Chamberlain. Ann Eliza Webb Young, *Wife Number 19* (Hartford, Connecticut: Dustin Gilman & Co., 1876), 417; Eighth Census (1860).

Charlotte Cobb. Stanley Hirshson, *Lion of the Lord* (New York: Alfred A. Knopf, 1969), 214; Ronald W. Walker, *Wayward Saints: The Godbeites and Brigham Young* (Urbana and Chicago: University of Illinois Press, 1998), 134–36, 325, 328–30, 355–56.

Mina A. Cook. Eighth Census (1860), 1:268, quoted in Hirshson, 219.

Margaret G——. Samuel Hawthornthwaite, quoted in Hirshson, 216.

Talula Gibson. R. Lanier Britsch, *Unto the Islands of the Sea* (Salt Lake City: Deseret Book, 1986), 118–24; Eighth Census (1860), 1:270, line 4; Hirshson, 218; Walker, *Wayward Saints*, 136–37.

Maria Lawrence. Ancestral File; Hirshson, 200; Kate B. Carter, ed., *Brigham Young: His Wives and Family*, (Salt Lake City: Daughters of Utah Pioneers, 1990), 21–22; Leonard J. Arrington, *Brigham Young: American Moses*, (New York: Alfred A. Knopf, 1985), 421; Leonard J. Arrington, conversations with Jeffrey O. Johnson, 1986; Dean Jesse, "Brigham Young's Family: The Wilderness Years," *BYU Studies* 19 (summer 1979): 475–99; *Woman's Exponent* 14:38; Linda King Newell and Valeen Tippetts Avery, *Mormon Enigma: Emma Hale Smith*, 144; Todd Compton, *In Sacred Lonliness: The Plural Wives of Joseph Smith* (Salt Lake City: Signature Books, 2000), 473–79.

Eleanor Jane McComb McLean. Ancestral File; Hirshson, 217; Richard Burton, *City of the Saints* (n.p., n.d.), 474; Norman F. Furniss, *The Mormon Conflict 1850–1859* (New Haven: Yale University Press, 1960), 89–90.

Sarah Ann McDonnal. Ancestral File; Hirshson, 221.

Susan Taffindor. Eighth Census (1860), 1:268, quoted in Hirshson, 219.

Two Sioux Indians. Hall, *Abominations of Mormondom Exposed*, quoted in Hirshson, 214; Jeffrey O. Johnson, interviews with Colleen Whitley, 1998–2001.

Jane Watt. The New York Times, 1 May 1858, quoted by Hirshson, 216; Ron Watt, Historical Department of the Church of Jesus Christ of Latter-day Saints, Salt Lake City, Utah, telephone interview with Colleen Whitley, 1999. Watt is currently working on a life of George Watt and has conducted extensive research in the family.

Eliza Y. Young. Eighth Census (1860), 1:268, quoted in Hirshson, 219.

Notes

PREFACE

1. Susa Young Gates, *Unique Story—President Brigham Young* (Salt Lake City: Daughters of Utah Pioneers, 1990), 79.

2. Brigham Young was appointed "a committee of one" to build a public bathhouse at the warm springs north of Salt Lake City; today the building houses the Utah Children's Museum. Journal History of the Church of Jesus Christ of Latter-day Saints (Liverpool and London: LDS Booksellers, 1855–1886), microfilm, Historical Department of the Church of Jesus Christ of Latter-day Saints, Salt Lake City, Utah, 17 February 1849.

3. Leonard J. Arrington, *Brigham Young: American Moses* (New York: Alfred A. Knopf, 1985), 206.

4. For a complete discussion of the problems of Brigham Young's will, see Leonard J. Arrington, "The Settlement of Brigham Young's Estate, 1877–1879," *Pacific Historical Review* 21 (1952): 1. One simple but obvious error in one printed form of the will is the bequest of property to Brigham's son Weber, a misprint of the name Heber. Brigham Young, will, Utah State Historical Society, Salt Lake City, pamphlet 3857.

5. Several other women requested that they be sealed to Brigham after his death, but since he did not provide houses for them while they lived, they are not included here.

CHAPTER 1

1. Al Church, "Stalking the Wild Gentile," *Network* 5 (September 1981): 17.

2. Ann Eliza Webb Young, *Wife Number 19; or, The Story of a Life in Bondage, Being a Complete Exposé of Mormonism and Revealing the Sorrow, Sacrifices, and Suffering of a Woman in Polygamy* (Hartford, Connecticut: Dustin Gilman & Co., 1876).

3. Stanley Hirshson, *Lion of the Lord* (New York: Alfred A. Knopf, 1969).

4. Mabel Young Sanborn, comp., *Brigham Young's Wives, Children, and Grandchildren* (Salt Lake City: Gaylen S. Young, 1940).

5. Irving Wallace, *The Twenty-seventh Wife* (New York: Simon & Schuster, 1961).

6. Leonard J. Arrington, *Brigham Young: American Moses* (New York: Alfred A. Knopf, 1985).

7. Brigham Young, et al., *Journal of Discourses*, 26 vol. (Liverpool: LDS Booksellers Depot, 1854–1886), 13:173.

8. Historian's Office, Journal, 31 January 1857, Archives of the the Church of Jesus Christ of Latter-day Saints, (hereafter cited as LDS Church Archives), Salt Lake City, Utah.

9. Young, et al., *Journal of Discourses*, 14:162.

10. Susa Young Gates, "Recollections," typescript, Utah State Historical Society, Salt Lake City, n.d., 74.

11. Clerk's report of Brigham Young's interview with Horace Greeley, 13 July 1859, Brigham Young Collection, LDS Church Archives, Salt Lake City, Utah.

12. Brigham Young, "Speech, 6 April 1845," *Times and Seasons* 6 (1 July 1845): 955.

13. Greeley, interview.

14. Gates, 4.

15. Mary Cable, "She Who Shall Be Nameless," *American Heritage* 16 (February 1965): 165.

16. Joseph F. Smith, *Plural Marriage Affidavit Books*, 2 vol., holograph, Historical Department of the Church of Jesus Christ of Latter-day Saints, Salt Lake City, Utah, 1:48, 50; 2:12, 16.

17. Susa Young Gates and Mabel Young Sanborn, "Brigham Young Genealogy," *Utah Genealogical and Historical Magazine* 11 (April 1920): 127.

18. Mary Elizabeth Rollins Lightener, Autobiography and Diary, Special Collections, Harold B. Lee Library, Brigham Young University, Provo, Utah, n.d., 25.

19. Elizabeth Terry Heward, "Autobiography," in *Parshall Terry Family History* (Salt Lake City: Mr. and Mrs. Terry Lund, 1956), 73.

20. Gates, 74.

21. Brigham Young Papers, LDS Church Archives, Salt Lake City, Utah.

22. Brigham Young Papers.

23. Divorce certificates, Brigham Young Papers, LDS Church Archives, Salt Lake, City, Utah.

24. Arrington, 373.

25. Mary Ann Clark Powers, letter to Young, 18 June 1851, Brigham Young Papers, LDS Church Archives, Salt Lake City, Utah.

26. Hannah Tapfield King, "Autobiography," LDS Church Archives, Salt Lake City, Utah, circa 1864–1872.

27. Nauvoo Temple Records, 2 February 1846, Church of Jesus Christ of Latter-day Saints Family History Library (hereafter LDS Family History Library), Salt Lake City, Utah.

28. Brigham Young Papers.

29. Family group sheet, LDS Family History Library.

CHAPTER 2

1. Brigham Young, et al., *Journal of Discourses*, 26 vol. (Liverpool: LDS Booksellers Depot, 1854–1886), 11:295.

2. "Paul Bunyan," *Microsoft Encarta 98 Encyclopedia Deluxe Edition,* Microsoft Corporation, Redmond, Washington.

3. Brigham Young, *Manuscript History of Brigham Young, 1801–1844,* ed. Elden Jay Watson (Salt Lake City: Smith Secretarial Service, 1968), 1.

4. Leonard J. Arrington. Preface to *Brigham Young: American Moses* (New York: Alfred A. Knopf, 1985), cover, xvii.

5. Mary Van Sickle Wait, *Brigham Young in Cayuga County: 1813–1829* (Ithaca, New York: DeWitt Historical Society of Tompkins County, 1964), 1.

6. Ibid.

7. *Greenfield (Massachusetts) Gazette and Courier,* 23 August 1880. Extracts from the address of Honorable Clark Jillson at the centennial of Whitingham, Vermont, 18 August 1880, on Town Hill; located in Marjorie W. Graves File, Whitingham Town Clerk's Office.

8. The author traveled a thousand miles by rental car to visit and photograph the sites of Brigham Young's homes, May 1999 and September 1999. She visited Whitingham, Vermont, September 1999. Location and directions reverified with Whitingham Town Office (802-368-7887) on 1 December 2000.

9. Richard F. Palmer, telephone interview with author, July 1999. The author had several e-mail and telephone communications during the summer of 1999 with Mr. Palmer, who is co-author of *Brigham Young: The New York Years* and has seen these early postcards. When the author was photographing this monument, a woman living just east of the monument informed her that the monument had been stolen two weeks before. She said, "But the owner of the property and monument knew who had stolen it. He said, 'It was those Mormons!' and called them, demanding they bring it back. They did." The author, having traveled two thousand miles by air and seven hundred miles by rental car to photograph it, was happy it was back in place for her photo opportunity.

10. Whitingham Town Office, telephone interview with author, 1 December 2000.

11. Susan Easton Black and Larry C. Porter, *Lion of the Lord: Essays on the Life and Service of Brigham Young* (Salt Lake City: Deseret Book, 1995), 3.

12. Doris Kirkpatrick, "Where Was Brigham Young Born Anyway?" *Battleboro (Vermont) Reformer,* 1 July 1983, 15.

13. *Greenfield (Massachusetts) Gazette and Courier,* 23 August 1880.

14. Black and Porter, 9.

15. Ibid., 11; for a detailed discussion of this alternative birthplace, see Black and Porter's collection of essays, *Lion of the Lord.*

16. Ibid., 8. The transactions of John Young buying land from and selling it back to his brother-in-law, Joseph Mosely, are recorded in "Whitingham Deeds," microfilm, Genealogical Department Archives, Church of Jesus Christ of Latter-day Saints, Salt Lake City, Utah, 18 November 1800, 675.. Some dispute exists over how much Young paid Mosely for this land, $50 or $100. Porter claims that the record clearly stipulates the cost of the land was $100, which was an equitable price. Land in the Whitingham area sold during the early 1800s from $1 to $3 per acre. The property was deeded back to Joseph Mosely, also recorded in "Whitingham Deeds," 24 December 1802, 821.

17. Ibid., 8.

18. Wait, 3. Wait quotes from a book entitled M. R. Werner, *Brigham Young* (New York: Harcourt, Brace and Company, 1925). Wait does not offer complete documentation in her manuscript.

19. Wait, 4. Wait quotes Gates and Widtsoe saying that Brigham's older sister Fanny milked the cow. See Susa Young Gates and Leah D. Widtsoe, *The Life Story of Brigham Young* (New York: Macmillan, 1931). See also Black and Porter, 5; and Joseph Young, Sr., Journal, Archives of the Church of Jesus Christ of Latter-day Saints (hereafter cited as LDS Church Archives), Salt Lake City, Utah, 4–7.

20. Brigham Young, "Introduction," in *Manuscript History of Brigham Young, 1801–1844,* ed. Elden Jay Watson (Salt Lake City: Smith Secretarial Service, 1968), iv.

21. Wait, 4. Wait quotes Gates and Widtsoe saying the older boys helped their father with the farming.

22. Joseph Young, Sr., Journal, 10–11.

23. Black and Porter, 9.

24. Young, et al., 5 January 1860, *Journal of Discourses,* 10:360.

25. Brigham Young, "Introduction," iv.

26. Ibid.

27. B. H. Roberts, *A Comprehensive History of the Church of Jesus Christ of Latter-day Saints,* 6 vol. (Provo, Utah: Brigham Young University Press, 1977), 287.

28. Arrington, 9. See also S. Dilworth Young, *Young Brigham Young* (Salt Lake City: Bookcraft Publishers, 1962), 16–18.

29. Ibid., 10.

30. Richard F. Palmer and Karl D. Butler, *Brigham Young: The New York Years* (Provo, Utah: Charles Redd Center for Western Studies, Brigham Young University, 1982), 88.

31. Franklin Wheeler Young, "Young Family Genealogy," LDS Church Archives, Salt Lake City, Utah, 13.

32. Palmer, interview, July 1999.

33. Correspondence between Richard F. Palmer and Mrs. Vaughn Fargo, town historian, Smyrna, New York, as quoted in Palmer and Butler, 3.

34. Two maps, one of Smyrna in 1875 and another current map, were sent to the author by Sherburne town historian Rose Wellman, letter, 7 February 2001. Cold Brook Road has been renamed Cole Road. This explains why the Young references are to Cold Brook, not Cole Road.

35. Roy Gallinger, "Here's How an 'Ordinary Boy' Became Top Religious Leader," in book published prior to 1960, located in Chenango County Historian's Office, Norwich, New York. Arrington records that the journey took place in the spring of 1804.

36. Ibid.

37. *Chenango (Norwich, New York) Union,* 8 May 1883, in Lathrop Scrapbook, 59, 66–67, Sherburne Public Library, Sherburne, New York, as quoted in Palmer and Butler, 3.

38. Palmer and Butler, 3.

39. Brigham Young, *Manuscript History,* 1. See also Brigham Young, "Introduction," iv. This second reference refers directly to Sherburne.

40. Arrington, 10.

41. Young, et al., 2 August 1857, *Journal of Discourses,* 5:97. See also 4:312 and 14:103.

42. Young, et al., 8 October 1868, *Journal of Discourses,* 12:287.

43. James A. Little, "Historical Items on the Life of Brigham Young," James A. Little Collection, LDS Church Archives, Salt Lake City, Utah, 2–3. James A. Little was a first cousin to Brigham Young.

44. Young, et al., 2 August 1857, *Journal of Discourses,* 5:97.

45. Fanny Young, letter to Phinehas Young, microfilm copy, Geneological Department Archives, Church of Jesus Christ of Latter-day Saints, Salt Lake City, Utah, 1 January 1845, as quoted in Arrington, 8. Rhoda was left behind in Hopkinton presumably to console Nabby's parents.

46. Franklin Wheeler Young, Journal, LDS Church Archives, Salt Lake City, Utah, 14.

47. Joseph Young, Sr., Journal, as quoted in Palmer and Butler, 3.

48. Wait, 9.

49. Ibid.

50. Palmer, interview, July 1999, and Butler, 3.

51. Wait, 9.

52. Journey by author to the site, 4 September 1999.

53. Isabelle H. Parish, Lansing town historian, *It Happened in Lansing* (Ithaca: Dewitt Historical Society of Tompkins County, 1964), 71. Parish recalls that Clarence Jefferson told her this information, saying his grandmother lived near and knew the Youngs. She used to tell him about them.

54. Ibid., 71

55. Richard Palmer informed the author that residents of Ithaca erected the new marker. E-mail, 8 June 1999.

56. Journey by author to the site, 4 September 1999. Another account, the *History of Tioga, Cheming, Tomkins, and Schuyler Counties* (Philadelphia: n.p., 1879), 520, states: "The cemetery adjoining J. W. Hamilton's farm was connected with the Methodist Episcopal Church. Brigham Young's mother is said to be buried here; but if so, no stone marks the spot. An account given by Dr. J. P. Barnum in *The New York Times*, 16 September 1877, locates the grave on Ben Wegger's farm near Lansing. As a child, Dr. Barnum lived a few miles from the Wegger farm and had often seen her grave.

57. Parish, 71.

58. Arrington, 11. Arrington does not quote a source here. Brigham states in the *Journal of Discourses*, 2 August 1857, 5:97, "Brother Heber [Kimball] and I never went to school until we got into 'Mormonism.' We never had the opportunity of letters in our youth."

59. Young, et al., 8 August 1869, *Journal of Discourses*, 14:103.

60. Young, et al., 15 August 1852, *Journal of Discourses*, 6:290.

61. Ibid.

62. Young, et al., 6 February 1853, *Journal of Discourses*, 2:94.

63. Young, et al., *Journal of Discourses*, 14:225.

64. Gates and Widtsoe, as quoted in Wait, 4–5.

65. Gates, 2–3, as quoted in Eugene England, "Young Brigham," (n.p., September 1977).

66. Young, et al., 15 August 1852, *Journal of Discourses*, 6:290.

67. J. P. Barnum, *The New York Times*, 16 September 1877.

68. Arrington, 12.

69. Palmer and Butler, 5. See also Brigham Young, "History of Brigham Young," *Latter-day Saints Millenial Star*, 25: 310–11.

70. Little, "Historical Items about Brigham Young," 2:3.

71. *History of Tioga, Cheming, Tomkins, and Schuyler Counties*, 664.

72. Ibid., 680.

73. James A. Little, "Biography of Lorenzo Dow Young," *Utah Historical Quarterly* 14 (1946): 130.

74. Palmer and Butler, 6.

75. Little, "Biography," 130.

76. Ibid., 130–31.

77. Young, et al., 25 May 1862, *Journal of Discourses*, 9:294. See also 2 August 1857, 5:97.

78. Arrington, 12.

79. Little, "Biography."

80. Ibid.

81. Young, et al., 6 November 1864, *Journal of Discourses*, 10:360.

82. Palmer and Butler, 3.

83. Sylvester J. Matthews, *The Antiquarian*, 18 January 1902.

84. Wait, 24.

85. Young, et al., 31 August 1875, *Journal of Discourses*, 18:76.

86. Wait, 24.

87. Benjamin F. Hall, "Genealogical and Biographical Sketch of the Late Honorable Elijah Miller," manuscript, Cayuga County Historian's Office, Auburn, New York, circa 1877, 80. Hall records, "In the fall of 1817, Jeffries was employed to paint the woodwork [of the Miller house on South Street] and he brought with him the renowned Brigham Young, then a journeyman of his, to assist him."

88. Wait, 31.

89. Walter K. Long, an eminent artist in charge of the Cayuga Museum of History and Art at the time Wait produced her monograph, reports that practically every old house in Auburn claims the distinction of a fireplace built by Brigham Young.

90. Wait, 24. Wait explains that the large supply of ready-to-install fireplaces is one explanation why everyone in Auburn claims the distinction of owning a mantelpiece carved by Young himself.

91. A sign marking the site of his residence informs that William H. Seward lived in the home from 1824 to 1872. Personal visit by author, 4–5 September 1999.

92. Wait, 30. Wait has drawn this material from William H. Seward, *Seward— An Autobiography* (Darby and Miller, 1891).

93. Palmer and Butler, 42–44, 50. Brigham worked on the Theological Seminary in 1820. This building is no longer standing. He worked on the Elijah Miller home in 1817. It is located in the heart of the city. The Brown home was located across from the Miller House on the corner of South and Grover Streets, where the New York Telephone office now stands. The Wadsworth home, located near Aurelius on West Genesee Street Road (old Seneca Turnpike), was torn down in 1974. The Abijah Miller home, built circa 1817, was located in Ludlowville. The Wait farmhouse, still standing, is located west of Auburn, near Aurelius, at 2009 West Genesee Street Road.

94. Nancy Wait, interview with author, 5 September 1999. Follow-up telephone interview with author, 13 June 2001. Current owners James and Nancy Wait say the long-standing tradition within the family holds that Brigham may have lived on the Wait property while he helped construct the farmhouse and barn.

95. Wait, 63. Mary Van Sickle Wait lived summers at the farmhouse "for about half a century." See *Auburn (New York) Citizen-Advertiser*, Saturday, 22 August 1964.

96. Samuel Hopkins Adams, "Unsung Eden," *Holiday Magazine* (June 1951), as quoted in Wait, 15–16.

97. David M. Dunning, *Auburn Advertiser-Journal*, 13 January 1927, as quoted in Palmer and Butler, 14. See also note 87. Dunning further recalled: "Sometime during the war, about 1862–63, one day a carriage drove up from the city and a gentleman announced himself as John Young, a son of Brigham Young. He was on his return from a trip to Europe and had been requested by his father to stop off at Auburn and find the Wadsworth place and see if any of the Wadsworths were still living there. He was told that my mother, a daughter of Joseph Wadsworth, was living there, and that her father died in 1855."

98. Young, et al., 20 April 1856, *Journal of Discourses*, 3:323.

99. Brigham Young, letter to George Hickox, 19 February 1876, Ontario County Historical Society, Canandaigua, New York.

100. Matthews, *The Antiquarian*, 18 January 1902.

101. *Auburn Daily Bulletin*, 31 August 1877.

102. William Hayden, "In the Days of Long Ago," *Port Byron Chronicle*, 5 March 1904.

103. Cayuga County Deeds, book Z, Cayuga County Courthouse Archives, Auburn, New York, 432–34, as quoted in Palmer and Butler, 18.

104. William Hayden, *Syracuse Sunday Herald*, 21 February 1904. See also an article by Hayden published in the *Deseret News*, 20 December 1913. Brigham lived for a time on the Hayden farm. William Hayden, born

in 1821, was only a boy when Brigham lived on the farm and around Port Byron. No doubt he was told many stories by his parents.

105. Hayden, *Syracuse Sunday Herald.*

106. Kate B. Carter, ed., *Brigham Young: His Wives and Family* (Salt Lake City: Daughters of Utah Pioneers, 1990), 11. See also Arrington, 15.

107. Gates and Widtsoe, 19.

108. Wait, 38.

109. Hayden, *Syracuse Sunday Herald.*

110. *Cayuga Patriot,* 3 November 1824.

111. Hayden, *Auburn Daily Advertiser,* 17 February 1904.

112. Maria Axton, interview with author, 29 May 1999.

113. Palmer and Butler, 94.

114. Axton, interview.

115. Palmer and Butler, 21.

116. Richard Palmer, e-mail to author, 10 October 1999. Mr. Palmer wrote that he had recently discovered a document in the New York State Library dated 1825. It was a bill from Brigham Young to the Canal Commissioners for work he performed during construction of the Erie Canal. "Quite a find!" Palmer said.

117. Matthew and Genevieve Uglialoro, interview with author in Uglialoros' home, 29 May 1999. The Uglialoros gave the author a tour of the home, pointing out all that is original to the home.

118. Ibid.

119. Brigham Young, letter to David B. Smith, 1 June 1853. LDS Church Archives, Salt Lake City, Utah, as quoted in Palmer and Butler, 23.

120. Palmer and Butler, 23.

121. Arrington, 16. Arrington's account is similar to Palmer's; however, he also includes Fanny, John Jr., and Lorenzo.

122. Palmer and Butler, 24.

123. John Fowler, *Journal of a Tour in the State of New York in the Year 1830* (London: n.p., 1831), 97.

124. Charles F. Milliken, *The Beginnings of Mormonism,* vol. 5 (Rochester, New York: Rochester Historical Society, Publication Fund Series, 1926): 42.

125. Personal visit by author to the Mendon home, now owned by the Hutchinsons, 29 May 1999.

126. Eileen Havens, fax to author, 6 July 1999.

127. Anna B. Yates, "The Pioneers of Mendon," *Honeoye Falls Times,* 2 February 1922, as quoted in Palmer and Butler, 25.

128. Charles F. Milliken, *The Beginnings of Mormonism,* 5:42.

129. George Washington Allen, "Brigham Young and Mormonism," manuscript in possession of J. Sheldon Fisher,

Valentown Museum, Fishers, New York, 5–6.

130. Havens fax.

131. The Heber C. Kimball home was located south of the John Young Sr. home, on the west side of the Mendon-Ionia Road, just north of Boughton Hill Road. It was across the street from the Tomlinson Inn. The Kimball home is no longer standing. Some foundation stones possibly can be seen near a yellow house that stands in close proximity to the Kimball site today. Personal visit by author. See also Havens fax.

132. Heber C. Kimball, "History," manuscript, book 94-B, Heber C. Kimball Papers, Historical Department of the Church of Jesus Christ of Latter-day Saints (hereafter cited as LDS Church Historical Department), Salt Lake City, Utah.

133. Brigham Young, *History of Brigham Young, Latter-day Saints' Millennial Star,* 132 vol. (Manchester and Liverpool: LDS Booksellers Depot, 1840–1870), 25:438.

134. Palmer and Butler note that "Number Nine" refers to the ninth township in the Phelps and Gorham Purchase land development, which at one time comprised 2.6 million acres. Franklin B. Hough, *Gazetteer of the State of New York* (Albany: n.p., 1872), 51.

135. Wait, 1.

136. Palmer and Butler, 26.

137. A letter of an unnamed correspondent in the *Canandaiga (New York) Ontario Republican Times,* 7 September 1857, reported that "Mrs. Young was sick, most of the time unable to do any work. . . ."

138. Gates and Widtsoe, as quoted in Wait, 61.

139. Allen, 5–6.

140. Arrington, 17.

141. Heber C. Kimball, 7 June 1862, *Journal of Discourses,* 9:329.

142. Undated clippings, *Ontario Republican Times.*

143. Rev. J. Willard Webb, "A Memorial Sermon—the Life and Character of George Hickox," undated newspaper clipping, LDS Church Historical Department, Salt Lake City, Utah. See also letter of George Hickox, 7 February 1876, and Brigham Young to George Hickox, 19 February 1876, Brigham Young Papers, LDS Church Archives, Salt Lake City, Utah.

144. Wait, 62. Wait refers to the "Brigham Young File" in the Ontario County Historical Museum, which contains a short dossier on Miriam Works. This document states that she died at the home of Heber C. Kimball, with her

husband, daughters, and Heber C. and Vilate at her side.

145. Visit to the cemetery by author, 29 May 1999.

146. Arrington, 30. Miriam Young was baptized three weeks after Brigham in May 1832.

147. Ibid., 33.

148. J. Sheldon Fisher, "Brigham Young as a Mendon Craftsman: A Study in Historical Archaeology," *New York History* 61 (October 1980): 435–46.

149. "Brigham Young's Home Yields 1st Wife's Ring?" *Salt Lake Tribune,* 28 July 1973. Critics of Sheldon Fisher claim that some of his artifacts may not be authentic.

150. Fisher, 444–45.

151. Arrington, 18.

152. Monroe County Deeds, Liber 28, Monroe County Clerk's Office, Rochester, New York. See also John Young Revolutionary War Pension File, W. 11908 BLWT 101, 305-160-55, National Archives, Washington, D.C.

153. Young, et al., 3 February 1867, *Journal of Discourses,* 11:295.

154. Ibid., 295–96.

155. Palmer and Butler, 27–29, cover the extent of Young's debts and how and when he repaid them.

Chapter 3

1. Brigham Young, *Manuscript History of Brigham Young, 1801–1844,* ed. Elden Jay Watson (Salt Lake City: Smith Secretarial Service, 1968), 6–7.

2. Leonard J. Arrington, *Brigham Young: American Moses* (New York: Alfred A. Knopf, 1985), 37.

3. Joseph Smith, *History of the Church* 1 (Salt Lake City: Deseret News, 1902): 146. Joseph Smith records in February 1831, "The branch of the church in this part of the Lord's vineyard . . . had increased to nearly one hundred members."

4. Arrington, 37.

5. Ibid., 36.

6. Brigham Young, et al., *Journal of Discourses,* 26 vol. (Liverpool: LDS Booksellers Depot, 1854–1886), 12:59.

7. Arrington, 37.

8. Young, *Manuscript History,* 7.

9. Lyle Briggs of Kirtland, Ohio, telephone interview with author, 12 February 2001.

10. Arrington, 37.

11. Briggs, telephone interview.

12. This book lists the date of Brigham's second marriage as 10 February 1834. Other sources list his marriage to Mary Ann on 18 February 1834. See also Kate B. Carter, ed., *Brigham Young: His Wives and Family* (Salt Lake City: Daughters of Utah

Pioneers, 1990), 12, Arrington, 37, and Brigham Young File, Lands and Records Office, Church of Jesus Christ of Latter-day Saints, Nauvoo, Illinois. An article in the *Cleveland Press*, 14 April 1982, states: "Records in the Geauga County courthouse show that Brigham, then 24 [wrong age—Brigham was almost 33], applied for a marriage license for himself and Mary Ann Angell, 18 [wrong age—Mary Ann was almost 31], on Feb. 10, 1834."

13. Carter, *Brigham Young: His Wives and Family*, 12. The material, which follows in the ensuing paragraph on Mary Ann Angell Young, is taken from this source.

14. Ibid., 12.

15. Arrington, 37.

16. Emmeline B. Wells, ed., "In Memoriam," *Woman's Exponent*, 15 July 1882, obituary.

17. Arrington, 37.

18. Carter, *Brigham Young: His Wives and Family*, 12.

19. Arrington, 37.

20. Young, *Manuscript History*, 7–8.

21. Carter, *Brigham Young: His Wives and Family*, 13.

22. Arrington, 38.

23. Ibid.

24. Young, et al., *Journal of Discourses*, 16 November 1856, 4:92.

25. Arrington, 45, 48.

26. Heber C. Kimball, "History," *Times and Seasons* 6:668. The original minutes for this meeting are in the Kirtland Record Book, Historical Department of the Church of Jesus Christ of Latter-day Saints (hereafter cited as LDS Church Historical Department), Salt Lake City, Utah, 147. See also B. H. Roberts, *A Comprehensive History of the Church of Jesus Christ of Latter-day Saints*, 6 vol. (Provo, Utah: Brigham Young University Press, 1977), 2:181–89.

27. Young, *Manuscript History*, 10.

28. Ibid., 12.

29. Arrington, 51.

30. Young, *Manuscript History*, 12.

31. Ibid.

32. Elwin C. Robison, *The First Mormon Temple* (Provo, Utah: Brigham Young University Press, 1997), 78.

33. Arrington, 51.

34. Robison, 78–80.

35. Arrington, 53. Although it is difficult to put a price tag on the construction of the Kirtland Temple, a guide at the site suggests the building cost between $40,000 and $70,000. On-site tour by author, 27 May 2001. Lachlan Mackay, historian and director of historical sites, Community of Christ, estimates the cost up to $100,000.

36. *Record Book of the Twelve*, minutes, 2 May 1835.

37. Young, et al., *Journal of Discourses*, 7:229 and 2:18.

38. Jonathan Crosby, reminiscence, LDS Church Historical Department, Salt Lake City, Utah. See also President's Office, Journal, 18 January 1860, Brigham Young Papers, Archives of the Church of Jesus Christ of Latter-day Saints, Salt Lake City, Utah.

39. Young, et al., *Journal of Discourses*, 2:19.

40. Brigham Young, letter to Mary Ann Angell Young, 3 June 1836, Philip Blair Collection, Marriott Library, University of Utah, Salt Lake City.

41. Ibid., 21 July 1836.

42. Deed recorded in *Geauga County Deed Books*, 25:168–69. Also, Briggs, telephone interview, 12 February 2001.

43. George H. Morse, "Morse Farm Settled in 1813 . . . Recollections of Local Folks . . ." *The Willoughby Republican* (29 July 1921). George H. Morse died one month after the article was published (Cleveland Necrology File, Cleveland Public Library).

44. Lake County Recorder's Office archivist, Dee Vihtelic, telephone interview with author, 15 June 2001. Dee Vihtelic verified that records show Ferry owned the large farm, 132.17 acres, UT Hotchless 101,102 in 1921. The land is now identified as Parcel 20A-028G-000010 on the tax map.

45. Lachlan Mackay, interview with author, 28 May 2001. See also Carl Anderson, telephone interview with author, 28 May 2001; Andrea Hunziker, personal discussion with author, 27 May 2001; and Lucy Wellhausen, telephone interview with author, 16 June 2001.

46. Wellhausen, telephone interview. The author informed Lucy Wellhausen that Mary Ann could have been the one to hide the dishes in the well in the Brigham Young Nauvoo home before she left the place, possibly for two reasons: one, to keep them from being used by the people taking over the property, and two, to protect them with the hope of someday retrieving them or having them brought to her.

47. Elwin C. Robison, interview with author, 24 July 2001. Dr. Robison, author of *The First Mormon Temple*, toured the Wellhausen home with the author, pointing out evidence for his early dating (1830s) of the home. He said there is sufficient evidence to date the home this early.

48. Ibid.

49. Briggs, interview, 28 May 2001.

50. "Little Red Schoolhouse," Myron Tanner Biography, 4. Given to author in July 2001 by Lyle S. Briggs.

51. Young, letter to Mary Ann Angell Young, 24 March 1837, .

52. Young, envelope of letter to Mary Ann Angell Young, 24 March 1837.

53. Brigham boasted that he could always win arguments. See, for example, his discussion with a professor about polygamy, 9 July 1843, in *Manuscript History*, 134–36. See also his reproof of an elder who attempted to instruct him how to preach, 8–9 October 1842, in *Manuscript History*, 123. See also *Journal of Discourses*, 4: 35. Brigham brags that he can charm potential converts.

54. Harriet Arrington, conversation with author, 18 September 1999. Mrs. Arrington told me this word exercise of Brigham's was Leonard's favorite anecdote of Brigham Young.

55. Arrington, 57, 59. Arrington records that several of the Twelve had signed their names to documents declaring Joseph to be a fallen prophet.

56. Young, et al., *Journal of Discourses*, 4:297 or 1:215 or 3:120–121??.

57. Young, *Manuscript History*, 23.

58. Ibid., 23–24.

59. Ibid., 24–25. Brigham Young was able to convince Tomlinson to sell his tavern-stand and secure the first bid, which Young promised him would be the best bid. Tomlinson gave Smith $300 of his profits to proceed on his journey.

60. Ibid., 25.

61. Arrington, 62.

62. Young, *Manuscript History*, 28.

63. Young, et al., 3 February 1867, *Journal of Discourses*, 11:296–97. See also 24 July 1854, *Journal of Discourses*, 2:18; and Brigham Young, "History," *Deseret News*, 17 February 1858, 393.

64. Brigham Young, letter to David B. Smith, 1 June 1853, Brigham Young Papers, LDS Church Historical Department, Salt Lake City, Utah.

65. Young, et al., 3 February 1867, *Journal of Discourses*, 11: 296–97.

66. Emmeline B. Wells, "Biography of Mary Ann Angell Young," *The Juvenile Instructor* 26 (1 January 1891): 18–19.

67. Young, *Manuscript History*, 28.

68. Wells, "Biography of Mary Ann Angell Young," 19. Joseph Smith issued Brigham this revelation on 17 April 1838. See also Smith, *History of the Church*, 3:23.

69. Young, *Manuscript History*, 29. Brigham stated that acts of the Missouri State Legislature backed up his claim that the angry mobs were paid by the state.

70. Arrington, 64.

71. Young, *Manuscript History*, 28–29, 32.

72. Smith, *History of the Church*, 3:175.

73. Arrington, 66.

74. Young, *Manuscript History*, 33.

75. Wells, "Biography of Mary Ann Angell Young," 19.

76. Young, *Manuscript History*, 34, 39. Morris Phelps was the great-great-grandfather of the author's husband, Robert H. Burgoyne, MD.

77. Joseph Smith, revelation, as recorded by Young, *Manuscript History*, 35, 37.

78. Young, *Manuscript History*, 41.

79. Annette Burton, telephone interview with author, 12 February 2001. Also, personal tour by author, 25 May 2001.

80. Wilford Woodruff, Journal, 2 July 1839.

81. Arrington, 74.

82. Joseph Smith, Journal, 5 August 1839.

83. Young, *Manuscript History*, 50.

84. Young, et al., *Journal of Discourses*, 13:211.

85. Young, *Manuscript History*, 50.

86. Young, letter to Mary Ann Angell Young, 15 September 1839.

87. Young, *Manuscript History*, 56–57.

88. Ibid., 61.

89. Ibid., 52–53, 58.

90. Ibid., 68–69.

91. Ibid., 69.

92. This phrase was used in an epistle in the first number of *Times and Seasons*: "To the Elders of the Church of Jesus Christ of Latter-day Saints, to the churches scattered abroad, and to all the Saints," which is printed in its entirety in Young, *Manuscript History*, 43–48.

93. Heber C. Kimball, letter to Vilate Kimball, 19 September 1840, Heber C. Kimball Papers, LDS Church Historical Department, Salt Lake City, Utah.

94. Young, *Manuscript History*, 69. See also Young, et al., 17 July 1840, *Journal of Discourses*, 13:211–12.

95. Ibid.

96. Young, *Manuscript History*, 71–72.

97. Ibid., 70.

98. Ibid.

99. Ibid., 77.

100. Young, letter to Mary Ann Angell Young, 2 June 1840.

101. Young, *Manuscript History*, 77.

102. Young, letter to Mary Ann Angell Young, 12 June 1840.

103. Young, letter to Mary Ann Angell Young, 20 June 1840.

104. Young, letter to Mary Ann Angell Young, 24 June 1840.

105. Young, letter to Mary Ann Angell Young, 12 November 1840.

106. Young, letter to Mary Ann Angell Young, 15 January 1841.

107. Ibid.

108. Ibid.

109. Dean C. Jessee, "Brigham Young's Family, Part 1, 1824–1845," *BYU Studies* 18, no. 3 (spring 1978): 321.

110. Mary Ann Angell Young, letter to Brigham Young, 15, 17, and 30 April 1841, as quoted in Jessee, 321–22.

111. Ibid., 322.

112. Young, *Manuscript History*, 96–97.

113. Arrington, 95.

114. Young, *Manuscript History*, 105, 109. See also "History of Brigham Young," *Deseret News*, 10 March 1858, as quoted in Jessee, 323.

115. Joseph Smith, revelation to Brigham Young, as quoted in Young, *Manuscript History*, 105.

116. Ibid., 105–6.

117. Young, *Manuscript History*, 109.

118. Brigham Young, Diary, 1837–1845.

119. Young, et al., *Journal of Discourses*, 3:266.

120. 183374 film, Special Collections, LDS Church Historical Department, Salt Lake City, Utah, 577. Alfa Jean Carter, interview with author, 27 July 2000.

121. Arrington, 102.

122. Young, *Manuscript History*, 134–35.

123. Biographical sketch of Lucy Ann Decker Young, "In the Long Ago," *The Paris*, Salt Lake City, Utah, n.d. This article was mailed to author by Alfa Jean Carter, historian for the Seeley family, 1 August 2000. All biographical material in this paragraph comes from this source.

124. Ibid. Other biographical data in this paragraph comes from this source.

125. Carter, telephone interview.

126. Arrington, 102.

127. Carter, telephone interview. Mrs. Carter's father was told by both Isaac and Harriet, children of Lucy by William, that William never abused their mother.

128. Ibid. See also notes supplied to author by Mrs. Carter.

129. Historic Nauvoo Land and Research Center handout, provided to author by Alfa Jean Carter, 1 August 2000.

130. Carter, *Brigham Young: His Wives and Family*, 13–14. See also appendix A.

131. See appendix A. The material which follows in this paragraph is taken from this appendix.

132. Ibid.

133. Young, *Manuscript History*, 124–25.

134. Ibid., 125.

135. Lester E. Bush, Jr., "Brigham Young in Life and Death: A Medical Overview," *Journal of Mormon History* 5 (1978): 79–103.

136. Young, *Manuscript History*, 130.

137. "The Brigham Young Home," Brigham Young File, Xerox record in the Lands and Records Office, Nauvoo, Illinois. The author copied this file on 25 May 2001.

138. Arrington, 105.

139. Ibid., 105.

140. Personal tour of property by author, 25 May 2001. Material on Brigham Young's Nauvoo home was verified with Carol Hill, Nauvoo Restoration, Inc. 15 March 2002.

141. Ibid., 105.

142. Mary Ann Angell Young, letter to Brigham Young, 17 August 1843, manuscript, LDS Church Historical Department, Salt Lake City, Utah.

143. Young, letter to Mary Ann Angell Young, 17 August 1843, manuscript, Yale University Library, Yale University, New Haven, Connecticut.

144. "Record of Deaths in the City of Nauvoo," manuscript, LDS Church Historical Department, Salt Lake City, Utah, as quoted in Jessee, 325.

145. Young, *Manuscript History*, 154.

146. Arrington, 110.

147. Young, letter to Mary Ann Angell Young, 12 June 1844, manuscript, original in possession of Dr. Wade Stephens, Bradenton, Florida, as quoted in Jessee, 326.

148. Ibid.

149. Arrington, 111.

150. Mary Ann Angell Young, letter to Brigham Young, 30 June 1844, manuscript, LDS Church Historical Department, Salt Lake City, Utah.

151. Young, *Manuscript History*, 171.

152. Arrington, 114.

153. Roberts, *History of the Church*, 7:230.

154. Mosiah Lyman Hancock, "Life Story of Mosiah Lyman Hancock," Special Collections, Harold B. Lee Library, Brigham Young University, Provo, Utah, 1965, 23.

155. Roberts, *History of the Church*, 7:231–36.

156. Editorial comment at the end of Young's *Manuscript History*, 173.

157. Ibid.

158. Arrington, 123.

159. Ibid., 123–24.

160. Roberts, *History of the Church*, 7:397–98.

161. Arrington, 124–25.

162. Smith, *History of the Church*, period 2, 7:523–33. Edmund Durfee was the author's great- great-great-grandfather.

163. Arrington, 125.

164. Ibid., 126.

165. Ibid.

166. Ibid., 126–27.

167. Young, et al., *Journal of Discourses*, 11:296–97.

168. Arrington, 127–29.

CHAPTER 4

1. Richard Poll, Thomas G. Alexander, Eugene E. Campbell, and David E. Miller, *Utah's History* (Provo, Utah: Brigham Young University Press, 1989), 117; James B. Allen and Glen

M. Leonard, *The Story of the Latter-day Saints* (Salt Lake City: Deseret Book, 1976), 220.

2. Ronald Anderson, president of the Overland Trails Association, interview with Judy Dykman, February 2000.

3. *Utah History Encyclopedia*, s.v. "Bountiful."

4. Nauvoo Visitors' Center information sheet, n.d.

5. Ibid.

6. More commonly called "drill," this is a heavy twilled linen or cotton cloth.

7. Irene Hascall Pomeroy, Camp of Israel, letter to Col. Wilson Andrews, New Salem, Massachusetts, 19 September 1846, letter number 12 in "Letters of Irene B. Hascall Pomeroy to Her Parents and Relatives in North New Salem, Massachusetts, Covering the Period May 1845–August 1854," typescript, Utah State Historical Society, Salt Lake City.

8. Leonard J. Arrington, Dean L. May, and Feramorz Y. Fox, *Building the City of God: Community and Cooperation among the Mormons* (Salt Lake City: Deseret Book, 1976), 42.

9. Richard E. Bennett, *Mormons at the Missouri, 1846–1852: "And Should We Die"* (Norman and London: University of Oklahoma Press, 1987), 25, 40, 250. One indication of their desperation is that included in the sale would be the now-completed temples at Kirtland and Nauvoo.

10. Leonard J. Arrington and Davis Bitton, *The Mormon Experience: A History of the Latter-day Saints* (New York: Alfred A. Knopf, 1979), 99.

11. Johanna Case Worden Keyes Teeples, personal history, spelling as in the original, in Loyd B. Keyes, *Keyes Family History* (privately published, 1985); copies in the Church of Jesus Christ of Latter-day Saints Family History Library (hereafter cited as LDS Family History Library), Salt Lake City, Utah; Utah State Historical Society, Salt Lake City; and Harold B.Lee Library, Brigham Young University, Provo, Utah. Johanna's daughter, Celia, identifies the man who took the farm as "Cherakey Walker." Celia Anzanette Keyes Taylor, personal history, also in *Keyes Family History.*

12. Bennett, 26.

13. Taylor, personal history.

14. Exodus 16:13; Taylor, personal history.

15. Lucy Bigelow Young, autobiography, unpublished. A full discussion of Brigham's wives' travels is contained in Dean C. Jessee, "Brigham Young's Family: The Wilderness Years," *BYU Studies* 19 (summer 1979): 57.

16. Brigham Young, Manuscript History of Brigham Young, January 1846 through July 1847, microfilm copy, Archives of the Church of Jesus Christ of Latter-day Saints, Salt Lake City, Utah 30–61. At this point Hastings was still proposing a shorter route to California by cutting through what is now northern Utah and Nevada; it was that route that later proved disastrous for the Donner Party.

17. Todd Compton, *In Sacred Loneliness: The Plural Wives of Joseph Smith* (Salt Lake City: Signature Books, 2000), 89–90; Kate B. Carter, ed., *Brigham Young: His Wives and Family* (Salt Lake City: Daughters of Utah Pioneers, 1990), 23.

18. Allen and Leonard, 227; S. George Ellsworth, *Utah's Heritage* (Salt Lake City: Peregrine Smith Inc., 1977).

19. Allen and Leonard, 230.

20. Poll, Alexander, Campbell, and Miller, *Utah's History,* 119.

21. For detailed information on Winter Quarters, see Jennifer L. Lund, "'Pleasing to the Eyes of an Exile': The Latter-day Saint Sojourn at Winter Quarters, 1846–1848," *BYU Studies* 39, no. 2 (spring 2000): 113.

22. Albert L. Zobell, Jr., *Sentinel in the East* (Salt Lake City: Nicholas G. Morgan, Sr., 1965), 62.

23. Bennett, 76.

24. Ibid.

25. Jennifer Lund, 113.

26. Bennett, 70, 141, 187; Jenny Lund, historian at the LDS Museum of History and Art, interview with Judy Dykman, 28 April 2000.

27. Bennett, 70; Zobell, 74–75.

28. Bennett, 12–13; Jenny Lund, interview.

29. Jenny Lund, interview.

30. Pomeroy, letter to Col. Wilson Andrews, New Salem, Massachusetts, April 1847, number 13 in Pomeroy letters.

31. Quincy is a small town notable for its charity in harboring refugees. Residents operated a station on the underground railroad and took in refugees ranging from Potawatomi Indians to persecuted Mormons. See *Deseret News,* 1 August 1999, LDS Church News sec. 1, and accompanying story.

32. Jeffrey O. Johnson, "Determining and Defining 'Wife': The Brigham Young Households," *Dialogue: A Journal of Mormon Thought* 20 (fall 1987): 61–62; Nora Lund, "History of Jane Terry Young," typescript, (unpublished, n.d.), 96–98.

33. Johnson, 68; Nora Lund, 98.

34. Nora Lund, 99–100. Emma displayed a particular tenacity: she was widowed in 1913 and wanting financial independence, at seventy five years of age she found a job in a shirt factory in Los Angeles doing piece work and invested her savings in real estate. "She died on Sunday, October 19, 1926, having been a self-supporting citizen to the very day of her death."

35. Carter, *Brigham Young: His Wives and Family,* 24–25.

36. Susa Young Gates, "Lucy Bigelow Young," typescript, Utah State Historical Society, Salt Lake City, 15–17 (hereafter cited as Gates, "Lucy Bigelow"). Lucy began this unpublished autobiography and her daughter, Susa, finished it following Lucy's death; copies now in possession of the Utah State Historical Society and Kari Robinson, president of the Daughters of Brigham Young.

37. Gates, "Lucy Bigelow," 17.

38. Ibid.

39. Arrington, 318–19.

40. Ancestral File; Mark Angus, *Salt Lake City under Foot* (Salt Lake City: Signature Books, 1993), 55; Miriam Murphy, "From Impulsive Girl to Patient Wife: Lucy Bigelow Young," *Utah Historical Quarterly* 45, no. 3 (summer 1977): 275; Johnson, 68. The Council House, designed by William Folsom, originally stood at 120 East 100 South. The sixty square foot building was made of stone quarried from Red Butte Canyon and served as both the Salt Lake City Hall and the Utah Territorial Capitol until 1894. The upstairs was used for religious ceremonies until the Salt Lake Temple could be completed. In 1962 the building was dismantled, each block of stone carefully coded, and then reassembled at 300 North State Street, across from the State Capitol Building. Now called the Council Hall, it houses the Utah Travel Council and the Utah Tourism and Recreations Center.

41. Orson F. Whitney, *Popular History of Utah* (Salt Lake City: *Deseret News,* 1916), 29.

42. Hal Knight and Stanley B. Kimball, *111 Days to Zion* (Salt Lake City: Deseret News Press, 1978), 2; Howard R. Lamar, *The Reader's Encyclopedia of the American West* (New York: Crowell, 1977), 772.

43. Whitney, *Popular History,* 30.

44. Doctrine and Covenants 136:8.

45. The initial wagon train included only two other women: Heber C. Kimball's wife, Ellen Sanders Kimball, and Lorenzo Snow's wife, Harriet Wheeler Young. Clara Decker Young, "A Woman's Experiences with Pioneer

Band," *Utah Historical Quarterly* 14 (1946): 173–76.

46. Ellsworth, 140; Murphy, 271–74; Bennett, 81.

47. There may have been up to eight more whose death dates and/or emigration records have not been found to this date.

48. Emily Dow Partridge, autobiography, quoted in Compton, 415.

CHAPTER 5

1. Some confusion exists in identifying exact addresses because the ground on which some homes stood has been split between two current properties or has been combined with another to accommodate a larger structure. In addition, in the early twentieth century Salt Lake County revised its street number system primarily to acknowledge the growing urbanization of what had been the "Big Field." Originally the land had been maintained in large parcels with streets much farther apart than those in the downtown area. Those original streets remain major thoroughfares today: the original Twelfth South is currently designated 2100 South; Thirteenth South is 2700 South; Fourteenth South is 3300 South; Fifteenth South is 3900 South; Sixteenth South is 4500 South. Steven Carr, *Holladay-Cottonwood Places and Faces* (Holladay: Holladay-Cottonwood Heritage Committee, 1976), 18.

2. Miriam Murphy, "From Impulsive Girl to Patient Wife: Lucy Bigelow Young," *Utah Historical Quarterly* 45, no. 3 (summer 1977): 274–75; "Mary Jane Bigelow" and "Lucy Bigelow Young," in Kate B. Carter, ed., *Brigham Young: His Wives and Family* (Salt Lake City: Daughters of the Utah Pioneers, 1990), 24–25; Emmeline Wells, "Our Picture Gallery—Lucy Bigelow Young," *Young Woman's Journal* 3, no. 4 (January 1892): 145; Vicky Burgess-Olsen, *Sister Saints* (Provo, Utah: Brigham Young University Press, 1978), 64–66.

3. Donna Smart, interview with Colleen Whitley, 1997; Marion McCardell, interview with Colleen Whitley, 2001.

4. Randall Dixon, "Emigration Canyon to City Creek," *Utah Historical Quarterly* (spring 1997): 158–60; S. George Ellsworth, Utah's Heritage (Salt Lake City: Peregrine Smith Inc., 1977), 153.

5. S. Kent Brown, Donald Q. Cannon, and Richard H. Jackson, *Historical Atlas of Mormonism* (New York: Simon & Schuster, 1994), 82, 85; Ellsworth, 153.

6. Brigham Young quoted in John S. McCormick, *Salt Lake City, The Gathering Place* (Woodland Hills, California: Windsor Publications, for the Utah State Historical Society, 1980), 16. The street numbers within Plat A remain the same today as they originally were laid out. Beyond 900 South, however, streets were much farther apart since the property itself was used for agriculture. Those steets were renumbered in 1906 or 1907 to the system currently in use: 900 South remained 900, but 1400 South became 3300 South, 1600 South became 4500 South, and so on. Roger Roper with Utah State Historical Society, interview with Judy Dykman, 22 May 2000.

7. McCormick, 16.

8. Mark Angus, *Salt Lake City under Foot* (Salt Lake City: Signature Books, 1993), 10; Leonard J. Arrington, *Brigham Young: American Moses* (New York: Alfred A. Knopf, 1985), 168; McCormick, 16. Those original surveys do not entirely match modern measurements made with far more sophisticated instruments. See Rebecca Walsh, "Off the Mark," *Salt Lake Tribune*, 20 February 2001, B1.

9. "What's Great about Salt Lake," *Salt Lake Tribune*, 5 July 1998, J1.

10. Margaret Truman, *Harry S. Truman* (New York: William Morrow, 1973), 78.

11. Arrington, *American Moses*, 168; Brown, Cannon, and Jackson, 85. In subsequent surveys, Plat C ran from 500 West to 1100 West, 500 North to 900 South; Plat D is the area that today is called the Avenues. Blocks there were one half the size of those in Plats A and B. For a more complete discussion of black settlement in Salt Lake City, see Henry Wolfinger, "Jane Manning James: A Test of Faith," in *Worth Their Salt: Notable but Often Unnoted Women of Utah* (Logan: Utah State University Press, 1996), 14.

12. Arrington, *American Moses*, 169; Marguerite Cameron, *This Is the Place* (Caldwell, Idaho: Caxton Printer, 1941); Ellsworth, 154; Orson F. Whitney, *History of Utah*, 4 vols. (Salt Lake City: George Q. Cannon & Sons, 1904), 42; Dennis Lythgoe, "Preserve the Historic Role of Pioneer Park," *Deseret News*, 30 July 1992, web edition, J1.

13. Whitney, *History of Utah*, 45.

14. Thomas Alexander, *Mormonism in Transition: A History of the Latter-day Saints, 1890–1930* (Urbana and Chicago: University of Illinois Press, 1986), 104; Arrington, *American Moses*, 146; Cameron, 204; Ellsworth, 154; Whitney, *History of Utah*, 45.

15. The Nauvoo Bell was brought to Utah in 1847 by the second pioneer company and hung in the Old Fort. The bell cracked while being rung in 1850 and was scheduled to be recast. Recasting a bell, however, requires a great deal of expertise, and there is no evidence that any among the pioneers had sufficient skill to perform the task. In any case, the Nauvoo Bell simply disappears from history shortly after 1850 and its exact fate is unknown.

In the last year, historians with the LDS Church Historical Department have determined that the bell now celebrated as the Nauvoo Bell came from a Protestant church in the Midwest and was transported by a pioneer company in 1850. Put into storage, it eventually turned up in the Deseret Museum. When it was found in the 1950s, someone concluded that it was the Nauvoo Bell. The LDS Relief Society raised money to build the carillon in which it now hangs on the west side of Temple Square. That bell announces each hour on KSL radio. Ron Watt, interview with Colleen Whitley, 5 February 2001; marker plate on the carillon; Whitney, *History of Utah*, 46.

16. Dean L. May, *Utah, A People's History* (Salt Lake City: University of Utah Press, 1987), 61.

17. Ernest H. Taves, *This Is the Place: Brigham Young and the New Zion* (Buffalo, New York: Prometheus Books, 1991), 73.

18. Arrington, *American Moses*, 147; Cameron, 204.

19. Arrington, *American Moses*, 168–69; Ellsworth, chap. 10; Edward W. Tullidge, *History of Salt Lake City*, (Salt Lake City: Utah Printing Company, 1886), 642.

20. Arrington, *American Moses*, 168–69; Tullidge, 643–45.

21. Dennis Lythgoe, "Preserve the Historic Role of Pioneer Park," *Deseret News*, 30 July 1992, web edition.

22. Linda Sillitoe, *A History of Salt Lake County* (Salt Lake City: Utah State Historical Society and Salt Lake County Commission, 1996), 48.

23. Whitney, *History of Utah*, 51; Chein Archuleta, "History of Pioneer Park," unpublished. Archuleta is a city employee who uses quiet moments to assemble a history of each park in the city.

24. Lythgoe.

25. Diane Urbani, "Pioneer Park: To Develop or Not?" *Deseret News*, 18 December 2000, B1; Lythgoe, C1; Archuleta. The theater replicas are discussed in the epilog. Pioneer buildings and replicas are now located at Lagoon amusement park in Farmington and at

Old Deseret Village in the mouth of Emigration Canyon.

26. Archuleta; Lythgoe.

27. The term "estate" has been applied to Brigham's property, but that suggests something far more elegant than the family farm it actually was.

28. Arrington, *American Moses*, 168–69; Cameron, 204.

29. Arrington, *American Moses*, 170. For a discussion of the problem from Emma's perspective, see Linda King Newell and Valeen Tippetts Avery, *Mormon Enigma: Emma Hale Smith* (New York: Doubleday, 1984), chap. 14.

30. For a full discussion of the difficulties in settling Brigham's estate, see Leonard J. Arrington, "The Settlement of Brigham Young's Estate, 1877–1879," *Pacific Historical Review* 21 (1952): 1–20.

31. Information for this map comes from Cameron, 202–12; Angus, 4; and observations and measurements by the authors. Building sizes and locations are approximate because exact measurements and even locations are not available on many of the early homes, and because some of the walls of early buildings apparently ran on lines identical to those of present buildings and they would disappear into each other if shown exactly. Distances on some buildings have simply been paced off.

32. Murphy, 274–75; Susa Young Gates, "Lucy Bigelow Young," typescript, Utah State Historical Society, Salt Lake City, 29 (hereafter cited as Gates, "Lucy Bigelow"); "The Deseret Museum," *Improvement Era* (September 1911), 954–55; *Deseret Evening News*, 28 June 1902, 11; *Utah Historical Quarterly* 10 (1942): 112–13.

33. Robert Tuttle, facility manager for the Church Office Building, telephone interview with Colleen Whitley, 21 July 1999.

34. Arrington, *American Moses*, 169; Gates, "Lucy Bigelow," 17, 32; photo collection, Utah State Historical Society, Salt Lake City, nos.

35. Gates, "Lucy Bigelow," 32–34.

36. Dean C. Jessee, "'A Man of God and a Good Kind Father':Brigham Young at Home," *BYU Studies* 10, no. 2 (2001): 28–29.

37. Carter, *Brigham Young: His Wives and Children*; Russel Arlington Mortensen, *Early Utah Sketches* (Salt Lake City: University of Utah Press, 1969), 31.

38. Gates, "Lucy Bigelow," 39.

39. Susa Young Gates, "Susa's Thoughts on the Wives of Brigham Young as She Saw and Remembered Them," typscript copy from Kari Robinson, historian and genealogist for the Brigham Young Family Organization, 1999.

40. Their silk won prizes at the Chicago World's Fair in 1893, but production ended a few years later when it proved economically infeasible.

41. Carter, *Brigham Young: His Wives and Children*, 23–24; Richard Poll, Thomas G. Alexander, Eugene E. Campbell, and David E. Miller, *Utah's History*, (Provo, Utah: Brigham Young University Press, 1989), 343.

42. When Utah became a state in 1896, it had no capitol building. For several years the legislature convened in several places, but especially in the city hall originally located at 100 South and State where the Federal Building now stands. In 1962 it was moved to 300 North State, across the street from the capitol, and today houses the Utah Travel Council.

When railroad magnate E. H. Harriman died in 1911, Utah collected a 5 percent inheritance tax from his estate—$798,000. That provided seed money for the building of a new capitol in Salt Lake City, completed in 1915. Today the State Division of Facilities Management administers the building, and in recognition that public buildings belong to the public, the capitol rotunda, like several other state-owned buildings, can be reserved by individuals and groups for dances,scouting award ceremonies, memorials, and similar gatherings. Angus, 57–58; "The Utah State Capitol Building: A Photographic Exhibit," Utah State Historical Society, Salt Lake City, 1998; telephone interviews with Naly Ellis, 1991; Carter, *Brigham Young: His Wives and Children*, 14; early Salt Lake City plat maps; Dixon, interviews; Tullidge, 640.

43. "Crismon Mill Site," Daughter of Utah Pioneers monument no. 43, erected 10 December 1938.

44. Young, quoted in Arrington, *American Moses*, 335.

45. Carter, *Brigham Young: His Wives and Families*, 14 15.

46. Gates, "Susa's Thoughts."

47. Arrington, *American Moses*, 169; Margaret D. Lester, *Brigham Street* (Salt Lake City: Utah State Historical Society, 1979), 32; Mortensen, *Early Utah Sketches*, 25; A. R. Mortensen, "The White House," unpublished article, Utah State Historical Society, Salt Lake City.

48. Mortensen, "The White House"; A. R. Mortensen, "The White House, It Was Brigham Young's 'Real' Home," *Salt Lake Tribune*, 19 May 1957, 25;

Floralee Millsaps, interview with Colleen Whitley, May, 2001.

49. Mortensen, *Early Utah Sketches*, 25; and Mortensen, "The White House"; Eleanor Young, "Old Houses Tell Romantic Story of Salt Lake," *Salt Lake Tribune*, 4 February 1934, 3; George Spencer Young, "Life Story of George Spencer Young," in *The Story of a Pioneer Family: George Spencer and Martha Rigby Young 1868–1958*, comp. family members (Bloomington, Idaho: privately published, n.d.), 2.

50. Carter, *Brigham Young: His Wives and Children*, 13.

51. Arrington, *American Moses*, 283. The Perpetual Emmigrating Fund loaned poor emmigrants enough money to travel to Utah. Once they had employment, they would repay the loan; that money was then loaned to other emigrants to help them make the trip.

52. For a complete discussion of the move, see Richard D. Poll, "The Move South," *Life in Utah* (Provo, Utah: BYU Studies, 1996), 115.

53. Letter from a Union soldier in *To Utah with the Dragoons and Glimpses of Life in Arizona and California 1858–1859*, ed. Harold D. Langley (Salt Lake City: University of Utah Press, 1974), 86.

54. Old-timers report that Johnston ordered wooden stakes painted red and placed at intervals to mark part of the north-south trail to Camp Floyd and that the trail is now known as Redwood Road. Charming though that story is, the road was probably named in a much more mundane manner. Jesse Fox Sr., who did much of the earliest surveying in early Utah, had his crew drive in redwood stakes to mark that important road. "The Redwood Line" then became the meredian line for surveys west of the Jordan River, so that surveyors did not need to continually cross the river to reach the original base line from the meredian marker on Temple Square. "The Utah War, Journal of Captain Albert Tracy," *Utah Historical Quarterly* 13, no. 1 (winter 1945): 301; Rowland Smart, interviews with Judy Dykman, 1998–99; Kristen Rogers, "Redwood Road: How Did It Get Its Name?" *Currents: News of the Utah State Historical Society* (February 2000): 3.

55. Thomas Alexander, *Mormonism in Transition: A History of the Latter-day Saints, 1890–1930* (Urbana and Chicago: University of Illinois Press, 1986), 124–25; Arrington, *American Moses*, 160–61, 170–94; Norman F. Furniss, *The Mormon Conflict,*

1850–1859 (New Haven, Connecticut: Yale University Press, 1960), 201–3; Donald R. Moorman and Gene A. Sessions, *Camp Floyd and the Mormons: The Utah War*, (Salt Lake City: University of Utah Press, 1992), 263; Poll, Alexander, Campbell, and Miller, *Utah's History*, 245; Ken Verdoia and Richard Firmage, *Utah: The Struggle for Statehood* (Salt Lake City: University of Utah Press, 1996), 59–62; Orson F. Whitney, *Popular History of Utah* (Salt Lake City: *Deseret News*, 1916), 161.

56. Whitney, *Popular History*, 177.

57. Moorman and Sessions, 273; Mortensen, *Early Utah Sketches*, 25.

58. George Spencer Young, 2.

59. Eleanor Young, "Old Houses"; "Mr. Megaphone Tells Tourists Many New Things about Salt Lake," *Salt Lake Herald Republican*, 23 April 1911, 18; Hampton C. Godbe, letter to John James, 27 March 1964; Mortensen, "The White House, It Was Brigham Young's 'Real' Home."

60. Mortensen, *Early Utah Sketches*, 25; and Mortensen, "The White House"; Whitney, *Popular History*, 171; Salt Lake Elks representatives, telephone interview with Colleen Whitley, 1999; Zions Securities, interview with Judy Dykman, 1999.

61. Angus, 14; Arrington, *American Moses*, 333.

62. Angus, 14; "Monuments—Eagle Gate" Daughters of Utah Pioneers files, Salt Lake City, n.d.

63. Brigham Young, "Last Will and Testament," in *A Believing People: Literature of the Latter-day Saints*, ed. Richard H. Cracroft and Neal E. Lambert (Provo, Utah: Brigham Young University Press, 1974), 110–11. Brigham included explicit directions on his funeral, burial clothes, and coffin.

64. Mary Henderson, *History of Utah, Historic Sites, and Landmarks*, vol. 1, bound typscript copy, Archives of the Church of Jesus Christ of Latter-day Saints, Salt Lake City, Utah, 13; Angus, 16–17. Brigham gave explicit instructions for his burial.

65. Arrington, *American Moses*, 330–33.

66. Henderson, 37; "Work of Tearing Down Old Brigham Young School House Has Commenced," *Salt Lake Herald*, 3 August 1902.

67. Angus, 15; Henderson, 37; "Mrs. Holmes to Tear Down School Built for Brigham Young's Children," unidentified newspaper clipping, Susanne Emery-Holmes Scrapbook, Utah State Historical Society, Salt Lake City, 3 August 1902; "Work of Tearing Down."

68. Cameron, 206; Mortensen, *Early Utah Sketches*, 35.

69. Willard Richards, the first editor of the *Deseret Evening News*, saw the initial edition of the weekly come off the press on 15 June 1850. The press was a wrought-iron Ramage, purchased in Philadelphia and brought west in one of the early wagon trains. When the federal troops invaded in 1857, the whole shop, presses and all, "went south" with the rest of the populace. The press was moved to Fillmore for protection. The press was returned to Salt Lake City and the *Deseret Evening News* continued as a weekly, in English with occasional columns in Danish to accommodate the influx of Scandinavian converts, until 21 November 1867. Arrington, *American Moses*, 267, 423; Wendell J. Ashton, *Voice in the West: Biography of a Pioneer Newspaper* (New York: Duell, Sloan and Pearce, 1950), 38, 145–46; Whitney, *Popular History*, 88.

70. Docent, Old Deseret Village, interview with Colleen Whitley, July 1999.

71. Mortensen, *Early Utah Sketches*, 35; *Utah History Encyclopedia*, s.v. "Hotel Utah."

72. Angus, 11–12; Wally Christiansen, project engineer, interviews with Colleen Whitley, 1999; information office, Joseph Smith Memorial Building, telephone interview with Colleen Whitley, 1999.

73. Whitney, *Popular History*, 62, 88.

74. Brigham's nephew and namesake, Brigham Hamilton Young, and Thomas Bullock set the type on a press made by Truman O. Angell. Notes for fifty cents and for one, two, three, and five dollars were hand printed on white paper and signed by Brigham Young, his counselor, Heber C. Kimball, and the church's presiding bishop, Newell K. Whitney. The first issue of 830 notes had a face value of $1,365. Most of the notes used pictures of Brigham Young, a temple, or animals.

   Bills from Kirtland Bank and bags of gold dust brought from California by members of the Mormon Battalion also supplemented the barter system in general use. Several attempts were made to turn that gold into coins, beginning in November 1848. The first coin was designed by Brigham Young, John Taylor, and John Kay, who also cut the dies, with the assistance of William Clayton. A young Scotsman, Robert Campbell, engraved the stamps. The crucibles were broken in December after coining 46 ten-dollar gold pieces. On one side the design reflected beliefs of the priesthood: a three point Phrygian crown over Jehovah's all-seeing eye, encircled with the words "Holiness to the Lord." The reverse had clasped hands, the words "Pure Gold," and the value of the coin. Ashton, 23; Whitney, *Popular History*, 62; *Utah History Encyclopedia*, s.v. "Coins and Currency."

75. Tuttle, interview.

76. George Spencer Young, 2.

77. The LDS Church now has its own legal services department in the Church Office Building rather than contracting with outside law firms. Reflecting the recent emphasis on temples, the physical facilities department has been divided in two: one to handle general construction and maintenance of wards, stake centers, and other buildings worldwide and one to direct the construction of new temples. A separate department oversees the ecclesiastical administration of temples; authorities there determine what goes on inside the temples once the physical facilities department finishes building them. Tuttle, interview; Robert Tuttle, memorandum to Colleen Whitley, 22 July 1999; "By Way of Introduction . . . General Church Office Building," booklet prepared for employees who would work in the new building, n.d.

78. The building is designed for efficiency, economy, and environmental protection; for example, all lights except those needed for security automatically turn off at 5 p.m.; late-stayers must switch theirs on again. The building was designed with demountable wall systems with panes of prefinished vinyl wall coverings, which makes changes relatively easy and efficient. Tuttle, interview; Tuttle, memorandum; "By Way of Introduction."

79. Cameron, 202, 212; Clarissa Young Spencer and Mabel Harmer, *Brigham Young at Home* (Salt Lake City: Deseret Book, 1974), 250; George D. Pyper, "Silk Culture in Utah," *The Contributor*, January 1881, 115.

80. Arrington, *American Moses*, 331; George Spencer Young, 2.

81. Mortensen, *Early Utah Sketches*, 51.

82. Allen D. Roberts, "The Chase Mill" (Salt Lake City: Daughters of Utah Pioneers, lesson for December, 1983), 138–47. Roberts, former architectural historian for the Utah State Historical Society, provides detailed information about the structure and mechanics of the mill and about the various archeological excavations of the area along with an excellent chronology and bibliography on the mill.

83. Roberts, 157.

84. Clarissa was the daughter of William Ross, first husband of Isaac Chase's wife, Phoebe Ogden.

85. Carter, *Brigham Young: His Wives and Family*, 17–18; *Biographical Sketches of Brigham Young and His Twenty-nine Wives* (Philadelphia: S. C. Upham, 1873), available in Hatch Room, Merrill Library, Utah State University, pamphlet 16902, unpaginated; Zina Young with Clarissa's children, photograph, Daughters of Utah Pioneers collection; Arrington, *American Moses*, 171.

86. Carol Edison, director of the Chase Home for the Utah Arts Council, telephone interview with Colleen Whitley, November 2001.

87. Mortensen, *Early Utah Sketches*, 51; Daughters of Utah Pioneers markers 96, 130, 229, in Gary L. Gregson, *Utah Roadside History: Historic Sites and Landmarks* (Provo, Utah: Community Press, 1995), 175.

88. Gates, "Susa's Thoughts."

89. Carter, *Brigham Young: His Wives and Family*, 21; Gates, "Susa's Thoughts."

90. Roberts, 137.

91. Archuleta; Mortensen, *Early Utah Sketches*, 51.

92. Carter, *Brigham Young: His Wives and Family*, 16. A replica of the Social Hall stands in Old Deseret Village.

93. Gates, "Susa's Thoughts."

94. Carter, *Brigham Young: His Wives and Family*, 16.

95. Angus, 18; *1885 Salt Lake City Directory*.

96. "Mrs. Cobb's First House South of Social Hall," *Salt Lake Daily Herald*, 14 June 1874.

97. Jeffrey O. Johnson, "Determining and Defining 'Wife': The Brigham Young Households," *Dialogue: A Journal of Mormon Thought* 20 (fall 1987): 60; Ronald W. Walker, *Wayward Saints: The Godbeites and Brigham Young* (Urbana and Chicago: University of Illinois Press, 1998), 136.

98. Cable, 50–55.

99. Carter, *Brigham Young: His Wives and Family*, 16; Walker, 136–37; *Biographical Sketches of Brigham Young and His Twenty-nine Wives*.

100. Beverly Becton, "Woman Suffrage in Territorial Utah," *Utah Historical Quarterly* 46 (spring 1978): 118; Mary Cable, telephone interview with Judy Dykman, July 2000; Walker, 136. Augusta was also reported to be a member of the Quincy family of Boston.

101. Carter, *Brigham Young: His Wives and Family*, 15.

102. *Biographical Sketches of Brigham Young and His Twenty-nine Wives*.

103. Bruce Clayton, Zion Securities, telephone interview with Colleen Whitley, 7 February 2001.

104. Arrington, *American Moses*, 420; Carter, *Brigham Young: His Wives and Family*, 19.

105. Gates, "Susa's Thoughts."

106. Young quoted by Arrington, *American Moses*, 169.

107. Angus, 8; Martha Sonntag Bradley, *ZCMI America's First Department Store* (Salt Lake City, Utah: ZCMI, 1991), 2, 26.

108. Carter, *Brigham Young: His Wives and Family*, 30; Brigham Young, will, Utah State Historical Society, Salt Lake City, pamphlet 3857.

109. Rosemary Larsen, customer service manager, Crossroads Mall, telephone interview with Colleen Whitley, 8 March 1999; Sillitoe, 207.

110. Alice Hansen, County Recorder's Office, interview with Colleen Whitley, 1998; Larsen, interview.

111. Carter, *Brigham Young: His Wives and Family*, 28; "Sarah M. Pratt Cast," *Salt Lake Daily Herald*, 2 December 1875; *Salt Lake City Directory, 1888*.

112. Newell and Avery, 49.

113. Carter, *Brigham Young: His Wives and Family*, 18.

114. Ibid.

115. Gates, "Susa's Thoughts."

116. *Salt Lake City Directory, 1890*, 658; Brigham Young, will; Carter, *Brigham Young: His Wives and Family*, 18–19. While the *Directory* lists her as "Emily B.," Emily Partridge was the only widow of Brigham Young with the name Emily alive in 1890.

117. Carter, *Brigham Young: His Wives and Family*, 19.

118. Ken Shields, manager of Broadway Center, telephone interview with Colleen Whitley, 14 February 2001.

119. Lester, 32; photo collection, Utah State Historical Society, Salt Lake City, nos. 7419 and 1720.

120. Arrington, *American Moses*, 334; Carter, *Brigham Young: His Wives and Children*, 31.

121. Arrington, *American Moses*, 373, 425.

122. Ann Eliza Webb Young, *Wife Number 19; or, The Story of a Life in Bondage, Being a Complete Exposè of Mormonism and Revealing the Sorrow, Sacrifices and Sufferings of a Woman in Polygamy* (Hartford, Connecticut: Dustin Gilman & Co., 1876). For a more complete discussion of her assorted suits and her claims about Brigham's property at the time, see Arrington, *American Moses*, chap. 20.

123. Brigham Young, will.

124. photo collection, Utah State Historical Society, Salt Lake City, nos. 7419 and 1720; Kate B. Carter, ed., *Our Pioneer Heritage*, vol. 1 (Salt Lake City: Daughters of Utah Pioneers, 1950), 128.

125. "Pioneer Home of Pres. Young Given to Village," *Deseret News*, 30 December 1952, A4.

126. *Pioneers* (Sons of Utah Pioneers magazine), (December 1956); Peter Freed, Lagoon Corporation, interview with Judy Dykman, February 2000.

127. Lester, 32; Orien Dalley, telephone interview with Colleen Whitley, 1999.

128. Lisa Johnson, "Artist in Residence," *Deseret News*, 4 July 1999, F1.

129. Jack Goodman, *As You Pass By* (Salt Lake City: University of Utah Press, 1995), 186.

130. National Register files, quoted in Goodman, 186; Tuttle, interview.

CHAPTER 6

1. Truman O. Angell, Journal, typescript, Archives of the Church of Jesus Christ of Latter-day Saints, Salt Lake City, Utah (hereafter, LDS Church Archives), 7–15 February 1852.

2. Orson F. Whitney, "Lorenzo Dow Young," in *History of Utah*, 4 vols. (Salt Lake City: George Q. Cannon & Sons, 1904), vol. 4.

3. Angell, 3 May 1853.

4. Ben Brown, comp., *The Journal of Lorenzo Brown, 1823–1900* (Salt Lake City: Heritage Press, n.d., circa 1980), 46–47.

5. Brown, 55–56.

6. Clarissa Young Spencer and Mabel Harmer, *Brigham Young at Home* (Salt Lake City: Deseret Book, 1974), 17.

7. Horace Greeley, letter, "Two Hours with Brigham Young," *New York Daily Tribune*, 13 July 1859; reprint, *Millennial Star* 21 (1859): 608–9; Scott G. Kenney, ed., Wilford Woodruff's Journal 1833–1898, 9 vol. (Midvale, Utah: Signature Books, 1983–1985), 13 July 1859.

8. Truman O. Angell's records for the Beehive House refer to ordering materials such as the logs needed for the rafters. He describes the various parts of the house, listing the barn as part of the house. Apparently during the process of construction some changes were made in the plan of the house. The kitchen may have originally been in the main part of the house with a wing containing a woodhouse and barn. There are early references to a store behind the President's House, so it may have been there early and then moved to the barn in the 1860s. That would explain why that section of the house is shaped like a barn or a carriage house. Such construction is not unusual. In New England, it was common to attach the barn to the house, usually with a wing that contained a kitchen and woodhouse.

While that pattern may have been used for the Beehive House, no one can be certain since no careful descriptions are extant from that period.

9. Spencer and Harmer, 28.

10. Ibid., 184.

11. The funeral of Mary M. Thatcher held in the Beehive House was reported in the *Deseret Evening News*, 17 July 1877.

12. Brigham Young, letter to Don Carlos Young, 16 February 1876, in Dean C. Jessee, *Letters of Brigham Young* (Salt Lake City: Deseret Book in collaboration with the Historical Department of the Church of Jesus Christ of Latter-day Saints [hereafter cited as LDS Church Historical Department], Salt Lake City, Utah, 1974), 269; Spencer and Harmer, 184.

13. Spencer and Harmer, 186; city directories show the Spencers living in the house through 1888.

14. Spencer and Harmer, 46; changes in the porch are evident from many photographs of the period.

15. *Deseret Evening News*, 4 December 1878; *Utah Enquirer*, 31 August 1888; *Salt Lake Herald*, 13 May 1888, 8; "The Beehive House Sold," *Deseret Evening News*, 30 January 1893; "Historic Old Mansion," *Salt Lake Tribune*, 1 February 1897; "John Beck's Plight," *Salt Lake Tribune*, 24 July 1898; "The Bee Hive House," *Salt Lake Herald*, 1 November 1898; "Sale of the Bee Hive," *Deseret News*, 20 December 1898.

16. "New Use for Bee-Hive House," *Deseret Evening News*, 24 June 1899; "Church Offices in Beehive House," *Salt Lake Tribune*, 25 June 1899; "President Snow in Historic Beehive," *Deseret Evening News*, 23 September 1899, 1.

17. "Beehive," *Deseret News*, 28 July 1904; photographs from the period show the changes.

18. "Beehive House Made Available for Working Girls," *Deseret Evening News*, 3 April 1920. A larger girls' home was never built.

19. "Historic Beehive House as Home for Girls," *Deseret Evening News*, 10 June 1920; "Famed Beehive House Closed as a Residence, *Church News*, 10 January 1959, 5.

20. "Historic Residence to Be Restored," *Church News*, 8 August 1959, 6; George Cannon Young, interview, typescript, LDS Church Archives, Salt Lake City, Utah; Judy Anderson, "Beehive House" (master's thesis, Brigham Young University, 1967). Information on the restoration described in the following paragraphs comes from these sources and the author's own observations.

21. "Tourists Visit Restored Beehive House," *Church News*, 12 August 1961, 4.

22. Angell, 3–4 January 1854, and 10 August 1854.

23. George A. Smith, letter to "Bro. Joseph," 28 June 1855, typescript, LDS Church Archives, Salt Lake City, Utah.

24. "City items," *Deseret News*, 18 July 1855.

25. Historian's Office, Journal, 20 October 1855.

26. Susa Young Gates, "Lucy Bigelow Young," typescript, Utah State Historical Society, Salt Lake City, 36, 39.

27. Spencer and Harmer, 24–26.

28. Kate B. Carter, *Heart Throbs of the West*, vol. 1 (Salt Lake City: Daughters of Utah Pioneers, 1939): 234.

29. Floor plans for the Lion House, Susa Young Gates Collection, Utah State Historical Society, Salt Lake City; Susa Young Gates, The Life Story of Brigham Young, draft copy, Susa Young Gates Collection, Utah State Historical Society, Salt Lake City, 16.

30. Spencer and Harmer, 30; *Millennial Star* 23 (1861): 477; photographs, LDS Church Archives, Salt Lake City, Utah.

31. Gates, 41; Spencer and Harmer, 28.

32. "Church Buys the Lion House," *Deseret Evening News*, 20 March 1900; "Church Buys Lion House," *Salt Lake Herald*, 21 October 1900.

33. William E. Felt, "The Inception and Growth of the LDS Business College," 1 February 1982, Salt Lake City, Utah, 91; Lynn M. Hilton, *The History of LDS Business College and Its Parent Institutions, 1886–1993* (Salt Lake City: LDS Business College, 1993), 102–3; "Old Rag Carpet of Pioneer Days," *Deseret Evening News*, 22 December 1906, 13; Harriet Page, "A Friendly Visit to a Friendly Place," *Deseret News*, 15 September 1934, 3; *The Gold and Blue* 4, no. 14 (July 1901) contains several photographs of the home during the period it served as part of the school. These sources along with the author's observations provide the information on the restoration given in the following paragraphs.

34. "Organization of Daughters of Pioneers," *Deseret Evening News*, 24 January 1907.

35. Monitor C. Noyce, "Will Remodel Lion House," *Deseret News*, 1 April 1966, B1.

36. The business department remains today as LDS Business College.

37. Hilton, 102–3.

38. Harrison R. Merrill, "Welcome, Come In," *Improvement Era*, May 1933, 394, 396; "Historic Lion House Becomes Center for Social Activities of Y.L.M.I.A.," *Deseret News*, 3 December 1932, 3.

39. "Church Closes Facilities at Lion House," *Deseret News*, 27 February 1964, B1; Noyce, "Will Remodel," B1; Monitor C. Noyce, "Lion House to Undergo Renovation," *Church News*, 9 April 1966, 10; Eleanor Knowles, "The Lion House Social Center Reopens," *Improvement Era*, October 1968, 26–28.

40. Knowles, 26–28.

CHAPTER 7

1. Susa Young Gates and Leah D. Widtsoe, *Life Story of Brigham Young* (New York: Macmillan, 1931), 343; Brigham Young Papers, Archives of the the Church of Jesus Christ of Latter-day Saints (hereafter LDS Church Archives), Salt Lake City, Utah.

2. Florence Jacobsen, "Restorations Belong to Everyone," *BYU Studies* 8, no. 3 (spring 1978): 279; Retta Blanche Davis Reese and Jubilee Committee, *Golden Jubilee—Forest Dale Ward, Granite Stake, 1896–1946* (privately published, n.d.), 12.

3. Leah Woolley, *Early History of Forest Dale* (privately published: Granite Stake of the Church of Jesus Christ of Latter-day Saints, 1981), 1; Reese and Jubilee Committee, 12.

4. The changes in street numbering in the Salt Lake Valley is discussed in chapter 5.

5. Woolley, 2.

6. Andrew Jenson, *Encyclopedic History of the Church of Jesus Christ of Latter-day Saints* (Salt Lake City: Deseret News Publishing Company, 1941), 843; Jay and Fae Heslop, *The Story of the Salt Lake Stake* (privately published: Salt Lake Stake of the Church of Jesus Christ of Latter-day Saints, 1997), 35.

7. Paul B. Cannon, "Summary History of the Brigham Young Forest Farm House," *Deseret News*, 28 April 1923.

8. Jacobsen, 278.

9. "Forest Farm Tidbits," Beehive House Historical File, Utah State Historical Society, Salt Lake City, 20 February 1979.

10. *Millennial Star*, 16 November 1885, 728, quoted in Woolley, 2.

11. George D. Smith, ed.,, *An Intimate Chronicle: The Journals of William Clayton* (Salt Lake City: Signature Books, 1995), 427–28. William Clayton described meeting the worn out teams hauling the sugar beet equipment to the Valley in September 1852. It was shipped to New Orleans on the

Rockaway from Liverpool, arriving in New Orleans April 25, and then taken on to the Salt Lake Valley in wagons. The load was so heavy and cumbersome and the journey so extremely difficult it did not arrive until November 1852.

12. J. M. Tanner, *History of James Jensen* (privately published, n.d.), copy on file with the LDS Family History Library.

13. Hamilton G. Park, quoted in Woolley, 3.

14. Tanner, as quoted in Wooley, 3.

15. Brigham Young promoted the industry. He described his cocoonery at Forest Farm as "100 feet by 20 feet" (Daughters of Utah Pioneers files on the Silk Industry). Tanner, quoted in Wooley, 12; Carter, *Our Pioneer Heritage*, vol. 8, 165. Information on activities at Forest Farm comes from interpretive documents at This Is the Place Heritage Park. These documents have been prepared to guide docents in their presentation of the history of the farm for visitors. Hereafter referred to as "Interpretive documents, This Is the Place Heritage Park."

16. "Silk Culture in Utah," in *Heartthrobs of the West*, ed. Kate B. Carter, vol. 11 (Salt Lake City: Daughters of Utah Pioneers, 1950), 56.

17. "Silk Culture in Utah," 56.

18. Woolley, 4, footnote.

19. Spencer and Harmer, 123; Interpretive documents, This Is the Place Heritage Park.

20. "Making the butter come" was a term used for when the clumps of butter began to form in the churn. It always seemed to take a long time and required constant churning motions.

21. Susa Young Gates, "Lucy Bigelow Young," typescript, Utah State Historical Department, Salt Lake City, 59 (hereafter cited as Gates, "Lucy Bigelow"). In a later description of the farm, Gates says the cabin was adobe. Gates and Widsoe, 343.

22. Gates, "Lucy Bigelow," 59–60; Interpretative documents, This Is the Place Heritage Park.

23. Hamilton Park, quoted in Reese, 3; Beatrice Cannon, quoted in Wooley, 6. Park, a Scottish convert of 1840, came to Utah in September 1854. Two years later he entered into the services of Brigham Young and was his business manager until called on a mission in 1869. During this time he was closely associated with most of the enterprises of Brigham Young. Cannon, daughter of John M. Cannon, whose residence was south of the farmhouse, said the walnut trees

on their lot were believed to mark the end of the avenue of trees which led to the farmhouse originally.

24. Interpretive documents, This Is the Place Heritage Park. The visitor is not identified.

25. Reese, 13.

26. Clarissa Young Spencer and Mabel Harmer, *One Who Was Valiant* (Salt Lake City: Deseret Book, 1974), 79–80.

27. Interpretive documents, This Is the Place Heritage Park.

28. Jacobsen, 278.

29. Interpretive documents, This Is the Place Heritage Park.

30. Spencer and Harmer, "One Who Was Valiant," in Kate B. Carter, ed., *Our Pioneer Heritage*, vol. 19 (Salt Lake City: Daughters of Utah Pioneers, 1976), 123.

31. Frank Halverson, interview with the author, 1950.

32. Tanner, quoted in Wooley, 5.

33. Gates, "Lucy Bigelow", 60–61.

34. The ten oldest daughters of Brigham Young had privileges the younger ones envied.

35. Julia Dean Hayne was a beautiful and gifted young lady, one of the most famous actresses of her day. Born in Pleasant Valley, New York, on 21 July 1830, she made her first appearance as Esmeralda in *Hunchback* at age sixteen. She married Dr. Arthur Hayne in Charleston, South Carolina, in 1855, but shortly afterward she was divorced in the Salt Lake City courts. *Stories from Your Museum*, Daughters of Utah Pioneers files, Salt Lake City, undated. Lurene Gates Wilkinson, granddaughter of Susa Young Gates, interview with the author, 1999.

36. Description from pioneer stories told to the author by grandparents.

37. "Interpretive documents, This Is the Place Heritage Park."

38. Young and Spencer, 72

39. Clarissa Young Spencer and Mabel Harmer, *Brigham Young at Home*, 72.

40. Spencer and Harmer, Brigham Young at Home includes descriptions of the life of the Young children.

41. Gates and Widtsoe, 343.

42. Ibid., 344.

43. These were coverings placed at the back of chairs, presumably to protect the furniture from the hair products used at the time, but included armrests as well, and were part of the decoration of many homes. Many were hand crocheted and very pretty.

44. Gates and Widtsoe, 345.

45. Ann Eliza Webb Young, *Wife Number 19; or, The Story of a Life in Bondage, Being a Complete Exposé of Mormonism*

and Revealing the Sorrow, Sacrifices, and Sufferings of a Woman in Polygamy (Hartford, Connnecticut: Dustin Gilman & Co., 1876), chap. 35. Ann Eliza and Emily Dow, quoted in Todd Compton, *In Sacred Loneliness: The Plural Wives of Joseph Smith* (Salt Lake City: Signature Books, 2000), 418. Farm work is hard, unquestionably, but pioneers were expected to accept hard work as part of life.

46. Gates and Widtsoe, 343.

47. Pedigree chart of Susannah Snively, Ancestral File, LDS Family History Library. Another spelling is given as Snevely (1693). It is noteworthy that the Snively/Schnerbli line continues back but the Heavenor line does not. It is listed as "Havener" in Carter, *Our Pioneer Heritage*, 1:428. Susannah's father Henry was born in Berne, Pennsylvania, 30 January 1763, and his father Hans Conrad Snively was born at Affoltern, Switzerland, 12 December 1728. Hans died in Keedysville, Maryland, 15 September 1804. Hans's father is listed as Hans Kaspar Schnebli, also of Affoltern, Switzerland, so it seems apparent the name was changed when the family immigrated to the American colonies. Susan's mother, Mary Heavenor, was born in Frederick, Maryland, 17 December 1774. Her parents are Johann Michael Hevner and Catherine Wagle, both born in Maryland.

48. Carter, *Our Pioneer Heritage*, 17:215.

49. Temple Index Bureau, LDS Family History Library; Susan Easton Black, ed., *LDS Memberships 1830–1848*, database, LDS Family History Library, Salt Lake City, Utah. These records also give the marriage date for Hannahetta or Henrietta and Susan as 2 November 1844. Black, 40:509.

50. The sisters are listed on Nauvoo City Tax Lists 1842 and in Nauvoo Property Transactions 1843. *Nauvoo Property Transactions, 1843, 1846*, Special Collections File, LDS Family History Library, Salt Lake City, Utah, compiled and catalogued during Nauvoo Restoration period.

51. A grandfather's clock owned by Susan was brought from Nauvoo to Salt Lake by oxen, now in possession of Jo Davies of Salt Lake. It still runs. The works were made in France and the cabinet work in England.

52. Carter, *Our Pioneer Heritage*, 1:428.

53. Carter, *Our Pioneer Heritage*, 17:215.

54. Jeffery Ogden Johnson gives the date of Susan's marriage to Brigham as 31 October 1844, citing Brigham Young's journal and Eighteenth Ward records.

The traditional date is 2 November 1844. See chapter 1 of this book.

55. Photocopy, typescript, Nauvoo Temple record 164.

56. *Pioneer Women of Faith and Fortitude*, ed. Mary Johnson, et al., vol. 4 (Salt Lake City: International Daughters of Utah Pioneers, 1998): 3520–21.

57. History of Hannahette Snively Pratt in Carter, *Our Pioneer Heritage*, 17:215. This quote is given with variations. In Carter, *Our Pioneer Heritage*, 17:215, it is suggested Susan didn't understand about polygamy and Hannahette is quoted as saying, "It's all for eternity, Susan." Then when Hannahette's first child was born Susan looked down with a wry smile and exclaimed, "Yes, Hannah. It's all for eternity."

58. Susa Young Gates, "Autobiography," and "Susa's Thoughts on the Wives of Brigham Young as She Saw and Remembered Them," in possession of Kari Robinson, great-great-granddaughter of Susa.

59. The sealing occurred in the Logan Temple, 19 June 1884, with Susan and Julia in person and Lorenzo Snow Young as proxy for Brigham Young (Film 178087, Special Collections, LDS Family History Library). In *Pioneer Women of Faith and Fortitude*, a sketch on Susanna notes Julia as a "foster daughter." Julia does not usually appear as one of Brigham Young's descendants and Susan is listed as Brigham's wife, with no issue.

60. Jo Davies, interview with the author, 1999.

61. Burton was born in Salt Lake, 18 May 1855, son of Robert Burton and Maria Haven. His father served as a military man, and was a friend of Brigham. Charles Burton served a mission to Australia. He was a businessman, joining the firm of Hardy Bros. & Burton in 1882. In 1885 he became the business manager of the *Salt Lake Herald*, which position he held for two years and then became the manager of the Salt Lake Theatre for the next ten years. He later worked as an assistant cashier at the State Bank of Utah, and then as cashier. He served as director on many boards, including Provo Woolen Mills, Salt Lake Livery and Transfer, Home Fire Insurance Co, Lehi Commercial and Savings Bank, Consolidated Wagon & Machine Co., and the Salt Lake Theatre. In 1896 he was appointed quartermaster-general on Governor Heber M. Wells's staff, and then adjutant-general of Utah. Following the sad death of Julia in 1889, he married Josephine Young Beatie, daughter of Bishop Walter J.

Beatie and another granddaughter of Brigham Young. They had a family who kept Julia's name in remembrance and cared for her keepsakes. Jo Davies, interview with the author, 1999.

62. In an attempt to help with her unspecified medical problems the Burtons went to Birmingham, England, where surgery was performed in November 1889. A cablegram sent to Salt Lake stated the surgery went well. A few days later on 29 November 1889, another cablegram arrived: Julia was in critical condition, and this was followed soon by another saying Julia had passed away and her husband would leave the following day to bring the deceased home. *Deseret Evening News,* 29 November 1889, reported, "The news of the death of one so aimable [*sic*] good and beloved will cause a great shock to the friends of the deceased and husband; who are a host. It is impossible for one acquainted with Mrs. Burton to think of her without emotion. She had been afflicted for years and bore her sufferings with phenomenal patience. The deepest sympathy will be felt for the bereaved husband. His trip to Europe was solely in the hope of obtaining aid for his wife. No one could have been more solicitous for his partner in life than he has been, every means within reach that had in it a prospect or probability of relief for her having been tried. Now his last effort has failed, and he returns with the lifeless remains of his wife, that her body may be interred in the home of her kindred and friends. God bless the memory of this tender hearted woman," *Deseret Evening News*, 29 November 1889.

An account of the funeral for Julia Young Burton is given in the *Deseret Evening News,* 16 December 1889. It was held in the Lion House, with Bishop Orson F. Whitney of the Eighteenth Ward conducting. The *Deseret News* gives the words to a hymn composed by Bishop Whitney for the occasion, and sung by the choir. The newspaper also describes how the large room at the Lion House was "tastefully draped with white, corresponding with the beautiful casket. There were many lovely floral decorations presented by family and friends. . . . A very large cortege followed the remains to the cemetery, where all that was mortal of one of the most gentle and lovable of her six was laid away to await the call of the final resurrection."

63. The Burton family also owned property near the Forest Farm. Eighteenth Ward records, LDS Family History Library.

64. Carter, *Our Pioneer Heritage,* 1:438.

65. Susan's death is noted briefly in the *Journal History of the Church of Jesus Christ of Latter- day Saints* (Liverpool and London: LDS Booksellers, 1855–1886): "Susan Snively Young, a widow of Pres. Brigham Young, died in Salt Lake City. 30 Oct. 1815–21 Nov. 1892." From a letter to the bishops of the church from Presiding Bishop Wm. B. Preston, 22 December 1898: "I take great pleasure in informing you that the late Susan Snively Young (widow of the late President Brigham Young) bequeathed to the poor of the Church . . . the sum of $1263.48 to be distributed at my discretion Herewith please find check . . . in the amount of $40.00 . . . the amount apportioned to your ward, with the request that you and your counselors distribute this sum to the worthy poor of your ward as occasion may require. . . ."

66. Charles Ora Card, *Diaries of Charles Ora Card,* ed. Donald G. Godfrey and Brigham Y. Card (Salt Lake City: University of Utah Press, 1993), chap. 1, 2, and 3. Charles Ora Card describes staying at the farmhouse occasionally when he was in the city when he was being sought by the federal officers during the polygamy era. However, it was subject to raids by the marshals, as were most hiding places. Card's wife was a daughter of Zina D. Huntington Young and a half-sister to Chariton Jacobs, Zina's son from her first marriage to Henry Jacobs. Card immigrated to Alberta, Canada, to escape the arms of the law, but was still acting as president of the Cache Stake and returned frequently. When he was back in Utah he was not immune to being arrested.

67. Reese, quoted in Woolley, 17.

68. Woolley, 8. Wooley cites county abstracts.

69. Thelma Woolley Fetzer, who grew up in Forest Dale Ward, interview with the author, January 2001.

70. Jacobson, 278.

71. Guests often visited the site before it was completely restored, and described entering the property through a big gate. Elaine S. LeSueur, interview with the author, 1999. LeSueur lived in the Forest Farm area as a young wife.

72. Jacobsen, 278.

73. Ibid.

74. Interview by author with supervisor/docent (name not available) of animals at new location of the farmhouse, 1988.

CHAPTER 8

1. *Deseret News,* 28 November 1921.

2. Susa Young Gates, "The Gardo House," *Improvement Era* 20 (1917): 1099–1103.

3. Doctrine and Covenants 124:22–23.
4. *Journal History of the Church of Jesus Christ of Latter-day Saints* (Liverpool and London: LDS Booksellers, 1855–86), 2 September 1873, microfilm, Historical Department of the Church of Jesus Christ of Latter-day Saints (hereafter cited as LDS Church Historical Department), Salt Lake City, Utah.
5. Clarissa Young Spencer and Mabel Harmer, *Brigham Young at Home* (Salt Lake City: Deseret Book, 1972), 219–21. Other accounts say that the house was called "Gardo" because it seemed to stand "guard" over the city.
6. Paul Anderson, "William Harrison Folsom: Pioneer Architect," *Utah Historical Quarterly* 43 (1975): 240–59. Gates, "The Gardo House," 1099–1103.
7. Nina Folsom Moss, *A History of William Harrison Folsom* (privately published biography, 1973), 33–54. Copy in possession of the authors.
8. Eugene Traughber, "The Prophet's Courtship: President Young's Favorite Wife, Amelia, Talks," *Salt Lake Tribune*, 11 March 1894. Typescript copy at Utah State Historical Society, Salt Lake City, MS A 578; *Deseret News*, 12 December 1910. In the Traughber interview, Amelia said she lived at the Lion House during her marriage to Brigham Young except for a short period when she resided at the Beehive House. When Brigham Young died, in 1877, she was living at the Lion House. This statement was later substantiated by William Rossiter, one of the administrators of Amelia's estate, after Amelia's death in 1910. See JH, 11 December 1910.

    However, it was Susa Young Gates's belief that Amelia moved out of the Lion House shortly before Brigham Young's death. See Susa Young Gates, *The Life Story of Brigham Young*, draft copy, Susa Young Gates Collection, Utah State Historical Society, Salt Lake City, B-95, box 8, folder 2.
9. Leonard J. Arrington, *Brigham Young: American Moses* (New York: Alfred A. Knopf, 1985), 421.
10. M. R. Werner, *Brigham Young* (New York: Harcourt, Brace and Company, 1925), 330–31. After her divorce, Ann Eliza Webb Young pursued a course of vengeance against Brigham Young and polygamy in general. In 1876, she published a book, *Wife Number 19*, that caused a public outcry and became one of the catalysts for more stringent legislation against polygamy. See Ann Eliza Webb Young, *Wife Number 19; or, The Story of a Life in Bondage, Being a Complete Exposé of Mormonism and Revealing the Sorrow, Sacrifices, and Sufferings of a Woman in Polygamy* (Hartford, Connecticut: Dustin Gilman & Co., 1876).

    Many of the luxuries Amelia enjoyed at the Lion House such as her piano, jewelry, and cologne were gifts from her father, William Harrison Folsom, not Brigham Young. See Spencer and Harmer, 80–81; and Gates, *The Life Story of Brigham Young*.
11. Spencer and Harmer, 64, 80–81, 219–21. According to Clarissa Young Spencer, "the frequently circulated statement that she [Amelia] was Father's 'favorite wife,' was a statement that was entirely without foundation." Clarissa also wrote that the nickname "Amelia's Palace" was the invention of a one-armed hack driver who used to drive tourists around the city.

    Gates, *The Life Story of Brigham Young*. Gates wrote the following about the Young household: "There may have been jealousy, I am sure of that—women are human. But Aunt Amelia herself refrained from any act or word that would give occasion to natural reactions in the household." According to Susa, Amelia won the respect and affection of her sister wives by her "consistent and modest deportment." Susa added, "Father went his quiet way and if he made any difference with his young wives Amelia and Mary [Van Cott], no doubt he did at times, my own keen childish eyes never detected that shade of difference."

    In another part of the manuscript, Susa acknowledged that Brigham Young may have had several "favorite" wives during his lifetime. She wrote, "Aunt Emmeline Free was, for a short time, rather a favorite with father because of her beauty, her quick wit and tactful approach. But, she was never a favorite with the other wives for she would not consider them as Aunt Clara Decker nor even as Aunt Amelia did when she was father's favorite wife. I use this term advisedly for father had perhaps the weakness of his strength and he could not pay equal attention to fourteen or fifteen women. So that two or three of his wives saw more of him, perhaps, than the others. I do not judge father for this, I merely state it as a fact."

    Deseret Evening News, 15 December 1910. At Amelia's funeral, Richard W. Young said, "She [Amelia] came into the family of President Brigham Young when he was nearly 60 years of age while she was young and attractive, but blessed with a mental grasp of the problems of the day. President Young's health was enfeebled on account of an onerous life and he needed great care. Aunt Amelia was a natural nurse and performed the duties expected of her in a most praiseworthy manner. . . . From these incidents came the report that Amelia was President Young's most favored wife. He however was an absolutely just man. . . . As the years grew on, however, the family learned to love Aunt Amelia. She was so just, so fair that I can truthfully say that she had the love of every member of the family."

    Heber J. Grant, who was also a speaker at the funeral, echoed Richard W. Young's sentiments. He said, "I believe no higher tribute could be paid Sister Amelia than the fact that President Brigham Young's wives loved his young wife."

    Traughber, "The Prophet's Courtship: President Young's Favorite Wife, Amelia, Talks," quotes Amelia as as saying, "I can't say he [Brigham Young] had any favorites." But, privately, she told friends she believed Emmeline Free Young was Brigham Young's favorite wife. See *California Inter-Mountain News*, 9 August 1949.
12. Leonard J. Arrington, "The Settlement of Brigham Young's Estate, 1877–1879," *Pacific Historical Review* 21 (1952): 1–20.
13. Gates, *The Life Story of Brigham Young*, 350–53.
14. George Reynolds, letter to Brigham Young, 6 June 1876, Letter Books, Brigham Young Papers, LDS Church Archives, Salt Lake City, Utah.
15. Joseph Heinerman, "Amelia's Palace," *Montana: The Magazine of Western History* 29 (1979): 54–63.
16. Melvin L. Bashore, "The 1876 Arsenal Hill Explosion," *Utah Historical Quarterly* 52 (1984): 246–55; *Salt Lake Herald*, 6 April 1876.
17. George Reynolds, letter to Brigham Young, 20 May 1876, Letter Books, Brigham Young Papers, LDS Church Archives, Salt Lake City, Utah.
18. Arrington, "The Settlement of Brigham Young's Estate," 1–20. According to Arrington, during the probate of Brigham Young's estate, it was discovered the Mormon prophet owed $1 million to the church. One of the credits the church granted the estate against this indebtedness was a $120,000 credit for the Gardo House.
19. Dr. Dee L. Folsom, interview with author, 23 September 1990, Salt Lake City, Utah; *Salt Lake Tribune*, 4 March 1912. There were at least two other residences designed by Folsom that were remarkably similar to the Gardo House. The first was the

Feramorz Little home located on 164 East and 100 South. The Little Mansion, constructed at the same time as the Gardo House, was also damaged during the Arsenal Hill Explosion in 1876. See Bashore, "The 1876 Arsenal Hill Explosion." It was also occupied by the Keeley Institute in 1902. The second was the George Q. Cannon home located on South Temple and 100 West, near Amelia's "Junior Gardo." See *Salt Lake Tribune*, 4 March 1912.

Harriet Amelia Folsom Young resided the rest of her life at the 100 West South Temple home her family provided for her after Brigham Young's death. She never remarried. Amelia is buried in the Salt Lake City Cemetery.

20. B. H. Roberts, *The Life of John Taylor: Third President of the Church of Jesus Christ of Latter-day Saints* (Salt Lake City: George Q. Cannon & Sons Co., 1892), 331.

21. JH, 27 December 1881.

22. Levi Edgar Young, "Historic Buildings of Salt Lake City," *Young Woman's Journal* 6 (1922): 309–11. Wilford Woodruff estimated the cost at $15,000; see Scott G. Kenney, ed., *Wilford Woodruff's Journal, 1833–1898*, 9 vols. (Midvale, Utah: Signature Books, 1983–1985), 2 January 1882.

23. *Salt Lake Tribune*, 3 February 1957; JH, 2 September 1873. Ramsey did woodwork for the Beehive House and Lion House. There is some question as to whether or not he did woodwork for the Gardo House. Ramsey moved from Salt Lake City to Richfield in 1874, which may have precluded him from working on the Gardo House. In addition, it has been noted that the style of woodwork in the Gardo House was dissimilar to that of Ramsey's work.

24. JH, 27 December 1881.

25. Ibid., 3 January 1882.

26. Matthias F. Cowley, ed., *Wilford Woodruff: History of His Life and Labors* (Salt Lake City: Bookcraft, 1964), 545.

27. Roberts, The Life of John Taylor, 331.

28. Kate B. Carter, comp., "Journal of Rachel Emma Woolley Simmons," *Heart Throbs of the West* 11 (1950):153–208.

29. *Daily Tribune*, 1 January 1882.

30. JH, 5 January 1882.

31. *Deseret News*, 5 January 1882.

32. Leonard J. Arrington, *Great Basin Kingdom: An Economic History of the Latter-day Saints, 1830–1900* (Lincoln: University of Nebraska Press, 1958), 354–71.

33. James B. Allen and Glen M. Leonard, *The Story of the Latter-day Saints* (Salt Lake City: Deseret Book, 1976), 381. Roberts, *The Life of John Taylor*, 331.

34. Ibid.

35. Richard D. Poll, Thomas G. Alexander, Eugene E. Campbell, and David E. Miller, *Utah's History* (Provo, Utah: Brigham Young University Press, 1978), 259–256.

36. Wilford Woodruff, Journal, 27 November 1882. LDS Church Historical Department, Salt Lake City, Utah, as cited by Heinerman, 54–63.

37. Bruce A. Van Orden, *The Life of George Reynolds: Prisoner for Conscience' Sake* (Salt Lake City: Deseret Book, 1992), 121–24.

38. Brigham Young, et al., *Journal of Discourses*, 26 vol. (Liverpool: LDS Booksellers Depot, 1854–1886), 153–54.

39. Roberts, *The Life of John Taylor*, 485.

40. Jessie L. Embry, *Mormon Polygamous Families: Life in the Principle* (Salt Lake City: University of Utah Press, 1987), 19–22.

41. Poll, Alexander, Campbell, and Miller, 259–65.

42. Mark Curtis, interview with Edith Smith Patrick, daughter of Joseph F. Smith, 26 April 1984, Bountiful, Utah, copy in Mr. Curtis's possession and in the LDS Church Archives, Salt Lake City, Utah.

43. John M. Whitaker, Journal, 21 May 1886, Special Collections, Harold B. Lee Library, Brigham Young University, Provo, Utah, as cited in Heinerman, 54–63.

44. Roberts, *The Life of John Taylor*, 490.

45. Heinerman, 54–63.

46. JH, 13 March 1885.

47. Whitaker, Journal, 21 May 1886, as cited in Heinerman, 259–65.

48. Kenney, 8:376.

49. Roberts, *The Life of John Taylor*, 392–400.

50. Thomas G. Alexander, *Mormonism in Transition: A History of the Latter-day Saints, 1890–1930* (Urbana and Chicago: University of Illinois Press, 1986), 3–11; Poll, Alexander, Campbell, and Miller, 259–65.

51. Kenney, 8:449.

52. Brian H. Stuy, ed., *Collected Discourses (1886–1889)*, vol. 1 (Burbank, California: B. H. S. Publishing, 1987), 39.

53. B. H. Roberts, *A Comprehensive History of the Church of Jesus Christ of Latter-day Saints*, Infobase: LDS Collectors' Library (Orem, Utah: Sonos Publishing Inc., 1991) ch 166: 194.

54. Kenney, 8:508. Arrington, Great Basin Kingdom, 368. JH, 17 November 1921.

55. Heinerman, 54–63.

56. Kenney, 508.

57. L. John Nuttall, Diary, 24 November 1889, as cited by Heinerman, 54–63.

58. Kenney, 5, 7, 17, 45, 57, 81, 117.

59. Alexander, *Mormonism in Transition*, 3–11; Roberts, *Comprehensive History*, 168: 218–19.

60. Joseph Fielding Smith, *The Life of Joseph F. Smith: Sixth President of the Church of Jesus Christ of Latter-day Saints* (Salt Lake City: Deseret News Press, 1938), 297; Doctrine and Covenants, Official Declaration, 291–92.

61. Abraham H. Cannon, Journal, 5 October 1890, Special Collections, Harold B. Lee Library, Brigham Young University, Provo, Utah, as cited in Heinerman, 54–63.

62. Ibid., 7 October 1890.

63. Heinerman, 54–63.

64. Alexander, *Mormonism in Transition*, 3–11.

65. James Henry Moyle, *Mormon Democrat: The Religious and Political Memoirs*, ed. Gene Sessions, LDS Church Historical Department, Salt Lake City, Utah, 1975, 177–81.

66. Ibid.

67. JH, 13 November 1891.

68. *Deseret Evening News*, 4 January 1892.

69. James T. White, *The Dictionary of American Biography*, vol. 25 (New York: Scribner's, 1936): 335–36.

70. Ibid.

71. Ibid; Mark Edward Lender, *The Dictionary of American Temperance* (Westport, Connecticut: Greenwood Press, 1984), 270–72; Cheryl Krasnick Warsh, "Adventures in Maritime Quackery: The Leslie E. Keeley Gold Cure Institute of Fredericton, N. B.," *Acadiensis* 17, no. 2 (1988): 109–30.

72. Warsh, 109–30; White, 335–36.

73. *Daily Tribune*, 1 January 1902.

74. Cowley, 580.

75. Daniel H. Ludlow, ed., *Encyclopedia of Mormonism*, vol. 2 (New York: Macmillan Publishing Company, 1992): 628, 1505.

76. Arrington, *Great Basin Kingdom*, 378.

77. Kenney, 315.

78. Ibid., 327. Keeley Institutes flourished throughout the United States, Canada, Mexico, and England until Keeley's death in 1900. Keeley left an estate valued at $1 million. By 1936, only the parent institution in Dwight, Illinois, and a branch in Los Angeles, California, were in operation. We have been unable to locate any current listings for Keeley Institutes.

79. Edward Leo Lyman, "Isaac Trumbo and the Politics of Utah Statehood," *Utah Historical Quarterly* 41 (1973): 128–49.

80. Ibid.

81. Ibid.
82. Ibid.
83. JH, 17 September 1899.
84. *The Argus*, 22 September 1894, as cited in Heinerman, 54–63.
85. Heinerman, 54–63.
86. JH, 17 September 1899.
87. Lyman, "Isaac Trumbo," 41:128–49.
88. JH, 17 September 1899.
89. Cannon, Journal, 21 November 1895, as cited in Lyman, 128–49.
90. Roberts, *A Comprehensive History* vol. 6, no. 174, 338–39.
91. *Daily Tribune*, 17 September 1899.
92. Lyman, 128–49.
93. JH, 5 February 1898.
94. Lyman, 128–49. Isaac Trumbo spent the remainder of his life in San Francisco. In 1911, he was evicted from his home for failure to pay an $18,000 mortgage debt. He was eventually forced to auction off many of his furnishings and art treasures, which were valued at $200,000. On 2 November 1912, Trumbo was the victim of a brutal beating and robbery and was left for dead on a San Francisco street. He never regained consciousness. Emma Trumbo remarried after her husband's death.
95. JH, 17 September 1897.
96. George M. McCune, "Alfred William McCune," privately published biography, 1972. Photocopy in authors' possession.
97. Ibid.
98. Ibid. See also Stewart L. Grow, "Utah's Senatorial Election of 1899: The Election That Failed," *Utah Historical Quarterly* 39 (1971): 30–39. Of all the candidates, McCune came closest to winning. As the possibility of his victory grew stronger, however, a Republican legislator accused McCune of trying to buy his vote. Investigations into the charges did not substantiate them but the damage had been done.
99. Ibid.
100. Gates, "The Gardo House," 1099–1103; Levi Edgar Young, "Historic Buildings of Salt Lake City," 6:309–11.
101. Jay Quealey, grandson of A. W. McCune, interview with author, 1990, Salt Lake City, Utah; notes in Ms. Brimhall's possession.
102. Gates, "The Gardo House," 1099–1103. Alfred William McCune and his wife resided in the McCune Mansion until 1920, when they moved to Los Angeles. When they left Utah, the couple donated their beautiful home to the LDS Church. Heber J. Grant publicly thanked the McCunes for their generous gift in the April 1921 general conference. He fur- ther noted that "There have been a great many people . . . who have urged me to move there [McCune Mansion] and use that magnificent house as the official residence of the President of the Church." Grant declined the invitation, believing that such a course of action would be a great waste of church members' money. The church later converted the mansion into the McCune School of Music and Art. The church's acquisition of the McCune Mansion, which was newer and more modern than the Gardo House, may have been one of the factors in the church's decision to demolish the Gardo House. After the death of his wife in 1924, McCune moved to France where he resided until his death in 1927. At the time of his death, his estate was valued at $15 million. The McCunes are buried in Nephi, Utah.
103. JH, 6 May 1901; Gates, "The Gardo House," 1099–1103.
104. Raye Carlson Price, *Diggings and Doings in Park City* (Salt Lake City: University of Utah Press, 1970), 27–32; Margaret D. Lester, *Brigham Street* (Salt Lake City: Utah State Historical Society, 1979), 111–20; George A. Thompson, Fraser Buck, *Treasure Mountain Home: Park City Revisited* (Salt Lake City: Dream Garden Press, 1981), 82–86. For a comprehensive history of the Silver Queen, see Judy Dykman and Colleen Whitley, *The Silver Queen: Her Royal Highness Suzanne Bransford Emery Holmes Delitch Engalitcheff* (Logan, Utah: Utah State University Press, 1998).
105. Dykman and Whitley. Dykman and Whitley believe that Susie's fortune was much less than the 50 million dollars reported by eastern and local newspapers.
106. Dykman and Whitley, 50–54.
107. Lester, 111–20; Price, 27–32.
108. *Elite*, 15 March 1902, 54–63.
109. *Salt Lake Tribune*, 27 December 1901; *Elite*, 15 March 1902; Silver Queen Scrapbook, 1902–1904, Utah State Historical Society, Salt Lake City, microfilm A 633.
110. Silver Queen Scrapbook, microfilm A 633.
111. Edith Smith Patrick, interview with author, 26 April 1984, Bountiful, Utah.
112. Silver Queen Scrapbook, microfilm A 633; JH, 1 January 1902.
113. Susanna Harris Hartman, interview with author, 2 October 1990, California.
114. *Deseret Evening News*, 17 May 1902; Silver Queen Scrapbook, microfilm A 633.
115. Silver Queen Scrapbook.
116. Ibid.
117. Ibid.
118. JH, 6 June 1917.
119. Ibid., 20 November 1917.
120. Ibid., 1 December 1917; Mrs. W. Mont Ferry, E. O. Howard, and R. J. Shields, *History of the Salt Lake County Chapter of American Red Cross, 1898 to 1919* (n.p., n.d.), 10, photocopy in possession of the authors.
121. Ibid; JH, 28 November 1921.
122. *Deseret Evening News*, 20 March 1920 and 4 May 1920. Colonel Edwin F. Holmes and Susie lived in their California home, El Roble, until Holmes's death in 1925. In 1930, Susie married a Serbian doctor named Radovan N. Delitch. The marriage ended in divorce two years later and Delitch later hanged himself in his cabin during an ocean cruise. Shortly after Delitch's death, Susie sold her California home, El Roble, and auctioned off her Rolls Royce, furniture, paintings, and the famous "Aida" piano. In 1933, Susie married Prince Nickolas Engalitcheff. The couple spent most of their time in California and Europe until Engalitcheff's death in 1935. When Susie died in 1942, at age eighty-three, she had spent almost all of her fortune. At her request, she was buried in Salt Lake City's Mount Olivet Cemetery alongside her first husband, Albion B. Emery. For many years, the exact location of her grave was kept a secret because of the persistent rumor she was buried in a silver dress and that there were silver dollars in her coffin.
123. *Deseret News*, 28 April 1920.
124. JH, 2 October 1920.
125. Ibid., 26 February 1921. According to the *Improvement Era* 29 (1925–1926): 517, "The work of breaking ground for the *Federal bank building*, corner of South Temple and State St., began on January 25, 1926." The Federal Bank Building has now been demolished and the site is now occupied by the twenty-six story Eagle Gate Plaza and Tower which was constructed in 1986.
126. Ibid., 10 March 1921 and 26 March 1921.
127. Ibid., 8 April 1921. During this time, the church was still in financial straits as a result of the antipolygamy legislation in the late 1800s. Stock market drops, the levying of federal income tax, and the expansion of the city's commercial district also made large mansions difficult to maintain.
128. Ibid., 17 November 1921 and 28 November 1921.
129. Silver Queen Scrapbook, microfilm A 633. The Daughters of Utah

Pioneers Museum, Beehive House, and Park City Museum all possess some furniture, clothing, and other memorabilia relating to the Gardo House and its occupants. On 6 August 1998 Judy Dykman presented a model of the Gardo House to the Daughters of Utah Pioneers Museum. It is now on permanent display at the museum.

CHAPTER 9

1. The pony express started providing mail service in 1861. It was in turn replaced by the telegraph in 1862 which carried brief messages at a cheaper rate. When the transcontinental railroad was completed in 1869, it provided Utahns the best and cheapest mail and freight service.

2. Thomas Alexander, *Utah, the Right Place: The Official Centennial History* (Salt Lake City: Gibbs Smith, 1995), 103–4; Leonard J. Arrington, *Great Basin Kingdom: An Economic History of the Latter-day Saints, 1830–1900* (Lincoln: University of Nebraska Press, 1966), 121, 113.

3. Alexander, *Utah, the Right Place,* 124–27; Arrington, 160–61, 170–94; Ken Verdoia and Richard Firmage, *Utah: The Struggle for Statehood* (Salt Lake City: University of Utah Press, 1996), 59–62.

4. At Mountain Meadows, near Cedar City, Utah, a group of Mormons, possibly allied with local Native Americans, assassinated the members of Baker-Fancher wagon train. John D. Lee was eventually executed as the leader of the group, the only person prosecuted for the massacre. Lee's prosecution came about, at least in part, from Connor's insistent efforts. The most complete work on the subject remains Juanita Brooks's *Mountain Meadows Massacre* (Norman: University of Oklahoma Press, 1961).

5. Brigham Young, et al., *Journal of Discourses,* 26 vol. (Liverpool: LDS Booksellers Depot, 1854–1886), 12:287, 8 October 1868.

6. Arrington, 113, 121; Elizabeth W. Kane, *Twelve Mormon Homes Visited in Succession on a Journey through Utah and Arizona* (Philadelphia: William Wood, l874), 8–16.

7. George Ellsworth, *Utah's Heritage* (Salt Lake City: Peregrine Smith Inc., 1977), 187.

8. George A. Smith, letter, 10 January 1871, in Florence Jacobsen, "Restorations Belong to Everyone," *BYU Studies* 18, no. 3 (spring 1978): 7–8.

9. Alfales Young, obituary. None of the sources on St. George or his mother mention him as being there.

10. Lucy Bigelow's girls found little social life for young people in St. George, so she set out to make some. She helped found the Union Club that offered young people picnics, dances, and oratory activities while stressing strong values and character development. A drama club opened about the time she arrived and she participated in several plays. Susa also made some good friends, including Elizabeth Claridge, who would eventually marry Alfred McCune; together they became one of the state's most wealthy and philanthropic couples. Vicky Burgess-Olson, *Sister Saints* (Provo: Brigham Young University Press, 1978), 67–68; Claudia Bushman, *Mormon Sisters: Women in Early Utah* (Logan: Utah State University Press, 1997), 66; Miriam Murphy, "From Impulsive Girl to Patient Wife: Lucy Bigelow Young," *Utah Historical Quarterly* 45, no. 3 (summer 1977): 281–84.

11. Emmeline B. Wells, "Lucy Bigelow Young—Our Picture Gallery," *Young Woman's Journal* 3, no. 4 (January 1892): 147.

12. Lucy Bigelow remained close to her children, especially her daughter Susa. She helped Susa by selling subscriptions door to door for the *Young Woman's Journal.* She assisted Susa in several other writing and teaching projects and was particularly involved in work for women's rights. Together Lucy and Susa traveled to conventions in the East and in Europe, working with suffragists including Susan B. Anthony. On one occasion both attended a women's rights convention in England and attended a reception hosted by Queen Victoria. Susa Young Gates, "Lucy Bigelow Young," typescript, Utah State Historical Society, Salt Lake City (hereafter cited as Gates, "Lucy Bigelow"); Historical marker for the Lucy Bigelow Young Home, 111 West St. George Boulevard, St. George, Utah.

13. Marlene Lucero, owner of the Dixie Trading Post, interview with Ann Best, June 2000.

14. Susa Young Gates and Leah Widstoe, *The Life Story of Brigham Young* (New York: Macmillan, 1931), 167, 359. An 1861 plat map of St. George shows where the Birch and Burgess homes were located. In a conversation with Bessy Gardner, a one-hundred-year-old resident of St. George, Judy Dykmam confirmed that these addresses were correct.

15. Examination of the property and interview with employees by Ann Best, June 2000.

16. Gary L. Gregson, *Utah Roadside History: Historic Sites and Landmarks* (Provo, Utah: Community Press, 1995), 86; Gates, "Lucy Bigelow."

17. Gates, "Lucy Bigelow."

18. Brad Westwood, Brigham Young University Special Collections, interview with Colleen Whitley, 1998; Jesse Embry, Redd Center, Brigham Young University, telephone interview with Colleen Whitley, 15 February 2001.

19. Tracy Hiatt, Provo Travelodge, interview with Colleen Whitley, 14 September 1998.

20. Faunda R. Bybee, *Then and Now: A Picture Book of Caribou County, Idaho* (privately published: Faunda R. Bybee, 1977), 369.

21. John Codman, "Soda Springs and Environs," *Idaho Yesterdays* 34, no. 1 (spring 1990): 23.

22. Lula Barnard, Faunda Bybee, and Lola Wallace, *Tosoiba* (Soda Springs, Idaho: Mead Camp, Daughters of Utah Pioneers, 1958), 91–104; Bybee, 369; Soda Springs, Idaho, website <www.ohwy.com/id/s/sodaspri.htm>; marker number 260, erected 1960 by Camp Mead, Daughters of Utah Pioneers, photograph in Bybee, 232.

23. Owners of the Brigham Young Motor Lodge, interviews with Judy Dykman and Colleen Whitley, December 1999.

EPILOGUE

1. *Utah History Encyclopedia,* s.v. "Salt Lake Theatre."

2. Both Vanderbilt and Hearst were wealthy members of that period in American history that Mark Twain labeled the "Gilded Age." Multi-millionaires in the period before income taxes, they built lavish, often excessive, homes.

Bibliography

ABBREVIATIONS

LDS Historical Department:
Historical Department of the Church of Jesus Christ of Latter-day Saints

LDS Church Archives:
Archives of the Church of Jesus Christ of Latter-day Saints

LDS Family History Library:
The Church of Jesus Christ of Latter-day Saints Family History Library

Alexander, Thomas. *Mormonism in Transition: A History of the Latter-day Saints, 1890–1930.* Urbana and Chicago: University of Illinois Press, 1986.

———. *Utah, the Right Place: The Official Centennial History.* Salt Lake City: Gibbs Smith, 1995.

Allen, James B., and Glen M. Leonard. *The Story of the Latter-day Saints.* Salt Lake City: Deseret Book, 1976.

Anderson, Judy. "Beehive House." Master's thesis, Brigham Young University, 1967.

Anderson, Paul. "William Harrison Folsom: Pioneer Architect." *Utah Historical Quarterly* 43 (1975).

Angell, Truman O. Autobiography. Holograph, LDS Church Archives, Salt Lake City, Utah, n.d.

———. Journal. Typescript, LDS Church Historical Department, Salt Lake City, Utah.

Angus, Mark. *Salt Lake City Under Foot.* Salt Lake City: Signature Books, 1993.

Archuleta, Chien. Histories of Salt Lake City Parks. Salt Lake City: Department of Public Services, 1998.

Arrington, Leonard J. *Brigham Young: American Moses.* New York: Alfred A. Knopf, 1985.

———. *Great Basin Kingdom.* Lincoln: University of Nebraska Press, 1966.

———. "The Settlement of Brigham Young's Estate, 1877–1879." *Pacific Historical Review* 21 (1952).

——— and David Bitton. *The Mormon Experience: A History of the Latter-day Saints.* New York: Alfred A. Knopf, 1979.

———, Dean L. May, and Feramorz Y. Fox. *Building the City of God: Community and Cooperation among the Mormons.* Salt Lake City: Deseret Book, 1976.

Ashton, Wendell J. *Voice in the West: Biography of a Pioneer Newspaper.* New York: Duell, Sloan and Pearce, 1950.

Auburn Daily Bulletin, 31 August 1877.

Barnard, Lula, Faunda Bybee, and Lola Wallace. *Tosoiba.* Soda Springs, Idaho: Mead Camp, Daughters of Utah Pioneers, 1958.

Barnum, J. P. *New York Times,* 16 September 1877.

Bashore, Melvin L. "The 1876 Arsenal Hill Explosion." *Utah Historical Quarterly* 52 (1984).

"Beehive." *Deseret News,* 28 July 1904.

"The Bee Hive House." *Salt Lake Herald,* 1 November 1898.

"Beehive House Made Available for Working Girls." *Deseret Evening News,* 3 April 1920.

"The Beehive House Sold." *Deseret Evening News,* 30 January 1893.

Beeton, Beverly. "Woman Suffrage in Territorial Utah." *Utah Historical Quarterly* 46 (spring 1978).

Bennett, Richard E. *Mormons at the Missouri, 1846–1852: "And Should We Die."* Norman and London: University of Oklahoma Press, 1987.

Biographical Sketches of Brigham Young and His Twenty-nine Wives. Philadelphia: S. C. Upham, 1873.

Black, Susan Easton, ed. *LDS Memberships 1830–1848.* Database. LDS Family History Library, Salt Lake City, Utah.

———, and Larry C. Porter. *Lion of the Lord: Essays on the Life and Service of Brigham Young.* Salt Lake City: Deseret Book, 1995.

"Bones Identified as Mother Angell's." *Salt Lake Tribune,* 26 April 1910.

Booth, Edith Harriett Young. "A Biographical Sketch of the Life of Oscar S. Young." Typescript LDS Church Historical Department, Salt Lake City, Utah, n.d.

Bradley, Martha. *ZCMI, America's First Department Store.* Salt Lake City: ZCMI, 1991.

———, and Mary Brown Firmage Woodward. *Four Zinas: A Story of Mothers and Daughters on the Mormon Frontier.* Salt Lake City: Signature Books, 2001.

Bransford, Suzanne. Scrapbook. Salt Lake City: Utah State Historical Society.

Brigham Young Forest Farminterpretive documents. Salt Lake City: This Is the Place Heritage Park.

"Brigham Young's Home Yields 1st Wife's Ring?" *Salt Lake Tribune*, 28 July 1973.

Britsch, R. Lanier. *Unto the Islands of the Sea.* Salt Lake City: Deseret Book, 1986.

Brooks, Juanita. *Mountain Meadows Massacre.* Revised edition. Norman: University of Oklahoma Press, 1961.

Brown, Ben, comp. *The Journal of Lorenzo Brown, 1823–1900.* Salt Lake City: Heritage Press, n.d.

Brown, S. Kent, Donald Q. Cannon, and Richard H. Jackson. *Historical Atlas of Mormonism.* New York: Simon and Schuster, 1994.

Burgess-Olsen, Vicky. *Sister Saints.* Provo, Utah: Brigham Young University Press, 1978.

Burton, Richard. *City of the Saints.* N.p., n.d.

Bush, Lester E., Jr. "Brigham Young in Life and Death: A Medical Overview." *Journal of Mormon History* 5 (1978).

Bushman, Claudia. *Mormon Sisters, Women in Early Utah.* Logan: Utah State University Press, 1997.

Bybee, Faunda R. *Now and Then: A Picture Book of Caribou County, Idaho.* Privately compiled and published: Faunda R. Bybee, 1977.

"By Way of Introduction . . . General Church Office Building." Salt Lake City: Church of Jesus Christ of Latter-day Saints, n.d.

Cable, Mary. "She Who Shall Be Nameless." *American Heritage* 16 (February 1965).

Cameron, Marguerite. *This Is the Place.* Caldwell, Idaho: Caxton Printer, 1941.

Cannon, Abraham H. Journal. Special Collections, Harold B. Lee Library, Brigham Young University, Provo, Utah.

Cannon, Paul B. "Summary History of the Brigham Young Forest Farm House." *Deseret News,* 28 April 1923.

Card, Charles Ora. *Diaries of Charles Ora Card.* Edited by Donald G. Godfrey and Brigham Y. Card. Salt Lake City: University of Utah Press, 1993.

Carr, Steven L. *Holladay-Cottonwood, Places and Faces.* Holladay, Utah: Holladay-Cottonwood Heritage Committee, 1987.

Carter, Kate B. "Journal of Rachel Emma Woolley Simmons." *Heart Throbs of the West* 11 (1950).

———. *Our Pioneer Heritage.* Salt Lake City: Daughters of the Utah Pioneers, 1958–1977.

———, ed. *Brigham Young: His Wives and Family.* Salt Lake City: Daughters of Utah Pioneers, 1990.

Case, J. Hogue. *Salt Lake Sketchbook.* Salt Lake City: Clyde E. Harvey, 1975.

Christensen, Rex LeRoy. "The Life and Contributions of Captain Dan Jones." Master's thesis, Utah State University, 1977.

Church, Al. "Stalking the Wild Gentile." *Network* 5 (September 1981)17.

"Church Buys Lion House." *Salt Lake Herald,* 21 October 1900.

"Church Buys the Lion House." *Deseret Evening News,* 20 March 1900.

"Church Closes Facilities at Lion House." *Deseret News,* 27 February 1964.

"Church Offices in Beehive House." *Salt Lake Tribune,* 25 June 1899.

"City Items." *Deseret News,* 18 July 1855.

Codman, John. "Soda Springs & Environs." *Idaho Yesterdays* 34, no. 1 (spring 1990).

Compton, Todd. *In Sacred Loneliness: The Plural Wives of Joseph Smith.* Salt Lake City: Signature Books, 2000.

Covered Wagon Women. Lincoln: University of Nebraska, 1997.

Cowley, Matthias F., ed. *Wilford Woodruff: History of His Life and Labors.* Salt Lake City: Bookcraft, 1964.

Cracroft, Richard H., and Neal E. Lambert. *A Believing People: Literature of the Latter-day Saints.* Provo, Utah: Brigham Young University Press, 1974.

Creer, Leland Hargrave. *The Founding of an Empire.* Salt Lake City: Bookcraft, 1947.

"Crismon Mill Site." Daughters of Utah Pioneers, monument #43.

Crockwell, James H. *Pictures and Biographies of Brigham Young and His Wives.* Salt Lake City: James H. Crockwell.

Crosby, Jonathan. Reminiscence. LDS Church Archives, Salt Lake City, Utah.

Cutler's Park, Nebraska. Death and burial records, 1846–1849.

"Death Beckons to Mrs. Young." *Salt Lake Tribune,* 12 December 1910.

"Death of a Veteran Lady." *Deseret Evening News* 35 (12 July 1886).

"Death of Clara D. Young." *Woman's Exponent,* 15 January 1889.

"Death of Lucy D. Young." *Deseret Evening News,* 24 January 1891.

"Death of Lucy D. Young." *Woman's Exponent,* 1 March 1891.

"Death of Mary V. Young." *Deseret Evening News,* 5 January 1884.

"Death of Sister Jones." *Deseret Evening News,* 6 May 1895.

"The Deseret Museum." *Improvement Era* (September 1911).

Dixon, Randall. "Emigration Canyon to City Creek." *Utah Historical Quarterly* (spring 1997)158.

Dykman, Judy, and Colleen Whitley. *The Silver Queen: Her Royal Highness Suzanne Bransford Emery Holmes Delitch Engalitcheff.* Logan: Utah State University Press, 1998.

Eighth Census (1860).

"Eliza B. Young Dies At Son's Home." *Deseret Evening News,* 21 August 1915, 16.

Ellsworth, S. George. *Utah's Heritage.* Salt Lake City: Perigrine Smith, 1977.

Embry, Jessie L. *Mormon Polygamous Families: Life in the Principle.* Salt Lake City: University of Utah Press, 1987.

Esshom, Frank E. *Pioneers and Prominent Men of Utah.* Salt Lake City: Utah Pioneers Book Publishing Co., 1912.

"Famed Beehive House Closed as a Residence." *Church News,* 10 January 1959.

Felt, William E. "The Inception and Growth of the LDS Business College." Typescript. LDS Church Historical Department, Salt Lake City, Utah, 1 February 1982.

Ferry, Mrs. W. Mont, E. O. Howard, and R. J. Shields. *History of the Salt Lake County Chapter of the American Red Cross, 1898 to 1919.* Photocopy.

Fisher, J. Sheldon. "Brigham Young as a Mendon Craftsman: A Study in Historical Archaeology." *New York History* 61 (October 1980).

"Forest Farm Tidbits." Utah State Historical Society, 20 February 1979; Beehive House Historical File.

Fowler, John. *Journal of a Tour in the State of New York in the Year 1830.* London: n.p., 1831.

Furniss, Norman F. *The Mormon Conflict 1850–1859.* New Haven, Connecticut: Yale University Press, 1960.

Gallinger, Roy. "Here's How an 'Ordinary Boy' Became Top Religious Leader." Chenango County Historian's Office, Norwich, New York.

Gates, Susa Young. "The Gardo House." *Improvement Era* 20 (1917).

———. *The Life Story of Brigham Young.* Draft copy. Susa Young Gates Collection, Utah State Historical Society, Salt Lake City.

———. "Lucy Bigelow Young." Typescript. Utah State Historical Society, Salt Lake City.

———. "Recollections." Typescript. Utah State Historical Society, Salt Lake City. N.d.

———. *Unique Story—President Brigham Young.* Salt Lake City: Daughters of the Utah Pioneers, 1990.

———, and Mabel Young Sanborn. "Brigham Young Genealogy." *Utah Genealogical and Historical Magazine* 11 (April 1920).

———, and Leah Widstoe. *The Life Story of Brigham Young.* New York: Macmillan, 1931.

The Gold and Blue 4, no. 14 (July 1901).

Goodman, Jack. *As You Pass By.* Salt Lake City: University of Utah Press, 1995.

Greeley, Horace. Letter. "Two Hours with Brigham Young." *New York Daily Tribune,* 13 July 1859. Reprint, *Millenial Star* 21 (1859).

Gregson, Gary L. *Utah Roadside History: Monuments, Markers, and Sites.* Provo, Utah: Community Press, 1995.

Grow, Stewart L. "Utah's Senatorial Election of 1899: The Election That Failed." *Utah Historical Quarterly* 39 (1971).

Hall, Benjamin F. "Genealogical and Biographical Sketch of the Late Honorable Elijah Miller." Manuscript. Cayuga County Historian's Office, Auburn, New York, circa 1877.

Hampton, Brigham Young. Diary. Holograph. LDS Church Historical Department, Salt Lake City, Utah.

Hancock, Mosiah Lyman. "Life Story of Mosiah Lyman Hancock." Special Collections, Harold B. Lee Library, Brigham Young University, Provo, Utah.

Hayden, William. "In Days of Long Ago." *Port Byron Chronicle*, 5 March 1904.

———. *Syracuse (New York) Sunday Herald*, 21 February 1904.

Heinerman, Joseph. "Amelia's Palace." *Montanta: The Magazine of Western History* 29 (1979).

Henderson, Mary. *History of Utah, Historic Sites, and Landmarks* Vol. 1. Bound typscript copy. LDS Church Historical Department, Salt Lake City, Utah.

Heward, Elizabeth Terry. "Autobiography." In *Parshall Terry Family History*. Salt Lake City: Mr. and Mrs. Terry Lund, 1956.

Hilton, Lynn M. *The History of LDS Business College and Its Parent Institutions, 1886–1993.* Salt Lake City: LDS Business College, 1993.

Hirshson, Stanley P. *The Lion of the Lord.* New York: Alfred A. Knopf, 1969.

Historian's Office. Journal. LDS Church Archives, Salt Lake City, Utah.

"Historic Beehive House as Home for Girls." *Deseret Evening News*, 10 June 1920.

"Historic Lion House Becomes Center for Social Activities of Y.L.M.I.A.." *Deseret News*, 3 December 1932.

"Historic Old Mansion." *Salt Lake Tribune*, 1 February 1897.

"Historic Residence to Be Restored." *Church News*, 8 August 1959.

"History of Brigham Young." *Deseret News*, 10 February 1858.

History of Tioga, Cheming, Tomkins, and Schuyler Counties. Philadelphia: n.p., 1879.

History of Tooele County. Tooele, Utah: Daughters of the Utah Pioneers, 1961.

Hodson, Paul W. *Never Forsake: The Story of Amanda Barnes Smith, Legacy of the Haun's Mill Massacre.* Salt Lake City: Keeban Publications, 1996.

Hoglund, Karl T., and Philip Notarianni. *The Avenues of Salt Lake City.* Salt Lake City: Utah State Historical Society, 1980.

"How One Wife Outwitted Brigham." *The Utah Magazine*, June 1947.

"Index to Nauvoo Endowments." LDS Family History Library, Salt Lake City, Utah.

Jacobsen, Florence S. "Restorations Belong to Everyone." *BYU Studies* 8, no. 3 (spring 1978).

Jenson, Andrew. *Encyclopedic History of the Church of Jesus Christ of Latter-day Saints.* Salt Lake City: Deseret News Publishing Company, 1941.

Jessee, Dean C. "Brigham Young's Family: The Wilderness Years." *BYU Studies* 19 (summer 1979).

———. *Letters of Brigham Young.* Salt Lake City: Deseret Book in Collaboration With the LDS Church Historical Department, 1974.

———. "'A Man of God and a Good Kind Father:' Brigham Young At Home." *BYU Studies* 40, no. 2 (summer 2001).

"John Beck's Plight." *Salt Lake Tribune*, 24 July 1898.

Johnson, Jeffrey O. "Determining and Defining 'Wife': The Brigham Young Households." *Dialogue: A Journal of Mormon Thought* 20 (fall 1987).

Johnson, Lisa. "Artist in Residence." *Deseret News*, 4 July 1999.

Johnson, Mary, ed. *Pioneer Women of Faith and Fortitude.* Salt Lake City: Daughters of Utah Pioneers, 1998.

Journal History of the Church of Jesus Christ of Latter-day Saints. Liverpool and London: LDS Booksellers, 1855–1886. Microfilm. LDS Church Historical Department, Salt Lake City, Utah.

Kane, Elizabeth W. *Twelve Mormon Homes Visited in Succession on a Journey through Utah and Arizona.* Philadelphia: William Wood, 1874.

Kenney, Scott G., ed. *Wilford Woodruff's Journal.* 9 Vol. Midvale, Utah: Signature Books, 1983–1985.

Keyes, Loyd B. *Keyes Family History.* Salt Lake City: privately published, n.d. Copies available through the LDS Family History Library, Salt Lake City, Utah.

Kimball, Heber C. "History." Manuscript. Heber C. Kimball Papers, LDS Church Historical Department, Salt Lake City, Utah.

———. Journal. LDS Church Historical Department, Salt Lake City, Utah.

King, Hannah Tapfield. "Autobiography." LDS Church Archives, Salt Lake City, Utah, circa 1864–1872.

Kirtpatrick, Doris. "Where Was Brigham Young Born Anyway?" *Brattleboro (Vermont) Reformer*, 1 July 1983.

Knight, Hal, and Dr. Stanley B. Kimball. *111 Days to Zion.* Salt Lake City: Deseret News, 1978.

Knowles, Eleanor. "The Lion House Social Center Reopens." *Improvement Era* (October 1968).

Lamar, Howard R., ed. *The Reader's Encyclopedia of the American West.* New York: Crowell, 1977.

Langley, Harold D., ed. *To Utah With the Dragoons and Glimpses of Life in Arizona and California 1858–1859.* Salt Lake City: University of Utah Press, 1974.

Lender, Mark Edward. *The Dictionary of American Temperance.* Westport, Connecticut: Greenwood Press, 1984.

Lester, Margaret D. *Brigham Street.* Salt Lake City: Utah State Historical Society, 1979.

Lightener, Mary Elizabeth Rollins. Autobiography and Diary. Special Collections, Harold B. Lee Library, Brigham Young University, Provo, Utah.

Little, James A. "Historical Items on the Life of Brigham Young." James A. Little Collection. LDS Church Archives, Salt Lake City, Utah.

———. "Biography of Lorenzo Dow Young." *Utah Historical Quarterly* 14 (1946).

Ludlow, Daniel H. *Encyclopedia of Mormonism.* New York: Macmillan Publishing Company, 1992.

Lund, Jennifer L. "'Pleasing to the Eyes of an Exile': The Latter-day Saint Sojourn at Winter Quarters, 1846–1848." *BYU Studies* 39, no. 2 (spring 2000).

Lund, Nora. "History of Jane Terry Young." Unpublished, n.d.

Lyman, Edward Leo. "Isaac Trumbo and the Politics of Utah Statehood." *Utah Historical Quarterly* 41 (1973).

Lythgoe, Dennis. "Preserve the Historic Role of Pioneer Park." *Deseret News*, 30 July 1992, web edition.

Madsen, Olive Virginia Grey. "Diana Chase Shaw." Typescript. LDS Church Historical Department, Salt Lake City, Utah, n.d.

"Mary Elizabeth Rollins Lightner." *The Utah Genealogical and Historical Magazine*, 17 July 1926.

Matthews, Sylvester J. *The Antiquarian*, 18 January 1902.

May, Dean L. *Utah: A People's History.* Salt Lake City: University of Utah Press, 1987.

———, and Feramorz Fox. *Building the City of God: Community and Cooperation Among the Mormons.* Salt Lake City: Deseret Book, 1976.

McCandless, Marjorie, and Utahna Frantz. "History of Jemima Angell Young." Typescript. LDS Church Historical Department, Salt Lake City, Utah, n.d.

McCormick, John S. *Salt Lake City, The Gathering Place.* Woodland Hills, California: Windsor Publications, for the Utah State Historical Society, 1980.

McCune, George M. "Alfred William McCune." Privately published, 1972.

Merrill, Harrison R. "Welcome, Come In." *Improvement Era* (May 1933).

Milliken, Charles F. *The Beginnings of Mormonism.* Rochester, New York: Rochester Historical Society, 1926.

Moorman, Donald R., and Gene A. Sessions. *Camp Floyd and the Mormons: The Utah War.* Salt Lake City: University of Utah Press, 1992.

Morse, George H. "Morse Farm Settled in 1813 . . . Recollections of Local Folks."

The Willoughby Republican (29 June 1921). Cleveland Necrology File, Cleveland Public Library.

Mortensen, Arlington Russel. *Early Utah Sketches*. Salt Lake City: University of Utah Press, 1969.

———. "The White House: It Was Brigham Young's "Real" Home." Unpublished article. Utah State Historical Society, Salt Lake City.

———. "The White House: It Was Brigham Young's 'Real' Home." *Salt Lake Tribune*, 19 May 1957.

Moss, Nina Folsom. *A History of William Harrison Folsom*. Privately published, 1973.

Moyle, James Henry. *Mormon Democrat: The Religious and Political Memoirs* Edited by Gene Sessions. LDS Church Historical Department, Salt Lake City, Utah.

"Mr. Megaphone Tells Tourists Many New Things about Salt Lake." *Salt Lake Herald Republican*, 23 April 1911.

"Mrs. Cobb's First House South of Social Hall." *Salt Lake Daily Herald*, 14 June 1874.

"Mrs. Holmes to Tear Down School Built for Brigham Young's Children." Unidentified newspaper clipping. Susanne Emery-Holmes scrapbook, Utah State Historical Society, Salt Lake City, 3 August 1902.

Murphy, Miriam. "From Impulsive Girl to Patient Wife: Lucy Bigelow Young." *Utah Historical Quarterly* 45, no. 3 (summer 1977).

Nauvoo Property Transactions, 1843, 1846. LDS Family History Library, Salt Lake City, Utah.

"Nauvoo Proxy Sealings, 1846." LDS Church Historical Department, Salt Lake City, Utah.

"Nauvoo Sealings and Adoptions." LDS Family History Library, Salt Lake City, Utah.

Nauvoo Temple Endowment House Register. LDS Family History Library, Salt Lake City, Utah.

Newell, Linda King, and Valeen Tippetts Avery. *Mormon Emigma: Emma Hale Smith*. Garden City, New York: Doubleday, 1984.

"New Use for Bee-hive House." *Deseret Evening News*, 24 June 1899.

Noyce, Monitor C. "Lion House to Undergo Renovation." *Church News*, 9 April 1966.

———. "Will Remodel Lion House." *Deseret News*, 1 April 1966.

"Old Houses Tell Romantic Story." *Salt Lake Tribune*, 4 February 1934.

"Old Rag Carpet of Pioneer Days." *Deseret Evening News*, 22 December 1906.

"One of the Pioneers." *Young Woman's Journal* 15 (1 Apr 1904).

"Organization of Daughters of Pioneers." *Deseret Evening News*, 24 January 1907.

Page, Alfene. *Woman's Exponent: Cradle of Literary Culture Among Early Mormon Women*. Master's thesis, Utah State University, 1988.

Page, Harriet. "A Friendly Visit to a Friendly Place." *Deseret News*, 15 September 1934.

Palmer, Richard F., and Karl D. Butler. *Brigham Young: The New York Years*. Provo, Utah: Charles Redd Center for Western Studies, Brigham Young University, 1982.

Parish, Isabelle H. *It Happened in Lansing*. Ithaca, New York: DeWitt Historical Society of Tompkins County, 1964.

"Passed into the Repose of Death." *Deseret Evening News*, 28 August 1901.

Philip Blair Collection. Marriott Library, University of Utah Library, Salt Lake City.

Photo collection. Utah State Historical Society, Salt Lake City, Utah.

Piercy, Frederick. *Route from Liverpool to Great Salt Lake Valley*. Ed. James Linforth. Liverpool: Franklin D. Richards; London: Latter-day Saints Book Depot, 1855.

"A Pioneer Speaks." *Improvement Era* 42 (July 1940).

"Pioneer Home of Pres. Young Given to Village." *Deseret News*, 30 December 1952.

Pioneers. Sons of Utah Pioneers Magazine, December 1956.

"Plural Marriage Affidavits." Book 1, LDS Church Historical Department, Salt Lake City, Utah.

Poll, Richard. "The Move South." In *Life in Utah*. Provo, Utah: BYU Studies, 1996.

———, Thomas G. Alexander, Eugene E. Campbell, and David E. Miller. *Utah's History*. Provo, Utah: Brigham Young University Press, 1989.

Pomery, Irene Hascall. "Letters of Irene B. Hascall Pomeroy to Her Parents and Relatives in North New Salem, Massachusetts, Covering the Period May 1845–August 1854." Typescript. Utah State Historical Society, Salt Lake City, Utah.

Pratt, Mary Ann Frost. "Biographical Sketch of Olive Gray Frost." *Historical Record* 6 (January 1887).

"President Snow in Historic Beehive." *Deseret Evening News*, 23 September 1899.

Price, Raye Carlson. *Diggings and Doings in Park City*. Salt Lake City: University of Utah Press, 1981.

Pyper, George D. "Silk Culture in Utah." *The Contributor*, January 1881.

Record of Members, Eighteenth Ward, Salt Lake Stake, Salt Lake City, Utah. LDS Family History Library.

Reese, Retta Blanche Davis. *Golden Jubilee, 1896–1946. Fifty Years of Progress of Forest Dale Ward, Granite Stake*. Privately published, n.d.

Reynolds, George. Letter to Brigham Young, 20 May 1876, 6 June 1879. LDS Church Archives, Salt Lake City, Utah.

Roberts, Allen D. "The Chase Mill." Salt Lake City: Daughters of the Utah Pioneers, lesson for December, 1983.

Roberts, B. H. *A Comprehensive History of the Church of Jesus Christ of Latter-day Saints* 6 Vol. Provo, Utah: Brigham Young University Press, 1977; Orem, Utah: Sonos Publishing Inc., 1991.

———. *The Life of John Taylor: Third President of the Church of Jesus Christ of Latter-day Saints*. Salt Lake City: George Q. Cannon & Sons Co., 1892.

Robison, Elwin C. *The First Mormon Temple*. Provo, Utah: Brigham Young University Press, 1997.

Rogers, Kristen Smart. "Redwood Road: How Did It Get Its Name?" *Currents: News of the Utah State Historical Society*, February 2000.

"Sale of the Bee Hive." *Deseret News*, 20 December 1898.

Salt Lake City Cemetery Records.

Salt Lake City Death Records, 1848–1884. LDS Church Historical Department, Salt Lake City, Utah.

Salt Lake City Directory for the Year Commencing August 1, 1885. San Francisco: U. S. Directory Publishing Company of California.

Salt Lake Endowment House Records. LDS Church Historical Department, Salt Lake City, Utah.

Sanborn, Mabel Young. *Brigham Young's Wives, Children, and Grandchildren*. Salt Lake City: Gaylen S. Young, 1940.

"Sarah M. Pratt Cast." *Salt Lake Daily Herald*, 2 December 1875.

"Silk Culture in Utah." In *Heartthrobs of the West*. Edited by Kate B. Carter. Vol. 11. Salt Lake City: Daughters of Utah Pioneers, 1950.

Sillitoe, Linda. *A History of Salt Lake County*. Salt Lake City: Utah State Historical Society and Salt Lake County Commission, 1996.

Smith, George A. Letter to "Bro. Joseph." Typescript. LDS Church Historical Department, Salt Lake City, Utah.

Smith, George D., ed. *An Intimate Chronicle: The Journals of William Clayton*. Salt Lake City: Signature Books, 1995.

Smith, Joseph F. Plural Marriage Affidavit Books. 2 vol. Holograph. LDS Church Historical Department, Salt Lake City, Utah.

Smith, Joseph Fielding. *The Life of Joseph F. Smith: Sixth President of the Church of Jesus Christ of Latter-day Saints*. Salt Lake City: Deseret News Press, 1938.

Soda Springs, Idaho, website. <www.ohwy.com/id/s/sodaspri.htm> [accessed 2001].

Spencer, Clarissa Young, and Mabel Harmer. *Brigham Young at Home*. Salt Lake City: Deseret Book, 1940. Reprinted several times.

————. *One Who Was Valiant*. Salt Lake City: Deseret Book, 1974.

Stories from Your Museum. Daughters of Utah Pioneers files, Salt Lake City, Utah, undated.

Stout, Wayne D. "William Henry Harrison Sagers." In *History of Tooele County* Tooele County Daughters of Utah Pioneers, 1961.

Stuy, Brian H., ed. *Collected Discourses (1886–1889)*. Vol. 1. Burbank, California: B. H. S. Publishing, 1987.

Tanner, J. M. *History of James Jensen*. Privately published, n.d., copy available through the LDS Family History Library, Salt Lake City, Utah.

Taves, Ernest H. *This Is the Place: Brigham Young and the New Zion*. Buffalo, New York: Prometheus Books, 1991.

Thatcher, Mary M. Funeral notice. *Deseret Evening News*, 17 July 1877.

Thompson, George A., and Fraser Buck. *Treasure Mountain Home: Park City Revisited*. Salt Lake City: Dream Garden Press, 1981.

"Tourists Visit Restored Beehive House." *Church News*, 12 August 1961.

Traughber, Eugene. "The Prophet's Courtship: President Brigham Young's Favorite Wife, Amelia, Talks." *Salt Lake Tribune*, 11 March 1894. Typescript. Utah State Historical Society, Salt Lake City, MS A 578.

Truman, Margaret. *Harry S. Truman*. New York: William Morrow, 1973.

Tullidge, Edward W. *History of Salt Lake City*. Salt Lake City: Utah Printing Company, 1886.

————. *Women of Mormondom*. New York: Tullidge and Crandall, 1877.

Tuttle, Daniel Sylvester. *Missionary to the Mountain West*. Salt Lake City: University of Utah Press, 1987.

Urbani, Diane. "Pioneer Park: To Develop or Not?" *Deseret News*, 18 December 2000.

"The Utah War, Journal of Captain Albert Tracy, 1858–60." *Utah Historical Quarterly* 13, no. 1 (winter 1945).

Van Orden, Bruce A. *The Life of George Reynolds: Prisoner for Conscience' Sake*. Salt Lake City: Deseret Book, 1992.

Verdoia, Ken, and Richard Firmage. *Utah: The Struggle for Statehood*. Salt Lake City: University of Utah Press, 1996.

Wait, Mary Van Sickle. *Brigham Young in Cayuga County: 1813–1829*. Ithaca, New York: DeWitt Historical Society of Tompkins County, 1964.

Walker, Ronald Warren. *Wayward Saints: The Godbeites and Brigham Young*. Urbana and Chicago: University of Illinois Press, 1998.

Wallace, Irving. *The Twenty-Seventh Wife*. New York: Simon & Schuster, 1961.

Walsh, Rebecca. "Off the Mark." *Salt Lake Tribune*, 20 February 2001.

Warsh, Cheryl Krasnick. "Adventures in Maritime Quackery: The Leslie E. Keeley Gold Cure Institute of Fredericton, N. B." *Acadiensis* 17, no. 2 (1988).

Webb, Rev. J. Willard. "A Memorial Sermon—the Life and Character of George Hickox." Undated newspaper clipping. LDS Church Historical Department, Salt Lake City, Utah.

Welling, Phoebe McLaughlin. "History of Isaac Chase." Typescript. LDS Church Historical Department, Salt Lake City, Utah .

Wells, Emmeline. "Biography of Mary Ann Angell Young." *The Juvenile Instructor* 26 (1 January 1891).

————. "Lucy Bigelow Young." *Young Woman's Journal* 3 (January 1892).

————. "In Memoriam." *Woman's Exponent*, 15 July 1882, obituary.

————. "Our Picture Gallery—Lucy Bigelow Young." *Young Woman's Journal* 3, no. 4 (January 1892).

————. "Zina D. H. Young: A Brief Sketch of Her Life and Labors." *Deseret Evening News*, 25 Jan. 1896.

Werner, M. R. *Brigham Young*. New York: Harcourt, Brace and Company, 1925.

"What's Great About Salt Lake." *Salt Lake Tribune*, 5 July 1998.

White, James T. *The Dictionary of American Biography*. New York: Scribner's, 1936.

Whitney, Orson F. *History of Utah*, 4 vols. Salt Lake City: George Q. Cannon & Sons, 1904.

————. *Popular History of Utah*. Salt Lake City: Deseret News, 1916.

Whittaker, John M. Journal. Special Collections, Harold B. Lee Library, Brigham Young University, Provo, Utah.

"Widow of President Brigham Young Who Died Last Night . . ." *Deseret Evening News*, 17 Jan. 1907.

Williams, Elsie M. "Biography of Joshua Sawyer Holman." Typescript. LDS Church Historical Department, Salt Lake City, Utah, n.d.

Wolfinger, Henry. "Jane Manning James: A Test of Faith." In *Worth Their Salt: Notable but Often Unnoted Women of Utah*. Logan, Utah: Utah State University Press, 1996.

Woodruff, Wilford. Journal. LDS Church Archives, Salt Lake City, Utah.

Woolley, Leah D. *Early History of Forest Dale*. Privately published, 1981.

"Work of Tearing Down Old Brigham Young School House Has Commenced." *Salt Lake Herald*, 3 August 1902.

Young, Amelia Folsom. Obituary. *Deseret Evening News*, 12 December 1910.

————. Obituary. *Improvement Era* 14 (1910).

Young, Ann Eliza Webb. *Wife Number 19; or, The Story of a Life in Bondage, Being a Complete Exposé of Mormonism and Revealing the Sorrow, Sacrifices and Sufferings of a Woman in Polygamy*. Hartford, Connecticut: Dustin Gilman & Co., 1876.

Young, Augusta Adams. Obituary. *Deseret Evening News*, 3 February 1886.

Young, Brigham. File. Lands and Record Office, Nauvoo, Illinois.

————. Journal. LDS Church Historical Department, Salt Lake City, Utah.

————, et al. *Journal of Discourses*. 26 vols. Liverpool: LDS Booksellers Depot, 1854–1886.

————. Letter to David B. Smith. 1 June 1853. LDS Church Archives, Salt Lake City, Utah.

————. Letter to Mary Ann Angell Young. 17 August 1843. Manuscript. Yale University Library, Yale University, New Haven, Connecticut.

————. *Manuscript History of Brigham Young, 1801–1844*. Edited by Elden Jay Watson. Salt Lake City: Smith Secretarial Service, 1968. Copy of original on microfilm, LDS Church Historical Department, Salt Lake City, Utah.

————. Papers. LDS Church Historical Department, Salt Lake City, Utah.

————. "Speech, 6 April 1845". *Times and Seasons* 6 (1 July 1845).

————. Will. Pamphlet 3857. Utah State Historical Society, Salt Lake City.

Young, Clarissa Decker. Obituary. *Deseret Evening News*, 7 January 1889.

————. "A Woman's Experience with Pioneer Band." *Utah Historical Quarterly* 14 (1946).

————. "A Young Women's Experience with the Pioneer Band." Bancroft Library, University of California, Berkeley, 1884.

Young, Eleanor. "Old Houses Tell Romantic Story of Salt Lake." *Salt Lake Tribune*, 4 February 1934.

Young, Eliza Nelson. Obituary, *Deseret Evening News*, 29 December 1885.

Young, Eliza Roxey Snow. Diary. LDS Church Historical Department, Salt Lake City, Utah.

————. Obituary. *Deseret News*, 7 December 1887.

Young, Emily Dow Partridge. "What I Remember." Typescript. LDS Church Historical Department, Salt Lake City, Utah, 1884.

————. Obituary. *Deseret Evening News*, 9 December 1988.

Young, Emmeline Free. Obituary, *Deseret Evening News*, 19 July 1875.

Young, Franklin Wheeler. Journal. LDS Church Historical Department, Salt Lake City, Utah.

————. "Young Family Genealogy." LDS Church Historical Department, Salt Lake City, Utah.

Young, George Cannon. Interview. Typescript. LDS Church Historical Department, Salt Lake City, Utah, n.d.

Young, Hannah Tapfield. "Autobiography." LDS Church Historical Department, Salt Lake City, Utah, circa 1864–1872.

———. Obituary. *Deseret Evening News*, 27 September 18863.

Young, Harriet Barney. Obituary *Deseret Evening News*, 11 February 1911.

Young, Harriet Cook. Obituary. Journal History of the Church of Jesus Christ of Latter-day Saints. Liverpool and London: LDS Booksellers, 1855–1886. Microfilm. Historical Department, Salt Lake City, Utah, 5 November 1898.

Young, Joseph, Sr. Journal. Archives of the Church of Jesus Christ of Latter-day Saints, Salt Lake City, Utah.

Young, Julia Foster. Obituary. *Deseret Evening News*, 17 January 1891.

Young, Levi Edgar. "Historic Buildings of Salt Lake City." *Young Woman's Journal* 6 (1922).

Young, Lydia Farnsworth. Obituary. *Deseret Evening News*, 6 February 1897.

Young, Lucy Bigelow. Obituary. *Deseret Evening News*, 4 February 1905.

———. Obituary. *Improvement Era* 8.

Young, Margarette P. W. "Autobiography of Margarette P. W. Young." Holograph. LDS Church Historical Department, Salt Lake City, Utah, n.d.

Young, Martha Bowker. Obituary. *Deseret Evening News*, 26 September 1890.

Young, Mary Ann Angel. Letter to Brigham Young, 17 August 1843. Manuscript. LDS Church Archives, Salt Lake City, Utah.

———. Obituary. *Deseret Evening News*, 28 June 1882.

Young, Mary Eliza Nelson. Obituary. *Deseret Evening News*, 29 December 1885.

Young, Mary Elizabeth Rollins Lightener. Autobiography and Diary. Special Collections, Harold B. Lee Library, Brigham Young University, Provo, Utah, n.d.

———. Obituary. *Woman's Exponent* 41 (January 1914).

Young, Naamah Carter. Obituary. *Deseret Evening News*, 6 August 1909.

Young, Rhoda Richards. Obituary, *Deseret Evening News*, 18 January 1879.

Young, S. Dilworth. *Young Brigham Young*. Salt Lake City: Bookcraft Publishers, 1962.

Young, Susannah Snively. Obituary. *Deseret Evening News*, 21 November 1882.

"Zina D. H. Young: A Brief Sketch of Her Life and Labors." *Deseret Evening News*, 25 January 1896.

Zobell, Albert L., Jr. *Sentinel in the East*. Salt Lake City: Nicholas G. Morgan, Sr., 1965.

About the Authors

SANDRA DAWN BRIMHALL, a Salt Lake native, holds a degree in mass communication from the University of Utah. She has published widely including articles in the *Salt Lake Tribune, Deseret News, Utah Historical Quarterly,* and LDS Church publications *Ensign* and *The New Era.* Interested in history and genealogy, she is currently editing her great-grandfather's journals, which give the viewpoint of a local leader in the LDS Church in Payson, Utah, for thirty years.

MARIANNE HARDING BURGOYNE was born in Hayden, Colorado, and educated in public schools until her junior year when she became a boarding student at Rowland Hall-St. Marks in Salt Lake City. She received her bachelor's degree from Brigham Young University and has completed her masters as well as her Ph.D. course work in English at the University of Utah. Widely published, she has written poetry, magazine articles, a novel, and, with her husband, professional articles in medicine and psychiatry. She is also a popular public speaker, currently conducting in-house symposiums for the Utah Opera Guild. Her forthcoming book, *Into the Okavango: The Africa Poems and Pictures,* will be published in December 2002.

MARK D. CURTIS is an architect licensed in Utah and California, currently residing in Sacramento, California. He has made extensive studies of many historic homes, often drawing architectural or floor plans based on his research.

W. RANDALL DIXON, a native of Jerome, Idaho, attended Ricks College and Brigham Young University. He holds a bachelor's degree in history and a master's in public administration. He is currently an archivist at the LDS Church Historical Department and has a particular interest in Salt Lake City, its early history, and its architecture. He has published articles in *Utah Historical Quarterly* and *Pioneer Magazine.*

JUDY DYKMAN has recently retired after teaching Utah history for thirty years at Churchill Junior High School. Her teaching excellence was consistently recognized by students and their parents and occasionally by others. She was named the school's outstanding teacher in 1995. She holds a bachelor's degree in history from Weber State University and a master's in history education from Brigham Young University. She is the author of *The Silver Queen,* a biography of Susanna Bransford, Park City silver heiress, and she provided the inspiration for and contributed chapters to both volumes of *Worth Their Salt: Notable but Often Unnoted Women of Utah.* A popular public speaker, she frequently works with the Utah Humanities Council Speakers' Bureau.

ELINOR HYDE is a native of Clarkston, Utah, and has studied at Brigham Young University. She is a member of the Utah State Poetry Society, the League of Utah Writers, and the National League of American Pen Women, having served as an officer and been honored with awards by the latter two. She has published articles in the *Salt Lake Tribune, Deseret News,* and several other papers. She has also written for LDS Church magazines, contributed to *Mormon Women Speak*, published poetry, several family and local histories, and a novel, *Canadian Windsong* (1987).

JEFFERY OGDEN JOHNSON was born and raised in Aurora, Utah. He received a bachelor's degree from Brigham Young University, then went to work for fifteen years for the LDS Church Archives. During that time, he completed the course work for a master's degree and took a year of leave to organize the Archives for the Cherokee Nation. He has been with the Utah State Archives for fourteen years, the last ten as director. He has published articles in *Sunstone* and *Dialogue: A Journal of Mormon Thought*, serving on the executive committee for the latter. His research into original marriage and LDS sealing records determined the definitive list of Brigham Young's wives.

KARI K. ROBINSON is a native of Salt Lake City and attended Brigham Young University, named for her third great-grandfather. A descendent of Lucy Bigelow, she is past president and currently historian for the Brigham Young Family Organization. She has written and published numerous family histories and, having served an LDS mission to Norway, she wrote a history of one of that nation's most noted immigrants, John A. Widtsoe, for St. Olaf College, Northfield, Minnesota.

COLLEEN WHITLEY, born and raised in Ogden, Utah, holds degrees from Weber (then College), the University of Utah, and Brigham Young University. She has taught in every grade level from elementary school through graduate students, Job Corps, and helped to open one of the first alternative high schools in the state. Currently she teaches for the English and Honors Departments of Brigham Young University and lectures for the Utah Humanities Council Speakers' Bureau. Widely published, she has written poetry, fiction, newspaper, journal, and magazine articles, edited two volumes of *Worth Their Salt: Notable but Often Unnoted Women of Utah*, and co-wrote *The Silver Queen*.

Index

All of Brigham Young's family, wives and children, are listed under "Young."

Adams, Abigail 114
Adams, Emily 121
Adams, Emma 121
Adams, John 114
Adams, John Quincy 114
Adams, Samuel 114
Adams, Samuel Hopkins 27
Aldrich, Joseph 222
Allen, George Washington 34–35
Allen, James B. 74
Alta Club 191
Amelia's Palace 173, 191, 193, 197
Angell, Abigail 222
Angell, Caroline Francis 222
Angell, Hiram 222
Angell, James 222
Angell, James William 222
Angell, Phebe Ann 222
Angell, Solomon 41, 222
Angell, Truman Osborn 97, 124, 128, 222
Angell, Washington M 222
Arrington, Leonard J. 13, 16, 37, 61, 229
Atlas, Illinois 50, 216
Auburn, New York 23–28, 31, 215
Aurelius, New York 24, 29
Avon, New York 41
Axton, Maria 30

Babbit, Almon W. 68, 229
Badlam, Alexander 186
Bair, John 79, 223
Barnum, J. P. 22
Barnum, P. T. 213
Barrymore, Drew 213
Barrymore, Ethel 213
Barrymore, John 213
Barrymore, Lionel 213
Beck, John 126
Beehive House 1, 96, 100, 124–29, 131, 132,
    150, 173, 174, 180, 194, 209, 212, 217
Bell, Philander 79, 223
Bell, William 100
Belvedere Apartments 113

Beneficial Life Insurance Company 118
Bernhardt, Sarah 213
Big Field 84, 88, 108, 147
Bigelow, Henry 182
Bigelow, Mary Gibbs 78
Bigelow, Nahum 78
Birch, Joseph 206
Bloomfield, New York 33
Boggs, Lilburn W. 50
Boise, Idaho 85
Bonney, A. 45
Booth, Edwin 41, 213
Booth, Lorenzo 41
Boston, Massachusetts 5, 16, 45, 64, 113, 114,
    195
Boston Symphony Orchestra 195
Brannan, Samuel 74
Bransford Apartments 103
Bransford, Susanna 103, 104, 191
Brigham Young Academy 103, 209, 213
Brigham Young Historic Park 103
Brigham Young Motor Lodge 211
Brigham Young University 103, 209, 213
British Columbia 190
Broadway Center 119
Brown, Hannah 24, 33
Brown, John 173
Brown, William 27
Bubb, John W. 196
Buchanan, James 97, 202
Bullock, Thomas 88
Burgess, Malancter 207
Burgoyne, Marianne Harding 122
Burke, Billie 213
Burton, Charles Samuel 169
Burton, Harold 213
Buttle, William 151

Caine, John T. 183, 186
Calcutta, India 190
Camp Floyd 98
Canandaigua, New York 14, 33, 35, 36
Cannon, Abram H. 182

Cannon, Angus M. 176, 177
Cannon, Frank J. 189, 190
Cannon, George M. 170, 171
Cannon, George Q. 175, 182, 183, 188–90
Cannon, George Y. 128
Canyon Creek Ward 148
Capitol Hill 85, 174
Capitol Theatre 213
Carnegie Hall 195
Carrington, Albert 14, 125
Carson Valley 186
Carter, Alfa Jean 61
Carter, Dominicus 223
Cayuga, New York 13, 14, 20, 23, 24, 26,
    30
Cedar City, Utah 69
Cedar Valley 98
Centerville, Utah 112
Chamberlain, Nancy 228
Chase, Isaac 6, 108, 109, 112
Chase, Madge Ferry 46
Chase Mill 108, 112, 123, 149, 217
Chastain, Junius Franklin 220
Chastain, William Lowery 220
Chastain, William Matthew 220
Chenango, New York 14, 17, 18
Chesney 208
Chicago, Illinois 61, 121, 173, 176, 184, 185,
    193
Chicago Tribune 185
Chicago World's Fair 121
Chief Walker 202
Chillicothe, Ohio 45–46
Church, Al 1
Churchill, Eliza 120
Church Office Building 92, 107, 108, 130
City Creek Canyon 101
Civil War 98, 106, 184, 192
Clark, Hyram 57
Clawson, Harriet Cornelia 223
Clawson, Helen Cordelia 223
Clawson, Hiram B. 100, 186, 187, 223
Clawson, John Reese 223

Clawson, Louisa P. 223
Clawson, Spencer 101, 125
Clawson, Susannah 223
Clawson, Zepheniah 223
Cleveland 40, 185
Cobb, Albert 219
Cobb, Brigham 113, 219
Cobb, Charlotte Ives 219, 228–29
Cobb, Ellen 219
Cobb, Henry 219
Cobb, James Thornton 219, 224
Cobb, Luella 224
Cobb, Mary Elizabeth 219
Codman, John 211
Cody, "Buffalo Bill" 213
Cold Brook, New York 17–20, 215
Cole, Thomas 222
Colebrook 94
Connor, Patrick 202, 210
Cook, John 229
Cook, John James 222
Cook, Mina A. 229
Cook, Sarah Ann 222
Corradini, Deedee 90
Council Bluffs, Iowa 68, 77
Crabtree, Charlie 163
Crismon, Charles 94
Crossroads Mall 117
Cumming, Alfred 97, 98

Daughters of Utah Pioneers 69, 101, 112, 118,
    213
Dean, Julia 163
Dee, James Edward 224
Dee, James L. 120
Dee, James Leach 224
Dee, Leonard Lorenzo 224
Delaware County, Pennsylvania 112
Decker, Charles 92
Decker, Harriet Page 61, 113
Decker, Isaac 5, 60, 62, 112
Decker, Vilate Young 35–37, 41, 44, 55, 92, 219
Deming, Moses R. 121, 224
Democratic Party 183
Denmark 162
Deseret Agricultural and Manufacturing
    Society 149
Deseret Bank 200
Deseret Book 114
Deseret Mandolin Orchestra 194
Deseret Mint 104, 106
Deseret News 91, 93, 104, 106, 123, 177, 178,
    180, 189, 200, 205
Deseret Silk Association 93, 154
Detroit, Michigan 195
Dilworth, Mary Jane 86
Drake, Orrin 20
Drury Lane Theatre 212
Dublin, Indiana 49, 216
Dunford, Morley 206
Dunklin, Daniel 41
Dunning, David M. 24, 27
Dunyan 154
Durfee, Edmund 66
Dwight, Illinois 184
Dyer, Frank H. 180–81, 183

Eagle Gate 100, 103, 104, 176
Eagle Gate Apartments 104
Edmunds Act 179
Edmunds-Tucker Act 181, 187, 191
Egbert, Heber C. 121
Eighteenth Ward 103, 169
El Roble 196
Elite 193
Elks Lodge 100
Emery, Albion 191, 192
Emigration Canyon 98, 171
Empey Cottage 121, 122, 218
Empey, Nelson P. 119, 121, 122
England 8, 11, 39, 51–57, 58–60, 68, 123, 185,
    207, 209
Erie Canal 28, 31
Estee, Morrill 182
Eureka, Utah 187
Evans, Oliver 109
Experimental Farm 149, 171, 217
Extermination Order 50

Fairbanks, Grant 101
Fairbanks, Justin 101
Fairmont Park 171
Family Cemetery 101
Family School 93, 95, 103
Fargo, Vaughn 17
Far West, Missouri 23, 49–51, 68, 77, 216
Federal Reserve Bank 200, 201
Ferguson 121, 125
Ferguson, James 121, 229
Ferris, Benjamin 228
First Encampment Park 84
First Presidency 52, 53, 106, 115, 166, 179,
    182, 183, 186, 189
Fisher, J. Sheldon 36
Fishers, New York 36
Florence, Nebraska 75
Folger, Sidney 117
Folsom, William Harrison 173, 175
Ford, Thomas 66
Forest Farm 97, 112, 122, 123, 147–151, 154,
    155, 157, 160, 162–164, 168, 170–72, 212,
    217
Forest Hills Golf Course 109
Fort Douglas 194, 202
Fowler, John 33
France 108, 150, 151, 154
Free, Absolom 115
Free, Betsy Strait 115
Free Will Baptists 41

Gardo 115, 117, 122, 173–89, 191–97, 200,
    201, 208, 212, 218
Gates Auto Sales 207
Genoa, New York 13, 14, 20, 23, 215
Gibbons, Ryan 85
Gibson, Talula 229
Gibson, Walter Murray 229
Glade, Earl J. 88
Godbe, William S. 228–29
Gould, Humphrey 14
Grandma's Tires 122
Grant, George 116
Grant, Heber J. 126, 179, 200

Grant, Jedediah 112
Gratix, Margarutte 229
Great Basin 69, 81, 82, 104, 202
Greek Orthodox Church 88
Greeley, Horace 5, 125
Greene, John P. 23, 33, 41
Greene, John Portineus 222
Greene, Mary Emma 222
Gribble, John 223
Groton, New York 20
Groves, John 223
Guild, Blanche Ferry 46

Half Acre, New York 24, 29, 215
Hall, Calvin 222
Hall, William 230
Hammer, Jabez 23
Hampton, Brigham Young 222
Hampton, Edalay Foster 222
Hampton, Jonathan 222
Hampton, Julia Anna 222
Hampton, Nephi 222
Hampton, Sarah Cerena 222
Hancock, Mosiah 65
Harris, Fisher 196
Hart, William 151
Haskins, Thomas W. 123
Hastings, Lansford 73
Haun's Mill 50
Havens, Eileen 33
Hawaiian Islands (see also Sandwich
    Islands) 207, 229
Hawthornthwaite, Samuel 229
Hayden, William 28–30
Haydenville, New York 28–30, 215
Hayselden, Fred H. 229
Heath, Perry S. 194
Heward, Elizabeth Terry 77
Hickox, George 36
Hirshorn, Stanley P. 229
Hodgkins 221
Hogle Zoo 112
Holmes, Edwin 103, 191, 192
Horace Roberts 79
Hotel Utah 104, 106
Huddart, Peter T. 194
Hughey, Dan 23
Hunt, Daniel Durham 79, 223
Hunziker, Andrea 46
Hunziker, James 46
Hussey, Warren 123
Hyde, Orson 59

Independence Hall 213
Iowa Territory 69
Ireland 184
Iron Mission State Park 69

Jacobs, Henry Bailey 12, 74, 93, 162, 222
Jacobs, Henry Chariton 162, 163, 222
Jacobs, Zebulon William 222
Jacobsen, Florence 171
Jeffries, John C. 25
Jennings, Priscilla 99
Jennings, William 99, 112, 176, 177
Jensen, Hyrum J. 170

Jensen, James 162
Jenson, Andrew 104
Jillson, Clark 15
Johnson, Benjamin F. 229
Johnston, Albert S. 97–99
Jolson, Al 213
Jonas, Alberto 195
Jones, Brigham 224
Jones, Dan 224
Jones, Ruth 224
Jordan River 98, 148
Joseph Smith Memorial Building 106

Kane, Thomas 98
Kanesville, Iowa 10, 68
Karl Maeser Building 213
Kaysville, Utah 181
Kearney, Stephen 75
Kearns, Thomas 192, 193
Keeley Institute 183–86
Keeley, Leslie Enraught 184
Kelsey, Catherine 223
Kelsey, Edson Shepherd 223
Kelsey, Eli 223
Kelsey, Eli Brazee 223
Kelsey, Fitch Woodruff 223
Kelsey, George William 223
Kelsey, Mary Jane 223
Kent, Daniel 23
Keyes, Elisha 72, 73
Keyes, Johanna 72, 73
Kimball, Heber C. 6, 33, 34, 36, 37, 39, 40,
    51, 53, 54, 67, 68, 79, 80, 94, 125, 177
Kimball, Vilate 37, 53
Kingsbury, Joseph C. 104
King, Andrew Crookson 224
King, Bertha Mary 224
King, Charlotte 224
King, Georgiana 224
King, Louisa 224
King, Margaret 224
King, Peter Tapfield 224
King, Thomas Owen 224
King, Thomas Owen Jr. 224
Kirby 123
Kirby, James 117, 224
Kirby, Luella 117, 204
Kirtland, Ohio 5, 11, 37–41, 44–49, 53, 60,
    216
Knapp, Marion 30

Lagoon 122
Lancashire, England 54, 207
Lansing, New York 20, 21
Lawrence, Maria 229
Lawrence, Sarah 229
LDS Church 37, 45, 78, 84, 91–93, 96, 99,
    101, 104, 106–108, 113–115, 117–119, 130,
    131, 150, 162, 168, 171, 175, 209, 210, 213
Lee, Ann 64
Lewis, Canaan 224
Lewis, David Thomas 224
Lewis, Eliza 224
Lewis, John 224
Lewis, Lewis 224
Lewis, Sarah Elizabeth 224

Lewis, Thomas 224
Liberty Park 112, 123, 149
Lightner, Adam 11, 221
Lightner, Adam, Jr. 221
Lightner, Algernon Sidney 221
Lightner, Caroline Keziah 221
Lightner, Charles Washington 221
Lightner, Elizabeth 221
Lightner, Florentine Mattheas 221
Lightner, George Algernon 221
Lightner, Mary Rollins 221
Lightner, Miles Henry 221
Lion House 93, 95, 96, 100, 103, 119, 124,
    125, 127–131, 137, 155, 159, 169, 174, 180,
    212, 217
Little, Jesse 73, 74
Liverpool, England 54, 56, 58
Locke, New York 20
Log Row 92–94, 96, 119, 124, 129, 155, 217
London, England 191, 212
Lott, Cornelius 147
Lund, A. H. 182
Lyman, Francis M. 177
Lyman, James Acy 220
Lyman, James Davis 220
Lynn, John D. 33

Mack, Jonathan 35
Maeser, Karl G. 103
Manchester, England 229
Manifesto 183, 185
Mansion House, see also White House 60,
    96, 97, 217
Manti, Utah 174, 207
Marks, Abigail 7, 29
Marsh, Thomas B. 40
Martin, Moses 229
Martin, Oramel 14
Matthews, James 220
Mayhew, Austin Ship 224
Mayhew, Caroline Abigail 224
Mayhew, Elijah 12, 224
Mayhew, Elijah Warren 224
Mayhew, Elisha 224
Mayhew, Laurana 224
Mayhew, Lucinda 224
Mayhew, Otto Lyman 224
Mayhew, Walter Franklin 224
McCune, Alfred William 189–191
McCune, Elizabeth 189–191
McCune Mansion 94, 191
McCune, Matthew 190
McCune, Sarah Elizabeth Caroline Scott
    190
McDonal, Sarah Ann 230
McKean 120
McLean, Albert 229
McLean, Ann Blanche 229
McLean, Eleanor Jane McComb 229, 230
McLean, Fitzroy 229
McLean, Hector Hugh 229, 230
McMurray, Elizabeth 220
McMurray, Joseph 220
Meier and Frank 116
Mendon, New York 14, 33–37, 40, 49, 215
Merrill, M. W. 182

Mesa Verde 213
Michigan Conservatory of Music 195
Miller, Elijah 25, 27
Minersville, Utah 11
Mississippi River 50, 51, 69, 72, 73
Montana 123, 190
Montrose, Iowa 52, 73, 216
Moon, Benager 53
Moon, John 54
Mormon Battalion 75
Mormon Liberal Party 183
Mormon People's Party 183
Morrill Antibigamy Act 179
Morris, Richard P. 196
Morse, George H. 45
Morton, Abner 20
Mosley, Joseph 15
Moses, Julian 86
Mount Vernon 213
Mountain Meadows Massacre 202
Moyle, James Henry 183
Mt. Pisgah, Iowa 74, 75, 119
Murdock, Caleb 15
Murdock, Lucetta 53

Nauvoo 3, 5–8, 10–12, 46, 51, 53, 59–64, 67,
    68, 71, 72, 75, 86, 88, 96, 109, 112–15, 117,
    119, 120, 123, 147, 169, 173, 212, 216
Nauvoo Bell 86, 88
Nauvoo Temple 5, 7, 10–12, 51, 63, 67, 86,
    169
New Orleans, Louisiana 229
New York City, New York 192
Nibley, Charles W. 197
Niles Mandolin Orchestra 194

Oakland, Jack 117
Ogden, Utah 10
Old Fort 85–88, 93, 119, 217
Omahas 75
Osborne, Nathan 24, 25
Oswego, New York 33, 215
Owasco, New York 27, 28, 30

Page, John E. 51
Painsville, Ohio 40
Paris Brass Band 210
Paris, Idaho 210
Parish, Isabelle H. 20
Park City, Utah 191
Park, Hamilton G. 150
Parks, Charles 28, 29
Partridge, Edward 6, 23, 61, 81, 119, 168
Partridge, Emily 119, 229
Partridge, Lydia 119
Pasadena, California 196
Pearce, John 223
Penrose, Charles W. 180
People's Party 183
Perpetual Emigrating Company 181
Phelps, Morris 50
Philadelphia, Pennsylvania 123
Philips, Bruce Israel 10, 222
Picadilly Apartments 119
Pickering Township, Canada 229
Pine Grove, New York 23

Pioneer Memorial Theatre 213
Pioneer Park 85, 86
Pioneer Square 88
Plumas County, California 191
plural marriage 3, 5, 8, 10, 60, 79, 169, 185
Polk, James 74, 75
polygamy 60, 61, 82, 119, 121, 179, 181, 183, 202
Pomeroy, Irene Hascall 71, 77
Port Byron, New York 28, 30, 31, 33, 215
Potawatomi 68
Powers 221
Pratt, Orson 8, 51, 53, 54, 64, 84, 118
Pratt, Parley P. 10, 44, 50, 59, 117, 169, 229
President's Office 124, 125, 180
Preston, England 54
Preston, William B. 189
Primary 107
Providence, Rhode Island 41
Provo, Utah 207, 209, 213, 218
Purinton, Raymond A. 15
Pyper, George D. 107

Quebec, Canada 184
Queen Victoria 191
Quincy, Illinois 50, 77, 216

Rampton, Calvin 88
Ramsey, Ralph 100, 176
Red Butte 109
Red Cross 197
Reese, John 186
Relief Society 93, 94, 107
Republican Party 183
Reynolds, George 179
Rich, Charles C. 210
Richards, Franklin D. 177
Richards, Harry 211
Richardson, Rufus 37
Richmond, Missouri 191
Ridges, Joseph 173
Rigdon, Sidney 49, 51, 64–65
Rio Grande Railway Station 213
Roberts, B. H. 189
Roberts, Horace 223
Robinson, George W. 49
Romney, Miles 209
Rowe, Massachusetts 14
Rowland, Benjamin 123
Rowland Hall 122
Russell, Lillian 213

Sacramento, California 85
Sadawaga Pond 15, 215
Sagers, Joseph Ormal 118, 224
Sagers, Mary Maria 224
Sagers, Royal Barney 224
Sagers, Sarah E. 224
Sagers, William Henry Harrison 118, 223
Salt Lake City, Utah 8, 10, 12, 14, 59, 69, 79, 80, 82, 84, 85, 88, 91, 97, 98, 101, 112, 116–19, 123–25, 127, 128, 131, 147, 148, 162, 173, 174, 177, 182, 186–88, 193, 194, 197, 202, 204–10, 212, 213, 217–18
Salt Lake Telegram 201
Salt Lake Theatre 88, 99, 116, 173, 195, 212

Salt Lake Tribune 177–78, 185, 194, 197
Salt Lake Valley 8, 65–66, 79, 80, 87, 97, 147, 188, 202, 209
Salt Palace 118
San Francisco, California 176, 182, 187, 189, 200, 229
San Simeon 213
Sandwich Islands (see also Hawaiian Islands) 94, 229
Santa Clara, Utah 204
Schulkens, Steve 90
Schwartz, Agnes 179, 180
Schwartz, Mary 179
Scott, Sarah Elizabeth Caroline 190
Seattle, Washington 85
Seeley, Harriet 60, 219
Seeley, Isaac Joseph 49, 60, 219
Seeley, William 5, 60, 219
Seeley, William Jacob 60, 219
Sessions, Perrigrine 70
Seward Mansion 25–27
Seward, William H. 25–27
Shaw, William Montgomery 10, 220
Shaw, Ambrose "E" 220
Shaw, Annis 220
Shaw, Clarence 220
Shaw, Frank 220
Shaw, Geneva 220
Shaw, Ina 220
Shaw, Manley 220
Shaw, Romania 220
Shaw, Rosebell 220
Shaw, Tirzah 220
Shaw, William Dudley 220
Sherburne, New York 17, 18, 20, 38, 215
Sherman's march to the sea 184
Sherwood, H. G. 84
Sinclair, William J. 193
Sioux 75, 230
Smith, Alma Lamoni 223
Smith, Alvira Lavonna 223
Smith, Amanda Melvina 223
Smith, David B. 33, 49
Smith, Elias 125
Smith, Elijah 40
Smith, Emma 119, 229
Smith, George A. 53, 54, 64, 128, 205
Smith, Hyrum 64
Smith, John H. 177
Smith, Joseph 5, 6, 8, 11, 13, 39, 41, 42, 43, 44, 48–51, 59, 60, 62, 64, 65, 91, 106, 119, 173, 229
Smith, Joseph F. 126, 177, 179, 194
Smith, Ortencia 223
Smith, Sarah Marinda 223
Smith, Sardis Washington 223
Smith, Warren 50, 223
Smith, Warren Barnes 223
Smith, Willard Gilbert 223
Smoot, Abraham O. 148
Smyrna, New York 14, 17, 18, 20
Snively, Hannahetta 168–69
Snively, Henry 168
Snively, Mary 168
Snow, Erastus 180
Social Hall 112, 113

Soda Springs, Idaho 210, 211
Sons of Utah Pioneers 88, 121
Sorenson, Horace 122
Spencer, John D. 125
Sprague 117
Springfield, Illinios 169
Spry, William 197
Stanford, Leland 182
Stilson, William B 33
Stimpson Hill, Vermont 14, 15, 215
St. George, Utah 113, 168, 174, 204–9, 212, 218
St. George Tabernacle 209
St. George Temple 207, 209
St. Louis, Missouri 67, 77, 80, 116
Stringham, William Bryant 221
Sudbury, Samuel 180
Sugar Creek, Iowa 73, 77
Sugar House 121, 148, 170
Sugarhouse Park 122
Summerhill, New York 20
Switzerland 150

Taffindor, Susan 229–30
Tarbox, Elisha Terry 77, 223
Tarbox, George 77, 223
Taylor, John 51, 54, 55, 148, 175, 177–182
Teasdale, George 179
Temple Square 84, 88, 91, 106, 117, 173
Temple View Center 118
Terry, Hannah 77
Terry, Parshall 77
Thatcher, George W. 103
Thatcher, Moses 176, 177
This Is the Place 84, 104, 122, 171, 212
Tithing Office 91, 104, 107, 180, 181
Toomer, Sarah 230
Toronto, Canada 77
Tosoiba 210
Trumbo, Isaac 182, 186–90, 192
Turley 56
Tuttle, Daniel S. 123
Twiss, John Saunders 222
Tyrone, New York 23, 24, 33, 215

Uglialoro, Genevieve 31
Uglialoro, Matthew 31
University of Deseret 103, 206
University of Utah 103, 213
Ursenbach, Octave 150
Utah Arts Council 112
Utah State Capitol 197
Utah State Historical Society 90, 213
Utah Supreme Court 181
Utah War 97, 202, 209
Utes 87, 202

Van Buren, Arkansas 230
Van Cott, Lucy Sackett 117
Van Cott, John 117
Vanderbilt, Washington, George 213
Vernal Tabernacle 213

Wadsworth, Joseph 27
Wait farmhouse 27
Wait, Mary Van Sickle 13

Walker, Alfred 223
Walker, Diontha 223
Walker, Evaline 223
Walker, Hannah 223
Walker, John R. 223
Walker, Julian 223
Walker, Mary Ann 223
Walker, Nancy 223
Walker, Oliver 223
Walker, Sarah 223
Walker, William Cressy 223
Ward, David 78
Washington, D.C. 73, 74, 168, 183, 186, 187
Washington, George 16, 35, 213
Washington, Mary Ball 168
Washington, Utah 204, 209
Watt, George 123, 230
Watt, Jane 230
Webb, Chauncy W. 120
Webb, Eliza Churchill 120, 168
Weed, Gilbert 30
ellhausen, Charles 46
lhausen, Lucy 46
ells, Daniel H. 114, 115, 125, 177
ells, Heber M 194, 196
Weston 222
Wheeling, West Virginia 229
Whitaker, John 180
White House, see also Mansion House 96, 97, 99, 101, 124, 125, 212, 213
Whitesides, Morris 112, 221
Whitingham, Vermont 13–18, 215
Whitmarsh, William 221
Wicks 78
Wilcox, Frank 171
Wilcox, Gwen 171
Willoughby, Ohio 40
Winder, J. B. 183, 189
Winder, J. R. 189
Winter Quarters 8, 68, 69, 75, 77, 79, 80, 119, 216, 230
Woodruff, Wilford 51, 54, 148, 150, 179–83, 186, 189, 210
Woodstock, Virginia 168
Woodward, James B. 12, 222
Woolley Family 154
Woolley, Simmons, Rachel Emma 177
Works, Abigail 221
Works, Adeline 221
Works, Angeline 221
Works, Asa 30, 221
Works, Asa Jr. 221
Works, James Marks 221
Works, Jerusha 221
Works, Joseph Tuncliff 221
Works, Miriam Angeline 221
Works, Perthenia 221
World War I 196, 197

YLMIA (see also Young Women) 131
Young, Abigail Harbach Hall 222
Young, Abigail Marks 7, 17–18, 20, 29, 221
Young, Albert Jeddie 112, 220
Young, Alfales 93, 205, 223
Young, Alice Emma 97, 219
Young, Alma 220

Young, Alonzo 115, 221
Young, Alvah 220
Young, Amanda Barnes Smith 223
Young, Amy Cecelia Cooper Aldrich 222
Young, Ann Eliza Webb 1, 10, 120, 168, 174, 221, 224, 228
Young, Ardelle Elwin 115, 117, 221
Young, Arta De Christa 61, 219
Young, Augusta Adams 5, 61, 113, 219, 228
Young, Brigham 1–3, 5–8, 10–31, 33–69, 71–82, 88, 90–99, 101, 103–4, 108, 109, 112–131, 147, 149,150, 154, 157, 158, 162–164, 166, 168–175, 190, 201, 202, 204–214, 219–24, 228–30
Young, Brigham Heber 61, 219
Young, Brigham Jonathan 230
Young, Brigham Jr. 41, 64, 97, 219
Young, Brigham Morris 112, 220
Young, Caroline 119, 220
Young, Catherine Reese Clawson 223
Young, Charlotte Talula 113, 220
Young, Clarissa Blake 6, 220
Young, Clarissa Caroline Decker 5, 8, 61, 80, 87, 112, 113, 125, 220
Young, Clarissa Decker 80, 87, 112, 113, 220
Young, Clarissa Hamilton 61, 125, 154, 164, 219
Young, Clarissa Maria 109, 212, 220
Young, Clarissa Ross (Chase) 6, 61, 109, 220
Young, Cynthia Porter Weston 222
Young, Daniel Wells 114, 115, 221
Young, Diana Severence Chase Shaw 6, 10, 220
Young, Edward Partridge 6, 119, 220
Young, Eliza 229–30
Young, Eliza Babcock 10, 220
Young, Eliza Burgess 8, 205, 209, 223
Young, Eliza Roxcy Snow 6, 61, 94, 103–4, 220
Young, Elizabeth 8, 31, 33, 36, 41, 44, 55, 219
Young, Elizabeth Fairchild 6, 10, 220
Young, Elizabeth Jones 224
Young, Ella Elizabeth 8, 114, 121, 221
Young, Ellen Ackland Rockwood 221
Young, Emeline Free 117, 221
Young, Emily Augusta 119, 220
Young, Emily Dow Partridge 6, 61, 81, 119, 168, 220
Young, Emily Haws 221
Young, Emma Amanda 223
Young, Emmeline Amanda 114, 221
Young, Ernest Irving 61, 93, 219
Young, Eudora Lovenia 205–6, 222
Young, Eunice Caroline (Luna) 41, 97, 219
Young, Evelyn Louisa 93, 221
Young Family Cemetery 101
Young, Fannie (daughter) 8, 117, 224
Young, Fanny (sister) 18, 23, 33
Young, Fanny Decker 61, 93, 219
Young, Feramorz Little 61, 219
Young, George 77, 223
Young, George Cannon 101, 128
Young, George Henry 223
Young, George Spencer 97, 99
Young, George W. 8, 223
Young, Hannah Tapfield King 11, 224

Young, Harriet Amelia Folsom 174, 175, 224
Young, Harriet Barney 118, 223
Young, Harriet Elizabeth Cook 5, 61, 94, 103, 164, 219
Young, Hyrum 220
Young, Hyrum Smith 114, 221
Young, Ida 221
Young, Ina 205–6
Young, James Valentine 221
Young, Jane Terry 8, 77, 223
Young, Jeanette Richards 220
Young, Jedediah Grant 112, 220
Young, Jemima Angell 221, 222
Young, John 5, 15–18, 20, 23, 24, 29, 37
Young, John Willard 41, 55, 61, 99, 109, 126, 127, 170, 219
Young, Jonathan 230
Young, Joseph 15–19, 20, 23, 24, 33, 43, 58, 220
Young, Joseph A. 44, 97, 219
Young, Joseph Don Carlos 101, 119, 220
Young, Josephine 119, 220
Young, Julia 163, 169, 170, 220
Young, Julia Foster 222
Young, Lorenzo Dow 17, 18, 24, 41, 124, 221
Young, Louisa 17, 18, 23, 33
Young, Louisa Beaman 6, 61, 220
Young, Louisa Wells (Nelle) 114, 221
Young, Lucy Ann Decker 5, 7, 60–61, 92, 103, 125–26, 219
Young, Lucy Bigelow 8, 80, 82, 113, 168, 205, 207, 209, 223
Young, Lura 119, 220
Young, Lydia Farnsworth Mayhew 12, 224
Young, Mahonri Moriancumer 221
Young, Margaret Maria Alley 8, 221
Young, Margaret Pierce Whitesides 6, 61, 92, 93, 112, 130, 165, 224
Young, Marinda Hyde 114, 221
Young, Martha Bowker 221
Young, Mary Ann 7, 97, 219
Young, Mary Ann Angell 5, 7, 8, 10, 11, 40, 41, 44–47, 49, 50, 52–59, 62–64, 93, 97, 99, 103, 125, 126, 174, 175, 219, 222, 219
Young, Mary Ann Clark Powers 7, 10, 11, 221
Young, Mary Ann Turley 10, 222
Young, Mary Eliza 109, 220
Young, Mary Eliza Nelson Greene 10, 222
Young, Mary Elizabeth Rollins Lightener 6, 11, 61, 221
Young, Mary Ellen De La Montegue Woodward 10, 12, 222
Young, Mary Harvey 221
Young, Mary Jane Bigelow 8, 10, 78, 223
Young, Mary Oldfield Kelsey 223
Young, Mary Van Cott 117, 224
Young, Miriam 119, 220
Young, Miriam Angeline Works 5, 7, 29, 30, 33, 35–37, 40, 219, 221
Young, Moroni 220
Young, Naamah Kendel Jenkins (Twiss) 130, 222
Young, Nabbie Howe 112, 125, 220
Young, Nabby 17
Young, Nancy 23

Young, Nancy Cressy (Crissie) Walker 23
Young, Nathan 221
Young, Olive Andrews Smith 221
Young, Olive Gray Frost 6, 7, 61, 220
Young, Oscar Brigham 95, 200
Young, Phebe Ann Angell 7, 222
Young, Phineas 170, 224
Young, Phinehas 18, 23, 24, 33, 41
Young, Phoebe Louisa 220
Young, Rachel Maxfield 221
Young, Rebecca Greenleaf Holman 220
Young, Rhoda 18–20, 23, 33
Young, Rhoda Mabel 205–6, 223

Young, Rhoda Richards 222
Young, Ruth 115, 221
Young, Sally 219
Young, Sarah Malin 8, 81, 223
Young, Seymour B. 179
Young, Shermira 61, 219
Young, Susan Amelia (Susa) 2, 8, 22, 82, 93, 95, 112, 113, 115, 119, 125, 155, 158, 162, 165, 166, 168, 169, 190, 205, 206
Young, Susannah 18, 23, 24, 33
Young, Susannah Snively 61, 97, 165, 168, 170, 220

Young Women (see also YLMIA) 107, 125–27, 131, 197
Young, Valentine 221
Young, Vilate 35–37, 41, 44, 55, 92, 219
Young, Zina Diantha Huntington Jacobs 8, 11, 12, 74, 93, 94, 107, 109, 119, 150, 154, 162, 209, 222
Young, Zina Prescinda 222

ZCMI 96, 115–18, 182
Zion's Camp 41–43
Zions Securities 100, 114